GOOD WINE GUIDE

1991

The Sunday Telegraph
in association with WINE magazine

GOOD

WINE

Guide

1991

ROBERT JOSEPH

PAN BOOKS
London, Sydney and Auckland

Published in Great Britain 1990
by *The Sunday Telegraph*
Peterborough Court, At South Quay
181 Marsh Wall, London E14 9SR
in association with Pan Books

First edition published 1982
Copyright © *The Sunday Telegraph*
and Robert Joseph 1990

ISBN 0-330-31627-3

Designed by Peter Ward
Printed and bound in Great Britain by
BPCC Hazell Books
Aylesbury, Bucks, England
Member of BPCC Limited

CONTENTS

WINE WITH FOOD   66

THE WINES   69

THE STOCKISTS   115

A-Z of Wines and Wine Terms   229

INDEX   267

INTRODUCTION

With this, the eighth edition of *The Sunday Telegraph Good Wine Guide*, we are delighted to have been able to squeeze in a greater than ever number of merchants, without losing the pocket-book format that has made the *Guide* so successful.

Unlike any other currently available book, the *Guide* not only provides the answers to such questions as 'What is Alvarinho?' and 'What was the 1986 vintage like in Barolo?'; it also suggests specific wines, telling you where you can buy them and, in the case of our 500 recommended wines, precisely what they should cost. At-a-glance charts detail the services offered by wine merchants across Britain and the types of wines in which they specialise, and these merchants—more than 175 individual firms—each receive the *Guide's* report on later pages.

The wines recommended in the *Guide* have been chosen from the 2,000 award winners at the 1990 *WINE Magazine* International Challenge, the world's biggest comparative tasting. All were awarded commendations or medals for their quality, and for the value for money they represent — whatever their price.

While over 250 of the wines listed are on sale for less than £5 a bottle, our recommendations include bottles that cost as much as £20 or £30. These represent just as good value as the cheapest wines in the *Guide*.

In response to the ever-growing interest in the way food and wine go together, for every recommended wine there is a set of suggested styles of dish, based on the results of the food-and-wine tastings held each month for *WINE Magazine*.

And, for anyone who has ever wondered where to find the best wine glasses, infallible corkscrews, made-to-measure wine racks and computerised cellar books, there is a whole section of the *Guide* devoted to these matters.

As in the past, our aim has been to live up to the description applied to the *Guide* in 1988: `The only wine book anyone is likely to need.'

ACKNOWLEDGEMENTS

Each edition of the *Guide* provides a greater challenge, both in terms of
packing a quart of information into a pint pot, and in the task of selecting 500
of the best wines and some 180 of the best wine merchants in Britain. The fact
that we have managed to do so owes everything to the combined efforts of
the designer, Peter Ward, and of a team of people headed by Louise Abbott
— associate editor of the *Guide* since the 1988 edition — and Simon Woods,
coordinator of the 1990 *WINE Magazine* International Challenge, from
which the major proportion of the information in the book is derived. The
team that made it possible to transform well over 10,000 tasting notes into
the 500 wine descriptions that appear in these pages, consisted of Sophie
Abbott, Helen Boswell, Darren Conquest, Will Davenport, Jenny Jacoby,
Nikki Jacoby, John Kemp, Patrick Porritt and Ruth Sheard.

Equally essential were the members of the British and international
wine trade listed below who spent a week tasting their way through over
4,000 wines (and half of these twice) to select the 2,000 worthy of awards.

To ensure that the right bottles of wine were placed in front of the right
tasters at the right time, Charles Metcalfe led a team of wine enthusiasts consisting of: John Stott, research chemist; Ian Huggett, fireman; Hugh Boynton,
retired turf accountant; Darren Conquest, bar manager/wine writer; Chris
Hall, manager of an Augustus Barnett shop; Peter Bright, consultant civil
engineer; Michele Sandell, manager of a Wine Rack shop; Kathleen Gill, pot-
ter/glass blower; Will Davenport, winemaker; Patrick Porritt, trainee accountant and 1990 *Daily Telegraph* Wine Taster of the Year; Ruth Sheard, law
student; Richard Fawcett, lawyer; Richard Bailey, wine writer; Alison Tate,
photographer; Sandra Marshall, art teacher; Lucy Bailey, freelance journal-
ist; Dave Perrottet, TV producer and Steve Morris, photographer.

But for these people, for Margaret Rand and the staff of *WINE Magazine*,
Malcolm Casimir, Andy Turnbull, Matt Loney, Piers Russell-Cobb, An-
thony Rose of *The Independent*, Oliver Bennett, Judith Hannam at Pan and
Marilyn Warnick at Telegraph Books, this *Guide* would never exist.

THE TASTERS

Paul Abbott, Timothy Abegg, Jim Ainsworth, Colin Akers, Alexander
Allan, Simon Alper, Keith Anderson, P Aplin, Bill Ash, Tim Atkin, Angus
Avery, John Axon MW, Richard Bailey, Bill Baker, Adam Bancroft MW,
Abigail Barlow, Anne Barlow, Gavin Barlow, Ken Barlow, Stephen Barrett,
Giles Bartleet, David Baverstock, David Bedford MW, Gideon Beinstock,
Rowland Bennett, Edward Berry, Randall Bertao, John Bertaut, D Billing-
ham, Vicky Bishop, Peter Blackwell, John Blanchard, Helena Bogletti,
David Boobbyer, Paul Bowker, John Boyes MW, Mark Brandon, Gerard
Brisson, Jane Brocket, Tony Brown, Mark Brunel-Cohen, Neville Bryant,
Jim Budd, David Burns, Debra Buzan, David Bywater, Hugh Cameron,
Alistair Cameron, Christine Campadieu, Hugo Campbell, Alexandre Canetti,
Vincent Canti, Nicholas Carey James, David Carr Taylor, Sheila Cartwright,
Guy Chisenhale-Marsh, Giles Clarke, Oz Clarke, Stephen Clarke, Catherine
Clissold, Gordon Coates, Simon Cock, Michael Collier, Dirk Collingwood,
John Comyn, Matthew Cooper, John Corliss, David Courtenay-Clack, Nick
Cowley, Robin Crameri MW, Jan Critcheley-Salmonson MW, Alan Crowley,
David Curtis, Amanda Dale, Robert Dale, Mark Dally, Tracey Daniel,

Stephen Daniels, Christopher Davey, Martin Davis, Stephen Day, Sergio de Luca, Simon Deakin, Joanna Delaforce, Demitri Demetriou, Robert di Massimo, Richard Doughty, Rose-Marie Doughty, John Downes, Christian Dupont, Paul Dwyer, Alison Easton, Tony Eastwood, Chris Eatly, Kevin Ecock, Nick Elliott, Marcus Elwes, Jochen Erler, Grant Farquhar, Simon Farr, Alfie Fiandaca, Alex Findlater, Charlotte Fleming, Stuart Floyd, Chris Foulkes, Martin Fowke, Margaret Francis, Henry Fryer, Elizabeth Gabay, Brian Gates, Robert Geddes, Colin Gent, Rosemary George MW, Caroline Gilbey, Simon Gillespie, Claude Giret, William Glasson, David Gleave MW, Richard Gooch, Philip Goodband MW, Robert Gorton, Paul Gow, Nigel Gray, Peter Greet, Gerald Gregory, Mavis Grover, Julie Gubbins, Bill Gunn MW, Patricia Guy, Ted Hale MW, Aileen Hall, William Hancock, James Handford, Dennis Hare, Philip Harris, Mark Harrison, Chris Hartley, Richard Harvey MW, Robin Hasslacher, Michael Hasslacher, Peter Hastings, Jo Hawkins, Harold Heckle, Tony Hein, Andrew Henderson, Piarina Hennessey, João Henriques, Bill Hermitage, Jane Higgins, Rosamund Hitchcock, Rodney Hogg, Pamela Holt, Christian Honorez, Simon Hore, Terry Horton, Mark Hughes, Jane Hunt MW, Colin Hynard, Julio Illanes, Dominique Irigneau, R. Charles Jackson, Nicholas James, Darrell Jones, Robert Joseph; Renee Jurgelon, Jacqueline Kay, Rodney Kearns, Paul Kelly, John Kemp, Judy Kendrick, Tony Keys, James King, Ivan Kinsman, Jane Laird, Adrian Laird Craig, Adrian Lake, C Lake, Adrian Lane, Michael Larn, Nick Lawson, Charles Lea, Willy Lebus, Peter Ledgerwood, John Leighton, Nick Leonard, Edward Lewis, Mike Lintner, Michael Lo, J Lockspeiser, William Long, Wink Lorch, Chris Loveday, Luciana Lynch, Giles Macdonogh, Jane MacQuitty, Robert Mapley, Simon March, Nina Marklew, Adrian Markwell, Robert Marsden, Tony Mason, Philip Matthews, Richard Mayson, Andrew McCarthy, Kevin McKoen, Maggie McNie MW, Paul Merritt, Charles Metcalfe; Laurent Metge, Christopher Milner, Andrew Montague, Jacky Moore, Liz Morcom MW, Manuel Moreno, Nicky Moreton, John Morgan, Wendy Morison, Sarah Morphew MW, Jasper Morris MW, L A Morton, Angela Muir MW, Peter Muir, Chris Murphy, Monica Murphy, Francis Murray, Rudi Nassauer, Larry Naylor, Paul Newey, James Nicholson, Matthew Norton, Richard Nurick, Richard Osbourne, Mark O'Bryen, M P O'Connor, Tom O'Toole, Neil Palmer, Graham Pash, Richard Pass, Diana Paterson Fox, Luis Pato, Alistair Peebles MW, Mick Pickup, David Pinchard, Peter Charles Plodde, Lynn Power, Andrew Poxon, Keith Richard Price, John Radford, Lewis Ragbourn, Debbie Ralph, John Rawlings, Patrick Rennie, Guy Richardson, Bill Ridley, Gordon Ritchie, Geoffrey Roberts, Jeremy Roberts, Liz Robertson MW, Kevin Robinson, James Rogers, Charles Rolaz, Bill Rolfe, Anthony Rose, Vicky Ross, David Sandys-Renton, Michael Saunders, Hector Scicluna, Peter Scudamore-Smith, E D Searle, Paul Shinnie, John Shortt, Joanna Simon, Pat Simon MW, James Simpson, Stephen Skelton, Theo Sloot, Ian Smallridge, G V Smallwood, Derek Smedley MW, Andrew Smith, A Soldani, Neil Somerfelt MW, Jane Sowter, Richard Speirs, Stephen Spurrier, Jo Standen, Tim Stanley-Clarke, Paul Stead, Kit Stevens MW, Nigel Stewart, Paul Stratford, Clare Symington, Martin Symmington, Beverly Tabbron, Christopher Tatham MW, John Taylor, David Thomas, Ian Thompson, John Thorogood, Kim Tidy, Marcus Titley, Michael Trull, Philip Tuck, Neil Tully, J Twaites, Nick Underwood, T M Underwood, John Vaughan-Hughes MW, Helen Verdcourt, Gilles Vinet, Nick Wakefield, Robert Walker, Peter James Wall, Bill Warre MW, Marcia Waters, Tom Weir, Alan West, Robert West, Eric While, Anthony Whitaker, Fiona Wild, Kathy Wilken, Andrew Williams, Chris Williams, J G B Williams, Laurence Williams, Andrew Willy, Melanie Wood, Arabella Woodrow MW, David Woods, Simon Woods, Martin Wright, David Wrigley, Sarah Wykes, Margaret Wysynska, Chris Young.

THE
AWARDS

The recommendations both of wines and merchants that form the main body of this *Guide* are taken from the International Challenge tasting held annually by *WINE Magazine*. Since it was launched in 1985, this event has become the biggest international competition of its kind, bringing together the humblest of table wines, the classiest of Bordeaux châteaux and the newest wineries of the New World.

Unlike any other event of this kind, the Challenge tasting not only compares wines of similar styles, but it also considers them on the basis of the value for money they represent. This is not to say that recommended wines have to be inexpensive — simply that they have to be well worth their price whatever they cost.

The wines are entered — and judged — by representatives of every part of the UK wine trade, from the smallest English vineyard and one-man-band importer, to the most venerable of City merchants and the biggest High Street off-licence chains and supermarkets. In addition, an increasing number of overseas winemakers and trade members now make time to attend the event, contributing a truly international perspective to the judging. Following this, a full list of the wines that have received awards is sent to over 750 retailers (whether or not they competed), enabling them to indicate to us, should they so wish, those that they stock.

Where companies have submitted wines, we first compare the number of successful wines with the number entered into the Challenge — so the success rate of a merchant that was awarded 15 recommendations out of 25 entries is recognised as being greater than that of a firm that submitted 100, of which 30 won awards. Then we compare the total number of award-winning wines from each company with their full wine lists to see whether the recommended wines are representative of their range as a whole. Finally, we select the merchants that will feature in the *Guide*.

We automatically include most of Britain's larger supermarket and off-licence chains, simply because their ubiquitous presence in the High Street virtually guarantees that most readers will shop for wine there at one time or another. Our assessment of each firm appears in their individual entries.

More difficult is the task of selecting the best from Britain's wealth of independent merchants. Paramount in our considerations are the breadth of choice and the range of services offered to customers, though we naturally take account of the fact that, by definition, specialists cannot be expected to supply an across-the-board range. And while our regional awards reflect the national scope of the *Guide*, our category winners, for different styles of businesses, take account of the diversity of ways in which British wine drinkers may choose to shop for their wine.

THE SUNDAY TELEGRAPH GOOD WINE GUIDE / WINE MAGAZINE WINE MERCHANTS OF THE YEAR

These sought-after awards are made by an expert panel of judges consisting of: Jim Ainsworth, wine writer for *Punch*; Tim Atkin, wine writer for *The*

Guardian; Ruth Cobb, editor of *Wine & Spirit International* magazine; João Henriques of the Portuguese Government Trade Office; Brian Jordan, restaurateur-turned-wine writer; Maggie McNie MW, wine consultant; Kathryn McWhirter, wine writer of the *Sunday Independent*, and former editor of both the *Which? Wine Guide* and *Wine & Spirit* magazine; Charles Metcalfe of *WINE Magazine, Homes & Gardens* and Granada Television's *This Morning*; Rose Murray-Brown, wine writer for *The Scotsman* and *WINE Magazine*; Margaret Rand, editor of *WINE Magazine*; Anthony Rose, wine correspondent of *The Independent*; Joanna Simon, wine writer of *The Sunday Times*, and Tom Stevenson, author of the award-winning *Sotheby's Wine Encyclopaedia* (and former editor of the *Guide*).

REGIONAL AWARDS

Scotland- Joint Winners: Raeburn Fine Wines & Foods (see p.190) & Peter Green (see p.158)

While Peter Green has not only maintained but developed the outstanding list that gained him this same prize in 1990, Zubair Mohamed of Raeburn has transformed his family grocers into one of the best-stocked wine merchants, not only in Scotland, but in the British Isles as a whole. As we said last year, this is the only place in Britain where you can buy *en primeur* claret, top-class Burgundies and Loires — and fig-rolls and Brillo Pads.

Wales - The Celtic Vintner (see p.136)

Winner of this prize for the second year running, The Celtic Vintner stood out in poorly-served Wales last year, but has built on its success and is now performing to a truly national standard. One of the most successful merchants in the 1990 *WINE Magazine* International Challenge.

North of England - D Byrne (see p.132)

If The Celtic Vintner was successful in the Challenge, D Byrne was stunningly so. Accused by many of its fans of being 'too modest', this Clitheroe firm boasts one of the best lists in the country. Competition for our North of England award is extremely fierce, but nevertheless D Byrne stands out with a superb across-the-board performance.

East of England - Adnams Wine Merchants (see p.115)

A long-time favourite with its customers, locally and nationwide, Adnams beat off keen opposition in the Eastern Counties to take this year's prize. The fact that it can also supply fine, traditional ale and a range of wonderful kitchen equipment was not allowed to influence our judges, but they were dazzled by the quality of the list.

Central England - Tanners (see p.203)

Tanners take this prize for the second year running, a success welcomed by our judges, one of whom made the point that this family firm is one of the very few in Britain that still behaves like the best kind of traditional country wine merchant.

West of England - Christopher Piper Wines (see p.188)

The only wine merchant in Britain to belong to a Beaujolais producer, Christopher Piper has been quietly influential throughout the West Country, introducing private customers and restaurants to the delights of well-chosen, individual-estate wines. His success as a winemaker can be judged by the number of his colleagues who stock his Challenge award-winning Brouilly, Château des Tours.

South of England - Fullers (see p.152)

A firm that has for too long been overlooked, Fullers has been transformed over the last few years, thanks to the efforts of wine buyer Mark Dally. The shops often still lack the pizzazz of some of their neighbours in the High Street, but they have a surprisingly good range of wines —and very well trained staff.

London - Bibendum (see p.126)

A unique cross between a wine warehouse and a traditional merchant, Bibendum is a perfect example of the best kind of modern wine merchant. The list includes a range of really top-class Rhônes, for example, as well as exciting — and otherwise hard to find — New World wines.

CATEGORY AWARDS

Independent Merchant - Winecellars (see p.219)

It says much about the way David Gleave MW and Nick Belfrage MW have built up this young business that it was short-listed for an award in no less than three different categories: as a specialist in Italian wines, as a by-the-case warehouse (the prize it took in 1988) and as a London merchant. The award of Best Independent will suprise no one who knows Winecellars' range (which strays far beyond Italy) and the service offered by its staff.

Regional Chain - Joint Winners: The Wine Rack (see p.222) & E H Booth (see p.129)

Over the last year, the commitment of Thresher/Wine Rack wine buyer Kim Tidy and his team (including former Oddbins marketing expert Tim Waters) to compete head-on with the best in the country has become clear, both in the shops and in the success of The Wine Rack wines in the *Wine Magazine* International Challenge.

National High Street Chain - Oddbins (see p.183)

This year, for the first time, there was some support among our judges for a chain other than Oddbins; Thresher and Victoria Wine, it was acknowledged, have both improved enormously. Even so, there was no hesitation in making this award to Oddbins for the fourth year running. As one judge said, 'There is no-one else, no other option, no contest...'

By-the-Case - Majestic Wine Warehouses (see p.174)

By-the-Case winners in 1990, too, Majestic has consolidated a triumphant return to form with a tremendous range of carefully chosen, well-priced wines. Despite some strong competition this year from The Wine Society and Morris & Verdin, Majestic kept its lead at the front of the field with a very successful set of entries to the 1990 *WINE Magazine* International Challenge.

Supermarket - J Sainsbury (see p.195)

Sainsbury's and Tesco ran a very close race too, but the former just won that vital extra couple of votes. It was an executive of another retail chain who wrily said, 'we have customers, Sainsbury's have converts'. No company is doing more to convert the British public to an appreciation of a broad range of interesting wines.

Specialist - Valvona & Crolla (see p.210)

Edinburgh is a great place to live if you like Italian food and wine; Valvona & Crolla provide a glorious range of both, along with informative wine list descriptions to lead prospective explorers from Aglianico del Vulture to Vin Santo. One of the very few places in Britain that can provide the means of organising a comparative — and enjoyable — Frascati tasting.

WINE MERCHANT OF THE YEAR — ODDBINS

After four years of Martina Navratilova-like consistency, we were seriously tempted to rename this prize the Oddbins Trophy. Predictable its success may be — no other major chain stocks nearly as many medal-winning wines from the 1990 *WINE Magazine* International Challenge — but of our 13 judges, 12 independently voted Oddbins winner of this award.

WINES OF THE YEAR

When selecting the Wines of the Year, our criteria are not that they should be greatest or the most exquisite bottles on the market, but that they achieve the arguably more difficult feat of standing out from the crowd without being too esoteric; they must appeal to a wide range of tastes and suit a wide number of occasions; they must be well made, characterful, sanely priced and, in view of the rocketing sales of previous winners, widely available. In short, they are wines we would unreservedly recommend.

Red Wine of the Year — Barbera d'Asti 1988 (Viticoltori dell'Acquese)/Sainsbury's Barbera d'Asti.

Two or three years ago, if anybody had asked Britain's more knowledgeable wine writers to name the three most exciting wine countries in the world, I doubt if any of them would have included Italy in the list. Today, however, a new wave of producers throughout Italy have invigorated traditional wines and created new ones with an extraordinary range of styles and flavours. This Barbera is everything an inexpensive — and many a pricier — Italian red should be: spicy, rich and herby, with bags of deep, berryish flavour. *See p.104 for stockists.*

White Wine of the Year — Pinot Blanc 1989 (Cave Vinicole de Turckheim)

The Cave Vinicole de Turckheim is one of the most successful cooperatives in Alsace. Producer of the winner of the Late Harvest Trophy at the 1990 *WINE Magazine* International Challenge, it has achieved double honour with this White Wine of the Year.

The Pinot Blanc is an underrated variety, both in Alsace and in Italy, where it is called the Pinot Bianco. Examples like this creamy, gently spicy wine prove how deliciously rích Pinot Blancs can be. And how much easier they are to enjoy than some of the big, brassy Chardonnays that have grabbed so much of the critical attention over the last few years.

As in previous years, our choice of wine has obliged us to reveal one of the secrets of the wine trade: the fact that the same wine is often sold under different labels and under various producers' pseudonyms. In this instance, any Pinot Blanc 1989 whose label declares it to have been made by the Cave Vinicole de Turckheim, the Cave de Witzenheim or the Caves Weiss, will fit the above description of our White Wine of the Year. The same wine is also available under the Co-op's Pierre Chaumont label. *See p.72 for stockists.*

Rosé Wine of the Year — Piemontello Pink (Grants of St James's)

Our first ever Rosé of the Year will probably suprise some of the stuffier members of the wine trade. Rosé wines in general have gone out of fashion and a grapey, off-dry rosé in a bottle with a screw-cap might seem to be the last thing any self-respecting wine guide ought to be recommending.

Well, we have given Piemontello this award without any hesitation. Tasted blind at the Challenge, it won one of only 43 Gold Medals (out of over 4,000 wines tasted), delighting three sets of tasters with its simple, refreshing flavour. Not a wine to be taken too seriously, but one to be enjoyed by the glassful. *See p.89 for stockists.*

AVAILABILITY

Among the gratifyingly large number of letters we receive from readers of the *Guide*, there is the occasional complaint that one or other of the merchants named in the book has run out of stock of particular recommended wines. We should love to be able to avoid this happening, and to guarantee availability. Indeed, when compiling the lists of wines we recommend, we specifically ask the retailers to confirm that they have sufficient stock to ensure that the wine can still be bought in the spring of 1991. They should also be selling at prices quoted in the *Guide*, though obviously merchants may be affected by currency changes when they have to bring in fresh stock.

We pass these assurances on in good faith. Unfortunately, by its very nature, a particular vintage of any wine is a finite product. If sales of a car or a washing machine rise, the manufacturer can simply increase production; once the 5,000 or 500,000 bottles of 1982 Château X have been bought, however, no one can turn on a tap to make some more.

Last year, 35,000 people bought copies of this book. If only half of those readers purchased one bottle of some of our recommended wines, cellars could literally be emptied. Were we to restrict our recommendations to wines made in huge quantities, this would be a very dull book indeed.

However, it's worth remembering that only a minority of our wines have only one stockist, and of those, supermarket 'exclusives' are usually bought in large quantities. So, if another *Guide* reader has bought your allocation of 78 Gruaud Larose from your merchant, try shopping around — another outlet's range might include other attractions too.

HOW TO USE THE GUIDE

The *Guide* is split into three main sections. First, on p.69, is the list of 500 recommended wines (**The Wines**), divided by style and within those styles listed in order of price. With each are one or more stockist codes indicating where the wine may be bought. Every wine in this recommended wine section has a code number which features elsewhere in the *Guide*. For each wine, we list coded food styles, explained in detail in the **Wine With Food** chapter (p.16).

Secondly, the **Stockists** section (p.115) lists and describes 180 retail wine merchants alphabetically, and indicates the recommended wines they sell.

Finally, the **A-Z** includes definitions of 1,000 wine names and terms, recommended vintages, approximate prices and suggested producers and stockists. Where a wine features elsewhere in the *Guide* its code number will appear; otherwise a typical example and a stockist is given.

HOW TO READ THE ENTRIES

The Wines Listing

304[1] ROSSO SECONDO[2] Vinattieri[3] 1985[4] Tuscany[5] (It)[6]

£9.65[7]	☞BI[8]	🍽 j, k, m[9]

From a partnership of three of Italy's best wine experts, this is a deep purple, blackcurranty wine with dusky tannin and rich tarry fruit right to the finish - very New World style.[10]

1   The code number which refers to this wine throughout the book
2   The wine name
3   The producer, though with New World wines in particular, this may already have featured as an integral part of the wine name - for example: **MONTANA[3] SAUVIGNON BLANC[2]** 1989[4] Marlborough[5] (NZ)[6]
4   The vintage
5   The region in which the wine was made
6   The country in which the wine was made
7   The price we would expect you to pay, not an average price
8   The stockists - for codes see p.16
9   Foods with which this wine might go well - for codes see p.66
10 Tasting notes

Wine names printed in red indicate particularly good quality and value.

The Stockists' Listing

Recommended wines are listed beneath each merchant thus:

354 [1] **£10.75** [2] **CORNAS** [3], Guy de Barjac [4], Rhône [5] 1986 [6]

1 The code number — refer to **The Wines** for tasting notes
2 The price which the stockist charges for the wine
3 The wine name
4 The producer
5 The region
6 The vintage

Wine names printed in red indicate particularly good quality and value.

The A-Z Listing

Aglianico del Vulture (BASILICATA) [1] Full-bodied, best-known and best DOC red from this region, made from a grape used by the ancient Greeks **79 81 82** 85 88 [2] £££ [3] Fratelli d'Angelo 85 [4] (WCE, L&W) [5]

1 Words that appear in SMALL CAPITALS have their own entry elsewhere in the A-Z.
2 Only those vintages that are good have been listed. The years that appear in bold are ready to drink.
3 Price guide: £ = under £3, ££ = £3-5, £££ = £5-8, ££££ = £8-12, £££££ = £12 and over.
4 This is a recommended example of the wine. Where possible we recommend one of the *Guide*'s 500 wines, in which case it will appear as a number, for example 1 7 9.
5 Stockists — for an explanation of merchants' codes, see below. If the merchant is not featured in the *Guide*, its telephone number will appear.

Abbreviations for Stockists

A	Asda Stores Limited	*featured on page* 118
AB	Augustus Barnett Limited	123
ABY	Anthony Byrne Fine Wines	132
ADN	Adnams	115
AF	Alexr Findlater & Co Ltd	149
AHC	Ad Hoc Wines	115
AR	Arthur Rackham	190
AS	Andre Simon Shops Ltd	199
ASK	Askham Wines	119
AUC	Australian Wine Centre	120
AV	Averys of Bristol	121
BAT	The Battersea Wine Company	123
BBR	Berry Bros & Rudd	125
BD	Bordeaux Direct	129
BEN	Bennetts	124
BH	B H Wines	121
BI	Bibendum Wine Ltd.	126
BIN	Bin 89 Wine Warehouse	126
BLW	Blayneys	127

MERCHANTS' SERVICES AND SPECIALITY AREAS

The two charts on the following pages, introduced last year as a brand new feature to the Guide, have proved popular with those readers who requested an at-a-glance guide to the overall style of the merchants we recommend in later pages.

Should you have an acquired taste for,. or perhaps have newly been introduced to, and enjoyed, the wines of a particular area, the chart on p.32 listing which of our merchants consider this to be their 'speciality' field will point the way towards the source of further examples. The chart summarising services offered to customers on p.22 has also, as we hoped, been a salutary lesson to those firms — particularly in the High Street — who, with a little more effort, could make marked improvements in some of these areas.

Though of course one would not expect, for example, a supermarket to be able to offer the individual service available at a specialist wine merchant, there are cases where the High Street shop that has trained its staff to be informed and helpful can be a far more attractive proposition than the intimidatingly snooty specialist where one doesn't dare ask a vital question — 'Should I drink it now, or wait? — for fear of being thought ignorant.

Notes for merchants' services chart (p.22)

STYLE OF BUSINESS
It is sometimes difficult to tie merchants down and ask them to define their style of business coherently. Wine warehouses sell by the bottle, supermarkets run their own wine clubs and mail-order-only firms run in-store tastings. The information presented is the description given to us by each company, to which we would add the following interpretations.

National High Street: a large chain of off-licences covering a very substantial part of Britain — for example, Victoria Wine.

Regional High Street: a smaller chain confined to a particular region. In general, these should offer more of a specialist approach to selling wine. Awards in this category are always fiercely fought.

Wine club: either mail-order only, or a merchant with some sort of scheme (for which there may or may not be a fee) whereby members receive, for example, regular newsletters, priority on wine orders, discounts, invitations to tastings etc.

Wine warehouse: this once indicated a by-the-case-only operation, and though this still holds true for some, the term has become much looser, often being used simply to describe the general atmosphere of the shop.

BY-THE-BOTTLE
It can be infuriating, having trawled round a so-called wine warehouse dutifully making up a case, to discover that you could have just bought the

bottle you needed for Sunday lunch after all. And the '12 or nothing' rule can be equally frustrating when you just fancy trying a bottle of something new. However, most by-the-case outlets allow that case to be mixed, which gives a lot more pleasure in the choosing and drinking than a dozen frantic stops at the late-night grocers that happens to lie on your way home from work.

CREDIT CARDS

Many small merchants would rather offer customers a discount for cheque or cash than accept credit cards, thus saving themselves the paperwork and the commission levied by the card companies. Worth enquiring.

ACCOUNT FACILITIES

Personal account facilities are available at the merchant's discretion. References are usually needed.

DELIVERY

L = free local delivery; N = free national delivery, though in many cases a premium is paid for this service; that is, the price of wines delivered 'free' may be rather high. Firms that acknowledge this — e.g. Adnams, The Wine Society — offer a 'collection discount'. More detailed information can usually be found in the firms' individual entries.

CELLARAGE

The firm has, or has access to, secure, temperature-controlled storage for customers' wines. Charges vary.

INVESTMENT ADVICE

Advice on wines to lay down for future drinking or profit will be freely available. Many firms in this category have their own cellar schemes whereby customers are informed and/or assisted to take advantage of special purchases.

EN PRIMEUR

The firm will regularly offer and advise on *en primeur* (in-the-barrel) purchases, making all the necessary arrangements.

PARTY PLANNING

The reverse of the 'investment' coin; the company will give sensible and economical advice on wine styles, quantities per person, etc. Particularly valuable if the company also offers 'sale or return'.

TASTINGS

'In-store' means that informal tastings of opened or promoted wines take place, often on an ad hoc basis, so luck will prevail. 'Ticketed/tutored' tastings imply a more organised event, though not necessarily charged. Fuller details may appear under companies' individual entries.

When contemplating a major purchase, any good specialist merchant should, except in the case of the most expensive wines, be more than happy to open a bottle for tasting. (It's worth noting that if Scottish merchants seem a little reluctant to offer wines for tasting, this is not confirmation of a hackneyed racial stereotype but an indication that the merchant is unwilling to break Scottish laws by allowing you to drink on the premises. Some canny firms have devised cunning ways of getting round this.)

PAGE NUMBER

A full entry for this merchant, including address, opening hours and the *Guide's* report, will be found on this page.

		Nat. High Street	Reg. High Street	Ind. Merchant	Wine Club	Supermarket
AHC	Ad Hoc Wines			◊		
ADN	Adnams		◊	◊		
DAL	David Alexander			◊		
HAS	H Allen Smith			◊		
A	Asda Stores Limited					◊
ASK	Askham Wines			◊		
AUC	Australian Wine Centre			◊		
AV	Averys of Bristol			◊	◊	
BH	B H Wines			◊		
DB	David Baillie Vintners			◊		
BWS	The Barnes Wine Shop			◊		
AB	Augustus Barnett Limited	◊				
BAT	The Battersea Wine Company			◊		
BEN	Bennetts			◊		
BBR	Berry Bros & Rudd			◊		
BI	Bibendum Wine Ltd			◊		
BIN	Bin 89 Wine Warehouse			◊		
BND	Bin Ends			◊		
BLW	Blayneys		◊			
BTH	E H Booths					◊
BOO	Booths (of Stockport)			◊		
B&B	Bottle & Basket			◊		
BU	Bottoms Up	◊				
BRO	The Broad Street Wine Co.			◊		
BUD	Budgens					◊
ABY	Anthony Byrne Fine Wines			◊		
DBY	D Byrne & Co			◊		
CAC	Cachet Wines			◊		
CWG	Cadwgan Fine Wine			◊		
CWI	A Case of Wine			◊		
CVR	The Celtic Vintner			◊		
CDV	Champagne de Villages			◊		
CPL	Chaplin & Son			◊		
CNL	Connollys			◊		
C&B	Corney & Barrow			◊		
CWM	Cornwall Wine Merchants			◊		

Wine W'house	By The Bottle	No. of Branches	Credit Cards	Own Charge Card	Account Facilities	Mail Order	Delivery	Coll. Discount	Cellerage	Invest. Advice	En Primeur	Free Glass Loan	Glass Loan	Ice	Party Planning	Gift Mailing	Books	In-Store Tastings	Tutored Tastings	Page No.
◊	◊	1	◊		◊		L					◊		◊	◊	◊	◊	◊	◊	115
◊	◊	3	◊			◊		◊	◊		◊	◊				◊		◊	◊	115
	◊	1	◊		◊	◊	L			◊	◊	◊			◊		◊		◊	117
	◊	2	◊		◊	◊	L		◊			◊			◊	◊	◊	◊		117
	◊	190	◊																◊	118
		1			◊	◊	N			◊	◊	◊							◊	119
	◊	1	◊			◊	N	◊							◊	◊	◊		◊	120
	◊	1	◊		◊	◊	L	◊	◊	◊		◊	◊		◊	◊			◊	121
◊		1				◊	L					◊			◊	◊			◊	121
		1																		122
	◊	1	◊				L		◊	◊	◊	◊			◊	◊	◊	◊	◊	122
	◊	645	◊	◊			L				◊	◊		◊						123
	◊	1	◊				L			◊		◊			◊	◊		◊		123
	◊	1	◊		◊	◊	L	◊	◊			◊	◊		◊	◊				124
	◊	2	◊		◊	◊	N	◊	◊		◊		◊			◊	◊	◊	◊	125
◊	◊	1	◊		◊	◊	L	◊	◊	◊	◊	◊			◊	◊	◊	◊	◊	126
◊	◊	1			◊	◊	L		◊		◊	◊				◊	◊		◊	126
	◊	2	◊		◊		L		◊	◊		◊						◊	◊	127
	◊	190	◊		◊		L					◊			◊				◊	127
	◊	20	◊			◊	N					◊							◊	129
	◊	1	◊			◊						◊	◊		◊			◊	◊	128
	◊	1	◊				◊													130
		55																		130
		1	◊		◊				◊	◊	◊				◊	◊			◊	131
	◊	125	◊																	131
◊	◊	1	◊		◊	◊	L	◊	◊	◊	◊	◊			◊	◊		◊	◊	132
	◊	1			◊	◊	L		◊		◊	◊	◊			◊	◊			132
◊		1		◊		◊	L	◊	◊		◊	◊			◊				◊	134
	◊	2	◊				L		◊	◊	◊	◊	◊	◊	◊	◊	◊		◊	135
		1	◊		◊	◊	L		◊		◊	◊		◊	◊	◊	◊		◊	136
		1	◊			◊	L	◊	◊	◊		◊			◊	◊			◊	136
	◊	1	◊		◊	◊	L	◊	◊		◊			◊	◊	◊	◊	◊	◊	138
◊	◊	1	◊			◊	L	◊			◊	◊		◊	◊				◊	138
	◊	1	◊		◊	◊	L		◊	◊		◊		◊		◊	◊	◊		139
	◊	4	◊		◊	◊			◊	◊	◊	◊				◊	◊		◊	140
		1	◊		◊	◊	L		◊	◊	◊				◊	◊			◊	140

		Nat. High Street	Reg. High Street	Ind. Merchant	Wine Club	Supermarket
CGW	Cote Green Wines Ltd.			◊		
COV	County Vintners			◊		
CWS	Co-op					◊
CUM	Cumbrian Cellar			◊		
D	Davisons		◊			
DVC	Davy & Co Ltd					
ROD	Rodney Densem			◊		
PD	Peter Dominic	◊				
DRI	Drinksmart			◊		
DX	Drinkx plc			◊		
EP	Eldridge Pope			◊		
EBA	Ben Ellis & Assocs			◊		
EOO	Everton's of Ombersley			◊		
EVI	Evingtons			◊		
FAR	Farr Vintners			◊		
AF	Alex Findlater			◊		
FDL	Findlater Mackie Todd			◊		
FW	Flemings Wines			◊		
FWC	Fulham Rd Wine Centre			◊		
FUL	Fuller Smith & Turner		◊			
G	Gateway					◊
GON	Gauntleys Of Nottingham			◊		
MG	Matthew Gloag & Son			◊	◊	
GH	Goedhuis & Co			◊		
GHW	Grape Hive Wines			◊		
GI	Grape Ideas					
GNW	Great Northern Wine Co					
GRT	Great Western Wine, Bath			◊		
GWR	Great Western Wines, Reading			◊		
PTR	Peter Green			◊		
GRN	Greens			◊		
TGB	The Grog Blossom			◊		
HFV	Harcourt Fine Wines			◊		
HPD	Harpenden Wines			◊		
GHS	Gerard Harris			◊	◊	
HAR	Harrods			◊		

Wine W'house	By The Bottle	No. of Branches	Credit Cards	Own Charge Card	Account Facilities	Mail Order	Delivery	Coll. Discount	Cellerage	Invest. Advice	En Primeur	Free Glass Loan	Glass Loan	Ice	Party Planning	Gift Mailing	Books	In-Store Tastings	Tutored Tastings	Page No.
	◊	1	◊				L			◊		◊			◊	◊		◊	◊	141
◊		1		◊			L			◊	◊		◊		◊	◊	◊	◊		141
	◊	2400	◊															◊		139
	◊	1	◊		◊	◊	L		◊	◊		◊			◊	◊	◊		◊	142
	◊	78	◊		◊	◊	L					◊		◊		◊		◊		142
◊	◊	1	◊				L					◊				◊				143
	◊	1	◊		◊	◊	L			◊	◊		◊		◊	◊		◊		144
	◊	600	◊				L							◊	◊	◊		◊		144
◊	◊	1	◊						◊					◊	◊		◊	◊		145
	◊	2	◊			◊	N	◊	◊	◊	◊			◊	◊	◊		◊	◊	146
◊	◊	13	◊		◊	◊	L	◊	◊	◊			◊		◊	◊		◊	◊	146
		1		◊	◊	◊	L	◊	◊	◊			◊	◊	◊	◊	◊	◊	◊	147
	◊	4	◊					◊	◊	◊	◊			◊	◊				◊	148
	◊	1	◊				L	◊	◊	◊	◊			◊	◊	◊		◊	◊	146
		1		◊	◊	◊	L	◊	◊	◊							◊			149
◊		1	◊		◊	◊	L	◊				◊				◊				149
	◊	1	◊		◊	◊	N	◊	◊	◊			◊		◊	◊		◊	◊	149
	◊	1	◊				L			◊	◊	◊				◊	◊	◊	◊	150
	◊	1	◊			◊	L			◊	◊	◊		◊	◊	◊	◊	◊	◊	150
	◊	59	◊		◊		L					◊		◊				◊	◊	152
	◊	600	◊															◊		152
	◊	1	◊			◊	L	◊	◊	◊	◊			◊	◊	◊		◊	◊	153
	◊	1	◊		◊	◊	L	◊	◊	◊	◊				◊	◊	◊		◊	154
		1	◊		◊	◊	N	◊	◊	◊									◊	154
	◊	1	◊								◊				◊					155
◊	◊	2	◊		◊	◊	L	◊	◊	◊			◊	◊		◊	◊			155
◊	◊	1	◊		◊	◊	L	◊	◊	◊	◊	◊	◊			◊		◊	◊	156
◊		1	◊		◊	◊	L	◊	◊	◊	◊			◊	◊	◊	◊	◊	◊	157
	◊	1	◊			◊	N	◊								◊		◊	◊	157
	◊	1		◊	◊	◊	L			◊			◊						◊	158
		1	◊		◊	◊	L	◊	◊	◊		◊	◊			◊			◊	159
	◊	3	◊				L				◊		◊	◊	◊			◊		159
	◊	1	◊		◊	◊	L		◊		◊			◊	◊			◊		159
	◊	1	◊		◊		L				◊			◊	◊	◊	◊	◊	◊	161
	◊	1	◊	◊	◊	◊	L	◊	◊	◊	◊			◊	◊	◊	◊		◊	154
	◊	1	◊	◊	◊	◊				◊	◊					◊	◊	◊		161

		Nat. High Street	Reg. High Street	Ind. Merchant	Wine Club	Supermarket
RHV	Richard Harvey Wines			◊		
HV	Harveys of Bristol			◊		
HFW	Haughton Fine Wines			◊		
HHC	Haynes Hanson & Clarke			◊		
H&H	Hector & Honorez			◊		
HW	Hedley Wright			◊		
HEM	The Hermitage			◊		
H&D	Hicks & Don Ltd			◊		
HBV	High Breck Vintners			◊		
GHL	George Hill of Loughborough			◊		
JEH	J E Hogg			◊		
RHW	Rodney Hogg Wines			◊		
HOL	Holland Park Wine Co			◊		
HOP	Hopton Wines			◊		
HUN	Hungerford Wine Co			◊		
JOB	Jeroboams			◊		
J&B	Justerini & Brooks			◊		
K&B	King & Barnes			◊		
L&W	Lay & Wheeler			◊		
LAY	Laytons			◊		
LNR	Le Nez Rouge			◊		
LEA	Lea & Sandeman Co Ltd			◊		
LTW	The Littlewoods Organisation					◊
LWL	London Wine Ltd			◊		
LHV	Lorne House Vintners			◊	◊	
MWW	Majestic Wine Warehouses					
M&S	Marks & Spencer					◊
MC	The Master Cellar					
MCL	McLeod's			◊		
MM	Michael Menzel Wines			◊		
MIL	Millevini			◊		
MTL	Mitchells Wine Merchants			◊		
MOR	Moreno Wines			◊		
M&V	Morris & Verdin			◊		
MRS	Morrison Supermarkets Ltd					◊
JN	James Nicholson Wine Merchants			◊		

Wine W'house	By The Bottle	No. of Branches	Credit Cards	Own Charge Card	Account Facilities	Mail Order	Delivery	Coll. Discount	Cellerage	Invest. Advice	En Primeur	Free Glass Loan	Glass Loan	Ice	Party Planning	Gift Mailing	Books	In-Store Tastings	Tutored Tastings	Page No.
—		1				◊	◊ L	◊	◊	◊	◊			◊	◊	◊			◊	162
	◊	2	◊		◊	◊			◊	◊	◊				◊	◊	◊	◊	◊	162
—		1	◊			◊	L				◊				◊			◊	◊	163
	◊	1			◊	◊	N	◊		◊	◊	◊		◊	◊	◊		◊	◊	163
—		1	◊			◊	L	◊	◊	◊	◊				◊				◊	164
◊		1	◊	◊	◊	◊	L		◊	◊	◊			◊	◊	◊	◊	◊	◊	164
	◊	1	◊				L				◊				◊	◊	◊			165
		2	◊		◊	◊	L	◊	◊	◊	◊				◊				◊	166
◊		1	◊		◊	◊	L		◊	◊	◊			◊	◊			◊	◊	166
	◊	1	◊		◊		L	◊	◊	◊	◊				◊	◊	◊			167
	◊	1				◊	L		◊		◊				◊	◊			◊	167
		1	◊		◊	◊	L	◊					◊	◊	◊	◊				168
	◊	1	◊		◊	◊	L		◊	◊	◊			◊	◊	◊	◊	◊	◊	168
		1	◊			◊	L		◊	◊	◊				◊			◊	◊	169
	◊	1	◊		◊	◊	L		◊	◊	◊			◊	◊	◊	◊	◊	◊	169
	◊	2	◊		◊		L				◊				◊			◊		170
	◊	2	◊		◊	◊			◊	◊	◊	◊				◊			◊	170
	◊	1	◊								◊		◊	◊		◊			◊	171
◊	◊	2	◊		◊	◊	L		◊	◊	◊			◊	◊	◊	◊	◊	◊	171
	◊	1	◊		◊	◊			◊	◊	◊				◊			◊	◊	172
	◊	1				◊	L	◊		◊	◊				◊				◊	181
	◊	1	◊		◊	◊	L	◊	◊	◊	◊			◊	◊			◊	◊	172
	◊	91	◊	◊																173
◊		1	◊				L			◊				◊				◊	◊	173
◊		1				◊	L	◊				◊	◊					◊	◊	174
◊		33	◊		◊	◊	L				◊			◊	◊	◊	◊	◊	◊	174
	◊	1				◊														175
◊		1	◊			◊	L		◊		◊			◊	◊	◊		◊	◊	176
	◊	1	◊				L				◊				◊					177
	◊	1	◊		◊		L				◊				◊		◊			177
—		1				◊	L						◊							178
	◊	3	◊		◊	◊	L	◊	◊		◊				◊	◊	◊	◊	◊	179
	◊	2	◊				L				◊					◊		◊	◊	179
—		1			◊	◊	L		◊	◊	◊	◊				◊				180
	◊	50	◊								◊									180
	◊	1	◊			◊	N	◊	◊	◊	◊				◊	◊	◊	◊	◊	181

		Nat. High Street	Reg. High Street	Ind. Merchant	Wine Club	Supermarket
NIC	Nicolas			◊		
RN	Rex Norris			◊		
OD	Oddbins	◊				
OBC	The Old Butcher's Wine Cellar			◊		
OLS	The Old St Wine Co			◊		
ORG	Organic Wine Co			◊		
P	Parfrements			◊		
THP	Thos Peatling		◊	◊		
CPW	Christopher Piper Wines			◊		
TP	Terry Platt Wines			◊		
POW	Portland Wine Company			◊		
AR	Arthur Rackham			◊		
RAE	Raeburn Fine Wine & Foods			◊		
RAV	Ravensbourne Wine Co			◊		
RD	Reid Wines			◊		
REW	La Reserva Wines			◊		
RES	La Reserve			◊		
WRB	William Robbs					◊
RTW	The Rose Tree Wine Co.			◊		
SAF	Safeway	◊				◊
JS	J Sainsbury Plc	◊				◊
SAN	Sandiway Wine Co.			◊		
SEB	Sebastopol Wines			◊		
SK	Seckford Wines			◊		
SEL	Selfridges			◊		
SHV	Sherborne Vintners			◊		
AS	Andre Simon Shops Ltd		◊			
SV	Smedley Vintners,			◊		
SPR	Spar (UK) Ltd	◊				
SAS	St Albans Sherston Wine Co			◊		
FSW	Frank Stainton Wine Merchant			◊		
SOB	Stones of Belgravia			◊		
SUM	Summerlee Wines			◊		
WC	Sunday Times Wine Club				◊	
T&W	T&W Wines			◊		
TAN	Tanners of Shrewsbury			◊		

Wine W'house	By The Bottle	No. of Branches	Credit Cards	Own Charge Card	Account Facilities	Mail Order	Delivery	Coll. Discount	Cellerage	Invest. Advice	En Primeur	Free Glass Loan	Glass Loan	Ice	Party Planning	Gift Mailing	Books	In-Store Tastings	Tutored Tastings	Page No.
—	◊	5	◊			◊	L			◊	◊	◊			◊	◊	◊		◊	182
—	◊	1	◊			◊	L				◊	◊	◊		◊					182
—	◊	144	◊			◊	L					◊			◊	◊			◊	183
—	◊	1	◊				L			◊	◊	◊			◊	◊			◊	185
—	◊	1	◊			◊	◊ L			◊	◊	◊			◊	◊			◊	185
—		1				◊	L	◊	◊						◊	◊			◊	186
—		1				◊	N												◊	186
◊	◊	1	◊			◊	◊ L			◊	◊	◊	◊	◊	◊	◊	◊	◊	◊	186
—	◊	1	◊			◊	◊ L	◊	◊	◊	◊	◊				◊		◊	◊	188
—		1				◊	L													188
—	◊	3	◊				L					◊		◊				◊	◊	189
—	◊	14	◊		◊	◊					◊	◊	◊		◊			◊	◊	190
—	◊	1					L	◊	◊	◊	◊				◊			◊	◊	190
◊		1			◊	◊	L	◊		◊				◊	◊	◊		◊	◊	191
—	◊	1	◊			◊	◊ L			◊	◊	◊			◊		◊		◊	191
—	◊	1	◊			◊	◊ L					◊					◊	◊	◊	192
—	◊	4	◊			◊	◊ L			◊	◊	◊		◊			◊		◊	192
—	◊	2	◊	◊	◊	◊	L					◊	◊			◊	◊		◊	193
—	◊	1	◊		◊		L	◊	◊	◊	◊				◊	◊			◊	193
—	◊	288										◊							◊	194
—	◊	288															◊			195
—	◊	1	◊				L					◊							◊	196
◊		1	◊			◊	L ◊				◊	◊		◊					◊	197
◊		1	◊		◊	◊	L	◊	◊	◊	◊	◊	◊		◊				◊	197
—	◊	1	◊	◊	◊	◊	L			◊					◊	◊	◊	◊		198
—		1			◊	◊	L	◊	◊						◊					198
—	◊	3	◊		◊	◊	L			◊	◊	◊			◊	◊	◊		◊	199
◊		1			◊	◊				◊	◊	◊	◊		◊	◊				200
—	◊	2000	◊						◊											200
—	◊	1	◊		◊		L			◊		◊			◊	◊	◊	◊	◊	201
—	◊	1	◊				L							◊		◊	◊		◊	201
—	◊	2	◊		◊		L			◊	◊	◊		◊		◊				202
—	◊	1			◊	◊	L	◊	◊	◊	◊			◊	◊	◊		◊		202
—	◊	1	◊			◊						◊						◊		202
—	◊	1	◊			◊	◊ L		◊		◊	◊				◊	◊			203
◊		6	◊		◊	◊	L ◊			◊		◊		◊	◊	◊	◊	◊	◊	203

		Nat. High Street	Reg. High Street	Ind. Merchant	Wine Club	Supermarket
TO	Tesco					◊
TH	Thresher	◊				
UBC	Ubiquitious Chip Wine Shop			◊		
U	Unwins		◊			
UC	The Upper Crust			◊		
V&C	Valvona & Crolla			◊		
HVW	Helen Verdcourt			◊		
VW	Victoria Wine	◊				
LV	La Vigneronne			◊		
VER	Vinceremos Wines Ltd.					
VR	Vintage Roots			◊		
W	Waitrose Ltd					◊
WAW	Waterloo Wine Co.			◊		
WAC	Waters of Coventry			◊		
WES	Wessex Wines			◊		
WOC	Whitesides of Clitheroe			◊		
WID	Widcombe Wines			◊		
WIL	Willoughby's of Manchester			◊		
WDW	Windrush Wines			◊		
WBM	Wine Byre Merchants			◊		
WE	Wine Emporium					
WGA	Wine Growers Assoc.			◊		
WH	The Wine House			◊		
TWR	The Wine Rack		◊			
WSO	Wine Society, IEC				◊	
WCE	Winecellars			◊		
WIN	The Winery			◊	◊	
WFP	Wines from Paris			◊		
WOI	Wines of Interest		◊			
WIZ	Wizard Wine Warehouses			◊		◊
WWI	Woodhouse Wines			◊		
WRW	The Wright Wine Co			◊		
PWY	Peter Wylie Fine Wines			◊		
YAP	Yapp Bros			◊		
YFW	Yorkshire Fine Wines		◊			

Wine W'house	By The Bottle	No. of Branches	Credit Cards	Own Charge Card	Account Facilities	Mail Order	Delivery	Coll. Discount	Cellerage	Invest. Advice	En Primeur	Free Glass Loan	Glass Loan	Ice	Party Planning	Gift Mailing	Books	In-Store Tastings	Tutored Tastings	Page No.
	◊	360	◊															◊	◊	204
	◊	968	◊		◊		L					◊			◊	◊				205
	◊	1	◊	◊	◊		L			◊		◊	◊		◊	◊			◊	207
	◊	305	◊	◊	◊		L					◊			◊	◊	◊		◊	208
	◊	1	◊	◊	◊		L	◊	◊	◊	◊	◊	◊		◊	◊	◊	◊	◊	208
	◊	1	◊	◊	◊		N	◊	◊						◊	◊		◊	◊	210
		1		◊	◊		L								◊	◊	◊	◊	◊	211
	◊	900	◊	◊	◊											◊				212
	◊	1	◊		◊		L	◊		◊						◊	◊		◊	213
◊		1	◊		◊		L	◊				◊			◊	◊			◊	213
		1	◊		◊		N	◊				◊								214
	◊	90										◊			◊	◊				214
	◊	1	◊				L			◊		◊			◊			◊	◊	215
	◊	1	◊	◊	◊		L						◊			◊				216
		1		◊			L	◊							◊	◊	◊		◊	216
	◊	1	◊		◊		L					◊			◊	◊	◊	◊	◊	216
	◊	1	◊	◊										◊		◊				217
	◊	5	◊				L	◊		◊	◊				◊	◊	◊	◊	◊	218
	◊	1	◊	◊	◊		N	◊	◊	◊						◊	◊	◊	◊	218
	◊	1	◊	◊	◊		L	◊	◊	◊	◊	◊			◊	◊	◊	◊	◊	219
◊		1	◊	◊	◊		L	◊	◊	◊	◊	◊	◊		◊	◊	◊	◊	◊	220
	◊	1	◊		◊		L			◊						◊				221
	◊	1	◊		◊		L					◊			◊	◊	◊	◊	◊	221
	◊	28	◊	◊			L					◊			◊	◊	◊	◊	◊	222
	◊	1	◊		◊		N	◊	◊	◊	◊	◊			◊	◊	◊		◊	224
◊	◊	1	◊	◊	◊		N	◊	◊						◊	◊	◊	◊	◊	219
	◊	2	◊		◊					◊	◊	◊	◊		◊	◊	◊		◊	224
		1																		220
◊	◊	1		◊	◊		L	◊	◊	◊					◊	◊	◊	◊	◊	225
◊	◊	12	◊												◊	◊		◊	◊	226
	◊	1	◊	◊	◊		L	◊	◊	◊	◊	◊			◊	◊	◊	◊	◊	226
	◊	1		◊			L			◊		◊			◊	◊	◊		◊	226
	◊	1					L	◊	◊	◊										227
	◊	1	◊	◊	◊		L	◊	◊	◊	◊	◊	◊		◊	◊	◊	◊	◊	227
		2	◊	◊	◊		N	◊	◊	◊	◊							◊	◊	227

		Bordeaux	Burgundy	Rhone	Loire	Alsace
AHC	Ad Hoc Wines	◊	◊	◊	—	—
ADN	Adnams	◊	◊	◊	—	—
DAL	David Alexander	◊	—	—	—	—
HAS	H Allen Smith	—	—	—	—	—
A	Asda Stores Limited	—	—	—	—	—
ASK	Askham Wines	—	—	—	—	—
AUC	Australian Wine Centre	—	—	—	—	—
AV	Averys of Bristol	◊	◊	—	—	—
BH	B H Wines	—	—	—	—	—
DB	David Baillie Vintners	—	—	—	—	—
BWS	The Barnes Wine Shop	—	—	—	—	—
AB	Augustus Barnett Limited	—	—	—	—	—
BAT	The Battersea Wine Company	—	—	—	—	—
BEN	Bennetts	—	—	—	—	—
BBR	Berry Bros & Rudd	◊	—	—	—	—
BI	Bibendum Wine Ltd	◊	◊	◊	—	—
BIN	Bin 89 Wine Warehouse	—	—	—	—	—
BND	Bin Ends	—	—	—	—	—
BLW	Blayneys	—	—	—	—	—
BTH	E H Booths	—	—	—	—	—
BOO	Booths (of Stockport)	—	—	—	—	—
B&B	Bottle & Basket	—	—	—	—	—
BU	Bottoms Up	—	—	—	—	—
BRO	The Broad Street Wine Co.	—	◊	—	—	◊
BUD	Budgens	—	—	—	◊	—
ABY	Anthony Byrne Fine Wines	—	—	—	—	—
DBY	D Byrne & Co	◊	—	◊	◊	◊
CAC	Cachet Wines	—	—	—	—	—
CWG	Cadwgan Fine Wine	—	—	—	—	—
CWI	A Case of Wine	—	—	—	—	—
CVR	The Celtic Vintner	—	◊	—	◊	—
CDV	Champagne de Villages	—	◊	—	◊	—
CPL	Chaplin & Son	◊	◊	—	◊	◊
CNL	Connollys	—	—	—	—	—
C&B	Corney & Barrow	◊	◊	—	—	—
CWM	Cornwall Wine Merchants	—	—	—	—	—

Champagne	French Reg.	Germany	Spain	Portugal	Italy	Australia	New Zealand	California	Other U.S.	South America	England	Sherry	Port	Madeira	Organic	Ind. Domaines	Fine/Old Wines	Everyday Value	Half Bottles	Page No.
	◊																			115
			◊		◊													◊		115
																		◊		117
			◊	◊																117
																			◊	118
																				119
						◊														120
																				121
																				121
																				122
						◊	◊	◊											◊	122
																				123
																				123
						◊	◊	◊										◊		124
	◊																	◊	◊	125
				◊													◊	◊	◊	126
				◊	◊															126
				◊								◊								127
																				127
																◊		◊		129
						◊	◊													128
◊		◊																		130
																				130
																				131
	◊																	◊	◊	131
																				132
◊	◊	◊			◊							◊						◊		132
																				134
																				135
																				136
	◊		◊										◊	◊		◊		◊	◊	136
◊																◊			◊	138
◊		◊		◊	◊	◊	◊			◊		◊				◊		◊	◊	138
																◊				139
																		◊	◊	140
																				140

		Bordeaux	Burgundy	Rhone	Loire	Alsace
CGW	Cote Green Wines Ltd.	—	—	—		—
COV	County Vintners	—	—	—		
CWS	Co-op	—	—	—		—
CUM	Cumbrian Cellar	—	—	—		—
D	Davisons	—	—	—		
DVC	Davy & Co Ltd	—	—	—		—
ROD	Rodney Densem	◊	◊	◊	◊	◊
PD	Peter Dominic	—		—		
DRI	Drinksmart	—		—		—
DX	Drinkx plc	◊	◊			
EP	Eldridge Pope	◊	◊		◊	◊
EBA	Ben Ellis & Assocs	—		—		—
EOO	Everton's of Ombersley		◊			◊
EVI	Evingtons	—		—		—
FAR	Farr Vintners	◊	◊	◊		
AF	Alex Findlater	—		—		—
FDL	Findlater Mackie Todd	◊				—
FW	Flemings Wines	—		—		—
FWC	Fulham Rd Wine Centre	—		—		—
FUL	Fuller Smith & Turner	—		—		—
G	Gateway	—		—		—
GON	Gauntleys Of Nottingham	◊	◊	◊		—
MG	Matthew Gloag & Son	◊		◊		—
GH	Goedhuis & Co	—		—		—
GHW	Grape Hive Wines	—		—		—
GI	Grape Ideas	◊	◊	◊		—
GNW	Great Northern Wine Co	—		—		—
GRT	Great Western Wine, Bath	—		—		—
GWR	Great Western Wines, Reading	—		—		—
PTR	Peter Green	—		—		—
GRN	Greens	◊	◊	◊		—
TGB	The Grog Blossom	◊	◊			◊
HFV	Harcourt Fine Wines	—		—		—
HPD	Harpenden Wines	◊		—		—
GHS	Gerard Harris	◊		—		—
HAR	Harrods Ltd	—		—		—

Champagne	French Reg.	Germany	Spain	Portugal	Italy	Australia	New Zealand	California	Other U.S.	South America	England	Sherry	Port	Madeira	Organic	Ind. Domaines	Fine/Old Wines	Everyday Value	Half Bottles	Page No.
												◊								141
																				141
																				139
				◊	◊															142
																				142
																				143
◊						◊							◊			◊	◊			144
																				144
	◊																	◊		145
						◊	◊									◊	◊	◊		146
	◊	◊						◊				◊	◊			◊	◊		◊	146
																				147
◊		◊															◊			148
													◊	◊		◊	◊			146
													◊	◊		◊	◊			149
	◊			◊	◊	◊						◊								149
												◊						◊	◊	149
																				150
																				150
◊	◊		◊																	152
																				152
	◊					◊	◊						◊			◊	◊			153
							◊						◊	◊			◊			154
																				154
																				155
				◊						◊			◊			◊	◊	◊		155
							◊	◊	◊											156
																				157
																				157
																				158
◊																◊	◊			159
◊		◊		◊	◊	◊														159
		◊									◊						◊			159
																				161
																				154
																		◊		161

		Bordeaux	Burgundy	Rhone	Loire	Alsace
RHV	Richard Harvey Wines	◊	◊	◊	◊	
HV	Harveys of Bristol	◊				
HFW	Haughton Fine Wines					
HHC	Haynes Hanson & Clarke	◊	◊		◊	
H&H	Hector & Honorez		◊	◊	◊	◊
HW	Hedley Wright	◊				
HEM	The Hermitage					
H&D	Hicks & Don Ltd					
HBV	High Breck Vintners				◊	◊
GHL	George Hill of Loughborough					
JEH	J E Hogg					
RHW	Rodney Hogg Wines					
HOL	Holland Park Wine Co	◊			◊	
HOP	Hopton Wines	◊	◊		◊	
HUN	Hungerford Wine Co	◊	◊	◊		
JOB	Jeroboams					
J&B	Justerini & Brooks	◊	◊	◊		
K&B	King & Barnes					
L&W	Lay & Wheeler	◊	◊	◊	◊	◊
LAY	Laytons	◊	◊			
LNR	Le Nez Rouge		◊		◊	
LEA	Lea & Sandeman Co Ltd	◊	◊		◊	
LTW	The Littlewoods Organisation					
LWL	London Wine Ltd					
LHV	Lorne House Vintners				◊	
MWW	Majestic Wine Warehouses					
M&S	Marks & Spencer					
MC	The Master Cellar	◊	◊			
MCL	McLeod's					
MM	Michael Menzel Wines	◊	◊	◊	◊	◊
MIL	Millevini					
MTL	Mitchells Wine Merchants		◊			
MOR	Moreno Wines					
M&V	Morris & Verdin		◊		◊	◊
MRS	Morrison Supermarkets Ltd					
JN	James Nicholson Wine Merchants					

Champagne	French Reg.	Germany	Spain	Portugal	Italy	Australia	New Zealand	California	Other U.S.	South America	England	Sherry	Port	Madeira	Organic	Ind. Domaines	Fine/Old Wines	Everyday Value	Half Bottles	Page No.
	◊															◊				162
												◊	◊				◊			162
	◊					◊	◊		◊							◊	◊		◊	163
◊					◊															163
	◊																◊		◊	164
								◊				◊					◊			164
																				165
																				166
◊																◊		◊		166
																				167
																				167
																				168
◊						◊										◊	◊			168
◊																◊	◊			169
																◊	◊			169
◊																			◊	170
	◊	◊											◊			◊	◊		◊	170
																				171
◊	◊	◊	◊		◊	◊	◊	◊				◊	◊	◊		◊	◊	◊	◊	171
																◊				172
																◊				181
◊												◊	◊			◊	◊			172
	◊																		◊	173
																		◊		173
																◊				174
																◊		◊		174
																				175
														◊						176
																				177
◊		◊		◊								◊	◊	◊		◊	◊			177
				◊																178
◊		◊										◊								179
		◊										◊								179
								◊								◊				180
																				180
																				181

		Bordeaux	Burgundy	Rhone	Loire	Alsace
NIC	Nicolas	◊	—			—
RN	Rex Norris					
OD	Oddbins			◊		
OBC	The Old Butcher's Wine Cellar	◊	◊			
OLS	The Old St Wine Co				◊	—
ORG	Organic Wine Co					
P	Parfrements					
THP	Thos Peatling	◊	◊			
CPW	Christopher Piper Wines		◊	◊		
TP	Terry Platt Wines	◊	◊			
POW	Portland Wine Company					
AR	Arthur Rackham					
RAE	Raeburn Fine Wine & Foods	◊	◊	◊	◊	—
RAV	Ravensbourne Wine Co	◊	◊			
RD	Reid Wines	◊	◊	◊		◊
REW	La Reserva Wines					
RES	La Reserve	◊	◊			
WRB	William Robbs		—			—
RTW	The Rose Tree Wine Co.	◊	—			—
SAF	Safeway		—			—
JS	J Sainsbury Plc					
SAN	Sandiway Wine Co.					
SEB	Sebastopol Wines			◊	◊	
SK	Seckford Wines	◊				
SEL	Selfridges	◊				
SHV	Sherborne Vintners					
AS	Andre Simon Shops Ltd					
SV	Smedley Vintners,					
SPR	Spar (UK) Ltd					
SAS	St Albans Sherston Wine Co	◊	◊	◊		◊
FSW	Frank Stainton Wine Merchant					
SOB	Stones of Belgravia					
SUM	Summerlee Wines	◊	◊			—
WC	Sunday Times Wine Club	◊	—			—
T&W	T&W Wines	◊	◊	◊		◊
TAN	Tanners of Shrewsbury		—			—

Champagne	French Reg.	Germany	Spain	Portugal	Italy	Australia	New Zealand	California	Other U.S.	South America	England	Sherry	Port	Madeira	Organic	Ind. Domaines	Fine/Old Wines	Everyday Value	Half Bottles	Page No.
◊	◊																			182
																				182
◊	◊				◊	◊		◊	◊				◊						◊	183
																◊	◊			185
													◊					◊		185
															◊					186
																				186
						◊	◊						◊					◊		186
	◊															◊			◊	188
	◊																			188
																				189
																				190
					◊											◊			◊	190
			◊												◊					191
					◊			◊										◊	◊	191
		◊																		192
◊													◊			◊	◊			192
																				193
◊																				193
																				194
																			◊	195
			◊		◊						◊									196
	◊															◊		◊		197
					◊								◊			◊		◊	◊	197
◊																	◊			198
		◊																		198
																				199
	◊				◊															200
																				200
		◊		◊												◊				201
																	◊		◊	201
																				202
	◊															◊				202
	◊								◊							◊				202
◊		◊		◊			◊						◊	◊		◊	◊		◊	203
																				203

		Bordeaux	Burgundy	Rhone	Loire	Alsace
TO	Tesco					
TH	Thresher					
UBC	Ubiquitious Chip Wine Shop	◊	◊	◊		
U	Unwins					
UC	The Upper Crust	◊	◊		◊	◊
V&C	Valvona & Crolla					
HVW	Helen Verdcourt			◊		
VW	Victoria Wine					
LV	La Vigneronne					◊
VER	Vinceremos Wines Ltd.					
VR	Vintage Roots					
W	Waitrose Ltd					
WAW	Waterloo Wine Co.				◊	◊
WAC	Waters of Coventry					
WES	Wessex Wines					
WOC	Whitesides of Clitheroe					
WID	Widcombe Wines					
WIL	Willoughby's of Manchester	◊	◊			
WDW	Windrush Wines		◊			
WBM	Wine Byre Merchants	◊		◊	◊	
WE	Wine Emporium					
WGA	Wine Growers Assoc.	◊				
WH	The Wine House	◊				
TWR	The Wine Rack					
WSO	Wine Society, IEC					
WCE	Winecellars					
WIN	The Winery					
WFP	Wines from Paris					
WOI	Wines of Interest					
WIZ	Wizard Wine Warehouses					
WWI	Woodhouse Wines	◊				
WRW	The Wright Wine Co					
PWY	Peter Wylie Fine Wines					
YAP	Yapp Bros			◊	◊	
YFW	Yorkshire Fine Wines					

Champagne	French Reg.	Germany	Spain	Portugal	Italy	Australia	New Zealand	California	Other U.S.	South America	England	Sherry	Port	Madeira	Organic	Ind. Domaines	Fine/Old Wines	Everyday Value	Half Bottles	Page No.
																				204
																				205
		◊										◊				◊	◊	◊	◊	207
																				208
◊					◊	◊	◊					◊	◊			◊	◊	◊	◊	208
					◊															210
																				211
										◊										212
																				213
																				213
															◊	◊		◊		214
																				214
	◊					◊														215
																		◊		216
																				216
◊						◊	◊												◊	216
															◊					217
◊																	◊			218
	◊				◊		◊	◊												218
◊	◊	◊	◊									◊	◊			◊	◊	◊	◊	219
																				220
	◊				◊															221
			◊		◊	◊						◊				◊				221
																				222
																				224
						◊											◊		◊	219
																				224
																				220
					◊									◊	◊					225
																				226
	◊																		◊	226
																				226
																				227
																				227
																				227

THIS YEAR

In the words of the old joke, the only people who weren't confused about the goings-on in the wine world in 1990 were the ones who had absolutely no idea what was going on.

How often, for example, do retailers welcome a government-imposed increase in the price of their goods? But that was precisely what happened following the Chancellor of the Exchequer's decision to raise the rate of duty on wine. As one supermarket buyer gleefully explained, the £1.99 bottle of wine is dead. For, even before that increase, if you added together the current cost of bottles, corks, labels, shipping and duty, it was almost impossible for anyone to sell a decent wine for £1.99 unless somebody, somewhere was making a loss. And in a way, the consumer now gains too — the moment people have to spend over £2.01 for a bottle of wine they'll be far readier to look at wines selling for £2.29, £2.49 or even £2.99 — prices at which they can begin to get some really good quality stuff.

Mind you, even if Mr Major had left the duty rates as they were, the cost of most wines on the shelves would have to have risen fairly steeply, partly because of price rises imposed by the producers, and partly because of the relative weakness of sterling against other currencies. As another professional wine buyer reported on her return from a trip to southern France, the days of the cheap bottle of French wine are over — and similar complaints were made about Italy and Australia. Even the newly-liberated producers of Eastern Europe were beginning to mumble about the need to pull in more hard currency and to raise their often ludicrously low prices.

The only countries whose wines were on offer at roughly the same price as in 1989 were Spain and Germany. The Spanish had already had their silly hikes — and no one would let the Germans raise the cost of Liebfraumilch.

Among the prices that shot up were those of Champagne. Late in 1989 there were warnings that stocks were running low, that we were all drinking too much fizz and that rationing might have to be introduced. Early in 1990, fears of massive price rises were further fuelled by reports of frost damage in the vineyards and of the inability of the growers to agree on the price to be paid by the Champagne houses for their grapes.

Much will depend on the size of the crop this year, but everything would seem to suggest that prices (already up by 12-15% on last year) will continue to rise until, inevitably, they come tumbling down again.

Among Britain's retailers, Victoria Wine closed its 'up-market' chain of Gare du Vin shops, deciding instead to concentrate its attention on building the reputation of Victoria Wine itself. By contrast, Thresher forged ahead with its similarly up-market Wine Rack shops, and the owners of the Peter Dominic chain, Grand Metropolitan, threw everything they had at their new Hunter & Oliver— or 'Huntley & Palmer' as they have already been nicknamed— shops.

The rationale behind Victoria Wine's decision was that the UK market really didn't have room for another rival to Oddbins, and that the heavily-touted 'aspirational' boom led by Next, Sock Shop and Laura Ashley was now over. British consumers were turning back to the names they knew and trusted; Sainsbury's, Tesco, Marks & Spencer and Victoria Wine.

There is some evidence to support this view. In at least one area, the transformation of a Thresher shop into a smart new Wine Rack made for an overnight doubling of turnover at a rival chain's dowdy but well-stocked 'offy' on the other side of the road. This is not to say that the Wine Rack 'concept' is not proving successful — in fact, as this year's *Guide* award to the chain confirms, this is a very welcome newcomer to the High Street. Even so, there seems little question that there are a lot of traditional High Street customers who are still suspicious of smartness and newness.

In one case, at least, their caution might be wise. The Hunter & Oliver shops are certainly attractive — but are unfortunately full of carelessly selected wine because, in its haste to open all these shops, Grand Met has not yet thought it necessary to set up the kind of buying department that has done so much for Oddbins, Sainsbury and Tesco. Any Grand Met-share-holding readers may care to keep an eye on the progress of this new venture, in which investment has been estimated at £3.5m.

Confusion surrounds the kind of wine we've all been drinking too. On the one hand, there has been the growing strength of the New World — several London restaurants now offer a wider range of Australian Chardonnays than of white Burgundies. On the other, there has been a widely reported swing back to the 'classic' regions of Europe. So both France and New Zealand have increased exports of their wines to Britain.

To muddy the waters still further, the growth in the sales of these wines has to be set against the background of a slowing-down of wine consumption throughout the country. The Perrier- (or this year, Badoit-) with-lunch syndrome really does seem to have set in with a vengeance. Linked to this is a growing demand for flavour and value: if you're only going to have a glass or two of wine, you're less likely to tolerate being bored by it or overcharged. The countries and regions that will benefit most from this will be Australia, New Zealand, regions throughout Italy, France (particularly the Rhône, Alsace, the south, the south-west and the dry white Bordeaux appellations) and Washington State.

If the Germans pitch the prices and the quality of their new dry wines right (Sainsbury's Trocken is a good example) they could do well too; the future of their cheap, basic off-dry wines is more doubtful — particularly since there seems little chance that they can continue to produce them profitably. Spain's sparkling wines should go on making new friends, and a small number of producers in regions like Navarra will help to introduce these areas to wine drinkers who do not yet know them. Rioja, however, will have to look to its already faded laurels; too many of its wines are either dull or faulty.

California's problem will be the price of its wines. Affordable but rarely impressive wine can be made in the Central Valley and great wines can be produced in the Napa Valley, Sonoma and further south. Unfortunately, however, fixed costs in the Napa and Sonoma (interest payments on those designer wineries and $20,000-per-acre vineyards) are so high that it will be very difficult for most producers ever to offer inexpensive wine at truly competitive prices. Oregon's Pinot Noir producers have the same handicap — coupled with the additional hazards of an uncertain climate. The best hope for the USA at the moment is probably Washington State, where some terrific Sauvignons, Rieslings and Merlots are being made.

In South America, Chile will have to overcome this year's hiccup which saw wines from two of its best known bodegas removed from the shelves after having been discovered to contain sorbitol. There are good, untainted, producers in Chile (particularly Nogales/Montes, Cousiño Macul, Los Vascos and Errazuriz Panquehue), as there are in Brazil and Argentina — but far too few to build the once hoped-for strong following overseas. Or at least not at the speed that was anticipated last year.

The Eastern Europeans have to conquer problems of quality control (especially prevalent in Hungary) and UK consumers' unwillingness to buy better than basic wines. The 'estate' wines from Bulgaria are worth seeking out; too few people are doing so.

Lastly, there's the joker in the pack. If the British don't finally start to drink English wines now, with the great 1989 vintage, I fear they never will. But if they don't perhaps it won't matter — with wines this good, there should always be overseas wine lovers who'll give them a fairer chance.

WINE AND HEALTH

While British carnivores worried about whether they should or shouldn't tuck into a T-bone, the wine world had yet another of its quiet scandals. The men from the Ministry of Agriculture, Fisheries and Food drew attention to the fact that a small number of Chilean wines had been found to contain illegal levels of a substance called sorbitol with an eagerness which led some to suspect an attempt to distract public attention from meatier matters. In fact, the sorbitol saga failed to excite much attention among wine writers for the simple reason that, as a brief glance at the contents list of a wide range of foods reveals, this sweetener is wholly legal in all sorts of foods and drinks — from low-calorie fruit squash to 'luxury' chocolate and peppermints. The only physical effect sorbitol is known to have is that of a reliably efficient laxative.

Elsewhere, the alcohol and health debate heated up, especially in the USA, where signs warning pregnant women against drinking have become mandatory and where, in California, it is proposed that wine labels should inform prospective drinkers of the infinitesimal carcinogenic potential of the contents of the bottle. Suggestions that the cities of Los Angeles and New York should carry similar labels warning against breathing the atmosphere have fallen on deaf ears.

Research so far indicates that wine represents less of a carcinogenic risk than a great many of the other substances — food, drink and air — that we consume every day. By the same token, studies in southern France (as opposed to the beer-drinking north) provide evidence that moderate wine drinking may significantly reduce the risk of coronary heart disease.

ORGANIC WINES

This year, I asked the owner of one of the best-known châteaux in Bordeaux whether he was contemplating 'going organic'; his reply was a frank admission that he had absolutely no idea what organic winemaking might entail. When I went on to outline the set of criteria accepted by most members of the organic lobby — no synthetic herbicides or pesticides (apart from the traditionally-used copper sulphate); no chemical fertilizers; no chemical treatment or additives (apart from sulphur dioxide in doses way below those permitted by European law); fining by organic substances such as egg white, milk protein or bentonite clay; natural filtration and no pasteurisation — he scratched his head, thought for a moment and said: 'Well, if that's all being organic means, I could almost go green overnight.'

Sometime soon (this century?) the EC has promised a set of rules that will precisely define what is, and what is not, an organic wine. In the meantime, the vociferous gang of organic winemakers and their respective organisations will continue to snipe at each other instead of directing their energies towards the rather more useful goal of swelling their own, and their customers', ranks.

However, a major change in the fortunes of the organic lobby is already taking place. Producers have discovered that there's money to be made from all this greenery. A recent press release (on recycled paper) from the Cave des Vignerons de la Montagne d'Alaric in Corbières quite frankly states that its reasons for taking the expensive and financially hazardous step of choosing 'Le Bio' are 'Respect for Nature' and 'Economics'. While defining the latter, the release goes on to describe typical consumers of organic wines as 'young executives and active women...with an average to high level of income and an above average social level...'

No mention, one notes, of their being discerning wine-drinkers. Too many wine merchants are far too lenient towards the quality of the organic wine they buy. Like vegetarian restaurants that get away with serving flavourless nut-cutlets, they sell wine few people would normally want to drink, excusing themselves by saying : 'But if we restricted ourselves to *good* organic wines, we'd hardly be able to stock any at all.'

Fortunately, a growing number are following the example of Bruce Kendrick at Haughton Fine Wines, whose rule is quite unbending: make no more allowances for organic wines than you make for any others. Safeway, first of the major supermarkets to specialise in organic wines, is taking just this line — which explains why this chain's green wines are almost all red.

A selection of organic wines

For descriptions and lists of stockists for these wines, consult the section of the *Guide* entitled **The Wines** (p69), using the numbers given here.

LEARNING ABOUT WINE

Firstly, I must declare an interest. I teach at what I believe to be the two best wine schools in London: the Fulham Road Wine Centre and Leith's School of Food and Wine. The premise behind both the schools' classes is that wine should be unpretentious, unprejudiced and, above all, fun. Would-be wine snobs would be well advised to seek their learning elsewhere.

James Rogers, the man behind the Fulham Road Wine Centre courses, presents his students with the wines 'blind' and encourages them to decide which they prefer (and why) *before* they are told the identity of what they are tasting. People who thought that they hated German Riesling discover they like it; others find that they can save a small fortune buying New Zealand Sauvignon Blanc instead of Sancerre. Similarly, those who had mocked wine writers' more fanciful descriptions discover how useful adjectives such as 'petrolly', 'oily', 'spicy' and 'peppery' can be.

These evening courses cost £12-18 per session and succeed thanks to the enthusiasm of Rogers and his students ('participants' is a better word), the quality of the wines and the small numbers present (there are rarely more than 20 at any evening). For those who want more 'classical' training, both Christie's and Sotheby's have tastings of their own, usually of the kinds of wine you are likely to see at their auctions. These are often hosted by the winemakers themselves.

Anyone wanting to join the wine trade, however, should make for the Wine & Spirit Education Trust, where they could take the simple (very simple would be a fairer description) 'Certificate', the useful 'Higher Certificate' and the testing 'Diploma'. Only once you have leaped all three hurdles may you consider trying for the real high jump, the Master of Wine written and tasting exams. But be warned; fewer than 200 people have earned this qualification in three decades; every year, far more fail than pass.

There is, by the way, a tricky little Catch 22 about these trade qualifications: to take them you should be in the wine trade (or connected to it in some way), and to get into the trade, it helps to have the qualifications...

Courses

Fulham Road Wine Centre (071- 736 7009); Christie's Auction House (The Wine Department, 071-839 9060); Sotheby's (071-408 1100); Wine & Spirit Education Trust (071-236 3551); Leith's School of Food and Wine (071-229 0177).

Tastings

For many people, a course is quite unnecessary; a great deal can be learned on a more *ad hoc* basis by attending tutored tastings given by wine merchants such as: Adnams (0502 724222); The Wine Society (0438 741177); La Vigneronne (071-589 6113); Le Nez Rouge (071-609 4711); The Hungerford Wine Co (0488 83238); Helen Verdcourt (0628 25577); Les Amis du Vin (071-736 4020); Lay & Wheeler (Lucinda Clark, 0206 764446); Thos Peatling (0284 755948) and The Sunday Times Wine Club (0734 481711).

Whether you are attending a structured class or simply a tutored tasting, what you get out of it will depend on the person who is talking you through the wines. The following people are especially worth travelling to hear: David Molyneux-Berry MW, Liz Berry MW, Jane Hunt MW, Charles Metcalfe, Michael Schuster, John Vaughan Hughes MW, Maggie McNie MW, Angela Muir MW, Richard Harvey MW, Oz Clarke, Michael Broadbent MW, David Gleave MW, Pamela Vandyke Price, Serena Sutcliffe MW, David Peppercorn MW, Richard Hobson MW and Richard Mayson.

BUYING BY THE CASE - MERCHANTS, CLUBS WAREHOUSES

To listen to the wine warehouses and some of the wine clubs, the idea of buying a dozen bottles of wine at a time is something of a novelty. Of course, this is nonsense; if anything is a novelty, it is the freedom to walk into one of an ever-wider variety of shops and buy a single bottle of good wine. Historically, wine was always purchased in bulk — either by the barrel or by the case.

Today, wine drinkers may buy by the dozen for convenience or to save money; they should not be browbeaten into doing so. We were interested to find a number of companies who charge the same price by the bottle as by the case, and a growing number of so-called 'wine warehouses' which allow customers to walk out with just one bottle of wine.

Similarly, be a little wary of wine clubs associated with wine merchants. In some instances you may find yourself either paying a membership charge or committing yourself to buying a certain number of cases, when you could enjoy the greater freedom of picking up precisely the same wines at the same prices, by the bottle, in the merchant's shop.

Good wine clubs offer far more than the mail-order wine service that many good wine merchants offer as a matter of course. What you should expect from a wine club are services not available elsewhere, and hopefully exclusive advantages of membership. A number of clubs achieve some of these objectives; only The Wine Society, which genuinely belongs to its members, truly fits the bill.

However, you may prefer a club whose *raison d'être* is not geared towards purchasing — a local wine appreciation society, for example, many of whom organise not only informal meetings but tastings presented by merchants and producers and social events such as theme dinners. In addition to those listed below, clubs with vacancies for new members are regularly featured in the diary pages of *WINE* and *Decanter*.

Wine merchant clubs

The Wine Society (see p.224); Le Nez Rouge (see p.181); Les Amis du Vin (see p.118); The Sunday Times Wine Club (see p.202); The Vintner (see p.214).

Non-merchant wine clubs

The Alsace Club/Cofradia Riojana/Gallo Nero Wine Club (Martin Mistlin, 081-863 2135/081-427 9944); The Coonawarra/Zinfandel Club (071-497 1406/081-698 2504); The International Food and Wine Society (London branch, 071-373 5377); Lincoln Wine Society (0522 42077); North East Wine Tasting Society (Nigel Ellam, 091-438 4107); Northern Wine Appreciation Group (0484 531228); The Wine and Dine Society (071-274 9484); The Wine-tasters (081-997 1252); Evington Wine Society (Edwin Wood, 0533 416595).

BUYING AT AUCTION/ WINE INVESTMENT

Don't imagine that 'fine' clarets and ports are the only kinds of wine in which auction houses deal. Every time a restaurant or wine merchant goes bankrupt (an all-too-frequent occurrence), there is a strong likelihood that some of the contents of the cellar will end up under the hammer.

But if auctions can still be a source of bargain parcels of everyday wine, it is still worth keeping a careful check on what you may be paying per bottle. Read *WINE Magazine*, *Wine & Spirit* and *Decanter's* auction-price guides, consult Clive Coates' *The Vine* and Robert Parker's *Wine Advocate* newsletters for tasting notes, and take note of the auctioneers' own estimates. Auction fever is an infectious condition, and it is all too easy to forget that a 'bargain' £50 case of Chablis can be a little less of a snip by the time you have added on the 10% buyer's premium, 90p or so a bottle duty and 15% VAT, and driven to Edinburgh where it was 'lying' to pick it up.

Of these possible 'extras', the buyer's premium is the only one you should almost always take for granted; a large proportion of wines sold are not subject to VAT, and the number that are sold 'in bond' is really very small. But it is worth taking these factors into account.

Remember, too, that the rule of *caveat emptor* applies; the condition of the wine you buy — whatever its shoulder level — is not guaranteed. Be particularly wary, by the way, of any Bordeaux that has been returned from the USA, a country where fine wine is often appallingly mistreated.

Among fine wines today, the 1978 and 1979 clarets we recommended last year are still underpriced and, when compared with the prices of the 1988s and 1989s *en primeur*, the 1986s and 1985s look positively cheap. The 1984s and 1983s are already looking surprisingly mature, but the 1982s are holding up wonderfully and deserve to be left alone for a long while yet. The 1975s are finally 'coming round' but the 1970s are, if anything, getting tougher with age. Of older vintages, you could still pick up some affordable 1966 or 1964 Pomerols and St Emilions (rather than Médocs.)

Auction Houses

Christie's Auction House (The Wine Department, 071-839 9060); Sotheby's (071-408 1100); Colliers Bigwood & Bewlay (0789 69415); Lacy Scott (0284 763531); Lithgow Sons and Partners (0642 710158); Phillips (0865 723524); Jean Pierre et Fils (0273 38422); Roseberry's Fine Art Auction House (071-837 3418); P W Silverstone & Co (081-340 1858); International Wine Auctions (071-403 1140).

INVESTING IN WINE

Don't under any circumstances use the word 'investment' when talking to wine merchants or winemakers. Their financial livelihood may depend on the value of the wines they have made or bought going up, but they are not, you must understand, in the grubby business of *investment*.

On the other hand, if you aren't a wine merchant or maker, you might be forgiven for wondering why, every spring, you are bombarded by offers to sell you brand new *en primeur* Bordeaux at £200 a case that you couldn't even dream of drinking for a decade.

The answer, so far, has been that in the long term the value of vintage port and 'fine' wines (ones produced by well-known Bordeaux châteaux) has risen more reliably than the FT Index or a building society nest-egg.

But the key words are 'so far' and 'in the long term'. Bordeaux has recently had an unprecedented series of good, fairly large vintages — and a series of fairly spectacular price increases. A case of 1988 first growth claret would have cost you around £400 in 1989; in 1990, a case of the 1989 would have set you back no less than £500. There are those who look at these kinds of price rises, glance back at the current — relatively low — cost of 1986s, 1985s, 1978s and 1979s at auction, and wonder whether it all makes sense.

This year, some of those sceptics received a bit of support from an unexpected source — the very merchants who were busily offering them the *en primeur* wine often doubted the wisdom of buying it at these prices, and also questioned the widely-touted claims that this was the 'Vintage of the Century'. Those merchants could afford to be frank with their advice; few of their customers were in any mood to listen. They just wanted to leap on to the *en primeur* bandwagon — no matter what it cost.

If you do want to buy the kinds of wine whose value is most certain to rise, avoid any temptation to take a punt on this or that 'new' California winery or hitherto little-known Médoc château. Stick to blue-chip first

STARTING A CELLAR   49

growths and vintage port from the best producers. I know that, by saying this, I am perpetuating the way in which a small number of wines get all the attention at auction and *en primeur* but, after years of writing, for example, that prices of fine sweet German wines are 'bound to shoot up to their proper level', I have cynically come to believe that the system is unbeatable.

My guess is that people who bought first-growth 1989s now have an asset whose value is bound to appreciate; those who bought the pricier second, third, fourth and fifth ones may find that they would have been wiser to wait for two or three years until those same wines hit the open market. But why should anyone worry? After all, if they're not *investing* in the stuff, the fact that its value may drop a bit oughtn't to worry them.

The following companies should all offer good advice on wine investment: Hungerford Wine Co (see p.169), who this year guaranteed to offer the lowest *en primeur* prices in Britain, Justerini & Brooks (see p.170) who put together 'portfolios', The Wine Society (see p.224), Lay & Wheeler (see p.171) and Berry Bros & Rudd (see p.125).

Specialists in fine, rare and old wines

See the *Merchants' specialities* chart, plus: Patrick Grubb Selections (0869 40229); The Wine Treasury (071 730 6774); Bute Wines (0700 2730); The Champagne and Caviar Shop (071 626 4912); The Old Maltings Wine Co Ltd (0787 79638); Wine on the Green (071 794 1143); Nigel Baring (071 724 0836); Domaine Direct (071 837 3521); William Rush (0753 882659);

WINE TOURS

Wine tours are rather like any other holiday organised for a group of like-minded people. They can be gloriously successful — or extraordinarily tedious. But earnest wine buffs are probably no more boring than earnest opera fans, bird watchers or train spotters. In our experience, the enjoyment of such tours depends only partly on one's fellow travellers; a much greater influence is the way in which the tour has been organised. The best wine tours we have come across are the ones put together by World Wine Tours (0865 891919) and The Sunday Times Wine Club (see p.202).

Other tour companies

Tanglewood Wine Tours (09323 48720); Arblaster and Clarke Wine Tours (0730 66883); Classic Wine Tours (0626 65373); Moswin Tours Ltd (0533 719922); Vacances Cuisine (010 33 94044977); Wine Trails (081-463 0012); Knights of Languedoc (071-704 0589); Vintage Wine Tours (0225 315834); Francophiles (0272 621975); Boose Breaks (0730 66883); Excaliber Holidays of Distinction (0202 298963); Allez France (0903 742346); Bordeaux Wine Holidays (0782-612015); Ian Dickson Travel (031 556 6777); Grants of St James (0483 64861); Graham Faithfull Activity Holidays (0780 66280); Vinescapes (0903 744279); Citalia (081-686-5533).

STARTING A CELLAR

In an ideal world, we would all live in homes with proper cellars. In France and Italy, most apartment blocks have handy stores in their basements; and in Switzerland, where nuclear shelters are obligatory, there can be hardly anyone who hasn't got a small area in which to stock his or her radiation-proof lead wine racks (which presumably means that if anyone ever does press the button, there will be some pretty good drinking going on down there beneath Bern and Basel).

In Britain, however, cellars of any kind are a rare luxury and most people who want to allow even a dozen or so bottles to grow old in peace have to use their ingenuity to find a suitable corner for them. For those readers who find themselves in that situation, the following do's and don'ts may be useful.

Avoid areas in which the temperature varies; constant warmth is better than the variations usual in a kitchen, for example. Avoid areas which are too dry; well-insulated cupboards and attics can be ideal cellars, but be sure to keep the humidity up with a sponge left in a bowl of water. Try to find a space where there is at least some air movement; cut air holes in cupboards if necessary. If the area you have chosen is damp, remember not to leave wine in cardboard boxes. It sounds obvious, but even experienced wine buffs have lost wine by letting it fall from soggy boxes.

Purpose-built cellars and racks exist. Spiral Cellars Ltd (037 284 2692) will sell you a kit (and install it, if you like) which can be sunk into the ground beneath the floor of your kitchen or garage — or in the garden. Wine racks that can be custom-built to fit awkwardly shaped areas are available from Majestic Wine Warehouses and most other helpful wine merchants. To buy direct, contact: CS Racks (0725 21858), RTA Wine Racks (032 878 292), A & W Moore (0602 607012).

A cellar book provides an invaluable means of keeping track of your wines, and elegant ones have been produced by Hugh Johnson (published by Mitchell Beazley) and by Grants of St James's. These make fine Christmas or birthday presents, but for your own use a simple exercise book can perform the same function. Simply rule it up to allow space for you to indicate where and when you bought each wine; the price you paid for it; its position in your racks; each time you remove a bottle; tasting notes; and the guests to whom you served it.

Incidentally, don't worry overmuch about trying to keep all your wines of a particular type in the same part of the rack; unless you have almost unlimited space, you'll only find yourself having to shuffle your bottles around the racks every time a new case arrives. One very effective way to avoid this is to use a system based on the old game of 'battleships'. Each vertical row of holes is given a letter of the alphabet, while each horizontal row is allocated a number. So, the third hole down of the third row from the left would be C3, a code you can allocate to the wine it contains. If you want to go beyond 26 rows, simply move on to AA1.

For the high-tech wine lover who would rather keep his information on disk, there is now a handy, purpose-built database that can be used on IBM compatible PCs. Available from Ant Software (0524 666128), it costs around £20. Finally, if you would prefer not to store your wine in your own home, there is always the option of leaving it in the cellars of the merchants from whom you bought it (see our *Merchants' services* chart on page 22) or renting space at Smith & Taylor (071-627 5070) or at Abacus (081-991 9717).

GLASSES

There is so much nonsense talked about the 'right' glasses for the 'right' wine that we are tempted not to discuss this at all. Our advice is to use any kind of clear glass whose rim has a smaller circumference than its bowl, and which is large enough to hold more than a few mouthfuls.

The ultimate tasting (and drinking) glasses are probably the widely available ones produced for this purpose by the Austrian firm of Riedel. But they are as pricy as they are beautiful and delicate. More affordable and almost as attractive glasses can be bought (in quantities of at least six per style) from Harvey Reed (071-731 0879). We would recommend the Magnum range from Royal Leerdam; these were the ones very happily used by tasters at the 1990 *WINE Magazine* International Challenge.

If you are tempted by antique glasses ('collectables' whose prices are rising fast), try Richard Kihl (071-586 3838); The Barnes Wine Shop (see page 122) or The Fulham Road Wine Centre (see page 150).

VINOUS GIFTS

An increasing range of often very silly and occasionally quite kitsch gifts is now available. For sensible selections, try The Fulham Road Wine Centre, who also offer a range of always-acceptable antiquarian wine books. These and old maps can also be bought from Wine Arts (0264 58036).

CORKSCREWS

The best corkscrew of all is made by Screwpull (081-847 2493) and is produced in a variety of different versions, including a very pricy semi-automatic example. These are available from Richard Kihl (071-586 3838), Harvey Reed (071-633 9020), John Jenkins (0730 80811), La Vigneronne (see p.213), Berry Bros & Rudd (see p.125), Bordeaux Direct (see p.129), branches of Liberty's, John Lewis, Habitat and many other stores.

WINE PRESERVATION DEVICES

The Vacuvin is widely available and has been proven to work well, as does the more sophisticated (and more expensive) Wine-keeper from Anthony Byrne Fine Wines (see p.132).

LOW- AND NON-ALCOHOL WINE

Sales of these styles have not exploded in the way that many members of the trade expected — possibly because many of Britain's would-be wine drinkers don't actually enjoy the liquid sherbet 'n' cardboard flavour associated with most of them. There are still producers throughout the world who are busily seeking the holy grail of 'lo-alc' wine that actually tastes vaguely like the stuff it is trying to replace. For the moment at least, the grail remains beyond their reach. However, for those who want to offer one of these wines to party guests this Christmas, on page 114 we have listed a set of the best that are currently on offer. Our advice is to stick to the lightest, simplest and most unashamedly Asti-like.

BUYING ABROAD

Within a very few years (if the Eurocrats have their way) British wine lovers will be able to shoot through the tunnel to the Continent, fill their boots with wine and zoom straight back without so much as a wave to the Dover customs officers. I'll believe it when I see it. For the moment at least, duty-free imports are limited to just over 10 bottles of wine per adult traveller, provided those bottles were not bought in a duty-free shop, and that no fortified wines or spirits are being imported at the same time. Beyond those 10 bottles, the Chancellor gets his slice of duty — and of VAT at 15%, chargeable on the value of the wine and on the duty itself (in other words, he taxes his own tax). Buying at the major hypermarkets on the French coast is undoubtedly convenient; it is also a good way to end up with some pretty unimpressive wine. Bear in mind that Gallic supermarket buyers are a lot less quality-conscious than their UK counterparts, and that most of their British customers care little about the stuff with which they fill their trolleys.

The time to buy from any French supermarket is just before Christmas, when they sell some very classy wine at knock-down prices as loss-leaders to attract local custom. Otherwise, do what the French do: buy direct from the grower. For more than 60 litres you will need a VA form to confirm that the wine is drinkable. If the value of the shipment is over £200, you must also have a C10 or C12 form, which you will, of course, have remembered to pick up at the port of departure. And don't forget to ask for a T2 form before you leave France; you'll need it on your way back into Britain.

		PARTY PLANNING - WINES FOR LESS THAN £3.00
£1.59	496	GOLDENER OKTOBER LIGHT WHITE, St Ursula Weinkellerei
£1.69	498	ST MICHAEL SPARKLING APERITIF BLUSH, Klosterhof
£2.25	230	GATEWAY LAMBRUSCO ROSE, Donelli Vini
£2.39	198	SAINSBURY'S MOSELLE
£2.49	383	VALPOLICELLA CARISSA, Pasqua
£2.50	244	BOTRYS RED, Botrys SA
£2.55	199	SAINSBURY'S MORIO-MUSKAT
£2.59	245	DOMAINE DES LENTHERIC GRENACHE MERLOT, Lentheric Pierre & Fils. 1988
£2.59	366	MILION PINOT NOIR, Navip, 1986
£2.65	325	SAINSBURY'S COTES DU RHONE
£2.67	419	CASTILLO DE ALHAMBRA, Vinicola de Castilla, 1989
£2.69	27	SAINSBURY'S VIN DE PAYS DES COTES DE GASCOGNE 1989
£2.69	266	PLOVDIV CABERNET SAUVIGNON, Bulgarian Vintners 1985
£2.75	267	VIN DE PAYS DE L'AUDE CABERNET SAUVIGNON, Paul Boutinot 1987
£2.79	384	SAINSBURY'S CANNONAU DEL PARTEOLLA, 1987
£2.79	28	VIN DE PAYS DES COTES DE GASCOGNE PLAIMONT, 1989
£2.80	445	CHATEAU DES TOURS, STE-CROIX-DU-MONT, 1986
£2.89	231	PIEMONTELLO PINK
£2.89	246	CABARDES, CHATEAU VENTENAC, 1989
£2.89	385	SAINSBURY'S DOLCETTO D'ACQUI, 1988
£2.95	439	MOSCATEL DE VALENCIA, Vicente Gandia 1988
£2.95	205	BINGER ST ROCHUSKAPELLE SPATLESE, Rheinberg Kellerei, 1988
£2.95	465	SAINSBURY'S AGED AMONTILLADO
£2.99	116	DOMAINE DE MONTMARIN SAUVIGNON, Vin de Pays des Côtes de Thongue, 1989
£2.99	356	ST MICHAEL GRAPE SELECTION GAMAY, Vin de Pays de l'Ardèche,
£2.99	386	CANTINA SETTESOLI ROSSO, 1987
£2.99	326	COTES DU VENTOUX, Paul Boutinot, 1989
£2.99	466	ST MICHAEL FINO SHERRY, Williams & Humbert
£2.99	268	ST MICHAEL GRAPE SELECTION MERLOT, Vin de Pays de l'Aude,
£2.99	269	HOUSE CLARET, Peter Sichel

The numbers printed next to each wine will enable you to find descriptions and stockists for them in the section of the *Guide* entitled *The Wines* (p69).

THE COUNTRIES

Australia

Australia's winemakers are producing more reliable value-for-money flavour per glass than their counterparts anywhere else on earth. And it's not only tasters at wine competitions (in Britain as much as down under) who are impressed. Five years ago, Australian wine was almost impossible to find in Britain. Today, it's on the lists of almost every good wine merchant, and in the cellars of most good restaurants. And there's a growing number of people who have switched allegiance to Australia from France, Spain and Germany. Even if one or two wine writers are getting bored with these wines, Britain's wine drinkers are doing no such thing.

1990 will have produced good wines throughout Australia, making up for the disappointments of 1989. And there are some great 1988s, 1987s and (tremendous) 1986s just waiting to come on stream.

Specialist stockists

See the chart on p32, plus: The Wine Spot (061 748 2568); Bow Wine Vaults (071-248 1121); Nobody Inn (0647 52394); Peter Watts Wines (03765 61130); Croque en Bouche (06845 65612); Fortis Ltd (0742 642227); Patrick Grubb Selections (0869 40867); Domaine Direct (071-837 3521/1142).

Austria

The Austrian comeback, like the male contraceptive pill, is declared imminent every year. And it never quite happens. But watch this space, because a small number of 'new-style' Austrian wines are already slipping into this country, and they bear no resemblance at all to the cheap mock-Germans which (adulterated with 'anti-freeze') got the Austrians into so much trouble a few years ago. Today's Austrian wines — especially the ones made in 1989 and 1988 — are rich, clean and dry; if they compete with examples from any other country, it is probably France. But the people who ought to worry are the Germans, because Austria's climate gives it every advantage over its would-be dry-winemaking neighbour.

Specialist stockists

A L Vose (044 84 3328); Alston Wines (091 384 3379); Premier Wines (0294 602409); Caxton Tower (071-381 6505).

Eastern Europe and the USSR

Curiously, the extraordinary upside-down, inside-out changes that have taken place in Eastern Europe have had less of an immediate effect on the export of wine than on that of most other goods; there can be very few British wine drinkers who have never drunk Bulgarian Cabernet Sauvignon, Bull's Blood or Laski, Olasz or Lutomer Rizling.

Eastern European winemakers, with help and encouragement from Western customers, have gradually built up a successful export trade based, in the case of the red wines at least, on wines of reasonable quality. The next hurdle will be to break into the slightly higher price-bands. Bulgaria, as always ahead of the pack, has already launched a range of 'estate' wines, but they have yet to catch on with people now accustomed to washing down their 'spag bol' with £1.99 bottles of Bulgarian 'Cab Sauv'. What the Eastern Europeans need is greater marketing skills and improved quality control...

And what of the long-awaited arrival of high-quality Russian wine? Well, it's still awaited. And Bottom's Up's inexplicable offering of a range of overpriced, oxidised examples from that country will have done little to whet anyone's appetite for any further shipments.

Specialist stockists

Bulgaria: Majestic Wine Warehouses (see p.174); Davisons (see p.142); Oddbins (see p.183); Peter Dominic (see p.144). Also Wines of Westhorpe (0283 820285).

Hungary: Hicks & Don Ltd (see p.166); Cumbrian Cellar (see p.142); Selfridges (see p.198); Peter Green (see p.158).

USSR: Peter Dominic (see p.144).

Yugoslavia: Teltscher Brothers (071-987 5020); Vitkovitch Bros (071-261 1770).

England

John Gummer, Minister for Agriculture, is a supporter of the English wine industry. I know this to be so because, on June 21 1990, he made a speech encouraging England's winemakers to 'take steps to put their wine on the same footing as the "Appellation Contrôlée" wines of France'.

Well, on behalf of the wine growers of England, I'd like to say: 'Thanks a lot, John — but could you do something a little more useful? Like having a word with your friends at the Treasury and persuading them to give those wine growers the support enjoyed by their counterparts in Europe?'

German wine growers building or altering their wineries currently receive 81% capital grants towards their costs. When they want to restructure and/or replant their vineyards, they receive DM31,000 per hectare; when they or their French neighbours want to borrow money, they pay only 7% or 8% interest.

English wine growers have to pay duty on the wine they hold in stock and they have to pay business rates, rather than the cheaper farm rates, on their wineries. They also have to compete against so-called 'British' wine made from imported grape concentrate.

They badly need help. With a few exceptions, England's wine growers are an innately disorganised bunch who could do with a little more than pious words of approval and encouragement.

Specialist stockists

See the chart on p.32, plus: English Wine Centre (0323 870532); Nobody Inn (0647 52394).

France

In1989, harvesters went out into fields throughout France armed with the knowledge that they were going to pick the vintage of the century. After all, hadn't the press been full of reports that this was the ripest, earliest year since the great 1949? And, as everyone knew, winemaking today is so much better than it was 40 years ago — *ergo*, 1989 was beyond compare. US critics helped to bolster this reputation, audibly describing the new Bordeaux as tasting 'ossome'.

Now that the wines have been allowed to speak for themselves, a slightly different picture has emerged. 1989 was certainly a good year throughout France and some truly great wines were produced. To call it the Vintage of the Century, and to suggest that its wines are universally better than those of years like 1928, 1945, 1961, 1985 and 1988 is, however, as silly as it is premature. Throughout the country, winemakers were confronted by a problem frequently encountered in the New World: the grapes often ripened *too* well, producing wine that's soft and better suited for early drinking than for long-term cellarage.

Alsace

Every dog, they say, has his day; the Alsatians might be forgiven for wondering if theirs would ever dawn. As each year has brought its 'new discovery' of this or that previously unknown winemaking region of Albania or Zimbabwe, the winegrowers of Alsace have shrugged their shoulders and stoically accepted that their role in life is to be treated as a misunderstood vinous no man's land between Germany and France.

This year, at last, the proud inhabitants of this region have begun to receive some of the recognition they deserve. The 1989 vintage was probably as great here as it was anywhere in France, and the quality of many of the wines produced from late-harvested grapes is stupendous. Wine drinkers throughout the world who have been introduced to buttery, spicy, tropical flavours by New World Chardonnay have found that Alsace has been making wines in just this kind of style in the Old World for generations. We are delighted to encourage an even greater number of people to discover the flavour of modern Alsace by making a really first-class example our White Wine of the Year.

This award winner, the 1989 Alsace Pinot Blanc from the Cave Vinicole de Turckheim is typical of the richness and intensity of flavour achieved in this vintage — and of the region as a whole.

Of previous Alsace vintages, the 1988s are showing well, there are some good 1987 Rieslings and lovely, long-lived 1986s. The 1985s and 1983s, though often delicious, can be over-ripe and lacking in freshness.

Specialist stockists

See the chart on p.32, plus: Fortnum & Mason (071-734 8040); Curzon Wine

Co (071 499 3327); O W Loeb (071 928 7750); Farthinghoe Fine Wine & Food (0295 710018); Borg Castel (025 485 2128); Bute Wines (0700 2730).

Bordeaux

`The cracking summer of '89 caused some exaggerated claims to be made for the quality of the vintage, mostly by the non-wine press.' This quote, from a leading London merchant, ought to set the tone for 1989 Bordeaux. There is nothing wrong with this year's wines, and some of them will undoubtedly be among the greatest of the decade (all right, 'of the century' if you insist). But it's a variable vintage and there will be a fair number of instances in which the less hyped, 20% less expensive 1988s will outclass them. As may the far less hyped, far less expensive 1986s. Buy yourself some 1989s *en primeur* if you like to be in at the start of every new vintage and if money's no real object. But just remember that your bank manager — and your wine merchant if he was really honest about it — might advise you to dispose of your cash more prudently.

Vintages to buy

1988s — red and white; 1987s — for immediate, delicious drinking; the still-underrated 1986s for long-term storage; and the constantly enjoyable 1985s. There are some bargain 1984s to be had — again for early drinking — and some 1983s look cheap by comparison with more recent vintages. But beware of the way the 1983s are maturing; this looks like being a far shorter-lived year than the still-impressive 1982s.

Specialist stockists

See the chart on p.32, plus: Ilkley Wine Co (0943 607313); Bedford Fine Wines (0234 740387); Curzon Wine Co (071 499 3327); Henry Townsend (04946 78291); Market Vintners (071-248 8382); Nickolls & Perks (0384 394518); SH Jones (0295 51177); Stephen Porter Wines (0452 618772); Andrew Gordon Wines (0306 885711); Pavilion Wine Co (071-628 8224); Nigel Baring (071 724 0836); Classic Wines (081 500 7614); Fine Vintage Wines (0865 724866); Friarwood (071-736 2628); Kurtz & Chan (071-930 6981); Andrew Mead Wines (05476 268); Townend & Sons (0482 26891); Whittalls Wines (Château Pleck) (0922 36161); Ballantynes of Cowbridge (04463 3044); David J Watt (021 643 5160); David Baker (0656 50732); Buckingham Vintners (0753 21336); Bute Wines (0700 2730); Balls Brothers (071 739 6466); Richard Granger (091 281 5000); Wine on the Green (071-794 1143); Patrick Grubb Selections (0869 40229).

Burgundy

1989 was probably not a great year for red Burgundy (though great reds and whites will certainly have been made), but it was a vintage whose wines have the ready, immediate appeal of 1979, with perhaps a little more substance. 1979 produced some top-class whites, and so may 1989, though there are fears that some of these may have been just a shade too ripe; more like the blowsy 1985s than the well-structured 1986s.

As for 1988, this increasingly looks as though it really was a great red Burgundy vintage, rivalling the tremendous, ripe, well-structured 1985s. Some of the whites may outclass the 1989s but many, like the 1987s, will not go far beyond middle age.

Specialist stockists

See the chart on p.32, plus: Curzon Wine Co (071-499 3327); Henry Townsend (04946 78291); Market Vintners (071 248 8382); Nickolls & Perks (0384 394518); O W Loeb (071-928 7750); Classic Wines (081-500 7614); Domaine Direct (071-837 3521); Ferrers le Mesurier (08012 2660); Friarwood (071-736 2628); Ingleton Wines (0621 52421); Kurtz & Chan (071-930 6981); Andrew Mead Wines (05476 268); William Rush (0753 882659); Ballantynes of Cowbridge (04463 3044); Bute Wines (0700 2730); Patrick Grubb Selections (0869 40229); Richard Granger (091 281 5000); The Wine Treasury Ltd (071-823 6402); Domaine Direct (071-837 3521/1142).

Champagne

Every year the growers of Champagne and the Champagne houses to whom they sell a large proportion of their crop get together and sign a contract that fixes the price to be paid for the region's grapes. Except in 1989, when the growers, like militant miners, simply refused to sign the contract as it was proposed to them. The result was stalemate and the prospect of still more price rises. The fact that 1989 was a year of tremendous quality merely helped to boost the Champenois' confidence. Previous experience would, however, suggest that, in the case of Champagne at least, prices that go up will eventually come down again...

Specialist stockists

See the chart on p.32, plus: Bart's Cellars (081-871 2044); Curzon Wine Co (071-499 3327); Nickolls & Perks (0384 394518); The Champagne House (071-221 5538); Champagne & Caviar Shop (071-626 4912); Richard Granger (091 281 5000).

The Loire

If anywhere potentially had the Vintage of the Century in 1989, it was probably the Loire, a region whose Chenin Blanc and Cabernet vineyards need every little glimmer of sunshine they can get. Lovers of luscious sweet Vouvray, Bonnezeaux and Quarts de Chaume should grab any '89 vintages of these wines they see; people who enjoy the crunchy blackcurrant flavours of Chinon and Bourgueil should seek these out too.

The warm weather did less of a favour to the Sauvignons of the Upper Loire; some of the Sancerres and Pouilly Fumés lack the tangy bite they ought to have. For these, 1988 was a far better, crisper year.

Specialist stockists

See the chart on p.32, plus: Ian Howe (0636 704366); Ilkley Wine Co (0943 607313); Prestige Vintners (081 989 5084); Christopher Milner Wines (071-266 2245); F & E May (071 405 6249); Locke's (0962 60006); Mentzendorff & Co (071-222 2522); Ferrers le Mesurier (08012 2660); Sapsford Wines (0920 67040); GE Bromley (0533 768471); Croque en Bouche (06845 65612); Richard Granger (091 281 5000).

The Rhône

For the northern Rhône, 1989 was undoubtedly a first-class vintage, though one whose wines will almost certainly enjoy shorter lives than the more finely structured 1988s. Still, if that means early-drinking Hermitage, who's to complain? Down south, while Châteauneuf-du-Pape produced great wine, the quality of Côtes du Rhône and Côtes du Rhône-Villages was far more variable because the drought conditions often made for tough, tannic, fruitless wines. 1988 reds from the north and south are looking increasingly good, but the whites of that year should be treated with caution.

Specialist stockists

See the chart on p.32, plus: Ian Howe (0636 704366); Market Vintners (071-248 8382); O W Loeb (071-928 7750); Croque en Bouche (06845 65612); Richard Granger (091 281 5000); Bute Wines (0700 2730); Wine on the Green (071-794 1143).

Germany

'For the first time I'm genuinely optimistic; we're beginning to see more and more people making an effort to think about quality - and wanting to make a change.' Steve Clarke of Tesco's rekindled belief in the potential of the Germans to put their wine industry to rights came after 'so many years of going to Germany and getting frustrated by producers' unwillingness to listen'. There are still countless problems to be resolved. The revision of the German wine laws last year was an opportunity wasted; the new legislation is almost as flawed and quality-unconscious as the old one. The industry is still largely run by— and for — the country's least ambitious cooperatives. The mass of Germany's wines are still poor and cheap, and there is still too keen a desire to foist overpriced, tooth-strippingly acidic 'trocken' (dry) wines on to unsuspecting foreigners.

Even so, a pair of good vintages —1988, and the only slightly less uniformly impressive 1989 — has helped to remind everyone of the kind of wines the Germans ought to make. As has the threat by a growing number of producers to stop behaving like law-abiding Germans and to follow the example of their Italian neighbours in making wines that stand quite outside the craziness of the legislation. Sichel, inventors of Blue Nun, are leading the way with a very smartly packaged wine called Novum. Clearly intended for chic restaurants that would never dream of offering Blue Nun, Novum is 'only' a *Tafelwein* (a table wine) while Blue Nun, like every other Liebfraumilch, is a *Qualitätswein* — an officially recognised 'quality' wine.

The day that it will truly be possible to say that Germany counts among the quality-wine-producing nations in the way it most fundamentally did earlier this century, will be the day that a greater number of people find its wines *interesting*. It is very revealing that, while Sainsbury has launched a series of books on the wines of France, Italy, Spain, Portugal and the New World, there are no plans to include Germany on the list. Sainsbury's customers (a very representative set of British wine drinkers, one might suppose) are not reckoned to be as keen to learn more about German wine as they are to build up their knowledge of Portuguese Bairrada, Spanish Toro and Italian Gattinara.

Specialist stockists

See the chart on p.32, plus: The Wine Spot (061 748 2568); AL Vose (044 84

3328); Henry Townsend (04946 78291); O W Loeb (071-928 7750); Robert Mendelssohn (081-455 9895); S H Jones (0295 51177); The Wine Schoppen (0742 365684); Borg Castel (025 485 2128); Douglas Henn-Macrae (0622 70952); G E Bromley (0533 768471); Dennhöfer Wines (091 232 7342).

Greece

Good bottles of Greek wine are still all too rare — both in Britain and Greece — but progress is finally being made towards dragging Hellenic winemaking into the late 20th century. Château Carras has led the way with its Cabernet Sauvignon, but there are now a growing number of improving wines that really do stand comparison with good examples from other countries — as was demonstrated by the Greek successes in the 1990 *WINE Magazine* International Challenge.

Specialist stockists

The Greek Wine Centre (0743 64636); Hicks & Don Ltd (see p.166); Cumbrian Cellar (see p.142); Selfridges (see p.198); Peter Green see (p.158).

India

The range of Indian wine on sale in Britain remains limited to the potentially excellent but variable *méthode champenoise* Omar Khayyam. Readers interested in tasting India's other red and white wines will have to go to the subcontinent. One screw-cap bottle of each should amply suffice.

Specialist stockists

Adnams (see p.115); Cumbrian Cellar (see p.142); Selfridges (see p.198).

Israel

Israel, one of the countries that has, for many years, produced some of the most reliably poor wines in the world, is gradually getting its vinous act together. New winemaking techniques and greater quality control have allowed wineries like Gamla and Yarden to make Cabernet Sauvignons and Sauvignon Blancs of a calibre that can compete with some well-known Californians. For a taste of the traditional wine Israel can still produce when it wants to, try a range from the Carmel winery. They'll give you a fair idea of why so few British retailers have been tempted to stock Israeli wines.

Specialist stockists

Selfridges (see p.198); Tesco (see p.204); Peter Hallgarten (071-722 1077).

Italy

In 1989, the buzz winemaking nation was Australia; in 1990, wine merchants and writers who had only just mastered the pronunciation of

Aboriginal wine names such as Pirramimma and Botobolar were now busily studying maps of Tuscany, Piedmont and the South Tyrol. It's tempting to give the World Cup at least some of the credit for this sudden upsurge of interest in Italian wine; after all, hosting the Americas Cup certainly did the Australians no harm.

In fact, however, it is Italy's new generation of winemakers who deserve all of the praise that their country's wines are getting; they are producing some of the most exciting — and characterful — wines in the world. The renaissance of Italian wine — its transformation from straw-covered flasks and mouth-numbingly tannic Barolos to the flavour-packed, fruity, spicy, oaky competition-winners of today — has been entirely due to the efforts of these wine growers, and to their readiness to combine a lack of reverence for silly Italian wine laws with respect for the unique flavours of ancient local grapes.

Despite a far less climatically helpful series of vintages than has been enjoyed by France, the young (and the young in spirit) growers and winemakers have taken a fresh look at the kinds of grapes— often the clones of grapes — they have planted and at the way their wines should be fermented and matured. The first regions to break this new ground were Tuscany and the South Tyrol; today, the focus has shifted to Piedmont, where previously intractable grapes like the Barbera, Nebbiolo and Dolcetto are being coaxed into producing flavours few people suspected they had. It is against this background, and against tough competition from France and Australia, that we were delighted to make two very different Italian wines, the 1988 Barbera d'Asti from the Viticoltori dell' Acquese, and Piemontello Pink, our Red and Rosé Wines of the Year.

Both of these wines are not only delicious, but also very affordably priced, unlike some of Italy's other high-flying wines. Following the example set by the Spanish, who raised the prices for the wine they made in their frankly bad 1988 vintage, the Italians took the decision to ask more for their 1989 wines, despite the fact that theirs was one of the few parts of Europe that had a bad harvest. The only part of Italy that nature allowed to make really good red wine in 1989 was Piedmont; almost everywhere else, the rain spoiled quality. 1988 and 1985 are the vintages to look out for, and 1986s are generally better than 1987s.

Specialist stockists

See the chart on p.32, plus: The Wine Spot (061 748 2568); The Wine Shop (0847 8787); Cantino Augusto (071-242 3246); Italian Wine Agencies (081-459 1515); Continental Wine House (071-262 2126); Caledonian Wines (0228 43172); Gardavini (081-549 2779); Wineforce (071-586 5618); Organics (071-381 9924).

New Zealand

Still tiny by any standards, the New Zealand wine industry was dismissed this year by one Frenchman as a 'drop in the bucket of the world's wine'. Well, perhaps, but size isn't everything. Over the last two or three years, the Kiwis have not only taken a disproportionately high number of medals at international tastings, they have also attracted the ultimate compliment: foreign investment. The Champagne houses are already arriving, as are Australians such as the ever-dynamic Wolf Blass. As the world begins to tire of big, warm-climate wines, New Zealand will come into its own; the exciting Chardonnays, Sauvignons and Rieslings we are already seeing only scratch the surface of what New Zealand's producers will be making by 1995. New Zealand is rapidly proving to be a very high quality drop in the bucket.

Specialist stockists

See the chart on p. 32, plus: Kiwi Fruits (071-240 1423); Fine Wines of New Zealand (071-482 0093) and Hunters (081-891 0670).

Portugal

The hot weather in 1989 made for an early harvest of very ripe grapes. Skilled winemakers (of whom Portugal still has too few) will have produced attractive, deep-flavoured wines whose low acidity will make them easy to drink fairly young. In less careful hands, however, those same grapes will have produced tough, tannic juice that may never soften into anything attractive. The red vintages to pick for drinking today are the light-bodied 1984s and the excellent 1985s.

1989 looks unlikely to have produced any vintage port, so the value of the 1985s seems set to go on rising. The 1982 ports are beginning to soften up nicely, but the 1983s need to be forgotten about for a long while yet — as do most of the 1980s. 1977s are drinkable, but the best are far from ready. As for the 1975s, these are still alive but far from hearty. Drink soon.

Specialist stockists

See the chart on p.32, plus: D & F Wine Shippers (081-969 2277); Premier Wines (0294 602409); Nickolls & Perks (0384 394518); A O L Grilli (0580 891472); Edward Sheldon (0608 61409); Wapping Wine Co (071-265 0448); Classic Wines (081-500 7614); Fine Vintage Wines (0865 724866); Wineforce (071-586 5618); Wine Finds (0584 875582); Patrick Grubb Selections (0869 40229).

South Africa

The liberation of Nelson Mandela and the opening of discussions between the Pretoria government and the ANC have removed the stigma from South Africa for some consumers, and reawakened the possibility of a wider sale of Cape wines in Britain. So far, however, that's all it is: a possibility. Far too few really good South African wines are being produced, and even fewer have reached Britain. Few quality-conscious UK retailers see any need to stock most of the ones that are being imported at the moment. Someday, the winemakers of the Cape will produce good Cabernets, Chardonnays, Pinot Noirs, Sauvignon Blancs and late-harvest wines on a scale that will allow them to compete with the best in the world. But first they will have to revolutionise their over-controlled, over-subsidised industry - and begin to take a far greater interest in the wines that are being made in other countries.

Specialist stockists

La Vigneronne (see p213); Gordon & Macphail (0343 545111); Chester Fine Wine (0244 310455); Edward Cavendish & Sons (0703 870171); Henry C Collison (071-839 6047).

South America

Argentina

Now that peace has finally broken out once again between Britain and its long-time South American friend and trading partner, there is absolutely no reason why British retailers shouldn't begin to fill their shelves with bottles of Argentinian wine. Except for the fact that there aren't enough good ones produced to make it worth them doing so. Argentina is one of the world's five largest winemaking nations; its wineries are generally well equipped and the climate — particularly around Mendoza — is ideal for grape growing. All that's needed now is for more Argentinians to aspire to make stuff better than the fairly basic red and white they sell in South America. For a taste of what Argentina can produce when it takes the trouble, try the Weinert Cabernet Sauvignon 1983 described on p.92.

Brazil

Still very rare in Britain, Brazilian wines are bound to attract greater attention as a growing number of people become interested in South America. So far, the only ones in the UK are the soft, commercial Palomas range imported by A L Vose and a blackcurranty example sold by Victoria Wine, part of the proceeds from which go to help save the rain forests.

Chile

In the spring, Chile's wines appeared to be carving their way into the UK market very effectively. Sainsbury's own-label Chilean Cabernet Sauvignon was that company's second-best-selling red.

The came the bombshell. A set of wines had been found to contain sorbitol, a chemical that is acknowledged to occur naturally in tiny quantities in grapes, as well as in such fruits as apples, pears and blackcurrants. Its use in winemaking is, however, banned world-wide.

The Chileans did not help their case by claiming —as one firm's spokesman did — that the sorbitol had been added accidentally by winemakers who thought the stuff they were pouring into their vats was glycerol, another equally harmless, but equally illegal additive.

The question that few people asked, however, was why anyone in this perfect grape-growing climate needed to add anything to their wine in the first place. Had they asked, they might have been given the same answer that was given during the Austrian 'anti-freeze' scandal some years back: money. Or, to be more precise, the need to produce the kind of wine foreign buyers wanted, at the price they wanted to pay.

Tastings of some of Chile's other, unadulterated wines have left more than a few members of the UK wine trade wondering why Chilean wines have been getting such a favourable press. Chile can make first-class red wine without the help of illegal additives — as has been proven by estates like Cousiño Macul, Los Vascos and Montes, and by Errazuriz Panquehue. But it also produces large quantities of very dull stuff. Chile is no second Australia. Indeed, it's not even a second Bulgaria. At the moment, it is more likely to be treated as a 'poor man's Spain'. And given the appalling current state of Spain's red wine exports to Britain, that's hardly a role we would envy.

Specialist stockists

Argentina :H Allen Smith (see p.117); Grape Ideas (see p.155); Fulham Rd
  Wine Centre (see p.150).
Brazil: Victoria Wine; (see p.212); AL Vose (044 84 3328).
Chile: Tanners (see p.203); Asda (see p.118); Augustus Barnett (see p.123);
  The Wine Society (see p.224); Waitrose Ltd (see p.140); Cornwall Wine
  Merchants (see p140); A L Vose (044 84 3328); Grape Ideas (see p.155);
  Moreno Wines (see p.179); Oddbins (see p.183); Unwins (see p.208);
  Victoria Wine (see p.212); Bordeaux Direct (see p.129); EH Booth (see
  p.129); Wine Emporium (see p.220); Yorkshire Fine Wines (see p.227);
  Peter Dominic (see p.144); Peter Green (see p.158); Eldorobo Wines
  (081-740 4123); Hedley Wright (see p.164).

Spain

After silly and unwarranted price rises in 1989, the Spaniards won back a
few friends by not joining their French and Italian neighbours in the 1990
rush to demand an extra few pence per bottle. However, the Spanish
problem remains one of both image and product. It is no coincidence that
the one success story in Spanish wine is cava, Spain's alternative to Champagne. And the most successful cavas have been the ones that have moved
furthest from their traditional 'earthy' style.

1989 was a good vintage for most of Spain, with Navarra and Duero
reporting consistently fine wines and Rioja and Penedés complaining of
some variability of quality as a result of the combination of drought and hail.
Despite its poor reputation, the 1988 vintage produced some perfectly
acceptable Riojas, Navarras and Penedés wines, though all three regions
did far better in 1987, 1986 and 1985. 1984 and 1983 Riojas have little to be
said for them, but good examples of the 1982s are well worth looking out for.

Specialist stockists

See the chart on p.32, plus: The Wine Spot (061 748 2568); Premier Wines
(071-736 9073); Arriba Kettle (0386 833024); Douglas Henn-Macrae (0622
70952); Mi Casa Wines (0298 3952); Paul Sanderson (031 312 6190); Wine
Finds (0584 875582); Wine on the Green (071-794 1143); Sainsbury Bros (0225
460481).

USA

This was the year when the gentlemanly world of the British wine trade was
introduced to US marketing — by means of an unprecedented £4.5m advertising campaign for the wines of the Californian giant E & J Gallo, featuring
two actors who portrayed Ernest & Julio, the company's aged founders, as
old peasants wearing mackintoshes and sombreros wandering through
their vineyards in the rain.

The Gallo wines — of which some are good and others (the Cabernet
and Chardonnay) are poor — are apparently not selling as rapidly in Britain
as the Gallos had hoped, but they are still very successful when compared
to most other imports from California. The problem with these is largely one
of value for money. California is making great wines in the £7-15 price

range, but far too few impressive ones in the vital £4-7.50 bracket — the one into which the Aussies are making such easy inroads.

But the price of California wines is likely to come down over the next few years for precisely the same reason that Ernest and Julio Gallo thought it worth spending all that money on trying to persuade us to drink their wine — and that reason is the near-desperate state of the Californian wine industry. On the one hand, every man and his dog is out there planting high-cost Chardonnay and Cabernet in high-cost land, creating the prospect of a glut of good wine. And on the other, there is the remorseless drive away from alcohol of any kind. When those two lines — of increased production and decreasing consumption — cross on the graph, the Californians will have no alternative but to drop their prices and begin thinking about exports.

Meanwhile, as the Californians (well, most of them) try to avoid thinking about the ghastly prospect of not being able to sell their entire production in San Francisco, their neighbours further north are quietly steeling the ground from under their feet. Washington State winemakers are already producing wines that are as good as many of those from California, but at half the price. They may not yet be able to compete with the very best of California, but give them time...

Specialist stockists

See the chart on p.32.

The Vintages

Quality ranges from 1–10, from the worst to the greatest respectively. Please note that these marks are all generalisms – good producers make good wine in bad years and bad producers can make even good years into a disaster.

	BORDEAUX RED	BORDEAUX WHITE-SWEET	BURGUNDY RED	BURGUNDY WHITE	RHONE RED	GERMANY WHITE	ITALY RED	SPAIN RIOJA	AUSTRALIA WHITE	AUSTRALIA RED	CALIFORNIA RED	PORT
1989	9△	9△	8△	9△	7△	9△	7△	7△	6△	6△	7△	
1988	8△	9△	9△	8△	8△	8△	9△	6△	8▲	8▲	7△	
1987	6△	5△	7▲	7●	6△	7▲	7△	8△	8▲	8▲	9△	
1986	8△	8△	8△	8▲	7△	7▲	7△	8△	7●	8▲	9△	
1985	8△	7△	9▲	7▲	8▲	8△	10△	7△	8●	8▲	9△	7△
1984	5▲	3△	6●	7▲	6●	5●	5●	7▲	8●	8▲	8▲	
1983	8△	9△	7▲	6●	9▲	9△	9▲	7▲		7●	6●	6△
1982	9△	4▲	5●	6●	7●	5▼	8●	9▲		8●	7●	6△
1981	8▲	5▲	4▼	8●	6●	6▼	7●	8▲				6▼
1980	5●	5●	8●	6▲	6●	5▲	7▲	7●			7▼	6△
1979	7▲	7●	7●	8●	7●	6▼	8▼	6●			7▼	
1978	8▲	4●	8●	8●	10▲	3▽	7▼	8●				6△
1977	4▼	2●	4▽	6●	4▼•	4▼	7▼	4▽				8△
1976	6●	8●	7▼	5▼	7▲	8●	4▽	6▼				
1975	7●	8●	2▽	5▽	3▽	8●	6▼	7▼				5●
1974	4▼	★	3▽	4▽	4▽	★	6▼	6▽				
1973	3▽	3▼	3▽	4▽	5●	★	4▽	8▼				
1972	3▽	★	8●	8▼	5●	★	3▽	3▽				
1971	6▼	8●	9●	8▼	9●	10▼	8▼	4▽				
1970	8●	6●	6▼	6▼	7●	★	8▼	9▼				8●
1969	★	3▼	8▼	8▼	8●	★	7▽	7▽				
1968	★	★	★	★	★	★	6▼	8▽				
1967	5▼	7●	5▽	5▼	7▼	★	7▼	6▽				6●
1966	7●	4▼	7▼	7▽	8▼	★	4▽	7▽				8●
1965	★	★	★	★	★	★	★	★				
1964	★	★	8▼	9▼	8▼	★	8▽	9▽				
1963	★	★	★	★	★	★	★	★				8●
1962	6▼	8●	6▽	8▼	8●	★	★	★				
1961	8●	7●	★	★	★	★	★	★				8▼
1960	★	★	★	★	★	★	★	★				
1959	7▼	★	★	★	★	★	★	★				

△ Still needs keeping
▲ Can be drunk but will improve
● Drinking now

▼ Should be drunk soon
▽ Probably over the hill
★ Bad year/don't buy/past it

Reproduced by kind permission of *WINE* magazine

WINE WITH FOOD

The first rule is...there are no rules. But we hope that we have provided suggestions, ideas and, above all, starting points for further experimentation in our recommendations for food and wine pairings throughout the *Guide's* pages. Below, we describe the food styles each letter refers to and, having consulted wine writers, chefs and 'foodies' alike, recommend not only the obvious perfect matchings but some unexpected successes too — just like those happy marriages that everybody said would never work. We also outline some of the more notorious pitfalls; though here, again, we would not wish to preach; one man's disastrous combination can be, like a peanut butter and jelly sandwich, another's all-time treat.

a	Smoked fish

b	Smoked meat

There are some wines which go equally well with smoked meats and fish — oaky whites and sherries, particularly finos, for example. With fish, a common mistake is to choose a light, lemony wine, thinking that it, like a wedge of lemon, will complement the dish. Head instead for a wine to match the smoky taste and oily texture — an oaky fat Chardonnay can fit the bill. Some of these also go well with smoked meats, but you might find a light red or a warm, spicy rosé equally appropriate.

c	Light starters

All the starters designed to clean and brace one's palate — dressed salads, anything with vinaigrette or citrus fruit — will render any wine unpalatable. For other dishes, one good idea is to try and make your pre-prandial glass of fizz or sherry last through to the main course and wine; otherwise, keep the strength of flavours in food and wine running in parallel — the subtle flavours of, for example, a vegetable terrine are easily overpowered.

d	Egg dishes

The slightest trace of 'egginess' in a fatter, fuller-bodied white wine will be horribly enhanced if drunk with eggs themselves. They need something absolutely clean and crisp, like a good Sauvignon, a Muscadet or even an English wine. Though it sounds unappealing, light reds are good with eggs too — a lightweight Burgundy or a northern Italian, perhaps.

e	White meat without sauce

By which we mean simply roast or grilled chicken, pork or veal, for which there is enormous choice. For duck or goose, choose a fatter, weightier white, a spicier red or, for duck without a fruity sauce, provide the missing ingredient with the ripest, fruitiest wine you can find.

f | Fish without sauce

The fishiness of plainly cooked fish is one determining factor — again, match the degree of flavour in fish and wine. Delicate fish need something like a light Chardonnay or a good Soave — nothing with overpowering acidity— while for oily types like sardines you need the oral equivalent of a finger bowl — Muscadet or Vinho Verde.

g | White meat or fish in a creamy sauce

Poached salmon in a cream sauce is so nice that it deserves to win — pick a softish wine like an unoaked Chardonnay or a good Italian white. Something less refined like a chicken can be given a worthier opponent with firmer acidity; a fresh, gooseberryish Sauvignon or a dry Vouvray .

h | Shellfish

Steely whites like Sancerre and Chablis are the classic choice for oysters (things are usually the classic choice for a good reason); richer shellfish can take on more benevolent styles. Anything with garlic, butter or aioli (or indeed all three) will fight to the death with most wines— take them by surprise with a fino sherry or retsina.

i | White meat or fish in a Provençale-type sauce

For these stronger, tangier sauces try a white wine with strong acidity and freshness. Alternatively, a well-structured, 'definite' red with strong fruit and some tannin would create a happy marriage.

j | Red meat

Plain roast lamb or beef deserves something elegantly spiffing. For cheaper cuts, particularly when casseroled, more rustic reds can be brought into play. Recipes from a particular region, say of France and Italy, usually (rather obviously) go well with that region's wines.

k | Game

Lighter game needs a fruity, not too woody red — a Merlot-based Bordeaux or a cru Beaujolais. Stronger meat — hung game and venison — needs stronger wine; big Italian and Portuguese reds, Rhônes, Zinfandels and Shirazes.

l | Spicy food

Gewürztraminer is the grape for Chinese food, but demi-sec Loire-styles can be good - a sweeter Chenin Blanc, or a really ripe Sauvignon. For curries, we'd recommend something ice-cold, flavourless and sparkling — lager.

m | Cheese

An exciting area, this, for vinous and fromagical research. At the end of your meal, you will (possibly) have several half-empty bottles and several different cheeses. We have enjoyed matching English wines with English cheeses, creamy French cheeses with red Burgundies and extremely smelly offerings with Sauternes, but you are limited only by your imagination.

n | Pudding

If it's stodgy and floury, you could drink Sauternes or some of the stickier Germans, but if you want a real treat, try a Madeira or a Rutherglen Muscat. If it's creamy, you have more of a problem. Try sweet wines made from Chenin Blanc or Sémillon, or a good quality sparkling wine or Champagne.

o | Fresh fruit and fruit puddings

Fresh fruit deserves a fresh fruity wine such as a Muscat (but not the Australian fortified ones) or German Riesling of Spätlese quality. With fruit puddings, try slightly sweeter Rieslings from Germany or the New World.

p | Chocolate

Chocolate *and* wine? Isn't that just a bit too hedonistic? Hardly any combinations seem to work. Brown Brothers Orange Muscat and Flora stands up well (just think of chocolate oranges), as do the fortified Muscats, but any wine of a subtle nature will suffer.

q | Non-food wines

Just as you don't have to drink wine with every meal, you don't have to eat with every bottle you uncork. How about a warming little Crozes-Hermitage on a cold winter's evening, or a big, beefy Californian Chardonnay (but hold the oak) while staying up to watch the Superbowl? Sounds good. There are also the more traditional non-food wines like German semi-sweeties — and then there is Champagne, which you can drink on any day with a 'd' in.

r | Party wines

I suppose these fit into three categories, the wines which you serve at parties, the wines you take to parties and the wines you bring back from parties. If you have the sort of parties where people actually notice what they're drinking, I feel sorry for you. There are many wines in this book which are not only fun but great value for money; see our list on p.52.

s | Special occasions

You've won the pools, the cat has had kittens, Auntie Gladys has left you her set of porcelain thimbles or you've just caught that episode of *Dallas* that you missed in 1983. Who cares what you drink, it's all going to taste good.

THE WINES

Sparkling Wine

As Champagne prices rise, there are only three options for fizz drinkers: a) give up on bubbles; b) seek out the best, least expensive alternatives to Champagne and c) go on drinking the stuff — but make sure that you are getting the best value for money.

For those readers who prefer options b) and c), the following list of sparkling wines should make life both more pleasurable and, hopefully, rather more affordable. From the simplest, sweetest, party Moscato to the richest, nuttiest, yeastiest vintage Champagne, each of these wines is packed with great value bubbles.

1 SAFEWAY MOSCATO SPUMANTE Santero Piedmont (It)

£3.15	✔ SAF LTW	🍽 o, r

A fascinating combination of candy-bars and flowers. Wonderfully refreshing and very emphatically grapey.

2 ST MICHAEL BLUSH FRIZZANTE (It)

£3.25	✔ M&S	🍽 o, r

Easy, vivid pink, gulpable fizz. Brilliant party fare.

3 YALUMBA ANGAS BRUT Barossa Valley (Aus)

£5.25	✔ OD AUC ADN NIC GHW GHS MC MWW POW D BOO BEN	
	FSW COV C&B BTH WGA GNW	🍽 o, q

A really full-flavoured fizz with 'dark, exotic fruit'.

4 ASTI MARTINI Martini & Rossi Piedmont (It)

£5.45	✔ VW TO SAN SAF OD CGW DRI ADN HPD MM TAN MC PD	
	AB TP POW DBY D U	🍽 c, q, r

Bags of bubbles — and grapey, sugared-almond fruit.

5 BRUT DE SAUMUR Caves des Vignerons de Saumur 1987 Loire (F)

£5.49	✔ MWW WBM MTL HAS	🍽 c, q

A rich, but bone dry alternative to Champagne, with lovely appley freshness.

6 CLAIRETTE DE DIE CUVEE IMPERIAL Union des Producteurs Rhône (F)

£5.99	✔ OD GHW L&W ROD	🍽 q, c

Crisp, lemony, and slightly melony fizz, with a creamy texture.

7 CREMANT DE BOURGOGNE ROSE Caves de Bailly 1987 Burgundy (F)

£6.50	✔ MWW JS UC HFW CAC WCE TH TWR W FUL WFP	
		🍽 c, q, o

A well-made wine. Light and biscuity with a touch of yeast.

8 VOUVRAY BRUT Huet Loire (F)

£7.99	✔ OD UBC RAE OLS	🍽 c, q

A really well-made wine with a deep golden colour, a lovely concentrated aroma of 'bluebells, pepper and salt', a rich, yeasty flavour and a smooth, long finish. Sparkling Vouvray at its very best.

9 WILSONS PINOT NOIR/CHARDONNAY Adelaide Hills (Aus)

£9.99	✔ OD AUC	🍽 o, q

A first class, biscuity Australian fizz made from the same blend as most Champagne. Beautifully balanced and refreshing.

10 CHAMPAGNE FORGET-BRIMONT 1ER CRU (F)

| £10.09 | ☞ TO | ⦿ q, s |

Decidedly not forgettable Champagne, with 'floral, sherbetty' flavours and plenty of appley bite. Perfect for parties.

11 CHAMPAGNE DE TELMONT BRUT (F)

| £10.85 | ☞ MWW | ⦿ a, c, q |

Rich, honeyed, apple nose. Full, richly 'earthy' flavour with good acidity and length. Could be worth keeping too...

12 SAINSBURY'S ROSE CHAMPAGNE (F)

| £11.45 | ☞ JS | ⦿ a, c, q, o |

Full and creamy with a hint of sweetness. A soft, stylish, elegant wine.

13 ASDA ROSE CHAMPAGNE (F)

| £11.99 | ☞ A | ⦿ a, c, q, o |

Fine and delicate with reasonable weight. Very, very dry.

14 LAY & WHEELER CHAMPAGNE EXTRA QUALITY BRUT Duval Leroy (F)

| £12.20 | ☞ L&W | ⦿ a, c, q |

Fine, fragrant, almost floral wine. Subtle and understated with a really stylish, biscuity finish.

15 THE SOCIETY'S CHAMPAGNE Alfred Gratien (F)

| £16.90 | ☞ WSO | ⦿ c, q |

This is a yeasty Champagne from Alfred Gratien, a traditional house that still uses oak barrels — hence the slightly oaky flavour.

16 CHAMPAGNE CUVEE DE RESERVE H Billiot (F)

| £14.77 | ☞ BI ADN RAE | ⦿ a, c, q |

From an individual estate, this is very, very classy fizz. It smells flowery and has a gorgeous, rich, buttery-biscuit texture and flavour.

17 CHAMPAGNE MARTEL MILLESIME 1985 (F)

| £14.99 | ☞ WAW | ⦿ c, q |

Lightweight, clean, good dry Champagne — ideal for weddings — or any occasion when a heavier wine might begin to pall.

18 ST MICHAEL ROSE CHAMPAGNE DE ST GALL Union Champagne (F)

| £14.99 | ☞ M&S | ⦿ a, c, q, o |

Dry, elegant and balanced with plenty of fruit and a toasty finish.

19 CHAMPAGNE POL ROGER DEMI-SEC (F)

| £15.75 | ☞ MWW MM MTL | ⦿ s, q, o |

Demi-sec fizz can be awful; this one's delicious, toffee-appley and biscuity, with just the right measure of balancing acidity.

20 CHAMPAGNE PHILIPPONNAT BRUT ROSE (F)·

| £15.90 | ☞ B&B GI BIN MM CNL | ⦿ o, q |

'Peaches and clotted cream'. Well balanced with a sherbety finish.

21 ST MICHAEL VINTAGE CHAMPAGNE DE ST GALL Union Champagne 1985 (F)

| £15.99 | ☞ M&S | ⦿ a, c, q |

Fresh, clean, yeasty nose. Classic and very elegant. Mildly toasted, yeasty biscuity flavour. Between dry and very dry.

22 CHAMPAGNE BRICOUT CARTE D'OR BRUT PRESTIGE (F)

| £16.50 | ☞ BWS CWM CGW UC BOO WCE OD BH CWG |
| | ⦿ s, q, a |

Rich, full and biscuity with slight floral hints and the potential to improve over the next 2-3 years.

23 CHAMPAGNE LAURENT PERRIER ROSE (F)

| £18.50 | ☞ TWR OBC MM NIC TAN GHS CNL LEA HOL GON |
| MWW RAV DBY M&V U SV SEB | ⦿ s, o, q |

Soft, rich and yeasty with lovely balance of fruit and acidity.

☞   For an explanation of stockist abbreviations, see page 17
⦿   For an explanation of food style codes, see page 65

24 **CHAMPAGNE LOUIS ROEDERER BRUT PREMIER** (F)

£18.75	TH TWR OBC ADN SUM K&B MM NIC TAN JS GHS MC UC	
HOL MWW RAV TP DBY M&VHW		s, q, c

Classic, full-bodied Champagne with lots of long, fruit flavour.

25 **CHAMPAGNE LANSON BRUT 1979** (F)

£20.00	TWR MM JS MTL BTH CPL	s, q, c

Glorious, deep-hued, rich, classy, vintage Champagne. It's soft, creamy flavours are at their peak right now but, in magnums, it could last another few years yet.

Richer dry whites

Chardonnay-and-oak have become something of a cliched couple. Nowadays, in fact, few winemakers have the courage to propose any kind of 'quality' dry white wine which has not enjoyed lengthy physical contact with a new oak barrel from one or other of France's more illustrious forests. Those oaky whites appear in the following section; in the next few pages, however, we consider a wide range of good wines which taste of very little or no oak at all.

26 **VIN DE PAYS D'OC** Les Chais Beaucairois Midi (F)

£2.49	U	c, d, f

Clean, ripe citrus fruit, with balancing acidity and good length.

27 **SAINSBURY'S VIN DE PAYS DES COTES DE GASCOGNE** Domaine Bordes 1989 South-West (F)

£2.69	JS	c, e, f, r

Oily, Sauvignon style. Honeyed, smoky apricot with a hint of sweetness and almost New World ripeness.

28 **VIN DE PAYS DES COTES DE GASCOGNE** Plaimont 1989 South-West (F)

£2.79	MWW AB GH OBC ADN TAN MC PD GON CWI M&V CAC	
WRB VW BUD L&W M&S CVR C&B FUL		c, e, f, r

Attractive, easy aromatic style, with some richness and a good balance of flavours.

29 **VIN DE PAYS DES COTES DE GASCOGNE** Dom de Perras 1989 South-West (F)

£3.29	HOL TGB HVW SAN CGW UC HOL POW DBY BOO WCE FW	
CVR BRO WOI ASK CWG		c, e, f, r

'Warm', soft, grassy wine with a fresh, gooseberryish tang.

30 **COTEAUX DE PIERREVERT LA BLAQUE** 1989 Miidi (F)

£3.29	VW	c, e, f, r

Maturing, full-bodied, with complex, smokey, beeswax flavours.

31 **CENTENARY SEMILLON** 1987 (Aus)

£3.50	VW NIC THP	a, e, g, i

Apricotty-peachy New World fruit; fat, with mature roundness.

32 **CHATEAU DE LA ROUERGUE** Barthe 1989 Bordeaux (F)

£3.69	TH TWR W	e, g, i, l

Fresh, ripe greengages and apricot with hints of aniseed. Lovely persistent mixture of fruit n' spice flavours.

33 **CANEPA VINO BLANCO** 1989 Maipo Valley (Ch)

£3.83	WC BD	c, e, g

Strongly aromatic — 'strawberries and green apples' — soft, fat-flavoured wine. One of Chile's better whites.

34 **CHARDONNAY** Wilhelm Walch Termeno 1989 Trentino-Alto Adige (It)

£3.99	W TO	e, g, i, l

Light, buttery, peachy aromas. Ripe and succulent taste. Soft, with good acidity and balance.

35 **TESCO AUSTRALIAN CHARDONNAY**

£4.05	←TO	🍴 e, g, l

The smell of marmalade and fresh yeasty bread has you reaching for your coffee cup. Rich, fruity and well-made.

36 **JURANCON SEC VIGUERIE ROYALE**   Les Vignerons des Coteaux   1988   South-West (F)

£4.21	←COV	🍴 c, e, f, g, r

Lots of complex fruit: 'floral hedgerows','spicy grapefuit'.

37 **HARDY'S BIRD SERIES CHARDONNAY**   1989   South Australia (Aus)

£4.29	←OD AUC DBY VW WAW BTH WRW	
		🍴 e, f

A fruit-packed wine with flavours of zesty lemon/lime citrus fruit. Ripe and juicy texture with a tropical fruit finish. Very New World.

38 **ALSACE TOKAY-PINOT GRIS**   Cave Vinicole de Turckheim 1988   (F)

£4.29	←OD VW GH UC HOL POW DBY BOO WCE FW HVW CVR	
LWL TH TWR SAN BRO HAS SHV ASK		🍴 e, g, i

Lots of fat succulent rose-petal and grape flavours; rich, strong wine, perfectly balanced by just enough acidity.

39 **HILL-SMITH PIGGOT HILL SEMILLON**   1988   South Australia

£4.29	←TH TWR BI	🍴 a, e, g, i

Warm toasted 'gunpowder' nose, crisp dry Semillon with all the complex, peachy, spicy ingredients of greatness. The flavour of the future?

40 **COOKS MARLBOROUGH SEMILLON**   1987   (NZ)

£4.29	←MC AB POW D WOC B&B	🍴 a, e, g, i

'Mouthwatering honey and primrose'; deep lemony green grass. This wine is full of concentrated ripeness. Some identified Chardonnay and some Pinot Gris, but all thought it rather wonderful.

41 **ALSACE PINOT BLANC**   Cave Vinicole de Turckheim 1989   (F)

£4.29	←U CGW SAS UC POW DBY BOO WCE OD HVW CVR TH TWR	
SAN DX BWS CWS ASK		🍴 e, g, i, l

White Wine of the Year

Made from one of the least appreciated varieties of all, this achieves the impossible feat of being both subtle and full- bodied. The fruit flavours are very delicate too, but they're there — and so is a spoonful or two of honey.

42 **ALSACE SYLVANER HEIMBOURG**   Cave Vinicole de Turckheim 1987   (F)

£4.50	←HVW CVR UC BOO	🍴 e, g, i, l

There's honey here too — with lots of fleshy citrus flavours. Honey and lemon? A fine example of a potentially dull grape.

43 **PINOT BIANCO**   Vigna al Monte   1989   Puglia (It)

£4.69	←BWS FWC WIZ C&B HOL WH	🍴 e, g, i, l

Fresh green grass, soft juicy melon and ripe apple flavours; mouthwatering Pinot Bianco, close to its best.

44 **MACON-LUGNY**   Eugène Blanc   1988   Burgundy (F)

£4.69	←OD	🍴 c, d, e, f, h

Clean, fresh fruit - 'grapefruit and guavas'. 'Explosions of flavours'. Good depth of fruit. Well-structured and stylish.

45 **MONTRAVEL SEC SEC SEC**   Cave Coop de St Vivien & Bonneville   1989   South-West (F)

£4.75	←BD WC.	🍴 c, e, f, r

Fresh, creamy, tropical fruit; fat, friendly and smooth; not nearly as dry as the name suggests.

46 **SOAVE CASTEGGIOLA**   G Rizzardi   1987   Veneto (It)

£4.90	←FUL MM RAV DVY BH	🍴 e, f, h

Toasty honey nose balanced by a crisp acidity — lovely Soave with a touch of age. From a pioneering organic estate.

47 LUGANA Ca Dei Frati 1989 Lombardy (It)

| £5.49 | ☞WCE UC EBA TO HEM H&D GNW CWG |
| | ⦿ c, d, e, f, g |

From the shores of Lake Lugana, this wine has perfect balance:
buttery, toasty pineapple fruit with lively fresh acidity.

48 MACON-VINZELLES Caves des Grands Crus 1987 Burgundy (F)

| £5.66 | ☞HFW GON CWI HW | ⦿ a, b, h, q |

Lovely soft wine with subtle, buttery-yeasty, honeyed fruit.

49 BABICH SEMILLON/CHARDONNAY 1989 Gisborne (NZ)

| £5.75 | ☞AB GHS UC BOO WOC CUM FSW HEM EVI WRW WFP |
| | ⦿ a, e, g, i |

The panel found a lot of herbal gooseberry and vine leaf flavours.
Typically New Zealand — very like Sauvignon Blanc.

50 SOAVE CLASSICO Pieropan 1989 Veneto (It)

| £5.75 | ☞WCE UC PTR CWG | ⦿ f, e, g, h |

Ripe, limey perfume, soft and grapey; fresh, full and well-made. From
the finest producer of 'proper' Soave.

51 PRELUDIO NO. 1 Tenuta di Torrebianco 1989 Puglia (It)

| £5.80 | ☞ JN HW GNW PTR | ⦿ c, e, f |

Peachy, ripe, banana fruit. Rich, rounded flavours.

52 HOUGHTON VERDELHO 1988 Swan Valley (Aus)

| £5.95 | ☞AUC DRI BOO CAC VW | ⦿ e, g |

Probably better known for its involvement in Madeira and Dão, the
Verdelho is a variety that takes a different shape at Houghton. The
wine has ripe, earthy melon fruit fattened by nutty butter flavours. It
has good acidity and could be kept.

53 SEPPELTS CHARDONNAY 1989 South-East Australia

| £5.99 | ☞AUC UC VW DAL THP | ⦿ e, f, g, m |

Rich, honeyed Chardonnay. Ripe, almost sweet fruit. Not subtle but
with concentrated flavours that are as distinctive as they are delicious.

54 POUILLY LOCHE CHATEAU DE LOCHE Caves des Grands Crus Vinzelles 1987
Burgundy (F)

| £6.50 | ☞TWR CGW CVR GI | ⦿ a, e, g |

Rich wine with slightly sweet, vanilla aromas. Pleasant, tropical,
lemony fruit with long, honeyed finish.

55 CHARDONNAY DI S MICHELE VIGNETO ZARAOSTI Roberto Zeni 1989 Trentino(It)

| £6.50 | ☞WGA TAN HW MIL V&C WSO | ⦿ e, g, i, l |

Ripe, apple and pear fruit flavours. 'Classy' and will develop.

56 LIBRARY COLLECTION CHARDONNAY Tiefenbrunner 1988 Alto Adige (It)

| £6.75 | ☞SHV HAS HEM POW FW | ⦿ e, g, i, l |

Light, clean, youthful aromas. Soft and approachable. Good acidity
and fresh, lemony fruit. Pleasing balance.

57 INNISKILLIN CHARDONNAY 1988 Niagara (Can)

| £7.25 | ☞AV FW WBM HOP PTR CWG WES |
| | ⦿ r, c, f |

From Canada's top producer, this wine has a light, grapefruit/peach
nose, medium body and is 'full of peachy flavour'.

58 MACON-CLESSE DOMAINE DE LA BON GRAN CUVEE TRADITION Jean
Thevenet 1987 Burgundy (F)

| £7.99 | ☞TAN HOP WDW | ⦿ g, e, f, i |

A spicy, creamy wine which, though not yet at its peak, already has a
wealth of creamy toffee and lime flavours.

(Arg) = Argentina; (Au) = Austria; (Aus) = Australia; (Bul) = Bulgaria; (Cal) = California; (Can) = Canada;
(Ch) = Chile; (F) = France; (G) = Germany; (Gr) = Greece; (Hun) = Hungary; (It) = Italy; (NZ) = New
Zealand; (P) = Portugal; (Rom) = Romania; (SA) = South Africa; (Sp) = Spain; (UK) = United Kingdom;
(US) = United States; (Yug) = Yugoslavia

59 **PINOT BIANCO** Jermann 1988 Friuli-Venezia Giulia (It)

£8.99	☞BWS FWC MIL V&C GNW	🍽 e, g, i, l

Jermann has a reputation for making adventurous wines with consistent high quality. This one has a rich, raisiny, dried apricot flavour and deep colour. Keep it for two years.

60 CHABLIS 1ER CRU FOURCHAUME Guy Mothe 1987 Burgundy (F)

£9.99	☞A HAR	🍽 e, f, g, h

A stylish, classic example of subtle white Burgundy with buttery richness and a beautiful full-flavoured finish.

61 **CHABLIS 1ER CRU VAILLONS** E Defaix 1985 Burgundy (F)

£11.80	☞GH UC TP D DAL	🍽 e, f, g, h

Classic, rich, buttery, toasted aromas of a top quality Chablis with some age. Ripe, fat fruit and fine underlying acidity.

Oaked whites

Oak lovers, this is your playground — from Meursault to Rioja, via white Bordeaux, Australia and California. But never fear. We are no slavish followers of fashion and we don't normally enjoy nibbling away at planks. If the wines we recommend in this section all smell and taste oaky, they all have more than enough fruit to balance that woodiness.

62 **KILLAWARRA CHARDONNAY** 1989 South Australia

£3.69	☞OD	🍽 a, b, i, l

Good New World style. Rich and buttery vanilla nose. Good opulent fruit on the palate. Clean with 'some style'.

63 **RIOJA BLANCO SECO MONTE REAL** Bodegas Riojanas 1986 (Sp)

£4.50	☞MOR MWW DBY	🍽 a, c, e

Lovely light nose with rich, flavoursome fruit and balanced oak. Super freshness. Traditional yet modern.

64 **HARDY'S NOTTAGE HILL SEMILLON** 1989 South Australia

£4.99	☞OD AUC	🍽 e, g, i, m

This wine is full of rich citrus fruit balanced by soft toasted oak flavours; it feels like oily butter in the mouth and is instantly appealing. Not for long term storage.

65 **VIN DE PAYS DES COTES DE GASCOGNE DOMAINE DU TARIQUET CUVEE BOIS** Grassa 1988 South-West (F)

£4.99	☞TH TWR GHS U BWS TO BBR BTH	
		🍽 e, f, g

A ripe fruity wine with good use of oak and a long finish which had some of our tasters asking 'Chardonnay?'

66 **ST MICHAEL AUSTRALIAN CHARDONNAY** Basedows 1988 Barossa Valley

£4.99	☞M&S	🍽 e, f, g

Rich, buttery-oaky wine. Not subtle but very tasty.

67 **CHATEAU BONNET RESERVE DU CHATEAU (OAK AGED)** Entre-Deux-Mers Lurton 1988 Bordeaux (F)

£4.99	☞TH TWR CAC	🍽 e, g, h, i

Ripe citric pineapple fruit with sweet oak and good acidity. A top Bordeaux producer shows that properly made Entre-Deux-Mers can have some class too.

68 **BERGERAC SEC DOMAINE DE GRANDCHAMP** Nick Ryman 1988 South-West (F)

£8.99	☞TH TWR UC	🍽 e, g, h, i

Soft 'Fume Blanc' smoky wine, with 'green tomatoes and peaches'; could easily be a high class white Bordeaux.

69 CHATEAU ROQUEFORT CUVEE PRESTIGE 1988 Bordeaux (F)

| £4.99 | ☞OD CPW | 🎧 e, f, g, h |

No-one questioned the quality of this fresh fruity wine - only when to drink it. Great drinking for the next few years.

70 **VERDICCHIO CA'SAL DI SERRA** Umani Ronchi 1986 Marches (It)

| £4.99 | ☞VW TAN JS UC MWW DBY OD MIL FSW HVW FUL PTR CWG FWC WES | 🎧 c, e, g |

Light, grapey and crisp with good balance and harmony of exotic fruit and wood. A rare example of a caringly made Verdicchio.

71 **MINERVOIS, DOMAINE DE LA TOUR BOISEE VIEILLI EN FUT DE CHENE** Jean Louis Poudou 1988 Midi (F)

| £5.00 | ☞WAW OLS | 🎧 f, g, i |

This smells soft and flowery and tastes softly oaky. Highly drinkable wine from a region far better known for its reds.

72 CHATEAU BAUDUC LES 3 HECTARES Entre-Deux-Mers 1989 Bordeaux (F)

| £5.18 | ☞CVR | 🎧 e, g, h, i |

Light, oily, fresh gooseberries, rich and aromatic with a long, crisp finish. Really mouthwatering Bordeaux Sauvignon.

73 **LINDEMANS BIN 65 CHARDONNAY** 1989 Murray River (Aus)

| £5.35 | ☞AB OD BU PD AUC DBY WOC CDV BEN WBM BWS DAL MCL BEF THP ROD | 🎧 e, g, i, m, s |

'Bananas and cream' with a clean, dry finish. A pleasant, balanced wine.

74 **RIOJA BLANCO SECO RESERVA** CVNE 1985 (Sp)

| £5.49 | ☞OD ADN MM GHW GHS PD UBC UC HOL POW WH CAC WRB WID HVW CVRBWS HAR AHC DAL | 🎧 a, c, e, m |

Soft, gently aged oak aromas and very buttery, clean, woody flavours. The oak is as dominant as it often is in old-fashioned Rioja, but there's plenty of freshness there too.

75 FIRESTONE CHARDONNAY 1987 Santa Ynez (Cal)

| £5.95 | ☞JS MC UBC UC TP POW CAC WRB LAV WIN | 🎧 a, g |

Buttery, oaky Chardonnay from one of the most reliable producers in southern California. (Yes, the Firestone in question is one of the tyre family — but the winery is Japanese-owned).

76 MONTROSE CHARDONNAY 1989 Mudgee (Aus)

| £5.99 | ☞CWG AUC DRT VER RAV DBY BWS BOO WH GHL DAL OBC | 🎧 e, g, i |

Exotic, pineapple fruit flavours with balanced acidity and lengthy flavour. Would keep for another year or so.

77 **KIES ESTATE SEMILLON/SAUVIGNON** 1988 Barossa Valley (Aus)

| £6.25 | ☞DB SAN DRI THP | 🎧 e, f, g, l |

Mouthfilling, honeyed fruit-and-nut, with rich vanilla oak.

78 **MITCHELTON MARSANNE** 1987 Goulburn Valley (Aus)

| £6.39 | ☞JS AUC DBY W GRT | 🎧 g, i, l, m |

'Elegant, floral honeysuckle rose, full, rich and quite oily'. 'Deep golden new oak', 'very together', 'big on flavour'. Made from a spicy grape usually associated with the Rhône.

79 CHATEAU TAHBILK MARSANNE-CHARDONNAY 1987 Goulburn Valley (Aus)

| £6.50 | ☞AUC DBY BEN CWG | 🎧 e, g, i, l |

Marsanne is a speciality of the Goulburn Valley. This blend feels full in the mouth, with chalky melon fruit and rich oak. Very fruity now, it will develop more complexity with keeping.

80 WOLF BLASS BARREL-FERMENTED CHARDONNAY 1988 South Australia

£6.55	☛VW AUC CGW MM AB POW DBY WH WOC WRB OD BEN CGW
B&B BH WRW THP MRS	1⊙l e, g, i, m

A rich tropical fruit style with attractive honeyed oak and high
balancing acidity. 'Delicious'.

81 STONELEIGH CHARDONNAY 1988 Marlborough (NZ)

£6.75	☛MWW MM UC POW DBY WH WAW L&W BEN TO TH TWR SEL
HAS B&B HOP DVY BH PTR CWG	1⊙l e, g, i, m

The 'top-of-the-range' wine from the better-known Cooks, this is a
very clean, buttery-pineappley Chardonnay from vineyards right
next door to those of Cloudy Bay.

82 WOLLUNDRY CHARDONNAY/SEMILLON 1986 Hunter Valley (Aus)

£6.95	☛L&W HUN	1⊙l e, g, i, o, q

Very ripe, full-bodied, oaky fruit with lots of buttery, pineappley
Chardonnay character.

83 MITCHELTON RESERVE CHARDONNAY 1988 Goulburn Valley (Aus)

£6.99	☛YFW HPD DBY WRB W AUC GRT
	1⊙l g, i, l, m

Ripe aromas of buttery oak and fruit with creamy vanilla.

84 SCHINUS MOLLE CHARDONNAY 1989 Mornington Peninsula (Aus)

£6.99	☛OD HFW AUC ADN CWI BOOWFP
	1⊙l g, i, l

Soft, richly oaked style with hints of tropical fruit.

85 JULIUS WILE CHARDONNAY 1986 (Cal)

£7.20	☛TWR UC HW	1⊙l a, g, i

An elegant wine with creamy oak and butter flavours. Good length.

86 MUSCADET DE SEVRE ET MAINE SUR LIE CHATEAU DE CHASSELOIR (OAK-AGED) 1987 Loire (F)

£7.49	☛CIW DRI GHS UC MWW DBY WH RN BEN HUN BND
	1⊙l g, u, q, s

Most Muscadet producers would hate this; they don't like the flavour
of oak. We do, however, especially in this 'buttery honeyed, lovely
rich' blend of yeasty dry Muscadet.

87 PENFOLDS CHARDONNAY 1988 South Australia

£7.79	☛OD AUC DBY WOC WRB SEB TH TWR THP GNW CPL ROD
	1⊙l a, g, h, r, s, q

The White Wine Trophy winner at the 1990 WINE Magazine International Challenge. Toasty, buttery, lemony and very rich wine.
Typically Australian, and extremely tasty.

88 CHATEAU COUHINS-LURTON Graves Lurton 1987 Bordeaux (F)

£7.99	☛THP TAN OD BI WSO	1⊙l e, f, g, u

Another great piece of winemaking by André Lurton. This is deep
coloured, with ripe, citric fruit and nice vanilla-y use of oak. It will
improve over the next two to three years.

89 CHATEAU LA LOUVIERE Graves Lurton 1986 Bordeaux (F)

£8.50	☛TH TWR TP SEL	1⊙l e, f, g, u

Green pea-pods and asparagus, with an attractive, spicy oak balance
and a lovely finish. Comparable to white Burgundy - at twice the price.

90 CHATEAU CONSTANTIN Graves 1986 Bordeaux (F)

£8.69	☛MWW UBC C&B BAT ABY	1⊙l e, f, g, u

'Toast and marmalade, soft and beautifully ripe', 'exotic tropical fruit
with lovely aged oak'. Absolutely at its peak, this wine is a real treat.

☛ For an explanation of stockist abbreviations, see page 17
1⊙l For an explanation of food style codes, see page 65

91 **DELATITE CHARDONNAY** 1989 Central Victoria (Aus)

| £8.75 | ☛ABY | ⭕e, g, l, m |

Soft, well balanced fruit, pineapples and vanilla. Balanced acidity and excellent finish.

92 **SIMI CHARDONNAY** 1985 Sonoma (Cal)

| £9.00 | ☛L&W DBY BEN SAN C&B GNW | ⭕e, g, l, s |

'Melons and pawpaws' with warm vanilla and melted butter. An elegant, classy wine. A rare opportunity to taste a great Californian wine at its mature best.

93 **POUILLY FUISSE** M Delorme 1985 Burgundy (F)

| £9.70 | ☛HFW CWI | ⭕a, b, e, f, g |

Baked apples with crisp acidity and underlying richness. Keep for 2 years to enjoy its full potential.

94 **CHARDONNAY PORTICO DEI LEONI** Vinattieri 1986 Veneto (It)

| £9.94 | ☛BI ABY | ⭕c, e, f |

Fat, toasty with a hint of apples and plenty of oak. Long finish.

95 **CLOUDY BAY CHARDONNAY** 1988 Marlborough (NZ)

| £10.50 | ☛ADN HAR DAL C&B L&W HPD TAN GHS UBC CNL MWW | |
| | DBY M&V HW BOO WWI WCE SEB WAW | ⭕e, g, i, q, s |

Spicy, vanilla with pineapple and lemon flavours. Good length and great potential. Keep 3-5 years. Unlike this winery's legendary but almost unobtainable Sauvignon, this is a wine you can buy as well as read about.

96 **MARTINBOROUGH VINEYARDS CHARDONNAY** 1988 Wairarapa (NZ)

| £10.70 | ☛HFW GON BOO L&W CPW | ⭕e, g |

Creamy and woody with plenty of Chardonnay fruit. Good acidity with clean, elegant finish.

97 **COLDSTREAM HILLS CHARDONNAY** 1988 Yarra Valley (Aus)

| £10.75 | ☛TWR AUC DBY HW OD FSW SHV THP | |
| | | ⭕e, f, g, s |

A smooth, rounded wine with subtle, Burgundian-style, raspberry 'n' vanilla flavours.

98 **GEOFF MERRILL CHARDONNAY** 1987 McLaren Vale (Aus)

| £10.99 | ☛ RES WAW AF AUC UC DBY WID SHV | |
| | | ⭕e, f, g |

Rich, peachy with some lemony fruit. Lovely balance and length.

99 **TREFETHEN CHARDONNAY** 1986 Napa Valley (Cal)

| £11.29 | ☛TWR ADN DBY WSO GRT WIN LAV | |
| | | ⭕e, f, g |

'Peaches and cinnamon', with great fruit concentration.

100 **PETALUMA CHARDONNAY** 1987 Adelaide Hills (Aus)

| £11.35 | ☛ AUC ADN POW DBY CVR THP GRT PTR LAV WIN | |
| | | ⭕e, f, g, i, m |

A well made Australian Chardonnay with rich, creamy fruit, balanced with great depth of flavour and acidity. Keep for at least another 5 years.

101 **MOUNTADAM CHARDONNAY** 1989 High Eden Ridge (Aus)

| £11.49 | ☛HFW OD HUN AUC GON CWI POW BOO BTH THP | |
| | H&D FWC | ⭕e, f, g, s |

An Australian Chardonnay that disproves the rule that Aussie whites have to be big, oaky and rich. This one is subtle and far more Burgundian in style. 'Lots of dimensions'; 'long, delicious, outstanding'; 'Creamy, buttery, oaky, elegant'.

102 **CRICHTON HALL CHARDONNAY** 1987 (Cal)

| £11.49 | ☛BTH HOL SEL | ⭕e, f, g |

Ripe apples and young oak with a long, spicy finish. Unusual.

103 VITA NOVA CHARDONNAY 1988 (Cal)

| £12.20 | ☛M&V FWC | 🎑 e, f, g, s |

Biscuity and roast almond flavours with hints of citrus fruits. Lovely soft finish.

104 VILLA MARIA BARRIQUE-FERMENTED CHARDONNAY 1987 Auckland (NZ)

| £13.50 | ☛FWC MM HVW | 🎑 e, g, q |

'Up-front' Chardonnay with tropical fruit and warm vanilla. Long buttery finish.

105 TARRAWARRA CHARDONNAY 1987 Yarra Valley (Aus)

| £13.60 | ☛FWC DBY SHV THP | 🎑 e, f, g, s |

Rich orchard fruits and pleasing creamy nuttiness. 'Classy style'.

106 LEEUWIN ESTATE CHARDONNAY 1984 Margaret River (Aus)

| £13.75 | ☛AUC DBY WH HAR DX GRT | 🎑 e, f, g, s |

Mature New World Chardonnays are a rarity. This one comes from a superstar winery in Australia whose vineyards were originally selected by Robert Mondavi when he was planning to make wine down under. It's creamy and lemony, with luscious flavours of toasted apricots. And 'very ready' to be drunk.

107 CULLENS CHARDONNAY 1987 Margaret River (Aus)

| £13.99 | ☛DX AUC UC BAT THP | 🎑 e, f, g, i |

'Lemon-butter and roasted chestnuts'; vanilla-creamy oak; 'very positive, almost jammy fruit'.

108 ROSEMOUNT ROXBURGH CHARDONNAY 1987 Hunter Valley (Aus)

| £14.95 | ☛TH TWR AUC UC GON MWW DBY WH CAC WCE WOC OD WBM SAN DAL GHW PTR | 🎑 e, g, l |

'Rich, resiny wood and sweet toasted oak'. 'A classic'.

109 CHATEAU DE FIEUZAL Graves 1986 Bordeaux (F)

| £15.00 | ☛HUN UC EBA ASK THP | 🎑 g, h, q |

'Rich buttered toast'; 'bags of everything' but still too young to be enjoyed at its best. Superlative Graves..

110 ZD CHARDONNAY 1987 Napa Valley (Cal)

| £15.00 | ☛MWW BWS | 🎑 e, g, m, q, s |

'Soft, vanilla ice cream'. Peachy aromas with a long, warm finish.

111 PULIGNY MONTRACHET Domaine Carillon 1987 Burgundy (F)

| £15.55 | ☛L&W WCE WDW | 🎑 g, q, e |

A classic white Burgundy with delicate fruit butter and some honey. Still young, it needs 3-5 more years.

112 CABREO LA PIETRA Ruffino 1986 Tuscany (It)

| £15.59 | ☛HAR V&C BTH | 🎑 e, f, g, q, s |

Spice and aniseed, with good balance and smooth, integrated oak.

113 MEURSAULT CLOS DU CROMIN O Leflaive 1986 Burgundy (F)

| £16.25 | ☛L&W | 🎑 g, q, s |

Rich depth of flavour with good acidity. Powerful and slightly oily. Will keep 3-5 years.

114 YARRA YERING CHARDONNAY 1987 Yarra Valley (Aus)

| £16.90 | ☛TAN LEA BEN AUC WFP CWG | 🎑 e, g, q |

Coconutty fruit and subtle vanilla oak. A young, complex wine which will develop over the next 3 years or so.

115 MEURSAULT Drouhin 1988 Burgundy (F)

| £16.99 | ☛OD MM L&W NIC GNW | 🎑 g, q, s |

'Honeydew melon' with discreet oak. Youthful and elegant. Will keep for 2-3 years.

(Arg) = Argentina; (Au) = Austria; (Aus) = Australia; (Bul) = Bulgaria; (Cal) = California; (Can) = Canada; (Ch) = Chile; (F) = France; (G) = Germany; (Gr) = Greece; (Hun) = Hungary; (It) = Italy; (NZ) = New Zealand; (P) = Portugal; (Rom) = Romania; (SA) = South Africa; (Sp) = Spain; (UK) = United Kingdom; (US) = United States; (Yug) = Yugoslavia

Dry Loire-style whites

When everybody finally grows bored of the flavour of the Chardonnay, we suspect that one of the directions in which they may turn is towards the traditional tastes of the Loire — in the form of the appley Chenin Blanc, the gooseberryish Sauvignon, and the yeastily dry wines of Muscadet. If and when they do — quite probably via some of the brilliant Loire-style Sauvignons now being made in New Zealand — you could have got there first, simply by discovering a few of the wines on the following pages for yourself.

116 DOMAINE DE MONTMARIN SAUVIGNON, VIN DE PAYS DES COTES DE THONGUE
1989   South-West   (F)

£2.99	◆TH TWR	⦶ d, e, f, g

Firm, fresh, fruity, clean, well-balanced and refreshing.

117 ANJOU BLANC CHUPIN G Saget 1989 Loire (F)

£3.45	◆GI WFP UC MWW B&B FUL	
		⦶ c, e, f, h

Rich, honeyed, banana and pineapple fruit, with refreshing acidity and an excellent lasting flavour.

118 MUSCADET CHATEAU DE LA MOUCHETIERE 1989 Loire (F)

£3.45	◆G SAF FSW	⦶ a, f, h, i

Clean and lean, fruity aromas with a bready yeast flavour and a fresh, tangy finish.

119 SAUMUR BLANC Caves des Vignerons de Saumur 1988 Loire (F)

£3.60	◆HAS POW WBM TO EVI SHV	⦶ c, e, f, h

Typical, steely, appley Chenin Blanc acidity is tempered here by some wonderful honeyed richness. Very complex and full-bodied.

120 SAUMUR BLANC CHATEAU DE VILLENEUVE Robert Chevalier 1988 Loire (F)

£3.99	◆SEB CPW	⦶ c, e, f, h

Rose petal and wood aromas give way to ripe apple and herb flavours; very full fruit; lasts well in the mouth.

121 TATACHILLA HILL CHENIN BLANC 1988 McLaren Vale (Aus)

£4.29	◆TH TWR UC	⦶ f, g, u

Rich, spicy fruit, fattened with vanilla and peach. Obvious New World winemaking has brought out the best from these grapes.

122 SAUVIGNON DE TOURAINE DOMAINE DE LA PRESLE Jean-Marie Penet 1988 Loire (F)

£4.45	◆SEB K&B HW HEM BAT CPW	⦶ a, b, e, f, h, i

A dry mouthwatering, appley wine with good acidity. Will improve over the next two years into an even more interesting drink.

123 SAINSBURY'S WASHINGTON STATE SAUVIGNON BLANC Columbia Crest 1987 (USA)

£4.49	◆JS	⦶ a, c, f, g, i

Well done to Sainsbury's for seeking out a wine from such a little-known region. 'Great, fat, gooseberry flavour'. Great value.

124 MUSCADET Bregeon 1988 Loire (F)

£4.50	◆H&H SEB FW	⦶ a, f, h, i

This wine has buckets of fresh ripe fruit and floral complexity. Very classy Muscadet with a marvellous palate-tingling bite.

125 VOUVRAY Chevalier de Moncontour Loire (F)

£4.50	◆TO BBR BH	⦶ c, e, f

This smells of honey-ripe baked peaches and has a juicy, rich, intense fruit flavour with some apricot 'noble rot' character. A really delicious wine which will continue to improve.

126 CHATEAU LA JAUBERTIE BERGERAC SEC Henry Ryman 1987 South-West (F)

| £4.50 | ☞VW MWW HBV WFP GNW | 🍴a, c, f, g, i, q |

Soft fruit with balanced acidity - stylish and interesting. Enjoyable now, it will improve over the next year or so.

127 MUSCADET DE SEVRE ET MAINE SUR LIE G Bossard 1989 Loire (F)

| £4.90 | ☞RAV VER OBC RAE WOC CUM BI VR CVR PTR A | |
| | | 🍴a, f, h, i |

'Sweet hay' aromas scented with honey; nice, fresh, clean floral fruit finishing with crisp acidity. From a producer with strong organic principles.

128 MUSCADET DE SEVRE ET MAINE Château de la Ragotière 1988 Loire (F)

| £4.99 | ☞AB HW | 🍴a, f, h, i |

Light, clean, dry, flowery wine, with bags of fruity intensity.

129 MONTANA SAUVIGNON BLANC 1989 Marlborough (NZ)

| £4.99 | ☞OD VW PD BWS WIZ DRI ADN HPD TAN WRB MC UC AB RAV | |
| | POW DBY D RN HW U | 🍴a, c, d, e, f, h, m, |

'Intense fruit implosion'; packed full of fresh clean-cut gooseberries with a light herbaceous feel. Very easy to drink, but a far more 'serious' wine than it seems.

130 SAUVIGNON DE ST BRIS DOMAINE DU RELAIS DE POSTE Luc Sorin 1989 Burgundy (F)

| £4.99 | ☞TH TWR | 🍴a, c, d, f, g, h, i |

A little-known Burgundian alternative to Sancerre, this is fresh, light and very ripe. Should develop during the next year.

131 QUINCY P & J Mardon 1988 Loire (F)

| £5.15 | ☞CDV OBC ADN LEA | 🍴a, c, d, f, g, h, i |

This well-made, fresh and lively young wine is full of character, with a seductive grapey taste to entice you all the more. A good value alternative to Sancerre

132 REUILLY H Beurdin 1988 Loire (F)

| £5.89 | ☞HV GH ADN WCE BWS | 🍴f, g, h, i |

A well-balanced, gooseberryish wine from the best producer in this little-known village, close to Sancerre and Pouilly.

133 HILL-SMITH ESTATE SAUVIGNON BLANC 1989 Barossa Valley (Aus)

| £6.25 | ☞AUC LWL POW HW WRB WBM SHV | |
| | | 🍴c, d, f, g, h, i |

'Is this Cloudy Bay?' wondered *Punch* writer Jim Ainsworth. High praise indeed for this crisp, fruity, violetty Sauvignon. It owes much to high altitude vineyards and good winemaking.

134 NOBILOS SAUVIGNON BLANC 1989 Marlborough (NZ)

| £6.45 | ☞AV AF DAL MWW OBC K&B MM UC DBY WH RN WID | |
| | GHL SAN SEL HEM WES EOO | 🍴a, c, d, e, f, h, q |

Oh, the green, green grass of home. This soft, rounded wine is jam-packed with green gooseberries, fresh apples and limes; a veritable verdant cocktail.

135 COOPERS CREEK SAUVIGNON BLANC 1989 Marlborough (NZ)

| £6.50 | ☞HAS POW HVW SHV | 🍴a, c, d, e, f, h, q |

Typical New Zealand Sauvignon. A smooth, crisp, herbaceous wine with the flavour of 'gooseberry fool'.

136 ADLER FELS SAUVIGNON BLANC 1987 Sonoma (Cal)

| £6.69 | ☞OD DRI PD FWC | 🍴f, g, h, i |

A rare, successful Californian Sauvignon from a winery perched on a precarious ridge. An 'extraordinary' mixture of 'asparagus and sweet-peas and soft, fresh gooseberries'. Will mature well.

137 POUILLY FUME VIEILLES VIGNES Caves de Pouilly sur Loire 1988 (F)

| £6.85 | ☞SAF FWC | 🍴f, g, i |

This clean, well-made wine has all the grassy, lemon-zesty aromas and dry, smoky taste of great, 'classic' Loire whites.

138 **HUNTERS SAUVIGNON BLANC** 1989 Marlborough (NZ)

£6.95	◆DB LWL YFW BEN DAL TP EBA DRI K&B UC HOL	
WH HVW CVR WBM SAN		⏴◯⏵c, f, f, g, h, i

A very worthy Gold Medal winner at the *WINE Magazine* International Challenge, this 'rich, silky' wine has all the gooseberries you could ask for - and a wonderful backbone of crisp acidity.

139 **SANCERRE** Henry Natter 1988 Loire (F)

£6.99	◆BI WOC L&W WOI	⏴◯⏵f, g, i, m

A fresh, subtly fruity example of Sancerre at its best.

140 **SANCERRE CLOS DE LA CROIX AU GARDE** Domaine H Pelle 1989 Loire (F)

£7.20	◆OD GH	⏴◯⏵f, g, h, i, m

'Real fresh gooseberries, not tinned!' said one taster; complex, and 'as finely-structured as a piece of sculpture'.

141 **SANCERRE DOMAINE DES P'TITS PERRIERS** A Vatan 1988 Loire (F)

£7.50	◆SAF	⏴◯⏵f, g, h, i, m

Strong and refreshingly crisp with a mouthwatering, almost tropical citric acidity - an example of classic, 'steely' Sancerre.

142 **POUILLY BLANC FUME DOMAINE CHAILLOUX** Châtelain 1987 Loire (F)

£7.99	◆D SAS MC GON DBY	⏴◯⏵f, g i

'Honey and gooseberry pie' wine, with a rich, full flavour.

143 **RONGOPAI SAUVIGNON BLANC** 1989 Waikato (NZ)

£8.50	◆HFW GON POW CWI BOO	⏴◯⏵c, d, f, g, h, i

Complex Kiwi Sauvignon with 'grapey smoothness' and 'just a background touch of sweet new oak'. Drink over the next 2-3 years.

144 **MOUNT HURTLE SAUVIGNON BLANC** 1989 McLaren Vale (Aus)

£8.99	◆RES WAW AF AUC UC WID DAL SHV	
		⏴◯⏵c, d, f, g, h, i

This fresh and zippy young wine, with its sharp lemony acidity, has a full, fat, gooseberry taste.

145 **POUILLY FUME BUISSON MENARD** Didier Dagueneau 1988 Loire (F)

£10.00	◆TH ABY OBC TWR	⏴◯⏵a, f, g i

Didier Dagueneau is one of the superstar producers of Pouilly Fumé. This wine is beautifully fresh, gooseberryish and lingering.

146 **POUILLY FUME SILEX** Didier Dagueneau 1988 Loire (F)

£22.95	◆TH ABY TWR	⏴◯⏵a, f, g i

Dagueneau's best. Even at over £20 for a bottle this is worth every penny. 'Silex' means 'flint' and refers to the flinty soil on which the grapes are grown - and the flinty flavour of the wine. Ultimate Pouilly Fumé.

Medium-dry whites

A very unfashionable part of the wine spectrum, this. And hardly surprisingly, because demi-sec wines in general are often so poor. But there are good, well-balanced examples which warrant tasting. Ah but, we hear you say, I don't like sweet wines. Fair enough; it's not for this *Guide*, or for anyone else, to dictate your tastes. All we'd ask is for all of you anti-sweetness wine drinkers who enjoy chocolate, puddings and sugar in your coffee to stop and wonder whether your insistence on wine being dry does

(Arg) = Argentina; (Au) = Austria; (Aus) = Australia; (Bul) = Bulgaria; (Cal) = California; (Can) = Canada; (Ch) = Chile; (F) = France; (G) = Germany; (Gr) = Greece; (Hun) = Hungary; (It) = Italy; (NZ) = New Zealand; (P) = Portugal; (Rom) = Romania; (SA) = South Africa; (Sp) = Spain; (UK) = United Kingdom; (US) = United States; (Yug) = Yugoslavia

not have at least a little to do with a desire not to appear unsophisticated...

147 RAMADA ALMEIRIM BLANCO (P)

| £2.49 | ☛PD | ￮ e, f, g, m |

Perfumed, slightly spritzy wine with crisp fresh fondant fruit. Excellent value from one of Portugal's most modern cooperatives.

148 PIERRE CHAUMONT ANJOU BLANC Remy Pannier Loire (F)

| £2.69 | ☛CWS | ￮ d, e, f, g |

A truly awful label, but first class, fresh, peachy, appley Chenin Blanc flavours. Perfect justification for blind tasting.

149 CHENIN BLANC E & J Gallo 1988 (Cal)

| £3.29 | ☛ A MRS BLW U CGW MC AB WWI WRB WID SEL THP | |
| | | ￮ c, f, g, i |

'Crisp crunchy melons', 'lively, grapefruity', 'just off-dry'.

150 VOUVRAY DEMI-SEC Les Caves des Viticulteurs 1988 Loire (F)

| £3.65 | ☛SAF EP | ￮ j, k, l |

Rich, complex, honeyed, floral. Sweet, but with a bit of bite.

151 COTEAUX DU LAYON ST-AUBIN DE LUIGNE Banchereau 1988 Loire (F)

| £3.89 | ☛MWW | ￮ c, f, g, i |

Powerful sweet wine, with oodles of honey and apple.

152 COOKS CHENIN BLANC 1987 Hawkes Bay (NZ)

| £3.99 | ☛MWW TAN MC PD POW TO B&B HOP GI CPL | |
| | | ￮ c, d, f, g, u, i |

Deep, 'broad, brown muscovado sweetness', and really rich fruit.

153 VOUVRAY CUVEE SELECTE Chainier 1985 Loire (F)

| £4.09 | ☛BUD | ￮ c, d, f, g, i |

Lemon and honey with a light clean sweetness, lovely and fresh.

154 JURANCON MOELLEUX CUVEE THIBAULT (BARRIQUE-AGED) Domaine de Bellegarde 1988 South-West (F)

| £4.99 | ☛OD | ￮ c, e, f, g, u |

Jurançon, in the Pyrenean foothills, used to be considered on a par with Sauternes. This has a wonderful concentration of rich fruit and good 'noble rot' peachy/apricot character. There's a bit of oak ('*barrique*') too. Beautiful.

155 MILTON VINEYARDS BARREL-FERMENTED CHENIN BLANC 1988 Gisborne (NZ)

| £7.20 | ☛VR ORG HFW L&W VER | ￮ e, f, g, m |

Golden, lightly oaky, rich, nobly-rotten New World wine from a New Zealander who's passionate about Chenin Blanc.

156 VOUVRAY DEMI-SEC CLOS DE BOURG Huet 1983 Loire (F)

| £8.30 | ☛BI ADN RAE HEM WSO OLS | ￮ j, k, l |

'Rich, biscuity, peachy fruit with young acidity'; great length of flavour - one to keep.

Aromatic whites

Misunderstood for much the same reason as sweeter wines are misunderstood, aromatic wines in general, and the Gewürztraminer in particular, rarely feature on most wine drinkers' top-tens. Admitting that you actually enjoy that perfumed, let-it-all-hang-out style is rather like stating that you are having an affair with the most brazen and promiscuous flirt in town.

☛   For an explanation of stockist abbreviations, see page 17
￮   For an explanation of food style codes, see page 65

Far better to stick to the more 'serious', acceptable flavours of the Chardonnay or Cabernet. Well, it's up to you. All we'd say is that not all aromatic wines are as flirtatious as you might imagine (some are fundamentally really quite serious); and those that are could give you a whole lot more fun at dinner than any number of more strait-laced bottles.

157 RETSINA OF ATTICA Kourtaki (Gr)

£2.99	☞AB CGW MM NIC JS BOO U CUM VW OD GHL TH TWR W	
MRS PTR		❍ a, b

If you like the taste of oil, turpentine, pine, eucalyptus and rosemary, you will love this well-made, characterful wine.

158 TESCO ALSACE GEWURZTRAMINER Kuen 1988 (F)

£3.95	☞TO	❍ e, g, l, m

Full-flavoured 'tropical fruit and spice' wine. Very typical.

159 TORRES GEWURZTRAMINER 1988 Curico (Ch)

£4.50	☞CVR DRI MC UC DBY	❍ a, l, m

A light, biscuity wine with a taste of pineapple. Less pronounced in its spiciness than most European versions.

160 ALSACE GEWURZTRAMINER Caves Coop des Viticulteurs d'Ingersheim 1987 (F)

£4.99	☞HV MC D	❍ e, g, l, m

Powerfully aromatic, ripe 'heavyweight', 'fruit-salady Gewürz'.

161 ALSACE GEWURZTRAMINER Dambach Louis Gisselbrecht 1988 (F)

£5.25	☞THP HW DVY BAT HUN MRS	❍ l, m

Young, spicy Gewürztraminer with good, oily richness held at bay by a tangy bite of acidity.

162 ALSACE AUXERROIS MOENCHREBEN RORSCHWIHR Rolly Gassmann 1987 (F)

£5.99	☞THP BI	❍ a, l, m

Rich, ripe wine with a touch of oak. Honeyed yet fresh. 'Full of life'. The Auxerrois is a rare Alsatian variety; Rolly Gassmann is one of the best producers in the region.

163 ALSACE GEWURZTRAMINER Pierré Frick & Fils 1988 (F)

£6.20	☞FW HFW VER	❍ a, l, m

Spicy, warm, tropical fruit wine. Soft, full and spicy.

164 ALSACE TOKAY-PINOT GRIS HERRENWEG Domaine Barmes-Buecher 1988 (F)

£6.40	☞H&H	❍ a, b, h

Very classy, gently spicy wine with a lovely smoky, perfumed aroma.

165 ALSACE TOKAY-PINOT GRIS RESERVE PERSONELLE Wiederhirm 1988 (F)

£7.18	☞HBV	❍ a, b, u

Lightly honeyed wine, with a 'rounded, full fruit flavour'.

166 MARK WEST VINEYARDS GEWURZTRAMINER 1988 Sonoma (Cal)

£7.50	☞ HOL DBY BOO BH PTR CWG LAV WIN	
		❍ a, l, m

Very New World style - fresh, sprightly fragrance; rich, fat sweetly ripe fruit with a bite of citrus acidity.

167 ALSACE GEWURZTRAMINER GRAND CRU KESSLER Schlumberger 1985 (F)

£11.55	☞L&W UC DBY BEN HAR BTH PTR FWC	❍ l, m

From a top class estate in the south of Alsace, and one of the region's best vineyards, this is still young, but already showing the rich depth of fruit that will emerge over the next five years.

168 ALSACE GEWURZTRAMINER SELECTION DE GRAINS NOBLES Cave Vinicole de Turckheim 1988 (F)

£15.00	☞CWG UC HOL DBY CVR BRO ASK CWG CWM	
		❍ k, l, i, s

A stunning wine, and a worthy winner of the *WINE Magazine* International Challenge 'Late-Picked' Trophy'. It's honeyed and very concentrated in its rich, spicy flavours. Tasters used expressions such as 'magnificent' and 'tremendous'. Beautifully well-balanced.

Grapey whites

Every time a wine writer describes a wine as smelling or tasting of strawberries, peaches or pepper, some wine drinker somewhere is almost sure to send in a letter pointing out that quality wines are not made from these fruits, and that the only growing thing they ought to taste of is grapes. In fact, of course, very few wines do taste grapey but, for the substantial number of people who wish they did, we've chosen a delicious set that is packed with the flavour of the vineyard.

169 TOLLEY'S PEDARE LATE HARVEST MUSCAT BLANC A PETITS GRAINS 1988 Barossa Valley (Aus)

£3.35	☞OD	🍲 e, k, m, n, o

Ripe, spicy and full of aromatic fruit. Slightly sweet but with sufficient balancing acidity to make this a delicious mouthful.

170 VIN DE PAYS D'OC LES TERRES FINES CEPAGE MUSCAT Delta Domaines 1987 Midi (F)

£3.79	☞TO	🍲 e, k, m

An unusually 'discreet' Muscat, with less grapey intensity than most. 'Subtle and elegant', with a long, dry finish.

171 MOSCATO D'ASTI Viticoltoro dell'Acquesi 1989 Piedmont (It)

£3.99	☞WCE UC HVW MG	🍲 q, r, o

Juicy, half-fizzy wine to delight anyone who likes the flavour of ripe Muscat grapes. Impeccably well-balanced.

172 JOAO PIRES WHITE TABLE WINE 1988 Palmela (P)

£4.49	☞MWW ADN JS GHS UBC CNL AB RAV DBY D BOO WWI VW WID OD HVW CVR EBA	🍲 m, n, q

Made by a young Australian, this is deliciously fruity, with an intriguing slight hint of green peppers.

173 VIN DE PAYS D'OC MUSCAT SEC Domaine de Coussergues 1989 Midi (F)

£4.92	☞WC BD	🍲 m, n, o

A light refreshing wine for a picnic or a winter party - with a delicate flowery smell and a taste of citrus fruit.

174 BROWN BROTHERS LATE HARVEST ORANGE MUSCAT & FLORA 1988 N E Victoria (Aus)

£9.78	☞VW TH TWR AUC DRI ADN HPD MM NIC GHW TAN GHS MC PD UBC CNL UC HOL BND	🍲 p, n, o

Packed with flavour and character, full, rich and luscious with a rich creamy taste which somehow never quite disappears...

175 QUADY ESSENSIA ORANGE MUSCAT 1987 (Cal)

£11.00	☞MWW NIC GHS UC WH WOC BEN BWS DAL HEM B&B HOP WRW THP MRS GNW ABY	🍲 o, p, n

'Thick', unctuous, honeyed wine with an immense concentration of orange flavour.

Dry Germanic Whites

The newest or, as the Germans and Alsatians would claim, one of the oldest styles of all, dry Riesling and Riesling-like wines are rapidly taking over from their sweeter equivalents, both in Germany where, unbelievably, two thirds of some estates' wines are now bone dry, and in England where producers have sensibly given up trying to mimic Liebfraumilch, The only problem with this style is that for 'dry' one often has to read 'raw' and 'unripe'. The examples we recommend below, however, are ripe and very delicious. Buy a couple and set up your own England v Germany taste-off.

176 SAINSBURY'S TROCKEN Rheinhessen (G)

£2.65 ☛ JS 🍴 e, r

A first class example of 'new style' German dry wine. It has spicy, pungent fruit with a hint of mangoes, lychees and honey and some refreshingly crisp, lemon acidity.

177 BADEN DRY ZBW (G)

£2.99 ☛ TO DRI MM NIC AB CUM OD MTL BTH CPW 🍴 c, q

From the southern, warmest part of Germany where the grapes ripen well, this has long lasting fruit flavours of soft fruit and gooseberry-like acidity.

178 WEISSER BURGUNDER DRY Rietburg 1986 Rheinpfalz (G)

£3.75 ☛ TO SAF 🍴 a, c, q

A clean, honest, straightforward wine with a touch of spice and soft, raisiny fruit.

179 WICKHAM VINEYARD MEDIUM DRY 1988 Hampshire (UK)

£3.75 ☛ GWR 🍴 a, c, q

Floral, lemony-minty, with heaps of summery aromas and flavours.

180 VILLA SACHSEN TROCKEN 1988 Rheinhessen (G)

£3.99 ☛ OD 🍴 a, c, q

An impeccably balanced, dry, appley wine from a very ripe vintage.

181 SEAVIEW RHINE RIESLING 1987 South East Australia

£3.99 ☛ AUC OD 🍴 a, e, f, q

An attractive fruit salad of grapefruit and pineapple with a hint of spice and lime. Rich and buttery, but with a crunchy bite of acidity. Like blackcurrants on hot buttered toast.

182 ALSACE RIESLING Seltz 1988 (F)

£4.15 ☛ MWW WAW OLS 🍴 a, b, e, g

A well-balanced wine with zippy acidity and a very long finish.

183 NUTBOURNE MANOR HUXELREBE 1989 Sussex (UK)

£4.50 ☛ CPL K&B SEL GWR HFV 🍴 c, e, f, q

An interesting mixture of 'guava' and 'blackcurrant', with young, sharp, orangey flavours. English wine at its fresh best.

184 ASTLEY HUXELVANER 1989 Worcestershire (UK)

£4.75 ☛ TAN GWR EOO 🍴 c, e, f, q

A light wine with a 'wild rose' scent, mouthwatering fruit and acidity. A wine many Germans would have liked to have made.

185 FREINSHEIMER GOLDBERG RIESLING TROCKEN KABINETT Lingenfelder 1987 Rheinpfalz (G)

£4.89 ☛ OD 🍴 c, e, f, g, l, r

Honeyed, petrolly and ripe lemony fruit - the hallmarks of first-rate Riesling. A very, very good wine.

186 ST MICHAEL ENGLISH WINE (Carr Taylor Vineyards) Kent (UK)

£4.95 ☛ M&S 🍴 c, e, f, q

Like a classy old Riesling, this smells of petrol and tastes attractively honeyed. Just off-dry and very well-made.

187 ORLANDO ST HELGA RIESLING 1986 Barossa Valley (Aus)

£4.99 ☛ OD AUC CWM 🍴 a, e, f, q

Barossa Riesling at its best. Petrolly flavours of German Riesling with the oiliness of Alsace. Great value.

188 PILTON MANOR DRY RESERVE 1987 Somerset (UK)

| £4.99 | ☞MWW GWR GRT WES | 🍽 c, e, f, q |

Tangy and spicy with a slight smell of blackcurrants. Well-balanced honeyed flavours.

189 STAPLE ST JAMES MULLER-THURGAU Staple Vineyards 1989 Kent (UK)

| £5.00 | ☞ HFV | 🍽 e, f, g |

Aromatic floral aromas of blackcurrant leaves, bananas and grapefruit. Crisp, fresh fruit with a high lemon acidity that will soften nicely during the next two to three years.

190 SHAWSGATE MULLER THURGAU 1989 East Anglia (UK)

| £5.25 | ☞L&W ADN GWR DAL | 🍽 e, f, g, q |

Ripe, spicy, clean, slightly sparkling wine. Particularly well-liked by one of the German tasters.

191 HENSCHKE RIESLING 1987 Barossa Valley (Aus)

| £5.50 | ☞L&W AUC | 🍽 c, e, f, q |

A clean, ripe wine with lots of apple flavours and enough acidity to keep it going for several years. Cheaper and tastier than many a Chardonnay.

192 ALSACE RIESLING RESERVE Schlumberger 1986 (F)

| £5.50 | ☞VW UC BEN | 🍽 a, b, e, g |

Lemon-gold colour with an aromatic, honeyed fruit nose. Dry, rich, clean and crisp. An ideal partner for light dishes.

193 OLD LUXTERS RESERVE Chiltern Valley Wines 1989 Buckinghamshire (UK)

| £5.99 | ☞ OBC FWC | 🍽 c, e, q |

Young, fruity and slightly minty. The perfect summer drink - but not till 1992. And a name that makes it sound just like a great, traditional ale.

194 DEINHARD HERITAGE SELECTION DEIDESHEIM 1987 Rheinpfalz (G)

| £6.50 | ☞MM TAN CNL CUM BEN FWC | 🍽 c, e, f, g |

Fresh floral wine with fresh citric (lime) acidity ,ripe fruit and the rich, mouth-filling texture of butter.

195 THREE CHOIRS BACCHUS 1989 Gloucestershire (UK)

| £6.75 | ☞ WIL PD MM GWR H&D GNW | 🍽 c, e, f, q |

Light clean, aromatic. Honeydew melon stuffed with sweet grapes.

196 ALSACE RIESLING GRAND CRU BRAND Cave Vinicole de Turckheim 1985 (F)

| £8.99 | ☞OD UC BOO FW ASK CWG | 🍽 c, h, m, q |

A classic Alsace Riesling from an excellent year. Oily/petrolly nose and mature, concentrated fruit flavours. Rich but dry. Perfect current drinking, but good for several years yet.

Medium Germanic Whites

The most abused wine style of them all, the one most people start with and grow out of, off-dry wines are too often made carelessly by producers who would rather be turning out drier or sweeter stuff. These wines are the honourable exceptions to that rule.

197 LOHENGRIN RUDESHEIMER ROSENGARTEN Rudesheimer Weinkellerei 1988 Nahe (G)

| £2.39 | ☞CWS | 🍽 e, g, l |

A lightly fruity, lightly citric wine with the clean, refreshing flavours of bitter lemon.

198 SAINSBURY'S MOSELLE Mosel-Saar-Ruwer (G)

| £2.39 | ☞JS | 🍽 e, f, r |

Typical off-dry Mosel (despite Sainsbury's 'French' spelling) with plenty of refreshing appley, grapefruity acidity.

199 SAINSBURY'S MORIO-MUSKAT Rheinpfalz (G)

£2.55	JS	c, m, q

Attractive and delicate with flowery aromas and good body.

200 TESCO BERNKASTELER KURFURSTLAY Moselland Mosel-Saar-Ruwer (G)

£2.59	TO	e, g

Clean, refreshing, fruity, deliciously simple, easy-drinking wine.

201 NAHE MEDIUM DRY MULLER THURGAU Nahe Winzer-Kellerein EG (G)

£2.69	TO	e, g, l

Appealing fruit flavours with freshness and bite.

202 RHEINPFALZ MEDIUM DRY SILVANER Deutsches Weintor (G)

£2.69	TO	e, g, l, q

Distinctive petrolly, grassy flavours with good finish.

203 ST JOHANNER ABTEY KABINETT Jakob Demmer 1988 Rheinhessen (G)

£2.75	G MTL	e, g, r, q

Refreshing, grassy aromas with good weight of fruit.

204 NIERSTEINER SPIEGELBERG KABINETT P J Steffens 1988 Rheinhessen (G)

£2.89	G	e, r

Pleasant flowery aromas with attractive fruit flavours.

205 BINGER ST ROCHUSKAPELLE SPATLESE Rheinberg Kellerei 1988 Rheinhessen (G)

£2.95	G	c, e, f, g

Full, almondy, rich wine with pungent aromas of orange zest.

206 KLUSSERATHER ST MICHAEL Zentrallkellerei Mosel-Saar-Ruwer 1986 (G)

£2.99	PD SV	e, r

A maturing, sweetly weighty wine with clean fruity flavours.

207 SAFEWAY GEWURZTRAMINER St Georg's Weinkellerei Rheinpfalz (G)

£3.45	SAF	e, g, q

Raisiny, spicy wine with a long, clean finish - and even a hint of dried apricotty noble rot. Suprisingly classy.

208 TESCO STEINWEILER KLOSTER-LIEBFRAUENBERG SPATLESE Deutsches Weintor Rheinpfalz (G)

£3.99	TO	e, r, q

Typical mouth-filling wine from the warm Rheinpfalz. Its slightly petrolly aromas suggest that it is quite mature, but there's some limey freshness there too.

209 SAINSBURY'S AUSLESE 1988 Rheinpfalz (G)

£3.99	JS	e, f, r, q

Great value mature wine, with lots of long, 'oily', petrolly flavours, luscious crisp sweetness and gentle soft acidity. An interesting wine and very true to type. Not for keeping though.

210 BIDDENDEN MULLER-THURGAU 1989 Kent (UK)

£4.25	RAV	c, e, g, l

Light and fresh with balance and a light fruitiness.

211 THAMES VALLEY VINEYARD SCHONBURGER MEDIUM 1989 Berkshire (UK)

£4.50	GWR HFV	c, d, e, f

Lychees, lemons and pineapples: fruit salad in a glass - from one of England's top producers

212 BINGER SCHARLACHBERG DRY RIESLING KABINETT Villa Sachsen 1986 Rheinhessen (G)

£4.69	TO	e, l, o

Made by one of the most reliable producers in the Rheinhessen. A

(Arg) = Argentina; (Au) = Austria; (Aus) = Australia; (Bul) = Bulgaria; (Cal) = California; (Can) = Canada; (Ch) = Chile; (F) = France; (G) = Germany; (Gr) = Greece; (Hun) = Hungary; (It) = Italy; (NZ) = New Zealand; (P) = Portugal; (Rom) = Romania; (SA) = South Africa; (Sp) = Spain; (UK) = United Kingdom; (US) = United States; (Yug) = Yugoslavia

mouth-filling blend of fruity, spicy flavours.

213 NIERSTEINER SPIEGELBERG KABINETT Guntrum 1988 Rheinhessen (G)

£4.75	D MC FSW CVR GHL MTL WRW CPW
	❏ c, d, e, f

Delicate fruit and spice flavours with a hint of asparagus.

214 ASTLEY MADELEINE ANGEVINE 1989 Worcestershire (UK)

£4.75	TAN EOO GWR
	❏ a, c, e, q

A stylish wine with ripe fruit and good acidity.

215 SICHEL RIESLING KABINETT 1988 Rheinpfalz (G)

£4.80	POW SHV
	❏ e, l, m, o

Herbaceous fruit with good body and fine, balancing acidity.

216 SCHARZHOFBERGER KABINETT KESSELSTATT 1988 Mosel-Saar-Ruwer (G)

£4.99	MWW BBR EP
	❏ e, g, m, o

Really distinctive, apricotty wine with intense lingering fruit.

217 KIONA LATE PICKED RIESLING 1988 Washington State (USA)

£4.99	OD
	❏ p, n, o, k

Rounded, full, wholesome wine, packed with guavas, pineapple and
grapefruit. Sweet and lush, with enough acidity to give a balance to
all these tropical delights.

218 GAU-BISCHOFSHEIMER KELLERSBERG RIESLING SPATLESE Kellerstaat 1988
Rheinhessen (G)

£4.99	MWW
	❏ c, e, f, g, u

Nicely balanced sweet wine, with floral citrus fruit and a lovely long
finish.

219 LAMBERHURST KERNER 1986 Kent (UK)

£5.25	GWR
	❏ c, q

A woody, New World-style wine with pronounced fruit flavours.

220 KREUZNACHER KAPELLENPFAD WEISSBURGUNDER SPATLESE E Anheuser
1986 Nahe (G)

£5.48	CGW
	❏ e, m, o, q

Rich, honeyed, treacley wine; fat, waxy and mouth-filling but with all
the acidity it needs to leave a dry clean taste in the mouth.

221 FORSTER JESUITENGARTEN RIESLING KABINETT Dr Burklin-Wolf 1988
Rheinpfalz (G)

£5.75	JS
	❏ e, l, o, q

Spicy, petrolly Riesling with lots of sharp lemony acidity. It shows
signs of slightly sweet, honey and melon flavours which will continue
to develop with further ageing.

222 SERRIGER HEILIGENBORN RIESLING SPATLESE Staatliche Weinbaudomanen
Trier 1983 Mosel-Saar-Ruwer (G)

£5.75	VW W
	❏ e, m, o, q

Serrig is a classic Riesling village on the Saar and 1983 is one of the best
recent vintages. This wine has sweet honey and apple fruit and a zingy
refreshing acidity. A touch of maturity gives it delicious bready, oily
complexity.

223 SCHLOSS BOCKEL-HEIMER KUPFERGRUBE RIESLING Von Plettenberg 1986
Nahe (G)

£5.80	HV
	❏ e, m, o, q

Mature, grapey, quite petrolly, 'ripe, everlasting' wine with a good
dry finish.

224 LAMBERHURST SCHONBURGER 1988 Kent (UK)

£6.00	UC HAR
	❏ c, q

Fruit salad flavours. An attractive, well balanced wine.

225 WEHLENER SONNENUHR RIESLING KABINETT Dr Loosen 1988 Mosel-Saar-Ruwer (G)

| £6.50 | ☛ADN JS UC DAL | 🍴 e, l, o, q |

Appealing bouquet of wild rose with a good balance of peachy fruit and acidity creating a lively, attractive wine.

226 MILTON VINEYARDS OPOU RIVER RIESLING 1989 Gisborne (NZ)

| £6.50 | ☛VR ORG HFW VER | 🍴 c, e, f, g |

A lovely fruity wine with a petrolly finish.

227 RUPPERTSBERGER GEISBOHL RIESLING SPATLESE Dr Burklin-Wolf 1985 Rheinpfalz (G)

| £6.99 | ☛OD | 🍴 c, e, f, g |

Generous, ripe, fruity wine with a smooth, 'rolling' texture, a strong golden colour and distinctive aromas of talcum powder.

228 GRAACHER HIMMELREICH RIESLING SPATLESE F W Gymnasium 1988 Mosel-Saar-Ruwer (G)

| £7.22 | ☛TAN CVR BWS EP | 🍴 c, e, f, g |

Light, soft, petrolly and apricot fruit. Sweet scent and green-gold colour.

229 KREUZNACHER BRUCKES RIESLING AUSLESE Schloss Plettenberg 1985 Nahe (G)

| £8.45 | ☛MWW DRI | 🍴 a, b, e, g, k, n |

A very classy Riesling that won itself a Gold medal at the *WINE Magazine* International Challenge. Spicy, peachy and with a rich, balanced flavour that lasts and lasts. All a German wine should be.

Rosés

Every year, I make the same plea. Rosé drinkers, come out of the closet and admit that you enjoy cool glasses of pink, fruity wine, that you aren't ashamed to order rosé in a restaurant on a warm summer evening when all around you are ordering Sancerre and Bordeaux rouge they don't really want. Nowadays, of course, the very word 'rosé' has been deemed to be naff; today's pink-drinkers apparently feel less embarrassed to ask for 'blush'.

230 GATEWAY LAMBRUSCO ROSE Donelli Vini Emilia-Romagna (It)

| £2.25 | ☛G | 🍴 o, q, r |

Clean, fresh and uncomplicated wine, with strawberry flavours and a welcome balancing acidity.

231 PIEMONTELLO PINK Piedmont (It)

| £2.89 | ☛VW SAF DBY WOC WRB TO G TH TWR MTL BTH MRS LTW | |
| | 🍴 o, q, r, s | |

Rosé Wine of the Year

A Muscatty delight, full of grapey freshness and with a slight sparkle. The perfect party wine at a great price. There's nothing remotely complicated about it, but it's one of the most easily enjoyable wines on the market.

232 SAINSBURY'S COTES DU LUBERON ROSE Domaine de Panisse 1989 Rhône (F)

| £3.19 | ☛JS | 🍴 c, e, l, q, r |

Fine, southern rosé from the producers of the successful Château Val Joanis. It has an onion skin colour, a light, fruity nose, a tangy flavour of redcurrants and a good dry finish.

233 WHITE GRENACHE E & J Gallo 1989 (Cal)

£3.29	🍷TH JS SAF TO A CGW DRI MC AB POW WWI U WRB VW	
WID	SEL MCL THP	🍽 c, d, q, r

Not white but most undeniably pink. Good strawberry, violets and
rose petal nose. Almondy, simple but attractive.

234 ST MICHAEL FRENCH COUNTRY ROSE Georges Duboeuf (F)

£3.49	🍷M&S	🍽 c, l, q, r

A lightly fruity rosé from the 'king of the Beaujolais'. Duboeuf's
Nouveau smells of boiled sweets - and so does this. Clean, dry,
good value for money.

235 FRONTON CHATEAU BELLEVUE ROSE 1988 South-West (F)

£3.59	🍷OD	🍽 c, l, q, r

Sweet, raspberry jam 'n' spice are the keynotes here. Powerfully good.

236 TORRES CABERNET SAUVIGNON ROSE 1989 Curico (Ch)

£4.20	🍷CVR GHS MC UC POW DBY BRO BAT PTR ROD	
		🍽 e, l, q

This smells of raspberries, but the flavour is of sweet cherries. There's
lots of fruity acidity too.

237 ST MICHAEL CALIFORNIA BLUSH The Christian Brothers (Cal)

£4.50	🍷M&S	🍽 e, l, q, r

Boiled sweets and raspberries – serve with a light pudding or
maybe a Danish pastry.

238 TOURAINE CABERNET ROSE Dorothy & Thierry Michaud 1989 Loire (F)

£4.50	🍷UC	🍽 c, l, q, r

Fresh, clean wine with sweet strawberry flavours and a crisp finish.

239 CHATEAU THIEULEY Bordeaux Clairet 1989 (F)

£4.59	🍷TH TWR GH ADN MWW CVR WSO	
		🍽 c, q, r

Long flavour of juicy, ripe raspberries.

240 CHATEAU LA JAUBERTIE BERGERAC ROSE Henry Ryman 1987 South-West
(F)

£4.60	🍷VW DBY HBV CVR WFP GNW	🍽 a, c, f, g, i, l, q

Almost too much flavour for a rosé; punnets of raspberries, full, long
finish. Definitely a 'food' wine.

241 ROSE DE PROVENCE CARTE NOIRE Les Maitres Vignerons 1989 (F)

£4.99	🍷CPW SAS LNR	🍽 c, l, q

'Vibrant' fruity nose and long, rich loganberry flavour.

242 PARKER VINEYARD BLUSH MACABEO/BASTARDO/VIOGNIER Randy Nacho
1987 San Atogen Valley (Cal)

£17.76	🍷FWC	🍽 a, s

As winemaker Randy Nacho says, the Romanian oak used for this
blend makes it an ideal accompaniment to marinated swordfish.

Country reds

A curious category, but a useful one nonetheless. In theory, it ought to
denote 'rustic' wines of the kind that we have all drunk and enjoyed on
holiday but can never manage to find when we get home. In practice, just
as country cottages are getting smarter, so too are the country wines. Some
of these, made from grape varieties a Bordelais or Burgundian (let alone a
Californian) wouldn't deign to pronounce, let alone plant, show real class.

243 BULGARIAN COUNTRY WINE MERLOT/GAMZA Suhindol (Bul)

£.2.99	🍷G DRI CWS MWW RAV POW DBY VW BUD WID CVR AHC	
FUL, BTH PTR WES GHW		🍽 c, e, i, k, m, q, r

Mature nose, soft, rounded fruit. Slightly off-dry, full-flavoured wine.

244 BOTRYS RED Botrys SA Nemea (Gr)

| £2.50 | ☛ TAN BOO DAL | ⦿ j, k. l, m, r |

Deep colour, rich fruity smell. Big, tannic and richly alcoholic. Long finish. Good value.

245 DOMAINE DES LENTHERIC GRENACHE MERLOT Lentheric Père et Fils 1988 Midi (F)

| £2.59 | ☛MWW | ⦿ e, j, k, l, m |

The sweet ripe, fruit of the Merlot combines with the spicy Grenache and some soft tannin in a most unusual blend. A Rhone-Bordeaux mix that isn't the usual Australian Cabernet-Shiraz.

246 CABARDES Château Ventenac 1989 Midi (F)

| £2.89 | ☛MWW | ⦿ e, j, k, m |

Still young and tannic but with plenty of well-balanced, rich fruit.

247 VRANAC Slovin 1986 Montenegro (Yug)

| £3.39 | ☛HAS DBY WOC BWS | ⦿ c, e, j, k, m q, r |

Ripe, plummy fruit with 'dry, dusky tannins'. A great value example of Eastern European winemaking at its best. Rich, characterful and mature. Wine that proves that Yugoslavia can make better wine than the Lutomer and Laski Rizling with which it is usually associated.

248 COTES DE GASCOGNE Domaine de Mathalin 1987 South-West (F)

| £3.42 | ☛HFW | ⦿ d, e, g, m |

Tangy, blackcurranty Cabernet Franc flavours give this the style of a refreshing 'mini-Bordeaux'.

249 COTES DU ROUSSILLON Château de Jau 1987 Midi (F)

| £3.49 | ☛OD | ⦿ e, j, r |

Pleasantly maturing, peppery wine, with good, sweet fruit.

250 COTEAUX DE MURVIEL DOMAINE DE LIMBARDIE Boukandoura & Hutin 1988 Midi (F)

| £3.50 | ☛TAN D ADN MC UC M&V WH SV L&W DVY SHV WSO FWC | |
| | | ⦿ e, j, k, m, q |

A clean, well-made wine with fresh, berry aromas, 'bags of fruit' and a bit of tannin. Seriously easy to enjoy.

251 CORBIERES Château du Luc 1988 Midi (F)

| £3.75 | ☛MWW POW | ⦿ c, j, k, m |

Young, with good all-round fruit and some tannin. Good value.

252 COTES DE BERGERAC PETITE BORIE M Sadoux 1987 South-West (F)

| £3.75 | ☛MWW | ⦿ d, e, g, q |

A big, plummy wine with blackcurrant aromas and a tobacco-ish, spicy aftertaste. Distinctive.

253 FITOU CHATEAU DE SEGUR Producteurs de Mont Tauch 1987 Midi (F)

| £3.99 | ☛BUD U | ⦿ c, j, k, m |

Nicely maturing wine with excellent, ripe tasting, almost jammy, fruit. Holiday wine to enjoy at home.

254 CAHORS Les Côtes d'Olt 1986 South-West (F)

| £4.25 | ☛U GHW BTH | ⦿ d, e, g, m |

A chocolate, cherry fruit wine with spice and some tannin. For drinking now or keeping for a while. Serious Cahors.

255 MINERVOIS Château de Blomac 1988 Miidi (F)

| £4.29 | ☛CUM EVI | ⦿ d, e, g, q |

This was nominated a 'barbecue wine' - robust, with good, ripe berry fruit and a hint of smoke - or was that from the barbecue?

256 CORBIERES CHATEAU HELENE VIEILLI EN FUT DE CHENE 1985 Midi (F)

☛ For an explanation of stockist abbreviations, see page 17
⦿ For an explanation of food style codes, see page 65

£4.35	☞WAW OLS	⦿ c, j, k, m

Pungent and spicy wine, with rich vanilla fruit. Very ripe but with an appealingly dry finish.

257 GROSSKARLBACHER OSTERBERG DORNFELDER Lingenfelder Rheinpfalz 1989 (G)

£4.49	☞OD	⦿ a, b, d, i, k, m, q

This is perfumed and blackcurranty with a slight hint of spice. Fruity and smooth stuff from an unusual German grape - and one of that country's best red winemakers.

258 VIN DE PAYS D'OC CUVEE DE L'ALLIANCE Cave de Limoux 1989 Midi (F)

£4.58	☞BD WC	⦿ j, k, l, m, q

A wine made by an Australian in France. Very blackcurranty, soft, full with a backbone of tannin. Well-balanced and approachable.

259 COTEAUX D'AIX EN PROVENCE Château Pigoudet Grande Réserve 1985 Midi (F)

£4.75	☞HAS WID MG POW BOO HEM	⦿ k, l, m, q

'Big and spicy'. 'A blackcurrant and bramble nose' with 'a hint of Cabernet?'

260 FAUGERES CHATEAU LA LIQUIERE V Gaillard 1988 Midi (F)

£4.75	☞FWC SV SHV	⦿ c, j, k, m

A youthful, berryish wine with great promise. Good fruit and a richly generous aftertaste.

261 BODEGAS Y CAVAS DE WEINERT CABERNET SAUVIGNON 1983 Mendoza (Arg)

£5.25	☞HV K&B COV BTH HV	⦿ j, k, l, q

'Absolutely magic' noted one taster. A mature, softly fruity example of good winemaking from Argentina.

262 CORBIERES CHATEAU DE LASTOURS (FUT DE CHENE) 1985 Midi (F)

£5.40	☞CAC SAS K&B UC POW DBY BOO WID TWR DAL ASK GNW	
		⦿ c, j, k, m

A gold medal château in the 1989 Challenge, this property is also a home for the mentally handicapped. Indeed, it is the residents who make the wine. This oaky example is spicy and concentrated, with lots of long-lasting, soft, juicy fruit flavours.

263 MADIRAN Château d'Aydie South-West 1988 (F)

£6.25	☞OD GHS LNR	⦿ j, k, l, m, r

A big, full, young wine, with an inky-black colour and and enormous depth of flavour. Should be kept for several years.

264 MAS DE DAUMAS GASSAC Vin de Pays de l'Hérault 1988 South-West (F)

£9.99	☞OD ADN TAN GHS UBC HOL GON SEB HVW VR SK WFP	
PTR		⦿ c, j, k, q

The 'Château Latour of southern France', this wine is so successful in France that bottles are often unobtainable there. It has an enticingly rich aroma with great depth of fruit and spicy cedar. It's very long too, and needs keeping.

265 J CARRAS GRANDE RESERVE 1975 Halkidiki (Gr)

£11.50	☞BOO	⦿ e, j

A rare chance to taste a quality Greek wine that has had a bit of age (rather than young, poorer ones that just taste as though they do). It's rich and ripely mature, but there's still a fair bit of tannin.

Cabernet and claret-style wines

There are so many comparable alternatives to Bordeaux nowadays, produced in so many different corners of the winemaking world, that an adventurous wine drinker could probably drink a different Merlot or

Cabernet every day for the rest of his or her life. We suspect that the experience would become a little boring after a while, but if one were to start with the wines on the following pages, there would be little reason for the attention to wander.

266 PLOVDIV CABERNET SAUVIGNON Bulgarian Vintners 1985 (Bul)

£2.69	☞BUD TH TWR OD DRI GHW SAF PD MWW RAV POW DBY
COV CVR AHC SAN DVY FUL D	🍴 c, e, j, k, m, q, r

Supple, weighty, 'old fashioned Bordeaux' style wine with 'savoury fruit and soft tannin'. Good value Bulgarian wine with a bit of class.

267 VIN DE PAYS DE L'AUDE CABERNET SAUVIGNON Paul Boutinot 1987 Midi (F)

£2.75	☞TGB SAN CGW UC DBY BOO CAC WCE HVW CVR
DAL HAS ASK SPR CWG CWM POW	🍴 j, k, l, m

Characterful wine with 'spicy, ripe onion fruit'. Mature and very ready to drink.

268 ST MICHAEL GRAPE SELECTION MERLOT Vin de Pays de l'Aude Foncalieu l'Aude Midi (F)

£2.99	☞M&S	🍴 j, k, l, m

This smells of leafy blackcurrants and cut grass, and tastes of crisp blackcurrants and spicy oak.

269 HOUSE CLARET Peter Sichel Bordeaux (F)

£2.99	☞MWW ADN TAN SEB BUD WBM DX HUN
	🍴 l, j, k, q, m

Intense soft, slightly peppery fruit with hints of toffee, oak, black-currants and raspberries. Super wine, super price.

270 NOGALES CABERNET SAUVIGNON Discover Wine 1988 Curico Valley (Ch)

£3.09	☞OD HW	🍴 j, k, m

From one of Chile's few individual estates, this has quite a bit of tannin but, as Jane Hunt MW, said, 'it's full of super-ripe, splendid fruit'. Try it with your oldest Cheddar.

271 BERGERAC CHATEAU LE CASTELLOT Domaine des Trois Templiers 1988 South-West (F)

£3.19	☞BUD	🍴 c, j, q

A wine with soft red plum aromas, a rich, jammy texture and just a touch of earthiness beneath the plummy, chocolate and spicy wood flavours. Full of lively, concentrated fruit that will improve for another two years.

272 CHATEAU LA TUQUE 1988 Bordeaux (F)

£3.19	☞JS	🍴 c, j, k, q

Spicy, fat, cedar and toast with lots of smoky cassis - intense long-lasting flavour in a wine which will keep a while.

273 ST MICHAEL CLARET Gallaire 1986 Bordeaux (F)

£3.29	☞M&S	🍴 c, j, k, q

Solid, curranty, soft and juicy. Bordeaux with a bit of tannin to let you know where it's from. It could keep too.

274 GATEWAY MEDOC Les Chais Beaucairois Bordeaux (F)

£3.35	☞G	🍴 c, j, k, q

The soft, jammy fruit is balanced here by spicy vanilla oak and just a bit of tannin. Ready now.

275 SANDEMAN CLARET 1986 Bordeaux (F)

£3.55	☞OD WRB	🍴 c, j, k, q

Floral violet aromas give way to rich, deep spicy fruit and a backbone of tannin. 'Sound, honest, young claret'.

276 CONCHA Y TORO MERLOT 1986 Maipo (Ch)

£3.89	☞U TAN BU CGW MM PD RAV DBY CUM GHW BAT H&D
BND CWM WAC	🍴 j, k, l, m

If you imagine the taste of the colour purple, you'll know this wine. Soft, sweet and clean, and full of blackcurrants.

277 SEAVIEW CABERNET SAUVIGNON 1985 South Australia

£4.29	☛AUC DBY WRB WAW OD EVI THP	
		ΙΟΙ j, k, l, m

Big, rich, ripe wine, packed with toffee and tar aromas and flavours of soft and sweet blackberries.

278 CHATEAU NICOT 1986 Bordeaux (F)

£4.30	☛L&W GH	ΙΟΙ c, j, k, q

Good, honest, fresh fruit with smooth tannin, clean and very attractive.

279 CHATEAU DE ELLIEZ 1983 Bordeaux (F)

£4.38	☛BBR	ΙΟΙ c, j, q

A big, alcoholic wine with fruit to match. It is showing a little age but still has some tannin and could be kept.

280 WOLF BLASS RED LABEL 1986 Barossa Valley (Aus)

£4.49	☛G POW	ΙΟΙ c, j, k, l, m

A rich, spicy and complex wine, heavy with fruit. Ready now but would benefit from another year or so.

281 CHATEAU TOUR MARTINES BORDEAUX SUPERIEUR 1983 (F)

£4.79	☛DRI WES	ΙΟΙ c, j, q

Bordeaux Supérieur can be such basic stuff that this ought to be used as a learning aid for other producers. Young, ruby-coloured, with rich, long, grassy, blackberry and blackcurrant fruit and a hint of oak. A winner.

282 MONTES CABERNET SAUVIGNON Discover Wine 1987 Curico Valley (Ch)

£4.95	☛HW SV POW T&W DBY BND	ΙΟΙ e, j, k, l, m

Pure blackcurrant aromas, soft and ripe, with a fine complexity of flavours - 'honey, figs, caramel','wood' and 'herbs'.

283 CHATEAU LA CLAVERIE (Francois Thienpoint) Bordeaux-Côte-de-Francs 1987 (F)

4.95	☛LNR HW LNR	ΙΟΙ j, k, l, m

Warm, fruity ripe and soft with a fairly hard, earthy texture which needs more time. A wine from a region to watch.

284 SPECIAL RESERVE STAMBOLOVO MERLOT Bulgarian Vintners 1985 (Bul)

£4.99	☛AHC DRI TAN AB MWW RAV POW DBY BOO WID OD BWS	
LWL WOI BBR SHV		ΙΟΙ j, k, l, m, o

Just ask for a bottle of 'stumble over' and you should end up with a lovely complex, fruity wine with smooth, sweet, oak flavours. 'Dill, mint, spicy fruit. Chewy tannins, with vanilla and butter'. A wine to prove that the Bulgarians can compete with the Australians too.

285 DAVID WYNN CABERNET 1986 High Eden Ridge (Aus)

£5.45	☛OD HFW BOO AUC CWI	ΙΟΙ j, k, m

Made at the superbly equipped Mountadam winery. This has sweet, smoky and long cassis flavours held together by firm tannins. Sheer class.

286 COLUMBIA CREST CABERNET SAUVIGNON 1985 Washington State (USA)

£5.79	☛DB OD DRI	ΙΟΙ j, m

Exciting, meaty, oaky Cabernet with lots of cassis fruit.

287 RAIMAT CABERNET SAUVIGNON 1985 Lerida (Sp)

£6.49	☛TH TWR VW FWC GHS WWI BWS HAR	
		ΙΟΙ e, j, k, l, m

A Spanish wine that's almost Australian in style, with heavy ripe berry flavours and a long smooth finish.

288 PETER LEHMANN CABERNET SAUVIGNON 1985 Barossa Valley (Aus)

£6.50	☛ BBR VER AUC OBC DRI UC RAV DBY WH BOO GHL	
CWG		ΙΟΙ j, k, m

Lots of mixed aromas and flavours. Pine needles, newly sawn oak and inviting plum-jam fruit. Complex, well-made wine.

289 CHATEAU BEAUMONT Cru Bourgeois Médoc Bordeaux 1986 (F)

£6.50	☛D SUM MC GON WAW WBM HAS LNR OLS GRT PTR HV EP
	🍽 e, j

'Ripe plums', 'minty aromas', 'soft vanilla oak'. A clean well-made wine that's almost ready for drinking but has great potential to improve with age.

290 FIRESTONE CABERNET SAUVIGNON 1986 Santa Ynez (Cal)

£6.55	☛TH TWR GHS MC UBC TP SV WOC COV HEM BH LAV WIN
	🍽 j, m

Soft, tightly-knit fruit with well-harmonised tarry oak. Quite forward and pleasing.

291 ALLANDALE CABERNET SAUVIGNON 1986 Hunter Valley (Aus)

£6.99	☛ MWW	🍽 j, m

A fully mature wine with lovely ripe berried fruit aromas and a long complex finish.

292 ORLANDO ST HUGO CABERNET SAUVIGNON 1986 Coonawarra (Aus)

£7.50	☛OD JS D SPR WCE AUC MC UBC DBY RN HW CAC WOC CVR
AHC HEM WOI	🍽 j, k, m

Packed with smoky, cigar-box aromas and fully ripe, blackcurrant fruit, with a lovely rich finish. Australian Cabernet at its best.

293 LE CARILLON DE L'ANGELUS (Château l'Angélus) St Emilion 1987 Bordeaux (F)

£7.65	☛FUL	🍽 j, m, s

Typical soft, slightly sweet Merlot, with good acidity. For drinking while waiting for Château l'Angélus's first wine to mature.

294 ROSEMOUNT SHOW RESERVE COONAWARRA CABERNET SAUVIGNON 1987 (Aus)

£7.85	☛MWW TH SAN GNW AUC UC WH BOO BND GRT ROD
	🍽 j, m

Dark, deep, ripe wine with intense blackcurranty fruit and plenty of tannin. Serious Aussie wine.

295 CHATEAU SOCIANDO MALLET Haut-Médoc Bordeaux 1986 (F)

£7.99	☛THP	🍽 e, j

A Cru Bourgeois that rarely gets the recognition it deserves. This is a super wine with flavours of dusty plums, cherries and chocolate. It's not ready yet but it will be perfect in the mid-1990s.

296 ST JULIEN Anthony Barton 1985 Bordeaux (F)

£7.99	☛L&W LEA WH BI	🍽 j, k, m

Dark, young cedar wood aroma and powerful blackberries. This is well-balanced, very good and needs a bit more time. A wine from the owner of Châteaux Léoville and Langoa Barton.

297 PENFOLDS BIN 389 SHIRAZ/CABERNET 1986 South Australia

£8.49	☛TH TWR AUC SAS MWW DBY WOC WRB SEB OD AHC EVI
THP GNW CPL ROD	🍽 j, k, m, s

Inky black. ('Is this a glass of Indian ink?', asked one taster). Completely packed with lots of firm, ripe liquoricey fruit. 'Soft, velvety and seductive'. Blissful now, but will improve over the next 3 years.

298 CHATEAU LA TOUR DE BY Haut-Médoc Bordeaux 1986   (F)

£8.50	☛THP K&B GHS UC SBW DBY WH U SV HBV DEN HAR HOP
ASK POW P	🍽 e, j

(Arg) = Argentina; (Au) = Austria; (Aus) = Australia; (Bul) = Bulgaria; (Cal) = California; (Can) = Canada; (Ch) = Chile; (F) = France; (G) = Germany; (Gr) = Greece; (Hun) = Hungary; (It) = Italy; (NZ) = New Zealand; (P) = Portugal; (Rom) = Romania; (SA) = South Africa; (Sp) = Spain; (UK) = United Kingdom; (US) = United States; (Yug) = Yugoslavia

Showing all the qualities this will need to become a great wine in 5
years or so. Extremely ripe plum and currant fruit with loads of
tannin, smoky cedary oak and a finish that goes on and on.

299 CHATEAU RAMAGE LA BATISSE Haut-Médoc 1985 Bordeaux (F)

£8.50	☛TH CNL HVW OBC CGW UC HOL POW DBY BOO WCE CVR	
TWR HAR HAS ASK GNW CWG		⦿ e, j

A meal in itself, with a slightly meaty character and flavours of
blackcurrants and herbs. It's deliciously soft and creamy and is quite
ready but it will keep.

300 CHATEAU DE PUY (Robert Amoreau) Bordeaux Supérieur 1982 (F)

£8.65	☛ORG WID B&B	⦿ c, j, q

A sweet blackcurrant, organic wine that is beginning to show some
maturity. You could drink it now but it's worth keeping.

301 DOMAINE DE MARTIALIS (Château Clos Fourtet) St Emilion 1986 Bordeaux (F)

£8.99	☛TH TWR UC •	⦿ j, m, s

A big, fat wine with chewy black cherry flavours and a hint of oak.
Nearly ready to drink.

302 CHATEAU CARONNE-SAINTE-GEMME Haut-Médoc, 1982 Bordeaux (F)

£9.00	☛WSO UBC WH B&B	⦿ j, k, m

Cassis, spice and oak; supple full flavours with concentration right
through to the finish.

303 ROUGE HOMME COONAWARRA CABERNET SAUVIGNON 1985 (Aus)

£9.50	☛AV DBY G AUC UBC UC GON WH WOC WAW L&W BEN	
FW CVR WBM EOO DAL HEM SHV	⦿ j, k, m	

Rich, ripe and mature with spicy, sweet fruit flavours and 'a hint of the
farmyard'. Beautifully well balanced.

304 ROSSO SECONDO Vinattieri 1985 Tuscany (It)

£9.65	☛BI	⦿ j, k, m

From a partnership of three of Italy's best wine experts, this is a deep
purple blackcurrant wine with dusky tannin and rich tarry fruit right
to the finish - very New World style.

305 CHATEAU MAUCAILLOU Moulis 1986 Bordeaux (F)

£9.95	☛JS DBY D	⦿ e, j, k, m

From one of the best properties in the undervalued village of Moulis.
Oz Clarke thought this, 'deep, dark and intense; quite attractive
without too much tannin; raspberry fruit and some full, supportive,
sweet oak - big, impressive and classy.'

306 CHATEAU HAUT-BAGES-LIBERAL Pauillac Bordeaux 1986 (F)

£10.90	☛SEB	⦿ j, k, m

This is very young and tannic at the moment but the rich, ripe fruit and
soft vanilla overtones are already evident and indicate good drinking
in 5 years. From the owner of the similarly excellent Château Chasse
Spleen.

307 LAKE'S FOLLY CABERNET SAUVIGNON 1987 Hunter Valley (Aus)

£10.99	☛L&W AUC	⦿ j, k, m

This wine is no one's folly, the colour of a healthy purple plum, with
an earthy smell of basil and brambles. Big and silky, dark intense
fruit with warming oak undertones, or, as one taster described
the aroma: 'hickory-smoked lemon fish'.

308 PETALUMA COONAWARRA CABERNET/MERLOT 1985 (Aus)

£11.50	☛AUC ADN CNL MWW DBY WH BEN BI CVR HAR AHC BBR	
GRT FWC LAV WIN	⦿ j, k, m	

A deep cherry colour, with a dusty vegetal aroma and hints of mature
wood. Peppered with ripe fruit and with a honey smooth texture.

309 CHATEAU HAUT-BAGES-AVEROUS (Château Lynch-Bages) Pauillac 1986
Bordeaux (F)

£11.50	☛CNL MWW POW WH VW TH TWR ABY
	❏ j, m, s

The second wine of Château Lynch-Bages. Ripe, cedar-oak on the nose with good up-front minty, blackcurrant flavour. Serve in 1993.

310 **CYRIL HENSCHKE CABERNET SAUVIGNON** Henschke 1986 Barossa Valley (Aus)

£11.99	☛L&W AUC BBR
	❏ j, k, m

Gorgeous, soft, balanced wine you could drink today - but you'd be missing heaps of blackcurrant enjoyment that will develop gradually over the next 5-6 years.

311 **CHATEAU HAUT-MARBUZET** St Estèphe Bordeaux 1985 (F)

£11.99	☛ SAS HPD UC GON DBY WRB HVW WBM G AHC MTL BTH
WRW	❏ j, k, m

Peapod and capsicum aromas, with strong smoky vanilla oak. Classy Bordeaux to drink in a few years.

313 **CHATEAU MOUTON-BARONNE-PHILIPPE** Pauillac Bordeaux 1986 (F)

£11.99	☛OD MM U MTL MCL B&B THP ROD
	❏ j, k, m

Mouton-Rothschild's younger brother has huge soft blackcurrant fruit. Still a little tough now, it will be very classy in 5 years.

312 **SIMI CABERNET SAUVIGNON RESERVE** 1981 Napa Valley (Cal)

£12.65	☛L&W C&B

Rich aromas of smoky hawthorn and blackcurrants. Weighty wine with very concentrated fruit. A Californian built to last.

314 **TORRES GRAN CORONAS BLACK LABEL** 1983 Penedés (Sp)

£15.00	☛THP MM TAN MC CNL UC DBY RAE WH HW WOC OD FSW
CVR GHL HAR MOR HOP GI WRW	❏ c, e, j, q

Unarguably one of Spain's top wines and a competitor to quite illustrious claret. It's soft, oaky, blackcurranty and mature.

315 **WYNNS JOHN RIDDOCH CABERNET SAUVIGNON** Coonawarra 1985 (Aus)

£15.99	☛FWC AUC DBY BBR THP
	❏ j, k, m

A deep, almost sweet, intensely blackcurranty wine; bags of flavour from one of Australia's Cabernet specialists. It's approachable now but should be a real beaut with a few years under the bed.

316 **PENFOLDS BIN 707 CABERNET SAUVIGNON** 1986 South Australia (Aus)

£18.65	☛AUC ADN MWW DBY WOC WRB WAW OD GNW CPL
	❏ j, k, l, m

Inky-dark with deep, smooth aromas of sweet, smoky oak. Solid fruit supported by strong tannins. Keep for another 3-4 years.

317 **MONDAVI CABERNET SAUVIGNON RESERVE** 1980 Napa Valley (Cal)

£18.95	☛MM UBC CNL WOC CVR EOO AHC PTR LAV WIN
	❏ j, k, l, m, s

Liquorice and worn leather aromas. A solid, deep wine with a mixture of cherries and blackcurrants that lasts for ages.

318 **CHATEAU L'EVANGILE** Pomerol 1987 Bordeaux (F)

£19.50	☛HUN	❏ j, m, s

Full, buttery fruit on the nose with lengthy blackberry flavours. Could - and should - be kept longer. Richly plummy, typical Pomerol.

319 **CHATEAU PICHON-LONGUEVILLE-BARON** Pauillac Bordeaux 1985 (F)

£20.00	☛VW LEA HOL DBY U EBA BBR THP CPL EP
	❏ j, k, m

Smoky, cedary, delicate Bordeaux with enough tannin to allow it to improve for at least the next 6 years. Sheer class.

320 **CHATEAU LYNCH-BAGES** Pauillac Bordeaux 1985 (F)

£22.95	☛VW TH TWR DRI SUM HPD MC CNL HOL AB POW D WH U MG
MTL SK BBR HUN	❏ j, k, m, s

A stylish claret with all the gorgeous approachability of the 1985

vintage. It shows its class with ripe minty blackcurrant and oaky
flavours, soft tannins and a long finish. Already lovely, it will be
stunning in 5-10 years.

321 CHATEAU GRUAUD-LAROSE (Cordier) St Julien Bordeaux 1978 (F)

£26.00	☞FWC L&W DRI GHS DBY AHC MTL HOP DX THP CWG EP	
		🍴 j, m

From an underrated vintage, this long-flavoured wine is still quite
tannic, but its mature, fruity, oaky flavours are ready to be enjoyed by
lovers of fine old Bordeaux.

322 CHATEAU FIGEAC St Emilion Grand Cru Bordeaux 1982 (F)

£32.00	☞VW MM WH U HEM GI LNR GRT CPW	
		🍴 j, m, s

Figeac is among the top properties in St Emilion and its wine contains
more Cabernet Sauvignon than most of its neighbours. The 1982 has
attractively soft spicy fruit, and although drinking beautifully now, it
will develop further.

Rhônes and spicy reds

After working your way through the 'claret-types' in the preceding section,
you probably need a mouthful of something different, something with a bit
more of a punch to it. Well, you've come to the right place; these wines, most
of which come from the Rhône or are made elsewhere from the Rhône
varieties, all share a single characteristic: spice. The red equivalents of up-
front Gewürztraminers, these are wine drinkers' wines; they are to an
inexpensive mellow Cabernet what a pint of Old Peculier is to Fosters.

323 COTEAUX DU TRICASTIN Cellier de l'Enclave des Papes Rhône (F)

£2.59	☞CWS OD	🍴 j, k, m

Light, peppery, mature, well balanced, very approachable wine.

324 COTEAUX DU TRICASTIN Vignerons de l'Ardèche 1989 Rhône (F)

£2.59	☞G	🍴 j, k, m

Maturing, pepper and cranberry flavoured wine. Light and smooth.

325 SAINSBURY'S COTES DU RHONE (F)

£2.65	☞JS	🍴 j, k, m

Young rich and peppery; great weight of strawberry fruit that will
develop a soft maturity with time.

326 COTES DU VENTOUX Paul Boutinot 1989 Rhône (F)

£2.99	☞MWW GHW ASK	🍴 j, k, m

Big bramble fruit; a soft, ripe, straightforward style.

327 COTES DU RHONE Château Joanny 1988 (F)

£3.09	☞SAF	🍴 j, k, m

Delicious, ripe, jammy fruit with soft oak edges.

328 VIN DE PAYS DE L'AUDE DOMAINE PERRIERE Jeanine Mercadier 1988 Midi (F)

£3.25	☞GH	🍴 j, k, l, m

Deep purple colour, intense blackberry fruit and soft tannin.

329 TRICASTIN DOMAINE DE RASPAIL J Jalifier 1988 Rhône (F)

£3.80	☞FW	🍴 j, k, m

Soft oaky nose; ripe developed blackberry; 'Typical Rhône Syrah'.

☞ For an explanation of stockist abbreviations, see page 17
🍴 For an explanation of food style codes, see page 65

330 COTES DU RHONE Château du Grand Moulas 1988 (F)

| £3.99 | ☛L&W ADN TAN CVR WBM FUL | 101 j, k, l, m |

Soft berry fruit, a touch of tannin, peppery and vegetal.

331 RASTEAU COTES DU RHONE VILLAGES Caves des Vignerons de Rasteau 1988 (F)

| £4.29 | ☛HVW CGW GHW PD UC HOL DBY CVR SAN BH GNW CWG |
| | 101 j, k |

Full, spicy wine with powerful ripe peppery fruit. This wine is still a little young but shows great complexity of flavour.

332 COTES DE PROVENCE DOMAINE DU JAS D'ESCLANS Lorges-Lapouge 1986 (F)

| £4.49 | ☛RAV VER HFW BOO | 101 j, k |

'Wonderful rich, smooth, black chocolate' - a big old fashioned wine with 'hot, leathery, jammy fruit', very intense, spicy liquorice and cinnamon, wood and tannin. Truly great style and complexity from a an under-rated appellation.

333 ST MICHAEL AUSTRALIAN CABERNET/SHIRAZ Penfolds 1987 South Australia

| £4.50 | ☛M&S | 101 j, k, l, m |

A long-lingering, typically Australian red with fruit and spice. Produced by Penfolds, the Antipodes' biggest and arguably best red wine maker.

334 COTES DU RHONE Domaine St Apollinaire 1988 (F)

| £4.55 | ☛JS OBC RAV VR CVR CPL | 101 j, k, l, m |

Sweet, slighty tarry wine with light peppery fruit and a long finish. Clean, fresh and organic.

335 FETZER LAKE COUNTY ZINFANDEL 1986 (Cal)

| £4.59 | ☛SAF TO LAV WIN | 101 j, k, l, m |

Fruity homemade jam with subtle oak overtones. Enjoy.

336 CROZES HERMITAGE Delas Frères 1988 Rhône (F)

| £4.99 | ☛AB SUM GHW DBY HW BOO DAL EVI GRT CWM |
| | 101 j, k, l, m |

Rich, smoky, meaty wine. Real quality and good value, from a very reliable producer. In 3 years it could be even better.

337 ROUGE HOMME SHIRAZ/CABERNET 1985 Coonawarra (Aus)

| £5.25 | ☛AV WRW ASK AUC GON DBY WAW BWS EOO SAN BRO SK |
| | FUL SHV ASK PTR FWC | 101 j, k, l, m |

A great, mature example of Australia's 'own' red blend, from the magic red soil of Coonawarra. Deep, berryish and very long-lasting. One to keep.

338 WYNNS COONAWARRA SHIRAZ 1987 (Aus)

| £5.49 | ☛VW TH AUC MM GON CUM TWR FWC |
| | 101 j, k, l, m |

Rich jammy cedarwood and spice, perfect acid and tannic balance. Talented winemaking for a very reasonable price.

339 PENFOLDS BIN 28 KALIMNA SHIRAZ 1986 South Australia

| £5.49 | ☛TH TWR AUC SAS MC MWW DBY D WOC WRB SEB OD EVI |
| | GNW CPL | 101 j, k, l, m |

A dark, intense, aromatic wine, smooth with ripe fruit. Another winner from the Penfolds collection. It'll grow over the next 2-3 years.

340 COTES DU RHONE Guigal 1986 (F)

| £5.49 | ☛OD OBC ADN MM DBY L&W HVW MG DAL HEM SK DX BAT |
| | OBC ABY | 101 j, k, l, m |

Sweet, soft and plummy with 'spicy chewing gum'. A classy mouthful from a top Côte Rotie producer.

341 VACQUEYRAS CUVEE DES TEMPLIERS Domaine le Clos de Cazeaux 1986 Rhône (F)

| £5.99 | ☛HFW L&W EVI | 101 j, k, l, m |

Deep, red-black wine from the hot, pebbley soil of the southern Rhône.

Rich, peppery and deliciously full-flavoured. A lovely, intense and smooth drink.

342 ST JOSEPH MEDAILLE D'ARGENT St Désirat 1986 Rhône (F)

£5.99	☛VW	❑ j, k, l, m

Soft, velvety, mature (and quite curious) flavours, including 'cedar wood jam' - with tannin to spare.

343 CROZES HERMITAGE Alain Graillot 1988 Rhône (F)

£6.75	☛YAP SEB WDW ABY	❑ j, k, l, m

Powerful and deep, berryish flavours, with a texture that's at once 'gritty and velvety'. Good ageing potential.

344 BOTOBOLAR ST GILBERT RED WINE 1987 Mudgee (Aus)

£6.75	☛RAV PD VR EVI B&B	❑ j, k, l, m

An unprepossessing bottle hides a rich wine full of blackberry flavours. And it's organic too.

345 BAILEYS BUNDARRA SHIRAZ 1986 Glenrowan (Aus)

£6.99	☛GON VER AUC ADN RAV BOO	❑ j, k, l, m

From a company best known for its liqueur Muscats, this is an old-fashioned Shiraz with all the leathery, smoky spice with which this variety is associated here and in the Rhône.

346 RYECROFT SHIRAZ 1986 McLaren Vale (Aus)

£6.99	☛AUC AS SF LAY LEA	❑ j, k, l, m

Suprisingly subtle, spicy, 'creosotey' and very fruity wine from the southern suburbs of Adelaide.

347 BREZEME CUVEE EUGENE DE MONTICAULT Jean-Marie Lombard 1985 Rhône (F)

£7.15	☛YAP DBY	❑ j, k, l, m

Spice, pepper, tar, rich black cherries, enormous strength of flavour which lasts and lasts. Despite its age this still needs longer to soften out.

348 CHATEAUNEUF-DU-PAPE DOMAINE FONT DE MICHELLE Gonnet 1985 Rhône (F)

£7.49	☛D MC L&W	❑ j, k, l, m

Warm, mature fruit with hints of charcoal. Really classy Châteauneuf du Pape; perfect for game.

349 RIDGE GEYSERVILLE ZINFANDEL 1987 Sonoma (Cal)

£8.29	☛OD LEA GON DBY SEB FSW HEM SHV LAV WIN	
		❑ j, k, l, m

Arguably California's best Zinfandel, this sent our tasters into raptures. 'Multi-dimensional yet harmonious', 'full and vibrant, spicy toffee, rich plums', 'very well-made, a quality wine'.

350 COTE ROTIE Miichel Bernard 1986 Rhône (F)

£9.39	☛TO	❑ j, k, m, s

Ripe, spicy maturing fruit with aromas of 'toffee, wood and vegetables'. Intensely chewy and superbly ready.

351 QUPE SYRAH 1988 (Cal)

£9.99	☛OD M&V WCE	❑ j, k, m, s

Deep purple colour; rich, heavy currants and dark spice. Very serious Californian Rhône from an equally serious winery.

352 HERMITAGE Cecile Mussel 1985 Rhône (F)

£10.39	☛TO	❑ j, k, m, s

No doubts here: 'rich tobacco, pepper, eucalyptus; many layered fruit...wonderful balance, length and concentration - super'.

353 ST JOSEPH CUVEE ANAIS DOMAINE DU CHENE Marc Rouvière 1987 Rhône (F)

£10.69	☛COV	❑ j, k, l, m

From vineyards close to Hermitage, this wine has well-developed, fresh new oak aromas with soft jammy strawberry fruit.

354 CORNAS Guy de Barjac 1986 Rhône (F)

£10.75	✒L&W ADN TAN HV WSO THP FWC
	⭑◯⭑ j, k, m, s

'Peppercorns and strong tobacco fruit flavours'. Starting to lose its shy youth but needs another 2-3 years to mature.

355 PENFOLDS MAGILL ESTATE 1986 South Australia

£15.99	✒AUC ADN DBY WOC WRB WAW OD
	⭑◯⭑ j, k, l, m, a

Wonderful fruit and vanilla/caramel aromas. Appealing, clean, rich fruit with 'good oak' and a 'touch of mint'. One of Australia's most serious wines; a stablemate of the great Grange.

Beaujolais and other Gamays

If I am tipping spicy reds as one of the next great trends, I'd put a fiver or two on the wines in this category - the lighter reds. Some of these are so tangily fruity and lightweight that you might almost imagine them to be white. Which is why a world full of white wine fanatics might turn their way.

356 ST MICHAEL GRAPE SELECTION GAMAY Vin de Pays de l'Ardèche Rhône (F)

£2.99	✒M&S	⭑◯⭑ c, e, g, j, k, l, q

A bargain alternative to Beaujolais, with flavours of cherries and strawberries. Very refreshing.

357 GAILLAC CEPAGE GAMAY Jean Cros 1989 South-West (F)

£3.95	✒ADN UBC RN WCE HAS H&D CPL
	⭑◯⭑ c, e, g, j, k, l, q,

Sweet, plummy fruit, with tar and spice. A real mouthful.

358 GAMAY DE L'ARDECHE Georges Duboeuf Rhône 1989 (F)

£3.99	✒ LNR LWL PD POW D WOC WRB SHV ABY
	⭑◯⭑ j, k, m, r

This has a ripe 'strawberry' feel to it with juicy flavours. But there's a bit of Rhône pepper too. Strawberries and pepper - delicious!

359 BEAUJOLAIS-VILLAGES Georges Duboeuf 1989 (F)

£5.30	✒TH ABY SAS SV WOC WRB FSW HVW LWL TWR EOO SHV
LNR	⭑◯⭑ c, e, g j, k, l, q,

Vivid purple wine, with fresh, fruity aromas of redcurrants and pear. Easy- drinking soft, lightweight wine.

360 BEAUJOLAIS ANCIENNE METHODE DOMAINE DES TERRES DOREES Jean Paul Brun 1989 (F)

£5.75	✒CDV	⭑◯⭑ c, e, g, i, l

An interesting young Beaujolais which is quite rich and soft but has an appealing sherbet-like edge to the raspberry fruitiness. The 'Ancienne' method, by the way, refers to a lower than usual addition of sugar to the vats - and thus a lower level of alcohol.

361 BROUILLY E Loron 1989 Beaujolais (F)

£5.89	✒U CUM THP HUN CPL	⭑◯⭑ c, e, g, j, l

Jammy raspberries and perfumed violets. Rich, exotic Gamay.

362 BROUILLY André Large 1989 Beaujolais (F)

£5.99	✒HHC WCE WOC	⭑◯⭑ c, e, j, l, m

Light cherry, soft silky strawberry fruit with hints of cloves.

363 REGNIE CRISTAL Georges Duboeuf 1989 Beaujolais (F)

£5.99	✒ LNR SAS GHW POW WRB EOO MTL ABY
	⭑◯⭑ e, j, l, m

Everything a young Beaujolais should be, fresh, clean, and just cram-packed with concentrated jammy fruit. Serve lightly chilled.

364 MORGON JEAN DESCOMBES Georges Duboeuf 1989 Beaujolais (F)

£6.75	☛TH ABY GHW POW DBY WOC WRB BEN FSW TWR EOO	
MTL MCL LNR GRT ABY		ΙΟΙ e, j, k, m

Jean Descombes is one of the finest producers in Morgon; his wines provide a perfect illustration of the way the wines of this village take on a chocolatey, cherryish intensity with age. This one is still young - and very intensely fruity.

365 FLEURIE LA MADONE Georges Duboeuf 1988 Beaujolais (F)

£7.49	☛D MC UBC WOC SEL MCL LNR	ΙΟΙ j, k, m

From one of the best vineyards in Fleurie, this has a sweet fruit nose with a hint of a prickle, full cherryish flavour and a smooth long aftertaste.

Burgundy and other Pinot Noirs

Still thought of as 'big and velvety' — presumably by people whose formative experiences have been of Burgundies which had shared their vats and barrels with a few gallons of deliciously dusky brew from North Africa — these should more realistically be described as more middle-to-featherweight. Whether they are made in Burgundy itself or, with increasing success, from the Pinot Noir elsewhere, these are all wines that ought to sing with bright, raspberry-plummy fruit.

366 MILION PINOT NOIR Navip 1986 Vranje (Yug)

£2.59	☛GHW SAF WH OD W	ΙΟΙ e, j, k, m, s

A good, maturing example of Eastern Europe's answer to Burgundy. Cleanly fruity, with a creamy texture. Good value.

367 BOURGOGNE PINOT NOIR Caves de Buxy 1987 Burgundy (F)

£4.99	☛G MWW RAV BUD P GHL TH TWR HEM W SPR CPW	
		ΙΟΙ c, j, k, m

'Super nose' with 'depth, fruit and tobacco'. Real 'farmyard' nose and 'good weight of fruit'. Excellent value.

368 TREFETHEN PINOT NOIR 1984 Napa Valley (Cal)

£8.50	☛VW ADN DBY AHC LAV WIN	ΙΟΙ j, k, m

Opulent New World fruit balanced by some dry earthiness. It is still quite tannic and the fruit is chewy. An assertive style well suited to food.

369 SANTENAY LE CHENAY Domaine Bernard Morey 1985 Burgundy (F)

£9.75	☛D MC	ΙΟΙ e, j, k, m

'Very mature farmyard and fruit aromas; light, fresh, well-balanced, with elegant style'. 'Lots of class'.

370 HICKINBOTHAM PINOT NOIR 1988 Geelong (Aus)

£10.45	☛L&W	ΙΟΙ j, k, m, r

A beautifully balanced young wine already showing richness of flavour but can be kept for three years or more. Good, concentrated blackberry fruit, and rich, velvety texture.

371 COLDSTREAM HILLS PINOT NOIR 1988 Yarra Valley (Aus)

£10.50	☛TWR AUC GHS CNL HOL HW OD FSW SHV THP	
		ΙΟΙ j, k, m, r

Made by Australia's top wine writer, James Halliday, this has lots of rich, ripe fruit and a touch of tannin.

372 SAVIGNY-LES-BEAUNE 1ER CRU LES LAVIERES Domaine Chandon de Briailles
1986 Burgundy (F)

£11.48	☛TO BAT THP	🍴 j, k, m

This smells quite mature, with aromas of burnt toffee, leather and
caramel. Good fruit, balance and a soft finish.

373 AU BON CLIMAT PINOT NOIR 1988 (Cal)

£11.75	☛BWS WFP M&V WCE EBA FWC	🍴 j, k, m, s

Rich and powerful New World style. Enticingly sweet, strawberry
jam nose and generous raspberry flavour. Lovely velvety texture.

374 NUITS ST GEORGES Alain Michelot 1986 Burgundy (F)

£14.31	☛LNR	🍴 j, k, m

Good Pinot aromas - ripe, soft fruits, slightly meaty and interesting
smoky, toasted flavours. Lovely concentration of fruit with balancing
oaky tannins. Keep for two years.

375 POMMARD CROIX BLANCHE Jacques Parent 1986 Burgundy (F)

£14.73	☛WIL GD TBS GHL	🍴 j, k, m

Gentle, ripe, oaky, sweet cherryish Pinot nose. Appealing ripe, strawberry fruit with soft tannins and fine balancing acidity. 'Great prom
ise' for drinking in 3 to 5 years.

376 CHAMBOLLE MUSIGNY Domaine Mâchard de Gramont 1986 Burgundy (F)

£15.25	☛D	🍴 j, k, m, s

'Fine, full and surprisingly mature, approaching optimum drinking'. Soft sweet fruit, with a spicy soft finish.

377 CALERA JENSEN PINOT NOIR 1987 San Benito (Cal)

£15.50	☛ADN LEA BOO WCE BEN BI LAV WIN	
		🍴 j, k, m, s

Generous, big, full, young, bitter-cherry flavoured wine with spicy
oak. Lovely rounded finish. Watch out Burgundy!

378 MONDAVI PINOT NOIR RESERVE 1986 Napa Valley (Cal)

£16.00	☛UC GON TP DBY WOC BEN CVR EOO HEM PTR FWC LAV WIN	
		🍴 e, j, k, m

'Sublime maturing Burgundy nose'. Lots of intense fruit, great length.

379 VOSNE-ROMANEE LES MALCONSORTS Moillard 1986 Burgundy (F)

£16.95	☛AB MTL ROD	🍴 j, k, m

'Extraordinary plummy nose'; 'spectacular, warm, earthy', with 'almost baked fruit' flavours.

380 VOSNE-ROMANEE 1ER CRU BEAUMONTS Daniel Rion 1986 Burgundy (F)

£18.99	☛GON OD JS UC M&V	🍴 e, j, k, m

Lots of fruit with 'assertive' oak. There is some tannin but the wine is
warm and velvety. The flavour goes on and on.

381 CLOS VOUGEOT GRAND CRU Château de la Tour 1982 Burgundy (F)

£20.00	☛HV OBC	🍴 j, k, m

Typical of the vintage, this has the pale orange colour and elegantly
vegetal aromas of a fully matured wine.

382 YARRA YERING PINOT NOIR 1987 Yarra Valley (Aus)

£26.95	☛AUC BEN FW BTH WFP	🍴 j, k, m

Deep colour and concentrated berry fruit aromas typical of New
World style. This wine scored highly with all tasters for its rich, yet
beautifully balanced fruit and its great length of flavour

(Arg) = Argentina; (Au) = Austria; (Aus) = Australia; (Bul) = Bulgaria; (Cal) = California; (Can) = Canada;
(Ch) = Chile; (F) = France; (G) = Germany; (Gr) = Greece; (Hun) = Hungary; (It) = Italy; (NZ) = New
Zealand; (P) = Portugal; (Rom) = Romania; (SA) = South Africa; (Sp) = Spain; (UK) = United Kingdom;
(US) = United States; (Yug) = Yugoslavia

Italian reds

A gloriously mixed bag here, but one in which every example bears at least some resemblance to its neighbours. These Italian reds come in all shapes and sizes, and are made from a range of (often unfamiliar) grape varieties, but they all have at least a measure of the herby-spicy character that makes them such a delicious accompaniment to food.

383 VALPOLICELLA CARISSA, Pasqua, Veneto (It)

£2.49	☞ CWS	❍ c, j, k, m, r

Aromas of cherry stones, peppercorns and light jammy fruit flavours make this wine a delicious drink.

384 SAINSBURY'S CANNONAU DEL PARTEOLLA, 1987, Sardinia (It)

£2.79	☞JS	❍ e, j, k

Fruity, with a hint of violets, rich and interesting.

385 SAINSBURY'S DOLCETTO D'ACQUI 1988 Piedmont (It)

£2.89	☞JS	❍ c, j, k, m

Italian wine at its inexpensive fruitiest and best. Lovely, intense cherryish, plummy flavours. Long, refreshing and satisfying.

386 CANTINA SETTESOLI ROSSO 1987 Sicily (It)

£2.99	☞M&S WRB V&C	❍ e, j, k

Masses of ripe, almost sweet, berry fruit with spicy wood, high acidity and some tannin. Best left for another year or two.

387 MONTEPULCIANO D'ABRUZZO Tollo 1987 Abruzzi (It)

£3.50	☞AB GHW MWW V&C DAL B&B ROD EP CPW	
		❍ e, j, k, m

Very young and strong with ripe, peppery berries; smooth and creamy at the moment, but will keep.

388 BARBERA D'ASTI Viticoltori dell'Acquesi 1988 Piedmont (It)

£3.65	☞WCE UC HVW MG HEM GI SPR CWG	
		❍ e, j, k

Red Wine of the Year

Deeply-coloured, very concentrated young wine with wonderful, unashamedly 'Italian' flavours of bitter fruit and herbs. It does need food to be enjoyed at its best and should be treated with care; as litttle as one mouthful could cause severe longing for a plate of antipasto.

389 BARDOLINO Fraterna Portalupi 1988 Veneto (It)

£3.99	☞THP SAS ADN OD V&C	❍e, j, k

Ruby-coloured, light, creamy wine with flavours of fruit and wood. Easily enjoyable.

390 CABERNET DEL TRENTINO Ca'Vit, 1987, Trentino-Alto Adige (It)

£4.19	☞LWL HEM SHV WSO WES	❍ e, j, k, l, m

Very typical Cabernet Franc, with fresh, grassy young cassis fruit, with just a little green pepper. Classic; satisfyingly refreshing.

391 TEROLDEGO ROTALIANO Gaierhof 1988 Trentino-Alto Adige (It)

£4.29	☞W MRS V&C MTL MRS	❍ c, e, j, k, l, m, r

Teroldego is a name to remember. This north-east Italian variety is almost only grown on flat land near the Noce and Adige rivers. It's mouthfillingly plummy and damsony, with a generous sprinkling of liquorice and vanilla spice.

392 BARBERA D'ASTI COLLINA CROJA Castelvero 1988 Piedmont (It)

£4.65	☞D	❍ e, j, k

Full, rich loganberry fruit, wrapped in a husk of fairly tough tannins at the moment. Needs another five years.

393 CORVO ROSSO 1987 Sicily (It)

£4.79	☛TH TWR MM TAN UC POW DBY U WRB L&W V&C PTR
	◎ e, j, k, l, m

Sicily's best known unfortified wine, this has rich, concentrated chocolatey fruit, a good level of acidity and some soft tannin.

394 QUATTRO VICARIATI Ca'Vit 1986 Trentino-Alto Adige (It)

£4.79	☛LWL HEM SHV	◎ j, k, l, m

'Grassy', 'robust' spicy flavoured wine with fresh acidity.

395 VALPOLICELLA CLASSICO Vigneti Mara Cesari 1987 Veneto (It)

£4.95	☛WH HW DVY	◎ c, e, j, k, l, m, r

A single-vineyard Valpolicella with big, fat tarry fruit and tobacco aromas. It tastes at once dry and intensely fruity.

396 NEBBIOLO DELLE LANGHE Berutti 1985 Piedmont (It)

£4.99	☛TH TWR	◎ e, j, k

'Super soft, vaporous';'almost sweet fruit ripeness'; great value.

397 RECIOTO DELLA VALPOLICELLA Cantine Sociale di Soave 1982 Veneto (It)

£4.99	☛TO CWM	◎ j, k, l, m, q

Gentle, sweet, raisiny wine mde from grapes that have been hung up to dry. The Italians call this 'Vino di Meditazione'.

398 FRANCIACORTA ROSSO Barone Pizzini Piomarta 1987 Lombardy (It)

£5.65	☛DVY	◎ e, j, k, l, m

An interesting combination of French and Italian grape varieties, showing some woody maturity and flavours of vanilla, tobacco, leather and chocolate.

399 CAMPO FIORIN Masi 1985 Veneto (It)

£5.95	☛AB MM DBY WH V&C SEL WFP CPW
	◎ e, j, k, l, m

Spicy, tarry aromas and concentrated sweet fruit, 'deep, lively and full bodied'. A consistently good wine from a top producer.

400 CABERNET RISERVA Lageder 1986 Trentino-Alto Adige (It)

£5.99	☛AB WCE V&C SPR	◎ e, j, k, l, m

Very ripe brambley wine with an almost 'New World' intensity of fruit. Soft, rich and balanced. Will improve over the next 3 years.

401 CHIANTI CLASSICO RISERVA DUCALE Ruffino 1986 Tuscany (It)

£6.29	☛MRS PD FDL RAV V&C MTL BLW
	◎ e, j, k, l, m

Full, rich chocolatey fruit. From one of Chianti's oldest wineries.

402 VINO NOBILE DI MONTEPULCIANO RISERVA Fattorio del Cerro 1985 Tuscany (It)

£6.50	☛WE MM MIL EBA WGA	◎ e, j, k, l, m

Quite a lot of Vino Nobile isn't very 'noble' at all. This one, however, is intensely packed with summery, herby flavours.

403 TANCA FARRA Sella e Mosca 1984 Sardinia (It)

£6.99	☛WGA HAR V&C MIL	◎ e, j, k, m

Spicy, cedary, sandalwoody. Soft, long and fruity. Great, satisfying, Sardinian wine.

404 DOLCETTO D'ALBA Coscina Francia Conterno 1985 Piedmont (It)

£7.59	☛TAN V&C	◎ e, j, k

Concentrated nutty, spicy wine with 'terrific, deep purple' colour. It's still very tannic but full of ripe, long, fruity flavour. Needs 3 to 5 years.

405 BAROLO RISERVA Borgogno 1982 Piedmont (It)

£7.99	☛WGA V&C TAN HW WGA BND CPL
	◎ j, k, m, s

Barolo for people who like buying 'Futures'. The fruit is ripe and silky, but the wine is still packed with tannin.

406 ROSSO CONERO RISERVA BARRIQUE Mecvini 1987 Marches (It)

£8.99	V&C	e, j, k, l, m

Ripe pungent berries with rich, warm, toasty oak, chewy tannins and a bite of acidity. A young wine which needs more time.

407 CASTELLO DI CAMIGLIANO ROSSO 1986 Tuscany (It)

£9.45	WGA HV BI	j, k, l, m

Intense maturing flavours of plums and cherries, wood and chocolate.

408 PRUNAIO Landini 1986 Tuscany (It)

£9.80	WH RN BWS	e, j, k, l, m

Soft, cherry and plummy fruit with some spice and noticeable tannin.

409 RECIOTO DELLA VALPOLICELLA Allegrini 1988 Veneto (It)

£10.29	WCE UC CWI V&C HEM CWG	j, k, l, m, q

Very, very, intense, beautifully balanced wine, packed with complex flavours of spice and raisins. A wine to turn to when you get bored with all those 'modern', oaky whites. Very, very satisfying.

410 MON PRA Conterno e Fantino 1987 Piedmont (It)

£10.99	OD BOO WGA V&C	e, j, k, l, m, s

Barolo producers are now breaking DOCG laws in the same way as their colleagues in Tuscany. Barbera, Nebbiolo and new oak go hand-in-hand in this 'excellent, opulent, expensive-tasting, spicy wine'.

411 BAROLO RISERVA Giacomo Conterno 1983 Piedmont (It)

£12.49	OD V&C	j, k, m, s

With the colour of 'deep dried blood', this is very big, tough and enormously tannic. It needs 3 to 5 years.

412 CEPPARELLO Isole e Olena 1986 Tuscany (It)

£12.50	WCE UC V&C HEM CWG	j, k, l, m, s

Morello cherry fruit and rich tannin. Pure Sangiovese from a great, innovative Chianti maker.

413 CABREO IL BORGO Ruffino 1986 Tuscany (It)

£15.69	BTH MRS BLW V&C BLW	e, j, k, l, m

Clean, ripe truffley wine. Slightly minty and herbal but with good fruit and tannin. Lovely.

414 TIGNANELLO Antinori 1985 Tuscany (It)

£15.95	TH TWR MWW CGW SAS MM TAN JS GHS MC UBC LEA UC	
	HOL DBY WH HW WCE SV VW	e, j, k, l, m, s

The *Wine Magazine* International Challenge Red Wine Trophy Winner. 'Deep, ruby red'; 'intense violets'; 'richly Italian, lovely fruit'; 'hint of vanilla oak'; 'ripe, subtle'. 'Tarry, new style, soft and sweet. Very good richness and black chocolate'.

415 BRUNELLO DI MONTALCINO MONTOSOLI Altesino 1985 Tuscany (It)

£16.55	WCE UC	j, k, m, s

Complex blend of rich, blackberry fruit, oak, chocolate and toffee. Lovely plummy fruit, slightly herbal with lots of vanilla.

416 BARBARESCO Gaja 1986 Piedmont (It)

£20.89	OD V&C	j, k, m

'Tannic, youthful, good fruit, needs time'. 'Lovely fruit balance, long aftertaste'. 'Yes! Nebbiolo? Tobacco. Light year? High tannin, good acid'. 'Very big, complex, expensive'. 'Opulent, spicy, exotic tannin, rich'. From the best producer in Barbaresco.

417 BAROLO MONPRIVATO G Mascarello 1985 Piedmont (It)

£23.50	WCE UC HEM WSO CWG EP	j, k, m, s

'Good depth, clean, rich and complex with young fruit. Rich and savoury, long and complete. Tannic but balanced'. Rich fruit - plums, chocolate and damsons.

418 SOLAIA Antinori 1986 Tuscany (It)

£37.00	RES AHC C&B UC V&C	j, k, m, s

Deep purple colour. Super Cabernet nose, sweet and ripe with good oak. 'Delicious', soft fruit flavours with notes of smoky oak. Well-balanced, soft enough to drink now but could be kept for 3-5 years. A modern Italian first growth?

Iberian reds

Spain and Portugal are rather like stables in which all but a handful of the horses have run at least one race too many. There are oodles of dull, workaday reds from both countries on the market, none of them objection-able, none of them worth thinking about while you drink them. The ones on these pages, however, are the stars; the great, mature thoroughbreds which can still win any race you put them in, and the bright, new, wines which, in their first few seasons, are already showing what Iberia could do if it tried.

419 CASTILLO DE ALHAMBRA Vinicola de Castilla 1989 La Mancha (Sp)

£2.67	DD JS OD	d, e, j, k, l, m

Spain's answer to Beaujolais? A former *Guide* Wine of the Year, this is still one of Spain's best value wines. Its deep vibrant cherry colour, its strong aromas of pear drops and grapes and its rich, fruity flavour all provide evidence that Spanish reds don't all have to be soft and oaky.

420 DON DARIAS VINO DE MESA Bodegas Vitorianas Alto Ebro (Sp)

£2.75	TO SAF TH TWR A	d, e, j, k, l, m

A warm, satisfying blend of coffee, black pepper and spicy oak. Ridiculously easy to drink. An example for other Spanish wine-makers to follow.

421 VINA ALBALI RESERVA Felix Solis 1983 Valdepeñas (Sp)

£3.35	BUD AB HOL MG PTR	c, d, j, k, l, m

Deep aromas, soft oaky, earthy and inviting flavours, with plenty of stout-hearted fruit... Perfect tapas fare.

422 ALMANSA MARIUS TINTO RESERVA Bodegas Piqueras 1982 (Sp)

£3.99	TAN UBC WH GHL SEL HEM EVI DVY	
		j, k, l

Blackberries and currant jam. Soft, warming. Will develop.

423 MEIA PIPA João Pires 1987 Palmela (P)

£3.99	OD	e, j, k, m

Blackcurrant fruit with oaky overtones. Excellent fruit and good acidity.

424 ROMEIRA GARRAFEIRA Cavas Velhas 1980 (P)

£4.29	JS PD MOR	e, j, k, m

Mouth-filling berry fruits; a typically Portuguese dry finish.

425 QUINTA DA BACALHOA 1987 Palmela (P)

£4.45	JS	j, k, m, q

Spicy, slightly tough fruity aromas with a whiff of smoke.

426 DAO PORTA DOS CAVALEIROS RESERVA Caves São João 1983 (P)

£4.65	WSO HV	j, k, l, m

Deep, dark stuff with dry blackberry fruit. Very tannic.

427 DUERO Bodegas Penalba 1985 (Sp)

£4.89	AB WH SHV	j, k, m, q

Ripe, fruity almost tropical aromas and flavours. Subtle oak.

428 QUINTA DE CAMARATE Fonseca 1985 Azeitão (P)

| £4.99 | ☛HAS ADN TAN UBC GON MWW POW DBY WH WCE HEM |
| B&B WRW GHW | 🍴 j, k, l, m |

Soft vanilla with good fruit. Rich and satisfying.

429 RAIMAT TEMPRANILLO 1987 Lerida (Sp)

| £4.99 | ☛OD TH TWR FWC | 🍴 e, j, k, l, m |

Rich, smooth, oaky wine with a big 'fruity' jam taste. Made from a
grape more usually found in Rioja.

430 RIOJA CRIANZA Navajas 1985   (Sp)

| £5.19 | ☛MOR MC MRS | 🍴 j, k, l, m |

Perfumed, floral aromas, strong tannin, citric, fruity acidity, smooth,
oaky, creamy.

431 LAR DE BARROS RESERVA Bodega Inviosa 1986 Extremadura (Sp)

| £5.30 | ☛SHV LV MOR HV MC SAS | 🍴 e, j, k, l, m |

Bright crimson, full, soft plummy wine with a hint of cedar wood. 'A
beautiful rich complexity of fruits'; 'a classic wine which will only
improve'. Rioja beware!

432 RIOJA RESERVA Beronia 1982 (Sp)

| £5.89 | ☛OD DBY WH BI GHL MTL PTR CPL |
| | 🍴 e, j, k, l, m |

Youthful, complex wine with fruit, almonds and minty oak.

433 RIOJA RESERVA ALBINA Bodegas Riojanas 1984 (Sp)

| £5.90 | ☛MOR B&B MTL | 🍴 e, j, k, l, m |

Flowery, young wine with succulent, rich ripe fruit. Seems to need
more time.

434 RIOJA Bodegas Remelluri 1985   (Sp)

| £6.90 | ☛FWC TAN WH SV SHV | 🍴 e, j, k, l, m |

Rich, rounded fruit with a hint of spice. Mellow in its maturity. Top
class Rioja from an individual estate.

435 GRANDE ESCHOLA Quinta do Cotto 1985 Douro (P)

| £7.65 | ☛OD ADN TAN WH BI PTR | 🍴 e, j, k, l, m |

A rich, fruity and peppery wine with plenty of weight. This
can be drunk now or left to develop for 2 to 3 years.

436 RIOJA RESERVA 904 La Rioja Alta 1976 (Sp)

| £10.65 | ☛THP J&B MOR YFW SAS ADN UBC LEA GON W H WAW BEN |
| BOO HAR SEL HEM | 🍴 j, k, l, m |

A supple, mature wine with great depth of fleshy, oaky, plummy fruit.
A stylish example to enjoy with the Christmas goose.

437 TINTO PESQUERA Fernandez 1986 Ribera del Duero (Sp)

| £10.90 | ☛OD ADN NIC TAN MC UBC GON DBY BOO SEB WAW HAR |
| SEL HEM WOI HAS | 🍴 j, k, m, s |

One of Spain's best and best-publicized wines, full of spicy, plummy
fruit, which will improve for the next 3 years.

438 FERREIRA BARCA VELHA Douro 1981 (P)

| £17.95 | ☛TWR GI | 🍴 e, j, k, l, m |

Rich, ripe, fine and fruity wine with a long clean finish. Portugal's
finest red?

Muscats

One of the least appreciated and most wonderful of all grape varieties, the
Muscat produces wines that are absolutely packed with the flavour of
grapes and raisins. Dry or sweet, fortified or unfortified, these are probably
the most drinkable examples of the kinds of wine our ancestors would have
drunk and enjoyed.

439 MOSCATEL DE VALENCIA Vicente Gandia 1988 (Sp)

| £2.95 | ☛FUL TAN TO | ◯n, o |

'Soft, melon fruit flavours'. Warm and stylish with good texture and excellent balance.

440 SAMOS NECTAR 10 YEAR OLD Cooperatives Vinicoles de Samos (Gr)

| £5.00 | ☛TAN WCE OD | ◯n, o |

Rich, concentrated and marmaladey with burnt raisin flavours.

441 MORRIS RUTHERGLEN LIQUEUR MUSCAT (Aus)

| £7.50 | ☛OD AUC UBC DBY CAC WCE COV CVR SK WFP MRS PTR |
| | ◯n, p, q |

Rich, nut brown colour with deep aromas of nuts and burnt sugar. Sweet, rich and spicy with a taste that lasts and lasts and lasts....

442 MUSCAT DE RIVESALTES Château de la Tuilerie 1988 Midi (F)

| £7.99 | ☛AV DAL FWC K&B DBY WH WID FW CVR GNW |

A lovely, perfumed wine with fresh orange aromas and clean finish.

443 CAMPBELLS RUTHERGLEN MUSCAT (Aus)

| £9.75 | ☛MWW AUC UC GON DBY AHC DAL DVY A |
| | ◯n, p, q |

'Fruit and Nut - with the milk chocolate!' Creamy, deep-flavoured, very sweet wine from one of the best producers in Rutherglen.

444 BAILEYS FOUNDERS LIQUEUR MUSCAT Glenrowan (Aus)

| £10.95 | ☛ CWG AUC OBC DRI VER UC GON RAV DBY BOO WOC |
| GHL DAL THP GNW | ◯n, p, q |

Wonderfully rich, Christmas-puddingy Muscat with refreshing lemon zesty freshness. Very exotic. Reputedly aphrodisiac.

Botrytis and all that rot

More decadent stuff. Like perfume and *The Archers* on Sunday, great botrytis-affected wines are among the world's indulgences. A decent bottle of red or white with the meal ought to be sufficient for any sensible human being. But then someone appears with a glass of well-chilled, deeply golden liquid which smells of apricots, flowers and honey - the kind of wine that *has* to feature in the armoury of every successful seducer Of course there are always bound to be a few people who can't stand sweet wine; Don Giovanni must have come across a few ladies who were tone deaf.

445 CHATEAU DES TOURS Ste-Croix-du-Mont 1986 Bordeaux (F)

| £2.80 | ☛MWW SUM BBR H&D | ◯m, o |

This wine, from vineyards just across the water from Sauternes, has rich, creamy-peach fruit and mouth-filling softness. Great value.

446 BOUVIER TROCKENBEERENAUSLESE Alexander Unger 1983 Burgenland (Au)

| £4.25 | ☛JS | ◯m, n, o |

Full, raisiny with honeyed botrytis. Sweet, golden syrup flavour. Classy.

447 CHATEAU DE BERBEC Premières Côtes de Bordeaux 1987 (F)

| £4.59 | ☛TH TWR SAF WCE W SPR MRS | ◯m, o |

Attractive, delicate, apricotty wine. 'Good all the way through'.

☛ For an explanation of stockist abbreviations, see page 17
◯ For an explanation of food style codes, see page 65

448 MONTANA LATE HARVEST RHINE RIESLING 1987 Marlborough (NZ)

| £4.99 | ☛OD SK | ◐ m, o |

Lovely, rich, grapey wine, starting to develop the petrolly character of aged Riesling coupled with some noble rot. It is luscious and sweet now but will become even more interesting in 1-2 years.

449 CHATEAU DES COULINATS Ste-Croix-du-Mont 1983 Bordeaux (F)

| £5.35 | ☛ HPD UC DBY WRB BEN GHL GI GRT CPL | |
| | | ◐ m, o |

'Tinned peaches in syrup'; soft, ripe, almost jammy with some botrytis. Good value.

450 DOMAINE DU NOBLE (Déjean Père & Fils) Loupiac 1986 Bordeaux (F)

| £5.75 | ☛WWI L&W BI FWC | ◐ m, o |

Bright gold colour, lovely sweet, creamy honey balanced with clean acidity. A good, inexpensive alternative to Sauternes.

451 CHATEAU LA NERE Dulac & Seraphon Loupiac 1986 Bordeaux (F)

| £5.99 | ☛ BUD BLW EP CPW | ◐ m, o |

A lovely, rich, peachy alternative to Sauternes - at a ridiculously low price. A wine to linger over.

452 PETER LEHMANN BOTRYTIS RIESLING 1984 Barossa Valley (Aus)

| £6.49 | ☛ AUC DRI VER RAV DBY BO GHL OBC CWG | |
| | | ◐ m, n. o |

A lovely, rich smell which many tasters described as 'Muscatty'. Good botrytis. Rich and full flavours with hints of caramel and raisins.

453 BONNEZEAUX Jean Godineau 1987 Loire (F)

| £6.99 | ☛WAW OLS LEA EOO | ◐ m, o |

Rich petrol, lemon-and-honey. Great potential but like most sweet Loires it needs more time.

454 TOKAY ASZU 5 PUTTONYOS 1981 Tokaji (Hun)

| £7.50 | ☛VW SEL DAL PD BBR WIL HPD TAN R&I | |
| | | ◐ m, o |

Wonderful, tangy, orangey, 'old-fashioned' wine. Great with chocolate.

455 KIONA ICE WINE RIESLING 1987 Washington State (USA)

| £8.99 | ☛OD | ◐ n, s |

Washington State is making a speciality of Riesling. This impeccably made New World version of traditional German Eiswein is quite extrordinary in its concentrated honey, toast and raisiny flavours.

456 THAMES VALLEY VINEYARD BOTRYTIZED SCHEUREBE 1989 Berkshire (UK)

| £9.00 | ☛ GWR HFV | ◐ m, n, o |

Lovely, floral, typically Scheurebe grapefruity fruit. A brilliant, unexpected achievement from one of the best English vineyards in a great vintage for England.

457 CHATEAU LE DRAGON Calvet 1987 Bordeaux (F)

| £9.99 | ☛TH TWR VW | ◐ n |

'Cooked pineapple and tinned mandarin oranges'. Well-balanced and elegant with good acidity to match the fresh peachy/apricot fruit. Rich but not cloying.

458 CHATEAU LAMOTHE-GUIGNARD Sauternes 1986 Bordeaux (F)

| £11.00 | ☛L&W AHC ROD | ◐ n, o |

Pungent aroma of pineapples and tropical (lychee) fruit. Attractive and richly sweet with good balancing acidity.

459 SICHEL BEERENAUSLESE Deidesheimer Hofstuck 1988 Rheinpfalz (G)

| £11.40 | ☛POW SHV | ◐ n |

Rich, honeyed aroma, concentrated with good botrytis. 'Voluptuous', richly-flavoured, marmalade-like, orangey, underlying acidity. Lovely, long finish.

460 CHATEAU RABAUD-PROMIS Sauternes 1986 Bordeaux (F)

| £14.90 | ☛THP DRI MWW RAE OD | 🍴 o, q, s |

Fascinating, unctuous, deep, raisiny smells and flavours. A backbone of alcohol and acidity contributing to a very, very classy wine.

461 RECIOTO DI SOAVE DEI CAPITELLE Anselmi 1987 Veneto (It)

| £15.90 | ☛SUM WCE OD V&C HAS ABY | 🍴 m, n, o |

Wonderful orangey, raisin aroma; rich fruit lightened by refreshing acidity. Lovely and not in the least cloying.

462 TORCOLATO Maculan 1986 Veneto (It)

| £17.00 | ☛ADN WCE OD CPW | 🍴 m, n, o |

From Maculan, one of the best producers in Veneto. This is an extraordinary intense, Muscatty wine, with flavours of dried apricot botrytis and toffeeish oak.

463 ZD LATE HARVEST RIESLING 1986 Napa Valley (Cal)

| £17.30 | ☛WIZ | 🍴 n |

Well-balanced, intensely sweet, with a marmaladey richness — a rare American example of a rare German style.

464 CHATEAU RIEUSSEC Sauternes 1983 Bordeaux (F)

| £27.50 | ☛D MC POW HW SEB OD FSW GI OLS EP FWC CWM | |
| | | 🍴 o, q, s |

Beautiful, golden colour, very, very concentrated and balanced wine. Apricotty, coconutty, complex flavours with bags of botrytis.

Sherry

Forget every glass of warm dry sherry you have ever been offered by vicars and university dons; obliterate from your mind the ancient half-full bottle of cream sherry which constituted Aunt Mildred's idea of hospitality. No, the sherries which feature on the next few pages are among the greatest wines in the world. Their flavour, dry or sweet, is unique. Like it or loathe it, you will never quite find its like anywhere else in the world. Sales are dropping every year, however, so unless we all show some of our enthusiasm by buying a bottle or two, this is an endangered species.

465 SAINSBURY'S AGED AMONTILLADO Jerez (Sp)

| £2.95 | ☛JS | 🍴 n, q, s |

A strong, lingering, fruity and nutty wine, well-made, with rounded and sweet flavours.

466 ST MICHAEL FINO SHERRY Williams & Humbert Jerez (Sp)

| £2.99 | ☛M&S | 🍴 a, b, m, q |

Marmaladey, more 'winey' than most finos. Perfect for the conversion of non-sherry drinkers.

467 SAINSBURY'S OLOROSO Jerez (Sp)

| £3.29 | ☛JS | 🍴 n, q |

Raisiny, sweet, toffeeish, very old-fashioned sherry. Astonishingly good value.

468 TESCO FINEST OLOROSO SECO Sanchez Romate Jerez (Sp)

| £4.29 | ☛TO | 🍴 a, b, d, m, q |

Rich leathery brown, dark, toasty aromas with a sweetish caramelly style and a dry, nutty finish.

469 ST MICHAEL RICH CREAM SHERRY Harveys Jerez (Sp)

| £4.29 | ☛M&S | 🍴 n, q |

Richly sweet with a complex blend of raisins, caramel and nuts. 'Would go very nicely with ice cream bombe'.

470 AMONTILLADO NAPOLEON Hidalgo   Jerez   (Sp)

£4.50	☛WWI ADN GHS	🍴 n, q

A smooth, mature treacle-toffeeish wine with a dry finish.

471 AMONTILLADO TIO DIEGO Valdespino   Jerez   (Sp)

£6.99	☛WSO GHW LEA DBY HW CUM HAR WSO OLS PTR	
		🍴 n, q

Warmly spicy, full of currants and toffee and a hint of caramel.

472 DON ZOILO VERY OLD FINO Jerez   (Sp)

£7.25	☛TGB MM JF GNW SEL MM GHW GHS MC UC DBY BEN HEM	
B&B GNW FWC		🍴 a, b , d, i, m, q

Juicy and smooth, yeasty, old-yet-fresh sherry. Classic fino, the
way the Spaniards like it.

473 DON ZOILO MANZANILLA Sanlucar de Barrameda   (Sp)

£7.25	☛BWS B&B WIL MM SEL MC DBY ABY	
		🍴 a, b, d, m, q

Yeasty, fresh baked bread and currants. 'Weighty', clean, crisp and
tingling.

474 DON LUIS AMONTILLADO Burdon   Jerez   (Sp)

£8.40	☛OD DRI UC DBY SHV	🍴 n, q

A great, complex concentration of flavours and textures. Big, fruity,
fresh and nutty. Hazelnut oil finish.

475 DOS CORTADOS Williams & Humbert   Jerez   (Sp)

£8.50	☛HAS MM B&B SHV PTR	🍴 q, s

Big, rounded fruit, long lasting and full of yeasty 'flor'.

476 MATUSALEM OLOROSO MUY VIEJO Gonzalez Byass   Jerez   (Sp)

£10.75	☛OD TWR DRI MM UC GON DBY RAE WH FW GHL TO HAR SEL	
MTL MOR SHV THP PTR		🍴 m, q, s

An extremely concentrated old wine full of nutty, Christmas pudding
flavour. Never-ending finish.

477 SANDEMAN ROYAL AMBROSANTE Jerez   (Sp)

£10.99	☛SEL LV UC HAR POW WRB	🍴 m, q, s

Creamy and nutty with a smooth balance of toffee and crisp acidity.

478 AMONTILLADO DEL DUQUE Gonzalez Byass   Jerez   (Sp)

£11.50	☛TWR OD TH DRI MM UC GON DBY RAE WH FW GHL MTL	
MOR WOI SHV THP PTR		🍴 m, n, q, s

Absolutely stunning. Deep, salty aroma with a hint of new leather.
Yeasty, bone dry, powerful.

Port and other fortified wines

If sherry is endangered, so too are most of the world's other fortified wines.
We live in a world in which a taste for alcohol and sweetness are increasingly treated as though it were a perversion. In this kind of climate, what
hope do sweet, fortified wines have? Vintage port is unthreatened (people
invest in it) and other, classier Tawny, Single Quinta and good Late Bottled
benefit from the fact that Vintage buyers tend to be attracted to other higher
quality ports. Other examples – Madeiras, Marsalas, Australian Liqueur
Muscats – find life a lot tougher. Which may help to explain why they are
so often such wonderful bargains.

(Arg) = Argentina; (Au) = Austria; (Aus) = Australia; (Bul) = Bulgaria; (Cal) = California; (Can) = Canada;
(Ch) = Chile; (F) = France; (G) = Germany; (Gr) = Greece; (Hun) = Hungary; (It) = Italy; (NZ) = New
Zealand; (P) = Portugal; (Rom) = Romania; (SA) = South Africa; (Sp) = Spain; (UK) = United Kingdom;
(US) = United States; (Yug) = Yugoslavia

479 MAVRODAPHNE Botrys SA Patras (Gr)

| £3.99 | 🖝TAN BOO | 🍽 m, n, q |

Full of warm, sweet blackcurrant jam and raisins with just a touch of toffee.

480 CASSONS FINE OLD RUBY PORT Smith Woodhouse Douro (P)

| £4.65 | 🖝CWS | 🍽 m, q |

Heavy, lingering aromas of currant fruit. Spicy and well balanced.

481 SAINSBURY'S RUBY PORT Douro (P)

| £4.79 | 🖝 JS | 🍽 m, q |

Soft inviting fruit aromas, smooth silky fruit. Balanced tannin and acidity.

482 SMITH WOODHOUSE RUBY PORT Douro (P)

| £5.45 | 🖝MWW DRI MC WWI U MTL HEM CWG CWM | |
| | | 🍽 m, q |

Does any one know if you can still buy chocolate covered plums? Because if you can't, this wine seems to be a good replacement.

483 TESCO LATE BOTTLED VINTAGE PORT (BOTTLED 1989) Smith Woodhouse 1984 Douro (P)

| £6.29 | 🖝TO | 🍽 m, q |

Young cherryish fruit with moist shag tobacco and old wooden chests.

484 YALUMBA CLOCKTOWER TAWNY Barossa Valley (Aus)

| £6.99 | 🖝AUC LAV WIN | 🍽 m, q |

A good example of Australian 'port' with ripe lush fruit and more than a hint of chocolate and figs.

485 THE SOCIETY'S CRUSTED PORT Douro (P)

| £7.95 | 🖝WSO | 🍽 m, q |

High, high, high society! A deep, dark, young colour with soft spicy cooked jammy fruit. Dry, but with a warming soft texture.

486 WARRE'S WARRIOR VINTAGE CHARACTER PORT Douro (P)

| £7.99 | 🖝 AB SEL DBY WH WID CVR HAR EVI | |
| | | 🍽 m, q |

Full, rich and fruity with a hint of bramble pie sweetness.

487 COSSART GORDON 5 YEAR OLD BUAL Madeira (P)

| £8.40 | 🖝TWR K&B UC DBY HW WCE SV CVR GHL EVI WOI H&D CWG | |
| CPW | | 🍽 n, q |

'Pleasant, well-balanced wine with soft, caramel and toffee flavours and a good, spicy palate'.

488 SMITH WOODHOUSE LATE BOTTLED VINTAGE PORT (BOTTLED 1984) 1979 Douro (P)

| £11.20 | 🖝VW CPL AF DRI GON HW CUM | 🍽 m, q |

Inky-dark and tannic with vanilla and violet flavours. Traditional late-bottled port with real fruity vintage character.

489 HENRIQUES & HENRIQUES 10 YEAR OLD SERCIAL Madeira (P)

| £13.06 | 🖝 RES ROD LV SHV ASK | 🍽 a, b, m, n, q |

Good dry style of Madeira with a hint of caramel and vanilla.

490 HENRIQUES & HENRIQUES 10 YEAR OLD MALMSEY Madeira (P)

| £13.06 | 🖝 RES ROD LV SHV ASK | 🍽 n, q |

Full of rich, raisiny, spicy flavour. Long, complex and woody.

491 WARRE'S QUINTA DA CAVADINHA 1979 Douro (P)

| £13.99 | 🖝AB TH TWR OD GI H&D DRI SUM NIC GON MWW HW | |
| CAC WOC CUM L&W FSW CVR G | | 🍽 m, q |

Soft, warming cherry and plum, with aniseed and dried fruit. Vintage quality at an affordable price.

🖝 For an explanation of stockist abbreviations, see page 17
🍽 For an explanation of food style codes, see page 65

492 BANYULS GRAND CRU SELECT VIEUX L'Etoile 1969 Midi (F)

| £14.99 | ✒HFW CWI | ❯❮ m, n, q |

France's answer to tawny port; this amber coloured wine smells of oranges and is so delicate in style that it barely seems fortified.

493 QUINTA DO NOVAL 20 YEAR OLD TAWNY PORT Douro (P)

| £20.99 | ✒ MM WOC EOO BAT WRW | ❯❮ m, q |

Firm, fruity, raisiny-rich fruit cake wine with a mellow and soothing texture.

494 WARRE'S FINE OLD PORT Douro (P)

| £28.99 | ✒THP | ❯❮ m, q |

A brambley-chocolatey mixture of tawny and vintage: 1966 vintage left in barrel for a decade. Great value, even at this price.

Low- and non-alcohol wines

Not a lot to say about these. They are the best of an uninspiring bunch devised, like caffeine-free coffee and sugar-free sweeteners, to serve the needs of people who are looking for a compromise. So far, the sweetener and 'decaff' manufacturers seem to have got their products rather more right than the low-'n'-non-alcohol brigade. But then, they've been at it for rather longer.

495 SAINSBURY'S MOSCATINO (It)

| £1.49 | ✒JS | ❯❮ o, q, r |

Soft, sweet, grapey, fizzy Moscato with delicious freshness.

496 GOLDENER OKTOBER LIGHT WHITE St Ursula Weinkellerei Rheinhessen (G)

| £1.59 | ✒HAS TO MRS OD W CWS VW FW BTH MRS CWS A |
| | ❯❮ c, o, q, r |

'Sweet, fizzy, juicy', 'very refreshing', 'richly grapey'.

497 LAMBRUSCO LIGHT (BLUSH WHITE) Giacobazzi Emilia-Romagna (It)

| £1.69 | ✒TH PD U TWR | ❯❮ o, q, r |

Blushing pink, with gentle, slighty sweet fruit and a dry finish.

498 ST MICHAEL SPARKLING APERITIF BLUSH Klosterhof (G)

| £1.69 | ✒M&S | ❯❮ q, r |

Another wine from the successful St Michael-Klosterhof team. Very pale pink colour, slight sparkle and soft gentle fruit.

499 PETILLANT DE RAISIN (3%) Listel Midi (F)

| £1.99 | ✒SAF A PD TO DAL VW SAS DRI HPD GHW TAN CNL AB RAV |
| BUD OD TH TWR | ❯❮ q, r |

Gently sparkling wine with an interesting aroma of 'dry honey' and very sweet grapey flavour with good, balancing acidity.

500 GRANTS OF ST JAMES MONTEVERDI ROSSO (3%) Piedmont (It)

| £1.99 | ✒VW TH DBY | ❯❮ q, r |

'Fizzy, cherry red, jammy strawberry fruit'; medium sweet, light and fresh.

THE STOCKISTS

AHC | Ad Hoc Wines

363 Clapham Rd, London SW9 (071 274 7433). Bulgarian capitalism in action: dynamic south London wine warehouse owned by Bulgarian Vintners. **Opening Hours**: 9am - 7.30pm Mon-Fri; 10am - 7.30am Sat; 11am - 3pm Sun. **Delivery:** Free locally; nationally at cost. **Tastings:** Regularly in-store, tutored tastings and theme dinners.

This is, hardly suprisingly, the place to come for the widest possible range of Bulgarian wines at, if grumbles from neighbouring retailers were to be believed, very reasonable prices. Apart from these wines, however, Ad Hoc offers a broad selection, including some particularly inviting Australians and Italians and Bordeaux of both fashionable and unfashionable vintages. A range that's almost majestic...

23	£16.89	**CHAMPAGNE LAURENT PERRIER ROSE**
74	£5.09	**RIOJA BLANCO SECO RESERVA**, CVNE 1985
172	£3.95	**JOAO PIRES WHITE TABLE WINE**, Palmela 1988
174	£4.20	**BROWN BROS LATE HARVEST ORANGE MUSCAT & FLORA**, N E Victoria 1988
243	£2.19	**BULGARIAN COUNTRY WINE**, Merlot/Gamza, Suhindol
266	£2.55	**PLOVDIV CABERNET SAUVIGNON**, Bulgarian Vintners 1985
284	£4.89	**SPECIAL RESERVE STAMBOLOVO MERLOT**, Bulgarian Vintners 1985
292	£5.99	**ORLANDO ST HUGO CABERNET SAUVIGNON**, Coonawarra 1986
297	£8.39	**PENFOLDS BIN 389 SHIRAZ/CABERNET**, South Australia 1986
308	£12.09	**PETALUMA COONAWARRA CABERNET/MERLOT** 1985
311	£11.29	**CHATEAU HAUT-MARBUZET, ST ESTEPHE**, Bordeaux 1985
317	£17.99	**MONDAVI CABERNET SAUVIGNON RESERVE**, Napa Valley 1980
321	£2.00	**CHATEAU GRUAUD-LAROSE (CORDIER), ST JULIEN**, Bordeaux 1978
368	£8.99	**TREFETHEN PINOT NOIR**, Napa Valley 1984
414	£15.59	**TIGNANELLO** Antinori, Tuscany 1985
418	£37.00	**SOLAIA**, Antinori, Tuscany 1986
443	£9.85	**CAMPBELLS RUTHERGLEN MUSCAT**
448	£9.65	**CHATEAU LAMOTHE-GUIGNARD**, Sauternes, Bordeaux 1986
499	£1.99	**PETILLANT DE RAISIN (3%)**, Listel, Midi

ADN | Adnams

East of England Wine Merchant of the Year

The Crown, High Street, Southwold, Suffolk IP18 6DP (0502 724222), & 109 Unthank Rd, Norwich NRZ 2PE (0603 613998) The acceptable face of brewery-owned wine retailing. Independent, wine-by-mail merchant, wine warehouse and kitchen utensil store. **Opening Hours** : Southwold:10am-6pm, Mon - Sat; Norwich 9am-9pmMon - Sat **Delivery:** Included in price for orders of 2 or more cases. Single case surcharge £3.50. **Tastings:** Tutored tastings and theme dinners galore. **Discounts:** Shop case prices are £3 less than mail order; 5% discount for orders of 12 cases and over.

'I have never believed that being representative is a virtue, if that means including dull bottles from dreary regions...Nothing is here "to fill a gap".' Simon Loftus's statement of principle in the 1990 Adnams list is fully supported by a stunning range of wines , and by the depth of his enthusiasm for everything from 1942 Castillo Ygay to 1989 Cloudy Bay.

Although Loftus's catering (the newly refurbished Swan and the Crown at Southwold) and writing interests have led him to hand over the tiller of the business to general managerAlastair Marshall, his imprint is still as evident in Adnams' wines, as in the most entertaining wine list of them all.

Returning to the *en primeur* fray after several years' influential and some might say laudable absence, Adnams has also broken new ground with an Organic Wine Declaration, signed by some 16 of its producers, including Domaine de Chevalier, JL Chave and Robert Mondavi (for his Opus One). And then of course there is The Grapevine Cellar & Kitchen Store, whose cookery utensils are quite as well chosen as the Adnams wines.

3	£5.95	**YALUMBA ANGAS BRUT**, Barossa Valley	
4	£5.20	**ASTI MARTINI**, Martini & Rossi, Piedmont	
16	£14.45	**CHAMPAGNE CUVEE DE RESERVE**, H Billiot	
24	£18.95	**CHAMPAGNE LOUIS ROEDERER BRUT PREMIER**	
28	£3.00	**VIN DE PAYS DES COTES DE GASCOGNE**, Plaimont, South-West 1989	
74	£5.50	**RIOJA BLANCO SECO RESERVA**, CVNE 1985	
84	£7.20	**SCHINUS MOLLE CHARDONNAY**, Mornington Peninsula 1989	
95	£9.95	**CLOUDY BAY CHARDONNAY**, Marlborough 1988	
99	£10.95	**TREFETHEN CHARDONNAY**, Napa Valley 1986	
100	£10.90	**PETALUMA CHARDONNAY**, Adelaide Hills 1987	
129	£5.05	**MONTANA SAUVIGNON BLANC**, Marlborough 1989	
131	£5.75	**QUINCY**, P & J Mardon, Loire 1988	
132	£5.10	**REUILLY**, H Beurdin, Loire 1988	
156	£7.75	**VOUVRAY DEMI-SEC CLOS DE BOURG**, Huet, Loire 1983	
172	£5.20	**JOAO PIRES WHITE TABLE WINE**, Palmela 1988	
174	£4.53	**BROWN BROS LATE HARVEST ORANGE MUSCAT & FLORA**, N E Victoria 1988	
190	£5.50	**SHAWSGATE MULLER THURGAU**, East Anglia 1989	
225	£6.50	**WEHLENER SONNENUHR RIESLING KABINETT**, Dr Loosen, Mosel-Saar-Ruwer 1988	
239	£4.55	**CHATEAU THIEULEY BORDEAUX CLAIRET** 1989	
250	£3.50	**COTEAUX DE MURVIEL DOMAINE DE LIMBARDIE**, Boukandoura & Hutin, Midi 1988	
264	£10.50	**MAS DE DAUMAS GASSAC**, Vin de Pays de l'Hérault, South-West 1988	
269	£3.20	**HOUSE CLARET**, Peter Sichel, Bordeaux	
308	£10.85	**PETALUMA COONAWARRA CABERNET/MERLOT** 1985	
316	£17.90	**PENFOLDS BIN 707 CABERNET SAUVIGNON**, South Australia 1986	
330	£3.95	**COTES DU RHONE**, Château du Grand Moulas 1988	
340	£5.65	**COTES DU RHONE**, Guigal 1986	
345	£7.15	**BAILEYS BUNDARRA SHIRAZ**, Glenrowan 1986	
354	£10.80	**CORNAS**, Guy de Barjac, Rhône 1986	
355	£16.90	**PENFOLDS MAGILL ESTATE**, South Australia 1986	
357	£3.95	**GAILLAC CEPAGE GAMAY**, Jean Cros, South-West 1989	
368	£9.25	**TREFETHEN PINOT NOIR**, Napa Valley 1984	
377	£15.20	**CALERA JENSEN PINOT NOIR**, San Benito 1987	
389	£4.50	**BARDOLINO**, Fraterna Portalupi, Veneto 1988	
428	£5.20	**QUINTA DE CAMARATE**, Fonseca, Azeitão 1985	
435	£8.65	**GRANDE ESCHOLA**, Quinta do Cotto, Douro 1985	
436	£12.85	**RIOJA RESERVA 904**, La Rioja Alta 1976	
437	£9.65	**TINTO PESQUERA**, Fernandez, Ribera del Duero 1986	
462	£18.45	**TORCOLATO**, Maculan, Veneto 1986	
470	£4.80	**AMONTILLADO NAPOLEON**, Hidalgo, Jerez	

DAL | David Alexander

69 Queen St, Maidenhead, Berks SL6 1LT (0628 30295). Independent merchant with sense of humour - 'minimum purchase one bottle'. **Opening Hours:** 10am-7pm Mon; 10am-8.30pm Tue-Thu; 10am-9pm Fri, Sat; 12-2pm Sun. **Delivery:** free locally and West London, nationally at cost. **Tastings:** regularly in-store plus tutored events. **Discounts:** 5% on mixed cases

An interesting operation that claims to be the 'only fully licensed really independent wine merchant in town'. There is undeniably a good all-round range here, though Bordeaux, Armagnac, malt whiskies and liqueurs are especially well represented. Value is high on the list of priorities and David Alexander is not afraid to stock better wines from lesser appellations, such as Delas Côtes du Rhône Villages, in preference to 'name' wines. Oh, and you can also buy draught beer by the pint and Dunkertons cider, made from apples such as Foxwhelp, Redstreak and Brown Snout.

23	£21.00	**CHAMPAGNE LAURENT PERRIER ROSE**
53	£6.20	**SEPPELTS CHARDONNAY**, South-East Australia 1989
61	£13.75	**CHABLIS 1ER CRU VAILLONS**, E Defaix, Burgundy 1985
73	£8.00	**LINDEMANS BIN 65 CHARDONNAY**, Murray River 1989
74	£5.45	**RIOJA BLANCO SECO RESERVA**, CVNE 1985
76	£7.50	**MONTROSE CHARDONNAY**, Mudgee 1989
95	£10.50	**CLOUDY BAY CHARDONNAY**, Marlborough 1988
108	£15.00	**ROSEMOUNT ROXBURGH CHARDONNAY**, Hunter Valley 1987
134	£7.00	**NOBILOS SAUVIGNON BLANC**, Marlborough 1989
138	£7.50	**HUNTERS SAUVIGNON BLANC**, Marlborough 1989
144	£9.75	**MOUNT HURTLE SAUVIGNON BLANC**, McLaren Vale 1989
174	£4.80	**BROWN BROTHERS LATE HARVEST ORANGE MUSCAT & FLORA**, N E Victoria 1988
175	£5.50	**QUADY ESSENSIA ORANGE MUSCAT** 1987
190	£4.75	**SHAWSGATE MULLER THURGAU**, East Anglia 1989
225	£5.80	**WEHLENER SONNENUHR RIESLING KABINETT**, Dr Loosen, Mosel-Saar-Ruwer 1988
244	£3.40	**BOTRYS RED**, Botrys SA, Nemea
262	£4.75	**CORBIERES CHATEAU DE LASTOURS (FUT DE CHENE)**, Midi 1985
267	£2.89	**VIN DE PAYS DE L'AUDE CABERNET SAUVIGNON**, Paul Boutinot, Midi 1987
303	£10.99	**ROUGE HOMME COONAWARRA CABERNET SAUVIGNON** 1985
336	£4.99	**CROZES HERMITAGE**, Delas Frères, Rhône 1988
340	£6.00	**COTES' DU RHONE**, Guigal 1986
387	£3.75	**MONTEPULCIANO D'ABRUZZO**, Tollo, Abruzzi 1987
414	£16.00	**TIGNANELLO**, Antinori, Tuscany 1985
442	£4.50	**MUSCAT DE RIVESALTES**, Château de la Tuilerie, Midi 1988
443	£9.75	**CAMPBELLS RUTHERGLEN MUSCAT**
444	£14.00	**BAILEYS FOUNDERS LIQUEUR MUSCAT**, Glenrowan
454	£7.40	**TOKAY ASZU 5 PUTTONYOS**, Tokaji 1981
491	£15.75	**WARRE'S QUINTA DA CAVADINHA**, Douro 1979
499	£1.99	**PETILLANT DE RAISIN (3%)**, Listel, Midi

HAS | H Allen Smith

24-25 Scala St, London W1P 1LU (071 637 4767) & also at 29 Heath Street, NW3 6TR (071 435 6845) & 56 Lamb's Conduit St, London WC1 (071 405 3106), Ancient and modern city stalwart. **Opening Hours:** 9.30am-6.30pm Mon-Fri; 10am-1pm Sat. **Delivery:** free in Central London, elsewhere depends on quantity. **Tastings:** regularly in-store. **Discounts:** 5% mixed case.

'A traditional merchant with an innovative flair.' Their own description is one with which we would find it difficult to argue. As we have reported in previous *Guides*, H Allen Smith gains greatly from its association with Viniberia and Ehrmanns, two of the most respected wholesalers in the business, and two of the best sources of Iberian and German wines. It would be mischievous for us to wonder which wines from the Royal warrant-holding list are delivered to the Queen Mother - and whether they include the Goldener Oktober Light, a low-alcohol wine for which the firm is UK agent.

5	£5.95	**BRUT DE SAUMUR**, Caves des Vignerons de Saumur, Loire 1987	
24	£19.95	**CHAMPAGNE LOUIS ROEDERER BRUT PREMIER**	
38	£5.30	**ALSACE TOKAY-PINOT GRIS**, Cave Vinicole de Turckheim 1988	
56	£5.65	**LIBRARY COLLECTION CHARDONNAY**, Tiefenbrunner, Trentino-Alto Adige 1988	
81	£6.95	**STONELEIGH CHARDONNAY**, Marlborough 1988	
119	£3.60	**SAUMUR BLANC**, Caves des Vignerons de Saumur, Loire 1988	
135	£4.60	**COOPERS CREEK SAUVIGNON BLANC**, Marlborough 1989	
172	£4.50	**JOAO PIRES WHITE TABLE WINE**, Palmela 1988	
247	£3.39	**VRANAC**, Slovin, Montenegro 1986	
259	£4.25	**COTEAUX D'AIX EN PROVENCE CHATEAU PIGOUDET GRANDE RESERVE**, Midi 1985	
267	£2.95	**VIN DE PAYS DE L'AUDE CABERNET SAUVIGNON**, Paul Boutinot, Midi 1987	
289	£6.90	**CHATEAU BEAUMONT**, Cru Bourgeois Médoc, Bordeaux 1986	
299	£9.95	**CHATEAU RAMAGE LA BATISSE**, Haut-Médoc, Bordeaux 1985	
357	£3.95	**GAILLAC CEPAGE GAMAY**, Jean Cros, South-West 1989	
414	£19.25	**TIGNANELLO**, Antinori, Tuscany 1985	
428	£4.60	**QUINTA DE CAMARATE**, Fonseca, Azeitão 1985	
437	£13.25	**TINTO PESQUERA**, Fernandez, Ribera del Duero 1986	
461	£18.95	**RECIOTO DI SOAVE DEI CAPITELLE**, Anselmi, Veneto 1987	
475	£8.50	**DOS CORTADOS, WILLIAMS & HUMBERT**, Jerez	
496	£1.59	**GOLDENER OKTOBER LIGHT WHITE**, St Ursula Weinkellerei, Rheinhessen	

LAV	Les Amis du Vin

19 Charlotte Street, London W1P 1HB (071 487 3419).
Up-market wine club and small shop,, belonging to Trust House Forte and associated with The Winery (q.v.). Most Les Amis wines are available from The Winery - and vice versa.

A	Asda Stores Ltd

Head Office: Asda House, Southbank, Great Wilson St, Leeds LS11 5AD (0532 435435). Increasingly up-market national supermarket chain with 190 branches. **Opening Hours:** Generally 9am - 8pm Mon - Fri; 9am - 9pm Thurs; 8.30am-8pm Sat. **Tastings**: Once every month in some stores.

As its new stores continue to spring up at the side of every motorway (the company has increased its empire by nearly 60 megastores since last year), Asda perseveres in its quest to interest its customers in the kinds of wines offered by Sainsbury, Tesco and Waitrose. The 'fine wines' list now features such rarities as 1984 Mouton Rothschild (at £30 a bottle), single-estate 1983 white Pernand-Vergelesses and the excellent Château Cruzeau Pessac-Léognan from André Lurton - not to mention the Challenge Gold Medal-winning Guy Mothe 1987 Chablis, Quality is still inconsistent across the range but progress is being made, and a welcome effort is being devoted to increasing the number of organic wines that are listed.

13	£11.99	**ASDA ROSE CHAMPAGNE**
60	£9.99	**CHABLIS 1ER CRU FOURCHAUME**, Guy Mothe, Burgundy 1987
127	£3.99	**MUSCADET DE SEVRE ET MAINE SUR LIE**, G Bossard, Loire 1989
129	£4.99	**MONTANA SAUVIGNON BLANC**, Marlborough 1989
149	£3.29	**CHENIN BLANC**, E & J Gallo 1988
233	£3.29	**WHITE GRENACHE**, E & J Gallo 1989
420	£2.39	**DON DARIAS VINO DE MESA**, Bodegas Vitorianas, Alto Ebro
443	£8.45	**CAMPBELLS RUTHERGLEN MUSCAT**
496	£1.59	**GOLDENER OKTOBER LIGHT WHITE**, St Ursula Weinkellerei, Rheinhessen
499	£1.99	**PETILLANT DE RAISIN (3%)**, Listel, Midi

ASK | Askham Wines

Askham, Via Newark, Notts NG22 0RP (077 783 659). Independent country merchant.**Opening Hours:** ring to arrange an appointment. **Delivery:** free nationally for orders over £50. **Tastings:** occasionally in-store plus tutored events.

At first sight, this Nottinghamshire merchant's list seems brief. It is only when you pick your way through it that you discover how carefully each selection has been made. The range is full of surprises, including wines from Rose Creek in Idaho and Jura dating back to 1964. It is easy to discern the skilful hand of Paul Boutinot among Askham's suppliers; his is the company that has made such a success of the Cave de Turckheim's Alsaces.

Askham may be able to boast another distinction; it might well be the only independent wine merchant to be run by the headmaster of an Independent School (which gives a whole new meaning to the words 'Class Growth').

29	£3.29	**VIN DE PAYS DES COTES DE GASCOGNE**, Domaine de Perras, South-West 1989
38	£4.29	**ALSACE TOKAY-PINOT GRIS**, Cave Vinicole de Turckheim 1988
41	£4.29	**ALSACE PINOT BLANC**, Cave Vinicole de Turckheim 1989
109	£15.00	**CHATEAU DE FIEUZAL**, Graves, Bordeaux 1986
134	£6.45	**NOBILOS SAUVIGNON BLANC**, Marlborough 1989
168	£15.00	**ALSACE GEWURZTRAMINER SELECTION DE GRAINS NOBLES**, Cave Vinicole de Turckheim 1988
172	£4.49	**JOAO PIRES WHITE TABLE WINE**, Palmela 1988
174	£4.89	**BROWN BROTHERS LATE HARVEST ORANGE MUSCAT & FLORA**, N E Victoria 1988
196	£8.99	**ALSACE RIESLING GRAND CRU BRAND**, Cave Vinicole de Turckheim 1985
262	£5.40	**CORBIERES CHATEAU DE LASTOURS (FUT DE CHENE)**, Midi 1985
267	£2.75	**VIN DE PAYS DE L'AUDE CABERNET SAUVIGNON**, Paul Boutinot, Midi 1987
298	£8.50	**CHATEAU LA TOUR DE BY, HAUT-MEDOC**, Bordeaux 1986
299	£8.50	**CHATEAU RAMAGE LA BATISSE**, Haut-Médoc, Bordeaux 1985
303	£9.50	**ROUGE HOMME COONAWARRA CABERNET SAUVIGNON** 1985
326	£2.99	**COTES DU VENTOUX**, Paul Boutinot, Rhone 1989
337	£5.25	**ROUGE HOMME SHIRAZ/CABERNET**, Coonawarra 1985
489	£13.06	**HENRIQUES & HENRIQUES 10 YEAR OLD SERCIAL**, Madeira
490	£13.06	**HENRIQUES & HENRIQUES 10 YEAR OLD MALMSEY**, Madeira

| AUC | Australian Wine Centre |

Down Under, South Australia House, 50 The Strand, London WC2 (071 925 0751). Specialist merchant buried in a cellar. **Delivery:** free nationally. **Tastings:** regularly in-store. **Discounts:** 5% collection discount.

The demise of Ostlers - reported in last year's *Guide* - and the closure of Alex Findlater's north London shop might have left those of the capital's Australian wine lovers who only want to buy a single bottle feeling rather at a loss. Fortunately, as many of them soon discovered, there was life after Ostlers - in the shape of The Drunken Mouse and the Australian Wine Centre, two companies that shared a common list of Antipodean wines. Today, the Drunken Mouse has been trapped by a major chain (rumour has it that the shop will soon become an Oddbins), and all Margaret Francis's efforts are directed towards the Australian Wine Centre 'down under' South Australia House. If you want it - and it's Australian - here it is, come and get it...

3	£5.99	YALUMBA ANGAS BRUT, Barossa Valley
9	£9.99	WILSONS PINOT NOIR/CHARDONNAY, Adelaide Hills
37	£4.99	HARDY'S BIRD SERIES CHARDONNAY, South Australia 1989
52	£6.99	HOUGHTON VERDELHO, Swan Valley 1988
53	£5.99	SEPPELTS CHARDONNAY, South-East Australia 1989
64	£5.49	HARDY'S NOTTAGE HILL SEMILLON, South Australia 1989
73	£5.49	LINDEMANS BIN 65 CHARDONNAY, Murray River 1989
76	£6.99	MONTROSE CHARDONNAY, Mudgee 1989
78	£6.69	MITCHELTON MARSANNE, Goulburn Valley 1987
79	£6.99	CHATEAU TAHBILK MARSANNE-CHARDONNAY, Goulburn Valley 1987
80	£6.99	WOLF BLASS BARREL-FERMENTED CHARDONNAY, South Australia 1988
84	£12.49	SCHINUS MOLLE CHARDONNAY, Mornington Peninsula 1989
87	£8.59	PENFOLDS CHARDONNAY, South Australia 1988
97	£11.49	COLDSTREAM HILLS CHARDONNAY, Yarra Valley 1988
98	£12.99	GEOFF MERRILL CHARDONNAY, McLaren Vale 1987
100	£11.99	PETALUMA CHARDONNAY, Adelaide Hills 1987
101	£13.99	MOUNTADAM CHARDONNAY, High Eden Ridge 1989
106	£13.99	LEEUWIN ESTATE CHARDONNAY, Margaret River 1984
107	£14.99	CULLENS CHARDONNAY, Margaret River 1987
108	£15.99	ROSEMOUNT ROXBURGH CHARDONNAY, Hunter Valley 1987
133	£7.99	HILL-SMITH ESTATE SAUVIGNON BLANC, Barossa Valley 1989
144	£9.99	MOUNT HURTLE SAUVIGNON BLANC, McLaren Vale 1989
174	£5.49	BROWN BROS LATE HARVEST ORANGE MUSCAT & FLORA, N E Victoria 1988
181	£4.99	SEAVIEW RHINE RIESLING, South East Australia 1987
191	£7.99	HENSCHKE RIESLING, Barossa Valley 1987
277	£4.49	SEAVIEW CABERNET SAUVIGNON, South Australia 1985
285	£6.99	DAVID WYNN CABERNET, High Eden Ridge 1986
288	£7.99	PETER LEHMANN CABERNET SAUVIGNON, Barossa Valley 1985
292	£7.99	ORLANDO ST HUGO CABERNET SAUVIGNON, Coonawarra 1986
294	£7.99	ROSEMOUNT SHOW RESERVE COONAWARRA CABERNET SAUVIGNON 1987
297	£7.99	PENFOLDS BIN 389 SHIRAZ/CABERNET, South Australia 1986
303	£9.99	ROUGE HOMME COONAWARRA CABERNET SAUVIGNON 1985
307	£11.99	LAKE'S FOLLY CABERNET SAUVIGNON, Hunter Valley 1987
308	£10.99	PETALUMA COONAWARRA CABERNET/MERLOT 1985
310	£11.99	CYRIL HENSCHKE CABERNET SAUVIGNON, Henschke, Barossa Valley 1986
315	£17.99	WYNNS JOHN RIDDOCH CABERNET SAUVIGNON, Coonawarra 1985
316	£18.99	PENFOLDS BIN 707 CABERNET SAUVIGNON, South Australia 1986
337	£5.49	ROUGE HOMME SHIRAZ/CABERNET, Coonawarra 1985
338	£5.49	WYNNS COONAWARRA SHIRAZ 1987
339	£5.99	PENFOLDS BIN 28 KALIMNA SHIRAZ, South Australia 1986

345	£7.49	**BAILEYS BUNDARRA SHIRAZ,** Glenrowan 1986	
346	£6.99	**RYECROFT SHIRAZ,** McLaren Vale 1986	
355	£17.99	**PENFOLDS MAGILL ESTATE,** South Australia 1986	
371	£11.49	**COLDSTREAM HILLS PINOT NOIR,** Yarra Valley 1988	
382	£26.99	**YARRA YERING PINOT NOIR,** Yarra Valley 1987	
441	£7.99	**MORRIS RUTHERGLEN LIQUEUR MUSCAT**	
443	£12.99	**CAMPBELLS RUTHERGLEN MUSCAT**	
444	£12.49	**BAILEYS FOUNDERS LIQUEUR MUSCAT,** Glenrowan	
452	£6.99	**PETER LEHMANN BOTRYTIS RIESLING,** Barossa Valley 1984	
484	£6.99	**YALUMBA CLOCK TOWER TAWNY,** Barossa Valley	

AV — Averys of Bristol

7 Park Street, Bristol BS1 5NG (0272 214141). Traditional merchant and a Bristol institution. **Opening Hours:** 9am-6pm Mon-Fri; 9am-5pm Sat. **Delivery:** free locally, nationally at cost. **Tastings:** regularly in-store plus tutored events. **Discounts:** negotiable.

Averys' reputation as a source for port, sherry, old Burgundy and Bordeaux is so firmly established that it may come as some suprise to many people to learn that this Bristol firm is actually far more active as a purveyor of the kind of New World Wines listed below. The Inniskillin Chardonnay is only one of six Canadian wines listed, alongside Californian wines like Sonoma-Cutrer and illustrious Australians such as Lindemans' Pyrus. But for real traditionalists, there is a range of old bottles - such as the 1875 vintage Bastardo Madeira, for example.

57	£7.22	**INNISKILLIN CHARDONNAY,** Niagara 1988	
134	£6.64	**NOBILOS SAUVIGNON BLANC,** Marlborough 1989	
303	£10.11	**ROUGE HOMME COONAWARRA CABERNET SAUVIGNON** 1985	
337	£5.25	**ROUGE HOMME SHIRAZ/CABERNET,** Coonawarra 1985	
442	£7.62	**MUSCAT DE RIVESALTES,** Château de la Tuilerie, Midi 1988	

BH — B H Wines

Boustead Hill House, Boustead Hill, Burgh-by-Sands, Carlisle, Cumbria CA5 6AA (0228 76 711). Independent merchant. **Opening Hours:** phone first to check. **Delivery:** free locally, nationally at cost. **Tastings:** occasionally in-store plus tutored events.

This Solway Firth independent merchant (the most north-westerly in the country) has received a great deal of well-earned praise for its reasonable prices; it deserves similar recognition for the quality of the wines it lists. From 1983 Château Branaire-Ducru (at £13) to Apremont (at £4.10), the excellent young-vines table wine from the La Chablisienne cooperative (at £4.49) and Ramos Pinto 20 year-old Quinta da Bom Retiro tawny (at £15.50), these are all precisely the kinds of affordable, high quality wine that makes this one of the best merchants in Britain.

22	£17.48	**CHAMPAGNE BRICOUT CARTE D'OR BRUT PRESTIGE**	
46	£4.44	**SOAVE CASTEGGIOLA,** G Rizzardi, Veneto 1987	
74	£5.16	**RIOJA BLANCO SECO RESERVA,** CVNE 1985	
80	£5.39	**WOLF BLASS BARREL-FERMENTED CHARDONNAY,** South Australia 1988	
81	£5.75	**STONELEIGH CHARDONNAY,** Marlborough 1988	
125	£4.54	**VOUVRAY, CHEVALIER DE MONCONTOUR,** Loire	

166	£8.06	MARK WEST VINEYARDS GEWURZTRAMINER, Sonoma 1988
174	£4.07	BROWN BROTHERS LATE HARVEST ORANGE MUSCAT & FLORA, N E Victoria 1988
266	£2.49	PLOVDIV CABERNET SAUVIGNON, Bulgarian Vintners 1985
290	£6.22	FIRESTONE CABERNET SAUVIGNON, Santa Ynez 1986
331	£4.29	RASTEAU COTES DU RHONE VILLAGES, Caves des Vignerons de Rasteau 1988

DB   David Baillie Vintners

At the Sign of the Lucky Horseshoe, Longbrook St, Exeter (0392 221345). Wholesale merchant with small retail line. **Opening Hours:** 9am-6pm Mon-Sat. **Delivery:** free for mainland UK. **Tastings:** to groups on request. **Discounts:** negotiable.

The retail arm of Horseshoe Wines' wholesale business, David Baillie has every reason to offer an impressive range of wines from Washington State, because this is a part of the USA in which they have several exclusive agencies. Apart from these, however, there are well chosen traditional selections from Burgundy, Bordeaux and Germany to satisfy the conservative wine drinkers of the West Country.

| 138 | £6.95 | HUNTERS SAUVIGNON BLANC, Marlborough 1989 |
| 286 | £5.79 | COLUMBIA CREST CABERNET SAUVIGNON, Washington State 1985 |

BWS   The Barnes Wine Shop

51 Barnes High St, London SW13 9LN (081 878 8643). Modern independent retailer with enthusiastic staff and customers. **Opening Hours:** 9.30am-8.30pm Mon-Sat; 12-2pm Sun. **Delivery:** free locally, nationally at cost. **Tastings:** bottles always open plus regular tutored events.

This little shop has become such an institution that is hard to believe that it is still one of the youngest merchants in London. Like *The Independent*, a newspaper we suspect many of the local customers read, Francis Murray's company has the feel of a business that has always been there. The Saturday morning informal tastings are so popular that a riverside wit was inspired to suggest that at least one Barnes resident had sold his weekend place in the country. The expected range of good, and often unusual, ready-to-drink wines was expanded this year to include a short list of emphatically unready 1989 *en primeur* Bordeaux. Barnes may have equals among Britain's independent wine shops; there is none that is better.

22	£14.95	CHAMPAGNE BRICOUT CARTE D'OR BRUT PRESTIGE
41	£3.95	ALSACE PINOT BLANC, Cave Vinicole de Turckheim 1989
43	£4.69	PINOT BIANCO, VIGNA AL MONTE, Puglia 1989
59	£8.95	PINOT BIANCO, Jermann, Friuli-Venezia Giulia 1988
65	£5.49	VIN DE PAYS DES COTES DE GASCOGNE DOMAINE DU TARIQUET CUVEE BOIS, Grassa, South-West
73	£5.49	LINDEMANS BIN 65 CHARDONNAY, Murray River 1989
74	£5.95	RIOJA BLANCO SECO RESERVA, CVNE 1985
76	£6.95	MONTROSE CHARDONNAY, Mudgee 1989
110	£16.45	ZD CHARDONNAY, Napa Valley 1987
129	£4.99	MONTANA SAUVIGNON BLANC, Marlborough 1989
132	£6.45	REUILLY, H Beurdin, Loire 1988
175	£10.95	QUADY ESSENSIA ORANGE MUSCAT 1987

228	£7.99	**GRAACHER HIMMELREICH RIESLING SPATLESE**, F W Gymnasium, Mosel-Saar-Ruwer 1988
247	£3.39	**VRANAC**, Slovin, Montenegro 1986
284	£4.99	**SPECIAL RESERVE STAMBOLOVO MERLOT**, Bulgarian Vintners 1985
287	£6.45	**RAIMAT CABERNET SAUVIGNON**, Lerida 1985
337	£5.45	**ROUGE HOMME SHIRAZ/CABERNET**, Coonawarra 1985
373	£11.75	**AU BON CLIMAT PINOT NOIR** 1988
408	£10.75	**PRUNAIO**, Landini, Tuscany 1986
473	£8.45	**DON ZOILO MANZANILLA**, Sanlúcar de Barrameda

AB	Augustus Barnett Ltd

Head Office: North Woolwich Rd, Silvertown, London E16 2BN (071 476 1477). Brewery-owned (Bass), 645 shop-strong High Street chain. **Opening Hours:** 10am-10pm Mon-Sat: 12-2pm Sun. **Delivery:** check for each outlet. **Tastings:** occasionally. **Discounts:** on mixed cases.

After the criticisms we have made in previous editions of the*Guide,* it is a real pleasure to be able to report that the management of Augustus Barnett has finally decided to compete with their more go-ahead neighbours in the High Street. Despite what must have been a distracting period when the company was openly for sale, Peter Carr MW, the wine buyer, has put together a generally creditable and occasionally very impressive range. Bass's disposal of most of its other wine interests has clearly allowedCarr the freedom not to have to buy 'in-house', and thus to purchase better wines.

4	£5.49	**ASTI MARTINI**, Martini & Rossi, Piedmont
28	£2.89	**VIN DE PAYS DES COTES DE GASCOGNE** Plaimont, South-West 1989
40	£4.25	**COOKS MARLBOROUGH SEMILLON** 1987
49	£5.99	**BABICH SEMILLON/CHARDONNAY**, Gisborne 1989
73	£5.19	**LINDEMANS BIN 65 CHARDONNAY**, Murray River 1989
80	£5.95	**WOLF BLASS BARREL-FERMENTED CHARDONNAY**, South Australia 1988
128	£4.79	**MUSCADET DE SEVRE ET MAINE**, Château de la Ragotière, Loire 1988
129	£4.79	**MONTANA SAUVIGNON BLANC**, Marlborough 1989
149	£2.99	**CHENIN BLANC**, E & J Gallo 1988
157	£2.55	**RETSINA OF ATTICA**, Kourtaki
172	£4.99	**JOAO PIRES WHITE TABLE WINE**, Palmela 1988
177	£2.79	**BADEN DRY**, ZBW
233	£2.99	**WHITE GRENACHE**, E & J Gallo 1989
284	£3.19	**SPECIAL RESERVE STAMBOLOVO MERLOT**, Bulgarian Vintners 1985
320	£17.45	**CHATEAU LYNCH-BAGES**, Pauillac, Bordeaux 1985
336	£4.39	**CROZES HERMITAGE**, Delas Frères, Rhône 1988
379	£16.95	**VOSNE-ROMANEE LES MALCONSORTS**, Moillard, Burgundy 1986
387	£2.99	**MONTEPULCIANO D'ABRUZZO**, Tollo, Abruzzi 1987
399	£5.69	**CAMPO FIORIN**, Masi, Veneto 1985
400	£5.99	**CABERNET RISERVA**, Lageder, Trentino-Alto Adige 1986
421	£2.95	**VINA ALBALI RESERVA**, Felix Solis, Valdepeñas 1983
427	£4.89	**DUERO**, Bodegas Peñalba 1985
486	£7.59	**WARRE'S WARRIOR VINTAGE CHARACTER PORT**, Douro
491	£11.49	**WARRE'S QUINTA DA CAVADINHA**, Douro 1979
499	£2.19	**PETILLANT DE RAISIN (3%)**, Listel, Midi

BAT	The Battersea Wine Company

4 Battersea Rise, London SW11 1ED (071-924 3631). Promising new, independent merchant.

Opening Hours: 12-9pm Mon-Fri; 10.30am-9pm Sat; 1-2pm & 7pm-10pm Sun. **Delivery:** free locally, elsewhere £5 per case. **Tastings:** monthly tutored tastings. **Discounts:** variable on whole cases.

After working as cellar manager for the Wine Society, Michael Gould has decided to start what he describes as a 'complete wine merchant's service' to customers living on both sides of this up-and-coming part of the Thames, and to City boardrooms. The list is quite adventurous, including magnums of 1982 Cahors and the rare Passing Clouds Shiraz-Cabernet from Australia as well as a commendable selection of young-to mature classics from Bordeaux and Burgundy. Prices are very fair.

74	£5.49	**RIOJA BLANCO SECO RESERVA**, CVNE 1985
90	£8.69	**CHATEAU CONSTANTIN**, Graves, Bordeaux 1986
107	£13.99	**CULLENS CHARDONNAY**, Margaret River 1987
122	£4.45	**SAUVIGNON DE TOURAINE DOMAINE DE LA PRESLE**, Jean-Marie Penet, Loire 1988
138	£6.95	**HUNTERS SAUVIGNON BLANC**, Marlborough 1989
161	£5.25	**ALSACE GEWURZTRAMINER DAMBACH**, Louis Gisselbrecht 1988
174	£4.89	**BROWN BROTHERS LATE HARVEST ORANGE MUSCAT & FLORA**, N E Victoria 1988
236	£4.20	**TORRES CABERNET SAUVIGNON ROSE**, Curico 1989
276	£3.89	**CONCHA Y TORO MERLOT**, Maipo 1986
340	£5.49	**COTES DU RHONE**, Guigal 1986
372	£11.48	**SAVIGNY-LES-BEAUNE PREMIER CRU LES LAVIERES**, Domaine Chandon de Briailles, Burgundy 1986
493	£20.99	**QUINTA DO NOVAL 20 YEAR OLD TAWNY PORT**, Douro

| **TBS** | **Thomas Baty & Son Ltd** See Willoughbys |

| **BEN** | **Bennetts** |

High St, Chipping Camden, Glos GL55 6AG (0386 840392). Blossoming independent merchant. **Opening Hours:** 9am-1pm & 2pm-5.30pm Mon-Sat. **Delivery:** free within 50 miles, nationally at cost. **Tastings:** regularly in-store plus tutored events. **Discounts:** 5% on mixed cases.

A five-year old merchant with all the bustling enthusiasm of children of that age, Bennetts makes its first entry into the *Guide* in some style. Like most value and flavour-oriented merchants, Charles Bennett has unsurprisingly made certain that his list is well filled with wines from the New World, but the traditional regions of Europe are well represented too, with such rare delights as Jean Bourdy's 1979 Château-Chalon Vin Jaune from the Jura. Future plans include a greater emphasis on 'fine and rare'.

3	£5.65	**YALUMBA ANGAS BRUT**, Barossa Valley
24	£18.25	**CHAMPAGNE LOUIS ROEDERER BRUT PREMIER**
73	£5.45	**LINDEMANS BIN 65 CHARDONNAY**, Murray River 1989
79	£6.90	**CHATEAU TAHBILK MARSANNE-CHARDONNAY**, Goulburn Valley 1987
80	£6.17	**WOLF BLASS BARREL-FERMENTED CHARDONNAY**, South Australia 1988
81	£6.60	**STONELEIGH CHARDONNAY**, Marlborough 1988
86	£8.44	**MUSCADET DE SEVRE ET MAINE SUR LIE CHATEAU DE CHASSELOIR (OAK-AGED)**, Loire 1987
92	£8.74	**SIMI CHARDONNAY**, Sonoma 1985
95	£9.95	**CLOUDY BAY CHARDONNAY**, Marlborough 1988

114	£16.90	**YARRA YERING CHARDONNAY**, Yarra Valley 1987
138	£6.99	**HUNTERS SAUVIGNON BLANC**, Marlborough 1989
167	£13.25	**ALSACE GEWURZTRAMINER GRAND CRU KESSLER**, Schlumberger 1985
174	£4.98	**BROWN BROTHERS LATE HARVEST ORANGE MUSCAT & FLORA**, N E Victoria 1988
175	£5.65	**QUADY ESSENSIA ORANGE MUSCAT** 1987
192	£7.03	**ALSACE RIESLING RESERVE**, Schlumberger 1986
194	£5.68	**DEINHARD HERITAGE SELECTION DEIDESHEIM**, Rheinpfalz 1987
303	£10.11	**ROUGE HOMME COONAWARRA CABERNET SAUVIGNON** 1985
308	£11.78	**PETALUMA COONAWARRA CABERNET / MERLOT** 1985
364	£6.95	**MORGON JEAN DESCOMBES**, Georges Duboeuf, Beaujolais 1989
377	£15.25	**CALERA JENSEN PINOT NOIR**, San Benito 1987
378	£15.99	**MONDAVI PINOT NOIR RESERVE**, Napa Valley 1986
382	£27.30	**YARRA YERING PINOT NOIR**, Yarra Valley 1987
436	£10.95	**RIOJA RESERVA 904**, La Rioja Alta 1976
449	£5.35	**CHATEAU DES COULINATS**, Ste-Croix-du-Mont, Bordeaux 1983
472	£7.20	**DON ZOILO VERY OLD FINO**, Jerez

BBR | Berry Bros & Rudd

3 St James St, London SW1A 1EG (071 839 9033) & The Wine Shop, Houndmills, Basingstoke RG21 2YB (0256 23566). Traditional family merchants since the 1690s. **Opening Hours:** 9.30am-5pm Mon-Fri. **Delivery:** free nationally. **Tastings:** regularly in-store plus tutored events. **Discounts:** 3% on two cases, 5% on five cases, 7.5% on ten cases.

Despite maintaining its Dickensian St James's shop, Berry Bros has cast off much of its 17th century trappings. The business is now fully computerised and such emphatically modern wines have been introduced as Vin de Pays des Côtes de Gascogne and Petaluma Chardonnay. But a careful reading of Berry's list reveals attitudes that are rather endearingly at odds with the current obsession with single-domaine, estate-bottled wines. If you want to buy 'London-bottled' wines and 'old-fashioned' Burgundy, from a truly courteous company, you should look no further.

24	£18.20	**CHAMPAGNE LOUIS ROEDERER BRUT PREMIER**
65	£5.52	**VIN DE PAYS DES COTES DE GASCOGNE DOMAINE DU TARIQUET CUVEE BOIS**, Grassa, South-West
125	£5.00	**VOUVRAY**, Chevalier de Moncontour, Loire
216	£6.65	**SCHARZHOFBERGER KABINETT KESSELSTATT**, Mosel-Saar-Ruwer 1988
266	£3.25	**PLOVDIV CABERNET SAUVIGNON**, Bulgarian Vintners 1985
279	£4.38	**CHATEAU DE ELLIEZ**, Bordeaux 1983
284	£5.98	**SPECIAL RESERVE STAMBOLOVO MERLOT**, Bulgarian Vintners 1985
288	£6.50	**PETER LEHMANN CABERNET SAUVIGNON**, Barossa Valley 1985
308	£12.95	**PETALUMA COONAWARRA CABERNET / MERLOT** 1985
310	£13.50	**CYRIL HENSCHKE CABERNET SAUVIGNON**, Henschke, Barossa Valley 1986
315	£15.20	**WYNNS JOHN RIDDOCH CABERNET SAUVIGNON**, Coonawarra 1985
319	£20.00	**CHATEAU PICHON-LONGUEVILLE-BARON**, Pauillac, Bordeaux 1985
320	£22.60	**CHATEAU LYNCH-BAGES**, Pauillac, Bordeaux 1985
445	£2.80	**CHATEAU DES TOURS**, Ste-Croix-du-Mont, Bordeaux 1986
454	£7.50	**TOKAY ASZU 5 PUTTONYOS**, Tokaji 1981

| BI | Bibendum |

London Wine Merchant of the Year

113 Regents Park Road, London NW1 8UR (071 586 9761). High-class by-the-case merchant
.**Opening Hours:** 10am-8pm Mon-Sat. **Delivery:** free within London, nationally at cost. **Tastings:**
regularly in-store plus tutored events.

In the eight years since it was launched, Bibendum has become one of the
best-known and best-appreciated merchants in London. Widely thought of
as a wine warehouse, this is in fact the modern equivalent of the ideal
traditional merchant, offering wines *en primeur*, cellar valuations and lots of
rare, old wines, ranging from a single bottle of Château Latour 1949 to a case
of 1978 Chablis Premier Cru from Moreau.

Esoteric wines like these, however, are a sideline to Bibendum's main
business of selling highly representative examples of the best of Burgundy,
the Rhône (a particularly impressive selection), Italy and the New World.
This, for instance, is the place to find the Cameron Pinot Noir - probably the
best produced in Oregon - and Elizabetta Fagiuoli's extraordinary Vernaccia di San Gimignano.

Bibendum is a company whose wines sometimes do not always dazzle
as brightly at blind tastings as those of some of their competitors, often
because of their subtlety of style. This year, though, the Wine Challenge saw
an impressive set of Bibendum award winners, the sheer range of which
says much about the company style. Bibendum remains one of the few wine
merchants from whom wine writers - and other merchants - like to buy their
wine.

23	£19.68	CHAMPAGNE LAURENT PERRIER ROSE
24	£18.89	CHAMPAGNE LOUIS ROEDERER BRUT PREMIER
39	£4.98	HILL-SMITH PIGGOT HILL SEMILLON, South Australia 1988
88	£8.83	CHATEAU COUHINS-LURTON, Graves, Lurton, Bordeaux 1987
94	£9.94	CHARDONNAY PORTICO DEI LEONI, Vinattieri, Veneto 1986
127	£4.95	MUSCADET DE SEVRE ET MAINE SUR LIE, G Bossard, Loire 1989
139	£7.56	SANCERRE, Henry Natter, Loire 1988
156	£8.87	VOUVRAY DEMI-SEC CLOS DE BOURG, Huet, Loire 1983
162	£6.37	ALSACE AUXERROIS MOENCHREBEN RORSCHWIHR, Rolly Gassmann 1987
296	£7.75	ST JULIEN, Anthony Barton, Bordeaux 1985
304	£9.65	ROSSO SECONDO, Vinattieri, Tuscany 1985
308	£12.43	PETALUMA COONAWARRA CABERNET/MERLOT 1985
377	£16.59	CALERA JENSEN PINOT NOIR, San Benito 1987
407	£9.45	CASTELLO DI CAMIGLIANO ROSSO, Tuscany 1986
432	£6.22	RIOJA RESERVA, Beronia 1982
435	£8.19	GRANDE ESCHOLA, Quinta do Cotto, Douro 1985
450	£5.75	DOMAINE DU NOBLE (DEJEAN PERE & FILS), Loupiac, Bordeaux 1986

| BIN | Bin 89 Wine Warehouse |

89 Trippet Lane, Sheffield S1 4EL (0742 755889). Independent one-man operation. **Opening Hours:**
11am-6pm Tue-Fri; 10am-1pm Sat. **Delivery:** free within South Yorkshire, nationally at cost.
Tastings: occasionally, by invitation. **Discounts:** negotiable on large orders.

In last year's *Guide*, we reported that Jonathan Park was installing a wine
bar in his wine warehouse. Today, that new venture is operational, allowing
customers to sample wines from Bin Ends' 350-strong list at their leisure.

The selection at any given time is generally good and fairly priced. Unfortunately, it tends to change very frequently (there are four lists a year) and quantities of specific wines are often limited. Which explains why it has been impossible for us to indicate specific recommendations.

BND | Bin Ends

83-85 Badsley Moor Lane, Rotherham S65 2PH (0709 367771) & Pavilion House, Oswaldskirk, York (04393 504). Independent merchant selling by the bottle in Rotherham and by the case in Oswaldskirk. **Opening Hours:** 10am-5.30pm Mon-Fri; 9.30am-12.30pm Sat. **Delivery:** free locally, nationally at cost. **Tastings:** regularly in-store plus tutored events. **Discounts:** 5% on unbroken cases.

Patrick Toone sells wine by the case as 'Patrick Toone Personal Wine Merchant' and by the bottle here at his South Yorkshire shop. The range is sound and well-structured without being exciting, including such familiar names as Rosemount, Concha y Toro, Berberana and Gallo, as well as a good set of single-domaine Burgundies.

23	£18.50	**CHAMPAGNE LAURENT PERRIER ROSE**	
24	£18.75	**CHAMPAGNE LOUIS ROEDERER BRUT PREMIER**	
74	£5.49	**RIOJA BLANCA SECO RESERVA**, CVNE 1985	
86	£7.49	**MUSCADET DE SEVRE ET MAINE SUR LIE CHATEAU DE CHASSLOIR (OAK-AGED)**, Loire 1987	
174	£4.89	**BROWN BROTHERS LATE HARVEST ORANGE MUSCAT & FLORA**, NE Victoria, 1988	
276	£3.89	**CONCHA Y TORO MERLOT**, Maipo 1986	
282	£4.95	**MONTES CABERNET SAUVIGNON**, Discover Wine, Curico Valley 1987	
294	£7.85	**ROSEMOUNT SHOW RESERVE COONAWARRA CABERNET SAUVIGNON** 1987	
405	£7.99	**BAROLO RISERVA**, Borgogno, Piedmont 1982	

BLW | Blayneys

Head Office: Riverside Rd, Sunderland SR5 3JW (091 548 4488). 190-branch specialist chain in Tyne and Wear and the Birmingham area. **Opening Hours:** 10am-10pm Mon-Sat: 12-2pm & 7pm-9.30pm Sun **Delivery:** free locally (certain branches), nationally at cost. **Tastings:** occasionally in-store plus tutored events. **Discounts:** 5% on 1-4 cases, 7.5% on 5+ cases.

Bill Ridley has no doubts about his objective for Blayneys: to 'catch up with - and then overtake - some of the more glamorous operators further south'. To judge by Blayneys' successes in the 1990 Challenge, this 190-branch chain is certainly heading in the right direction, though there is still a long way to go. The Italian selection is one of the strongest areas of the list, but there are some highlights among the Bordeaux, including a 1979 Château Gruaud Larose and 1978 Château Pavie at £16.99 and £19.45 respectively.

23	£18.85	**CHAMPAGNE LAURENT PERRIER ROSE**	
68	£4.08	**BERGERAC SEC DOMAINE DE GRANDCHAMP**, Nick Ryman, South-West 1988	
149	£3.29	**CHENIN BLANC**, E & J Gallo 1988	
174	£5.45	BROWN BROTHERS LATE HARVEST ORANGE MUSCAT & FLORA. N E Victoria 1988	
401	£6.75	**CHIANTI CLASSICO RISERVA DUCALE**, Ruffino, Tuscany 1986	
413	£15.69	**CABREO IL BORGO**, Ruffino, Tuscany 1986	
451	£5.59	**CHATEAU LA NERE**, Dulac & Seraphon, Loupiac, Bordeaux 1986	

BOO	Booths (of Stockport)

62 Heaton Moor Road, Stockport, Cheshire SK4 4NZ (061 432 3309). Independent family merchant. **Delivery:** free locally. **Tastings:** regularly in-store plus tutored tastings. **Discounts:** 5% on mixed case, 7.5% on unbroken case.

'We are fortunate that our customers are relatively well off...We find most of them are adventurous...In fact it is easier to sell a £6 sparkling wine from Australia or a £5 Corbières than a £6 Bourgogne Pinot Noir.' The general provisions store Graham and John Booth's father opened in 1955 in this Manchester and Stockport suburb has gradually been taken over by a range of wines that are ideally suited to all those well-heeled adventurous palates. A strong competitor to nearby Cadwgan - with the added attraction of a range of bread (including Ukrainian), cheese, smoked salmon and trout... The following list of Challenge Award winners speaks for itself.

3	£5.75	**YALUMBA ANGAS BRUT**, Barossa Valley	
22	£16.90	**CHAMPAGNE BRICOUT CARTE D'OR BRUT PRESTIGE**	
29	£3.30	**VIN DE PAYS DES COTES DE GASCOGNE**, Domaine de Perras, South-West 1989	
38	£4.40	**ALSACE TOKAY-PINOT GRIS**, Cave Vinicole de Turckheim 1988	
41	£4.00	**ALSACE PINOT BLANC**, Cave Vinicole de Turckheim 1989	
42	£4.40	**ALSACE SYLVANER HEIMBOURG**, Cave Vinicole de Turckheim 1987	
49	£5.50	**BABICH SEMILLON/CHARDONNAY**, Gisborne 1989	
52	£5.80	**HOUGHTON VERDELHO**, Swan Valley 1988	
76	£6.10	**MONTROSE CHARDONNAY**, Mudgee 1989	
84	£8.40	**SCHINUS MOLLE CHARDONNAY**, Mornington Peninsula 1989	
95	£9.40	**CLOUDY BAY CHARDONNAY**, Marlborough 1988	
96	£12.70	**MARTINBOROUGH VINEYARDS CHARDONNAY**, Wairarapa 1988	
101	£12.95	**MOUNTADAM CHARDONNAY**, High Eden Ridge 1989	
143	£9.40	**RONGOPAI SAUVIGNON BLANC**, Waikato 1989	
157	£2.95	**RETSINA OF ATTICA**, Kourtaki	
166	£8.75	**MARK WEST VINEYARDS GEWURZTRAMINER**, Sonoma 1988	
172	£4.80	**JOAO PIRES WHITE TABLE WINE**, Palmela 1988	
196	£8.99	**ALSACE RIESLING GRAND CRU BRAND**, Cave Vinicole de Turckheim 1985	
244	£3.00	**BOTRYS RED**, Botrys SA, Nemea	
259	£4.80	**COTEAUX D'AIX EN PROVENCE CHATEAU PIGOUDET GRANDE RESERVE**, Midi 1985	
262	£5.40	**CORBIERES CHATEAU DE LASTOURS (FUT DE CHENE)**, Midi 1985	
265	£12.30	**J CARRAS GRANDE RESERVE**, Halkidiki 1975	
267	£2.75	**VIN DE PAYS DE L'AUDE CABERNET SAUVIGNON**, Paul Boutinot, Midi 1987	
284	£5.60	**SPECIAL RESERVE STAMBOLOVO MERLOT**, Bulgarian Vintners 1985	
288	£5.00	**PETER LEHMANN CABERNET SAUVIGNON**, Barossa Valley 1985	
294	£7.60	**ROSEMOUNT SHOW RESERVE COONAWARRA CABERNET SAUVIGNON** 1987	
299	£8.50	**CHATEAU RAMAGE LA BATISSE**, Haut-Médoc, Bordeaux 1985	
332	£4.90	**COTES DE PROVENCE DOMAINE DU JAS D'ESCLANS**, Lorges-Lapouge 1986	
336	£4.80	**CROZES HERMITAGE, DELAS FRERES**, Rhone 1988	
345	£6.80	**BAILEYS BUNDARRA SHIRAZ**, Glenrowan 1986	
377	£16.00	**CALERA JENSEN PINOT NOIR**, San Benito 1987	
410	£12.50	**MON PRA**, Conterno e Fantino, Piedmont 1987	
436	£12.20	**RIOJA RESERVA 904**, La Rioja Alta 1976	
437	£10.20	**TINTO PESQUERA**, Fernandez, Ribera del Duero 1986	
444	£11.20	**BAILEYS FOUNDERS LIQUEUR MUSCAT**, Glenrowan	
452	£6.30	**PETER LEHMANN BOTRYTIS RIESLING**, Barossa Valley 1984	
479	£4.20	**MAVRODAPHNE**, Botrys SA, Patras	

BTH	E H Booth

oint Winner: Regional Wine Merchant of the Year.

Head Office: 4-6 Fishergate, Preston, Lancs PR1 3LJ (0772 51701).Classy supermarket chain with 0 shops in Lancashire, Cumbria and Cheshire. **Opening Hours:** 9am-5.30pm Mon-Fri; 9am-5pm Sat. **Delivery:** £5 per case for 1-4 cases, 5+ cases free nationally. **Tastings:** occasionally in-store plus tutored tastings.

Described in 1925 as 'Preston's high class family grocers', EH Booth has just celebrated its 143rd birthday; today, the present Edwin Booth would prefer his business to be thought of as a 'specialist supermarket'

EH Booth is the sort of company that is all too easily overlooked by wine enthusiasts (especially southern wine enthusiasts) who still find it hard to believe that supermarkets can take wine seriously. But just look at the award winning wines listed below, and look at Booth's 'Fine Wine' selection, which includes such wines as Château Montrose 1978, Grange 1980, Vega Sicilia 'Valbuena' 1985 and Pieropan Soave, as well as such sensibly afford-able wines as 1981 Mercurey from Labaume Aîné at £6.59 and Château Gruaud Larose 1980 at £11.75

This is a range which puts many far better-known and far more self-important merchants to shame.

3	£5.25	**YALUMBA ANGAS BRUT**, Barossa Valley	
23	£19.49	**CHAMPAGNE LAURENT PERRIER ROSE**	
25	£38.99	**CHAMPAGNE LANSON BRUT** 1979 (magnum)	
37	£4.95	**HARDY'S BIRD SERIES CHARDONNAY, SOUTH AUSTRALIA** 1989	
65	£4.49	**VIN DE PAYS DES COTES DE GASCOGNE DOMAINE DU TARIQUET CUVEE BOIS**, Grassa, South-West	
95	£9.75	**CLOUDY BAY CHARDONNAY**, Marlborough 1988	
101	£10.39	**MOUNTADAM CHARDONNAY**, High Eden Ridge 1989	
102	£10.99	**CRICHTON HALL CHARDONNAY** 1987	
112	£14.75	**CABREO LA PIETRA**, Ruffino, Tuscany 1986	
167	£10.25	**ALSACE GEWURZTRAMINER GRAND CRU KESSLER**, Schlumberger 1985	
174	£4.49	**BROWN BROTHERS LATE HARVEST ORANGE MUSCAT & FLORA**, N E Victoria 1988	
177	£3.25	**BADEN DRY**, ZBW	
231	£2.89	**PIEMONTELLO PINK**, Piedmont	
243	£2.32	**BULGARIAN COUNTRY WINE**, Merlot/Gamza, Suhindol	
254	£2.99	**CAHORS**, Les Côtes d'Olt, South-West 1986	
311	£11.99	**CHATEAU HAUT-MARBUZET**, St Estèphe, Bordeaux 1985	
382	£26.95	**YARRA YERING PINOT NOIR**, Yarra Valley 1987	
413	£15.69	**CABREO IL BORGO**, Ruffino, Tuscany 1986	
454	£6.99	**TOKAY ASZU 5 PUTTONYOS**, Tokaji 1981	
491	£14.49	**WARRE'S QUINTA DA CAVADINHA**, Douro 1979	
496	£1.65	**GOLDENER OKTOBER LIGHT WHITE**, St Ursula Weinkellerei, Rheinhessen	

BD	Bordeaux Direct

Head Office: New Aquitaine House, Paddock Rd, Reading, Berks RG4 0JY (0734 481711). Chain of six shops round the Reading area. **Opening Hours:** 10.30am-7pm Mon-Wed, Fri;10.30am-8pm Thu; 9am-6pm Sat. **Delivery:** free for orders over £50. **Tastings:** regularly in-store plus tutored events.

A confusing chain that claims not to be the retail arm of the *Sunday Times* Wine Club, but does seem to stock a remarkably similar range of wines to those offered by that mail order operation. French country wines tend to be the best buys but the quality of these (and some of the other other wines) is rarely high enough, nor the prices low enough for the chain to attract much more than its loyal local following.

33	£3.83	**CANEPA VINO BLANCO**, Maipo Valley 1989
45	£4.75	**MONTRAVEL SEC SEC SEC**, Cave Coop St Vivien & Bonneville, South-West 1989
173	£4.92	**VIN DE PAYS D'OC MUSCAT SEC**, Domaine de Coussergues, Midi 1989
258	£4.58	**VIN DE PAYS D'OC CUVEE DE L'ALLIANCE**, Cave de Limoux, Midi 1989

B&B | Bottle & Basket

15 Highgate High St, London N6 5JT (081 341 7018). Independent merchant. **Opening Hours:** 11am-3pm & 5pm-9pm Mon-Fri; 11am-9pm Sat; 12-3pm & 7pm-9pm Sun. **Delivery:** free locally. **Tastings:** regularly in-store. **Discounts:** 5% for case collection.

The hand-written Bottle & Basket list, with its headings from a John Bull printing set, looks like nothing so much as a bistro menu. Closer inspection, however, reveals this to be a most serious wine merchant with an across-the-board range of good value wines, but owner Fernando Munoz displays his origins (Madrid) with a very healthy Spanish selection including no less than four wines from Toro.

20	£16.06	**CHAMPAGNE PHILIPPONNAT BRUT ROSE**
40	£4.28	**COOKS MARLBOROUGH SEMILLON** 1987
74	£5.28	**RIOJA BLANCO SECO RESERVA**, CVNE 1985
80	£5.89	**WOLF BLASS BARREL-FERMENTED CHARDONNAY**, South Australia 1988
81	£5.61	**STONELEIGH CHARDONNAY**, Marlborough 1988
117	£3.42	**ANJOU BLANC CHUPIN**, G Saget, Loire 1989
152	£3.90	**COOKS CHENIN BLANC**, Hawkes Bay 1987
174	£4.56	BROWN BROTHERS LATE HARVEST ORANGE MUSCAT & FLORA, N E Victoria 1988
175	£5.51	**QUADY ESSENSIA ORANGE MUSCAT** 1987
300	£8.65	**CHATEAU DE PUY (ROBERT AMOREAU)**, Bordeaux Supérieur 1982
302	£11.02	**CHATEAU CARONNE-SAINTE-GEMME**, Haut-Médoc, Bordeaux 1982
313	£15.20	**CHATEAU MOUTON-BARONNE-PHILIPPE**, Pauillac, Bordeaux 1986
344	£6.94	**BOTOBOLAR ST GILBERT RED WINE**, Mudgee 1987
387	£2.47	**MONTEPULCIANO D'ABRUZZO**, Tollo, Abruzzi 1987
414	£16.53	TIGNANELLO, Antinori, Tuscany 1985
428	£4.37	**QUINTA DE CAMARATE**, Fonseca, Azeitão 1985
433	£5.90	**RIOJA RESERVA ALBINA**, Bodegas Riojanas 1984
472	£7.79	DON ZOILO VERY OLD FINO, Jerez
473	£7.79	**DON ZOILO MANZANILLA**, Sanlucar de Barrameda
475	£8.17	**DOS CORTADOS**, Williams & Humbert, Jerez

BU | Bottoms Up

Head Office: Astra House, River Way, Harlow, Essex CM20 2EA (0532 435435). As last year, still a complacent chain with 55 branches. **Opening Hours:** 10am-10pm Mon-Fri; 12-2pm & 7pm-9pm Sun. **Delivery:** free within 20 miles. **Tastings:** weekly in-store.

What on earth is going on here? 'Privatisation' - enforced autonomy from Peter Dominic, its big brother - ought to have done this Oddbins lookalike a favour. Bottoms Up had less award winners than Peter Dominic. Friendly shops and keen staff are being wasted by a management that seems to have no idea what it is doing. Why, for instance did anyone even consider the importation, let alone promotion, of stale, over-priced Russian wines?

| 73 | £5.35 | **LINDEMANS BIN 65 CHARDONNAY**, Murray River 1989 |
| 276 | £3.89 | **CONCHA Y TORO MERLOT**, Maipo 1986 |

BRO | The Broad Street Wine Co.

The Hollaway, Market Place, Warwick CV34 4SJ (0926 493951). Small, by-the-case only merchant with a good bin-end list. **Opening Hours:** 9am-6pm Mon-Fri; 9am-1pm Sat. **Delivery:** free for large orders. **Tastings:** to groups on request.

Russell Hobbs, the manager of this firm, must get terribly bored with jokes about kettles, so we won't make any here. We'll only say that Broad Street offers a good basic list (with attractive, if young, Burgundies from Joseph Drouhin), a selection of limited quantity bin-ends (recently including a couple of bottles of 1955 Bouchard Père Clos de Vougeot at £25 each) and one of the country's very best ranges of brandies, including no less than 15 different vintages of Hine Cognac, 24 of Larressingle Armagnac and nine old Calvados's, the oldest of which was distilled in 1926. Just the sort of stuff to get steamed up about...

29	£3.62	**VIN DE PAYS DES COTES DE GASCOGNE**, Domaine de Perras, South-West 1989
38	£4.83	**ALSACE TOKAY-PINOT GRIS**, Cave Vinicole de Turckheim 1988
95	£11.21	**CLOUDY BAY CHARDONNAY**, Marlborough 1988
168	£9.35	**ALSACE GEWURZTRAMINER SELECTION DE GRAINS NOBLES**, Cave Vinicole de Turckheim 1988
236	£4.50	**TORRES CABERNET SAUVIGNON ROSE**, Curico 1989
337	£5.24	**ROUGE HOMME SHIRAZ/CABERNET**, Coonawarra 1985

BUD | Budgens

Head Office: PO Box 9, Stonefield Way, Ruislip, Middx HA4 0JR (081 422 3422). Regional supermarket chain with 125 stores in the South-East, Norfolk and the Midlands. **Opening Hours:** 8.30am-8.30pm Mon-Fri; 8.30am-6pm Sat. **Tastings:** occasionally in-store.

Doing good by stealth, Sarah King, the wine buyer at Budgens, seems quietly to be transforming what was once a very pedestrian list into something that is really rather interesting. The list of successful wines drawn from Budgen's entry into this year's *WINE Magazine* International Challenge reveals the improvements Ms King has made to the list, introducing such novelties as New Zealand Sauvignon Blanc and the excellent Felix Solis Valdepeñas.

28	£2.55	**VIN DE PAYS DES COTES DE GASCOGNE**, Plaimont, South-West 1989
129	£4.99	**MONTANA SAUVIGNON BLANC**, Marlborough 1989
153	£4.09	**VOUVRAY CUVEE SELECTE**, Chainier, Loire 1985
243	£2.19	**BULGARIAN COUNTRY WINE**, Merlot/Gamza, Suhindol
253	£3.79	**FITOU CHATEAU DE SEGUR**, Producteurs de Mont Tauch, Midi 1987
266	£2.69	**PLOVDIV CABERNET SAUVIGNON**, Bulgarian Vintners 1985
269	£2.79	**HOUSE CLARET**, Peter Sichel, Bordeaux

271	£3.19	**BERGERAC CHATEAU LE CASTELLOT**, Domaine des Trois Templiers, South-West 1988
367	£4.65	BOURGOGNE PINOT NOIR, Caves de Buxy, Burgundy 1987
421	£2.99	**VINA ALBALI RESERVA**, Felix Solis, Valdepeñas 1983
451	£4.99	**CHATEAU LA NERE**, Dulac & Seraphon, Loupiac, Bordeaux 1986
499	£1.99	**PETILLANT DE RAISIN (3%)**, Listel, Midi

ABY | Anthony Byrne Fine Wines

88 High St, Ramsey, Huntingdon, Cambs PE17 1BS (0487 814555). Burgundy and Australia loving traditional merchant. **Opening Hours:** 9am-5.30pm Mon-Sat. **Delivery:** free locally and nationally for large orders, otherwise at cost. **Tastings:** bottles open every day plus tutored events.

Anthony Byrne is a tremendous Duboeuf fan, and his support for the Beaujolais merchant is regularly rewarded by success in comparative tastings. In the past, Byrne has been criticised for relying over-heavily on agencies like those for Duboeuf, Cuvaison from California and Delatite from Australia; wines from these producers still form a fundamental part of the list, but they are complemented by a growing range of single-estate wines from throughout the world. Like his namesake (see below) in Clitheroe, Mr Byrne is a wine merchant to watch.

28	£2.88	**VINS DE PAYS DES COTES DE GASCOGNE**, Plaimont, South-West 1989
90	£8.43	CHATEAU CONSTANTIN, Graves, Bordeaux 1986
91	£8.74	**DELATITE CHARDONNAY**, Central Victoria 1989
94	£9.79	**CHARDONNAY PORTICO DEI LEONI**, Vinattieri, Veneto 1986
145	£10.00	**POUILLY FUME BUISSON MENARD**, Didier Dagueneau, Loire 1988
146	£22.95	POUILLY FUME SILEX, Didier Dagueneau, Loire 1988
175	£8.67	**QUADY ESSENSIA ORANGE MUSCAT** 1987
309	£13.11	**CHATEAU HAUT-BAGES-AVEROUS** (Château Lynch-Bages), Pauillac, Bordeaux 1986
340	£6.08	**COTES DU RHONE**, Guigal 1986
343	£6.73	**CROZES HERMITAGE**, Alain Graillot, Rhône 1988
358	£3.85	**GAMAY DE L'ARDECHE**, Georges Duboeuf, Rhône 1989
359	£5.49	**BEAUJOLAIS-VILLAGES**, Georges Duboeuf 1989
363	£6.46	**REGNIE CRISTAL**, Georges Duboeuf, Beaujolais 1989
364	£6.75	**MORGON JEAN DESCOMBES**, Georges Duboeuf, Beaujolais 1989
461	£15.50	**RECIOTO DI SOAVE DEI CAPITELLE**, Anselmi, Veneto 1987
473	£6.27	**DON ZOILO MANZANILLA**, Sanlúcar de Barrameda

DBY | D Byrne & Co

North of England Wine Merchant of the Year

Victoria Buildings, 12 King St, Clitheroe, Lancs (0200 23152). Independent merchant, part one of the Clitheroe phenomenon. **Opening Hours:** 9am-6pm Mon-Wed, Sat; 9am-8pm Thu, Fri. **Delivery:** free within 50 miles, nationally at cost. **Tastings:** occasionally, tutored events on request.

Yes, there are slightly more wines recommended here than under the Oddbins entry - and this still represents only a fraction of an exemplary range of wines that won awards in the 1990 Challenge. Which explains why, in addition to D Byrne's award as Northern Wine Merchant of the Year, this company has also been given a special *WINE Magazine* Challenge Award.

When Andrew Byrne sent us his list, he asked us to bear in mind that it was 'quite dated; since its publication, we have expanded our Australian range ...' The pre-expanded list already contained no less than 178 wines. The Italian list seems modest by comparison - until you realise that the page at which you are looking covers only the Tuscan whites. A French red selection with 18 wines including 1985 Léoville Barton and 1988 Morgon Jean Descombes from Duboeuf looks good but sparse - but these are just the 'half-bottles'. Why Clitheroe should have two truly excellent merchants(*see* *Whitesides*) is a mystery; aren't all the best wine shops supposed to be in London?

	£4.85	**ASTI MARTINI**, Martini & Rossi, Piedmont
3	£18.39	**CHAMPAGNE LAURENT PERRIER ROSE**
4	£17.35	**CHAMPAGNE LOUIS ROEDERER BRUT PREMIER**
9	£3.29	**VIN DE PAYS DES COTES DE GASCOGNE**, Domaine de Perras, South-West 1989
7	£4.99	**HARDY'S BIRD SERIES CHARDONNAY**, South Australia 1989
8	£4.19	**ALSACE TOKAY-PINOT GRIS**, Cave Vinicole de Turckheim 1988
1	£3.95	ALSACE PINOT BLANC, Cave Vinicole de Turckheim 1989
3	£3.99	**RIOJA BLANCO SECO MONTE REAL**, Bodegas Riojanas 1986
8	£4.39	**BERGERAC SEC DOMAINE DE GRANDCHAMP**, Nick Ryman, South-West 1988
0	£4.09	**VERDICCHIO CA'SAL DI SERRA**, Umani Ronchi, Marches 1986
3	£5.19	**LINDEMANS BIN 65 CHARDONNAY**, Murray River 1989
6	£5.59	**MONTROSE CHARDONNAY**, Mudgee 1989
8	£6.20	**MITCHELTON MARSANNE**, Goulburn Valley 1987
9	£5.75	**CHATEAU TAHBILK MARSANNE-CHARDONNAY**, Goulburn Valley 1987
0	£5.49	**WOLF BLASS BARREL-FERMENTED CHARDONNAY**, South Australia 1988
1	£5.89	**STONELEIGH CHARDONNAY**, Marlborough 1988
3	£6.09	**MITCHELTON RESERVE CHARDONNAY**, Goulburn Valley 1988
6	£5.79	**MUSCADET DE SEVRE ET MAINE SUR LIE CHATEAU DE CHASSELOIR (OAK-AGED)**, Loire 1987
7	£7.59	PENFOLDS CHARDONNAY, South Australia 1988
2	£8.29	**SIMI CHARDONNAY**, Sonoma 1985
5	£8.89	**CLOUDY BAY CHARDONNAY**, Marlborough 1988
7	£10.75	**COLDSTREAM HILLS CHARDONNAY**, Yarra Valley 1988
8	£11.39	**GEOFF MERRILL CHARDONNAY**, McLaren Vale 1987
9	£11.35	**TREFETHEN CHARDONNAY**, Napa Valley 1986
100	£11.35	**PETALUMA CHARDONNAY**, Adelaide Hills 1987
105	£13.69	**TARRA WARRA CHARDONNAY**, Yarra Valley 1987
106	£11.85	LEEUWIN ESTATE CHARDONNAY, Margaret River 1984
108	£12.85	**ROSEMOUNT ROXBURGH CHARDONNAY**, Hunter Valley 1987
129	£4.75	**MONTANA SAUVIGNON BLANC**, Marlborough 1989
134	£5.69	**NOBILOS SAUVIGNON BLANC**, Marlborough 1989
142	£7.99	**POUILLY BLANC FUME DOMAINE CHAILLOUX**, Châtelain, Loire 1987
159	£4.49	**TORRES GEWURZTRAMINER**, Curico 1988
166	£6.99	**MARK WEST VINEYARDS GEWURZTRAMINER**, Sonoma 1988
167	£10.25	**ALSACE GEWURZTRAMINER GRAND CRU KESSLER**, Schlumberger 1985
168	£16.99	ALSACE GEWURZTRAMINER SELECTION DE GRAINS NOBLES, Cave Vinicole de Turckheim 1988
172	£4.35	**JOAO PIRES WHITE TABLE WINE**, Palmela 1988
231	£2.69	PIEMONTELLO PINK, Piedmont
236	£4.19	**TORRES CABERNET SAUVIGNON ROSE**, Curico 1989
240	£4.99	**CHATEAU LA JAUBERTIE BERGERAC ROSE**, Henry Ryman, South-West 1987
243	£2.39	**BULGARIAN COUNTRY WINE**, Merlot/Gamza, Suhindol
247	£3.49	VRANAC, Slovin, Montenegro 1986
262	£4.75	**CORBIERES CHATEAU DE LASTOURS (FUT DE CHENE)**, Midi 1985
266	£2.65	**PLOVDIV CABERNET SAUVIGNON**, Bulgarian Vintners 1985
267	£2.69	**VIN DE PAYS DE L'AUDE CABERNET SAUVIGNON**, Paul Boutinot, Midi 1987

276	£3.49	**CONCHA Y TORO MERLOT**, Maipo 1986	
277	£4.29	**SEAVIEW CABERNET SAUVIGNON**, South Australia 1985	
282	£4.79	**MONTES CABERNET SAUVIGNON**, Discover Wine, Curico Valley 1987	
284	£2.99	**SPECIAL RESERVE STAMBOLOVO MERLOT**, Bulgarian Vintners 1985	
288	£6.25	**PETER LEHMANN CABERNET SAUVIGNON**, Barossa Valley 1985	
292	£8.05	**ORLANDO ST HUGO CABERNET SAUVIGNON**, Coonawarra 1986	
297	£7.85	**PENFOLDS BIN 389 SHIRAZ/CABERNET**, South Australia 1986	
298	£7.39	**CHATEAU LA TOUR DE BY**, Haut-Médoc, Bordeaux 1986	
299	£8.05	**CHATEAU RAMAGE LA BATISSE**, Haut-Médoc, Bordeaux 1985	
303	£7.99	**ROUGE HOMME COONAWARRA CABERNET SAUVIGNON** 1985	
305	£10.25	**CHATEAU MAUCAILLOU**, Moulis, Bordeaux 1986	
308	£10.95	**PETALUMA COONAWARRA CABERNET/MERLOT** 1985	
311	£11.59	**CHATEAU HAUT-MARBUZET**, St Estèphe, Bordeaux 1985	
314	£13.39	**TORRES GRAN CORONAS BLACK LABEL**, Penedés 1983	
315	£14.59	**WYNNS JOHN RIDDOCH CABERNET SAUVIGNON**, Coonawarra 1985	
316	£18.65	**PENFOLDS BIN 707 CABERNET SAUVIGNON**, South Australia 1986	
319	£17.59	**CHATEAU PICHON-LONGUEVILLE-BARON**, Pauillac, Bordeaux 1985	
321	£23.00	**CHATEAU GRUAUD-LAROSE** (Cordier), St Julien, Bordeaux 1978	
331	£4.19	**RASTEAU COTES DU RHONE VILLAGES**, Caves des Vignerons de Rasteau 198	
336	£4.79	**CROZES HERMITAGE**, Delas Frères, Rhône 1988	
337	£4.99	**ROUGE HOMME SHIRAZ/CABERNET**, Coonawarra 1985	
339	£5.45	**PENFOLDS BIN 28 KALIMNA SHIRAZ**, South Australia 1986	
340	£5.89	**COTES DU RHONE**, Guigal 1986	
347	£7.15	**BREZEME CUVEE EUGENE DE MONTICAULT**, Jean-Marie Lombard, Rhône 198	
349	£9.29	**RIDGE GEYSERVILLE ZINFANDEL**, Sonoma 1987	
355	£17.65	**PENFOLDS MAGILL ESTATE**, South Australia 1986	
364	£5.65	**MORGON JEAN DESCOMBES**, Georges Duboeuf, Beaujolais 1989	
368	£8.29	**TREFETHEN PINOT NOIR**, Napa Valley 1984	
378	£11.19	**MONDAVI PINOT NOIR RESERVE**, Napa Valley 1986	
393	£4.35	**CORVO ROSSO**, Sicily 1987	
399	£5.35	**CAMPO FIORIN**, Masi, Veneto 1985	
414	£15.29	**TIGNANELLO**, Antinori, Tuscany 1985	
428	£4.39	**QUINTA DE CAMARATE**, Fonseca, Azeitão 1985	
432	£4.69	**RIOJA RESERVA**, Beronia 1982	
437	£10.69	**TINTO PESQUERA**, Fernandez, Ribera del Duero 1986	
441	£8.45	**MORRIS RUTHERGLEN LIQUEUR MUSCAT**	
442	£5.89	**MUSCAT DE RIVESALTES**, Château de la Tuilerie, Midi 1988	
443	£8.45	**CAMPBELLS RUTHERGLEN MUSCAT**	
444	£8.89	**BAILEYS FOUNDERS LIQUEUR MUSCAT**, Glenrowan	
449	£4.79	**CHATEAU DES COULINATS**, Ste-Croix-du-Mont, Bordeaux 1983	
452	£5.99	**PETER LEHMANN BOTRYTIS RIESLING**, Barossa Valley 1984	
471	£6.49	**AMONTILLADO TIO DIEGO**, Valdespino, Jerez	
472	£6.99	**DON ZOILO VERY OLD FINO**, Jerez	
473	£6.99	**DON ZOILO MANZANILLA**, Sanlúcar de Barrameda	
474	£8.19	**DON LUIS AMONTILLADO**, Burdon, Jerez	
476	£10.69	**MATUSALEM OLOROSO MUY VIEJO**, Gonzalez Byass, Jerez	
478	£10.69	**AMONTILLADO DEL DUQUE**, Gonzalez Byass, Jerez	
486	£6.35	**WARRE'S WARRIOR VINTAGE CHARACTER PORT**, Douro	
487	£9.09	**COSSART GORDON 5 YEAR OLD BUAL**, Madeira	
500	£1.99	**GRANTS OF ST JAMES MONTEVERDI ROSSO (3%)**, Piedmont	

CAC	Cachet Wines

Lysander Close, North York Trading Estate, Clifton, York YO3 8XB (0904 690090). Independent merchant selling by the case. **Opening Hours:** 9am-6pm Mon-Fri; 10am-4pm Sat. **Delivery:** free locally, nationally at cost. **Tastings:** occasionally in-store plus tutored events.

'We would never sell a bottle of wine we wouldn't drink ourselves.' Cachet's house maxim is one that a number of other merchants could do well to learn - particularly in view of another Yorkshire wholesaler's proud boast that, as one of the biggest importers of Laski Rizling, he had never tasted as much as a drop of the stuff.

But we admire Cachet's taste. We'd be very happy to drink almost everything on this list - from the Plaimont Côtes de Gascogne to the Château La Lagune 1978. The selection of halves is impressive too, including the delicious New Zealand Redwood Valley late-harvest Riesling.

7	£6.50	**CREMANT DE BOURGOGNE ROSE**, Caves de Bailly, Burgundy 1987	
28	£2.85	**VIN DE PAYS DES COTES DE GASCOGNE,** Plaimont, South-West 1989	
52	£5.95	**HOUGHTON VERDELHO**, Swan Valley 1988	
67	£4.75	**CHATEAU BONNET RESERVE DU CHATEAU (OAK AGED)**, Entre-Deux-Mers, Lurton, Bordeaux 1988	
74	£5.35	**RIOJA BLANCO SECO RESERVA**, CVNE 1985	
75	£6.70	**FIRESTONE CHARDONNAY**, Santa Ynez 1987	
108	£14.65	**ROSEMOUNT ROXBURGH CHARDONNAY**, Hunter Valley 1987	
262	£5.99	**CORBIERES CHATEAU DE LASTOURS (FUT DE CHENE)**, Midi 1985	
267	£2.69	**VIN DE PAYS DE L'AUDE CABERNET SAUVIGNON**, Paul Boutinot, Midi 1987	
292	£7.99	**ORLANDO ST HUGO CABERNET SAUVIGNON**, Coonawarra 1986	
441	£7.99	**MORRIS RUTHERGLEN LIQUEUR MUSCAT**	
491	£14.35	**WARRE'S QUINTA DA CAVADINHA**, Douro 1979	

CWG	Cadwgan Fine Wine

152a Ashley Rd, Hale, Altrincham, Greater Manchester WA15 9SA (061 928 0357) & 55 Spring Gardens, Manchester M2 2BZ (061 236 6547).Proud-to-be-northern independent merchant. **Opening Hours:** 11am-8pm Mon-Fri; 9am-8pm Sat. **Delivery:** free locally, nationally at cost. **Tastings:** regularly in-store plus tutored events. **Discounts:** 5% on unbroken cases.

Peter Williams is nothing if not a showman. Every June, residents of the wealthy Cheshire countryside around Hale and Knutsford are invited to attend the annual 'Cheshire Wine Festival', a Williams-conceived event at which for a mere £25 per person, the local populace can spend a Friday sipping and slurping their way through a few hundred different wines. These, as the following list demonstrates, are a pretty impressive bunch, as are the selections of Sèvre Crystal and Fruit in Armagnac...

22	£17.45	**CHAMPAGNE BRICOUT CARTE D'OR BRUT PRESTIGE**
23	£20.85	**CHAMPAGNE LAURENT PERRIER ROSE**
24	£20.95	**CHAMPAGNE LOUIS ROEDERER BRUT PREMIER**
29	£3.35	**VIN DE PAYS DES COTES DE GASCOGNE**, Domaine de Perras, South-West 1989
38	£4.75	**ALSACE TOKAY-PINOT GRIS**, Cave Vinicole de Turckheim 1988
47	£5.95	**LUGANA**, Ca Dei Frati, Lombardy 1989
50	£5.95	**SOAVE CLASSICO**, Pieropan, Veneto 1989
57	£5.99	**INNISKILLIN CHARDONNAY**, Niagara 1988
70	£5.25	**VERDICCHIO CA'SAL DI SERRA**, Umani Ronchi, Marches 1986
74	£5.85	**RIOJA BLANCO SECO RESERVA**, CVNE 1985
76	£6.75	**MONTROSE CHARDONNAY**, Mudgee 1989
79	£6.75	**CHATEAU TAHBILK MARSANNE-CHARDONNAY**, Goulburn Valley 1987
81	£6.85	**STONELEIGH CHARDONNAY**, Marlborough 1988
114	£16.79	**YARRA YERING CHARDONNAY**, Yarra Valley 1987

134	£6.65	**NOBILOS SAUVIGNON BLANC**, Marlborough 1989
166	£8.99	**MARK WEST VINEYARDS GEWURZTRAMINER**, Sonoma 1988
168	£18.99	**ALSACE GEWURZTRAMINER SELECTION DE GRAINS NOBLES**, Cave Vinicole de Turckheim 1988
196	£10.35	**ALSACE RIESLING GRAND CRU BRAND**, Cave Vinicole de Turckheim 1985
267	£2.99	**VIN DE PAYS DE L'AUDE CABERNET SAUVIGNON**, Paul Boutinot, Midi 1987
288	£7.15	**PETER LEHMANN CABERNET SAUVIGNON**, Barossa Valley 1985
299	£8.95	**CHATEAU RAMAGE LA BATISSE**, Haut-Medoc, Bordeaux 1985
314	£17.45	**TORRES GRAN CORONAS BLACK LABEL**, Penedes 1983
321	£24.90	**CHATEAU GRUAUD-LAROSE** (Cordier), St Julien, Bordeaux 1978
331	£4.65	**RASTEAU COTES DU RHONE VILLAGES**, Caves des Vignerons de Rasteau 1988
388	£3.45	**BARBERA D'ASTI**, Viticoltori dell'Acquesi, Piedmont 1988
409	£9.99	**RECIOTO DELLA VALPOLICELLA**, Allegrini, Veneto 1988
412	£12.99	**CEPPARELLO**, Isole e Olena, Tuscany 1986
417	£14.99	**BAROLO MONPRIVATO**, G Mascarello, Piedmont 1985
436	£11.95	**RIOJA RESERVA 904**, La Rioja Alta 1976
444	£11.95	**BAILEYS FOUNDERS LIQUEUR MUSCAT**, Glenrowan
452	£6.99	**PETER LEHMANN BOTRYTIS RIESLING**, Barossa Valley 1984
482	£6.55	**SMITH WOODHOUSE RUBY PORT**, Douro
487	£9.95	**COSSART GORDON 5 YEAR OLD BUAL**, Madeira
491	£17.25	**WARRE'S QUINTA DA CAVADINHA**, Douro 1979

CWI | A Case of Wine

Cwn Tawel, Horeb, Llandyful Dyfed SA44 4HY (055 932 3342). Farmer with wholesale and retail wine business selling by the mixed case. **Delivery:** free within Dyfed and nationally at cost. **Tastings:** regularly in-store plus own tutored tastings. **Discounts:** negotiable on large orders.

We might never have heard of A Case of Wine had owner Mike Dentten not volunteered his help for the 1990 *WINE Magazine* International Challenge. A genial Welshman who doesn't look like he has played a game of rugby in his life, Dentten somehow gives the impression that his wine interests take second place to his farm. Still, the range is carefully chosen, with several drawn from the range put together by Bruce and Judy Kendrick at Haughton Fine Wines (*q.v.*) - and if you need a sirloin of beef to accompany your David Wynn Cabernet Sauvignon, he will gladly supply that as well.

28	£3.40	**VIN DE PAYS DES COTES DE GASCOGNE PLAIMONT**, South-West 1989
48	£5.57	**MACON-VINZELLES**, Caves des Grands Crus, Burgundy 1987
84	£6.20	**SCHINUS MOLLE CHARDONNAY**, Mornington Peninsula 1989
93	£9.63	**POUILLY FUISSE**, M Delorme, Burgundy 1985
101	£10.20	**MOUNTADAM CHARDONNAY**, High Eden Ridge 1989
143	£7.92	**RONGOPAI SAUVIGNON BLANC**, Waikato 1989
285	£5.15	**DAVID WYNN CABERNET**, High Eden Ridge 1986
409	£9.25	**REC IOTO DELLA VALPOLICELLA**, Allegrini, Veneto 1988
492	£14.70	**BANYULS GRAND CRU SELECT VIEUX**, L'Etoile, Midi 1969

CVR | The Celtic Vintner

Welsh Wine Merchant of the Year

73 Derwen Fawr Rd, Sketty, Swansea, West Glamorgan SA2 8DR (0792 206661). Friendly, well-stocked independent merchant. **Opening Hours:** 8am-6pm Mon-Fri; weekends by arrangement.

Delivery: free within South Wales, nationally at cost. **Tastings:** occasional in-store tastings, outside events on request.

Even the briefest glances at the list of wines below will show you why the Celtic Vintner is our Welsh Wine Merchant of the Year for the second year in succession. 'Our policy will be to continue to buy only those wines we consider the best, most honest and good value from wherever and whomever. It is our wish to be like a restaurant whose menu changes as frequently as availability of fresh, "in-season" products dictates.' The list is not the longest we have seen, but it is well-packed with fascinating, carefully chosen wines such as the 1982 De Bortoli Botrytis Pedro Ximenez, and a range of ports from the house of Niepoort.

24	£18.40	**Champagne Louis Roederer Brut Premier**
28	£2.99	**VIN DE PAYS DES COTES DE GASCOGNE** Plaimont, South-West 1989
29	£3.11	**VIN DE PAYS DES COTES DE GASCOGNE**, Domaine de Perras, South-West 1989
38	£4.31	**ALSACE TOKAY-PINOT GRIS**, Cave Vinicole de Turckheim 1988
41	£4.03	**ALSACE PINOT BLANC**, Cave Vinicole de Turckheim 1989
42	£4.50	**ALSACE SYLVANER HEIMBOURG**, Cave Vinicole de Turckheim 1987
54	£5.75	**POUILLY LOCHE CHATEAU DE LOCHE**, Caves des Grands Crus Vinzelles, Bugundy 1987
72	£5.18	**CHATEAU BAUDUC LES 3 HECTARES**, Entre-Deux-Mers, Bordeaux 1989
74	£5.10	**RIOJA BLANCO SECO RESERVA**, CVNE 1985
95	£9.32	**CLOUDY BAY CHARDONNAY**, Marlborough 1988
100	£10.64	**PETALUMA CHARDONNAY**, Adelaide Hills 1987
127	£4.49	**MUSCADET DE SEVRE ET MAINE SUR LIE**, G Bossard, Loire 1989
138	£6.90	**HUNTERS SAUVIGNON BLANC**, Marlborough 1989
159	£4.31	**TORRES GEWURZTRAMINER**, Curico 1988
168	£18.11	**ALSACE GEWURZTRAMINER SELECTION DE GRAINS NOBLES**, Cave Vinicole de Turckheim 1988
172	£4.31	**JOAO PIRES WHITE TABLE WINE**, Palmela 1988
213	£4.31	**NIERSTEINER SPIEGELBERG KABINETT**, Guntrum, Rheinhessen 1988
228	£6.61	**GRAACHER HIMMELREICH RIESLING SPATLESE**, F W Gymnasium, Mosel-Saar-Ruwer 1988
236	£3.91	**TORRES CABERNET SAUVIGNON ROSE**, Curico 1989
239	£4.31	**CHATEAU THIEULEY BORDEAUX CLAIRET** 1989
240	£4.60	**CHATEAU LA JAUBERTIE BERGERAC ROSE**, Henry Ryman, South-West 1987
243	£2.31	**BULGARIAN COUNTRY WINE**, Merlot/Gamza, Suhindol
266	£2.61	**PLOVDIV CABERNET SAUVIGNON**, Bulgarian Vintners 1985
267	£2.70	**VIN DE PAYS DE L'AUDE CABERNET SAUVIGNON**, Paul Boutinot, Midi 1987
292	£7.48	**ORLANDO ST HUGO CABERNET SAUVIGNON**, Coonawarra 1986
299	£8.05	**CHATEAU RAMAGE LA BATISSE**, Haut-Médoc, Bordeaux 1985
303	£9.20	**ROUGE HOMME COONAWARRA CABERNET SAUVIGNON** 1985
308	£10.64	**PETALUMA COONAWARRA CABERNET/MERLOT** 1985
314	£15.52	**TORRES GRAN CORONAS BLACK LABEL**, Penedés 1983
317	£18.11	**MONDAVI CABERNET SAUVIGNON RESERVE**, Napa Valley 1980
330	£4.03	**COTES DU RHONE**, Château du Grand Moulas 1988
331	£4.26	**RASTEAU COTES DU RHONE VILLAGES**, Caves des Vignerons de Rasteau 1988
334	£4.60	**COTES DU RHONE**, Domaine St Apollinaire 1988
378	£8.91	**MONDAVI PINOT NOIR RESERVE**, Napa Valley 1986
441	£8.05	**MORRIS RUTHERGLEN LIQUEUR MUSCAT**
442	£4.20	**MUSCAT DE RIVESALTES**, Château de la Tuilerie, Midi 1988
486	£5.23	**WARRE'S WARRIOR VINTAGE CHARACTER PORT**, Douro
487	£9.20	**COSSART GORDON 5 YEAR OLD BUAL**, Madeira
491	£13.80	**WARRE'S QUINTA DA CAVADINHA**, Douro 1979

CDV	Champagne de Villages

9 Fore St, Ipswich, Suffolk IP4 1JW (0473 256922). Independent specialist merchant. **Opening Hours:** 9am-5.30pm Mon-Sat. **Delivery:** free locally, nationally £7 per case for 1-4 cases, 5+ cases free. **Tastings:** regularly in-store plus tutored events for outside organisations.

Despite its name, this East Anglian firm sells a good range of wines without bubbles - as the recommendations below demonstrate. Even so, Champagne is of course the speciality here, with a phenomenal list of individual estate-produced wines alongside all the inevitable Grandes Marques. And, for anyone who wondered why this region's wines all seem to be fizzy, there are also representative examples of its still reds, whites and rosés, even the best of which do much to justify the *méthode champenoise* process.

73	£5.95	**LINDEMANS BIN 65 CHARDONNAY**, Murray River 1989
131	£5.15	**QUINCY, P & J MARDON**, Loire 1988
360	£5.75	**BEAUJOLAIS ANCIENNE METHODE DOMAINE DES TERRES DOREES**, Jean Paul Brun 1989

CPL	Chaplin & Son

35 Rowlands Rd, Worthing, W Sussex BN11 3JJ (0903 35888). Independent merchant able to obtain most wines 'if they can be found'. **Opening Hours:** 8.45am-5.30pm Mon-Sat (closed for lunch). **Delivery:** free locally, nationally at favourable rates. **Tastings:** regularly in store plus tutored events. **Discounts:** 5% mixed case.

Through membership of several buying consortia, Tony and Bob Chaplin are able to secure small batches of wine at large batch prices. So while their list, though broad-ranging and sound, may not be the most adventurous in the world, they can usually track down any bottle you seek, and at a competitive rate.

25	£20.00	**CHAMPAGNE LANSON BRUT** 1979
87	£7.79	**PENFOLDS CHARDONNAY**, South Australia 1988
152	£3.99	**COOKS CHENIN BLANC**, Hawkes Bay 1987
174	£4.89	**BROWN BROTHERS LATE HARVEST ORANGE MUSCAT & FLORA**, N E Victoria 1988
183	£4.50	**NUTBOURNE MANOR HUXELREBE**, Sussex 1989
297	£8.49	**PENFOLDS BIN 389 SHIRAZ/CABERNET**, South Australia 1986
314	£15.00	**TORRES GRAN CORONAS BLACK LABEL**, Penedés 1983
316	£18.65	**PENFOLDS BIN 707 CABERNET SAUVIGNON**, South Australia 1986
319	£20.00	**CHATEAU PICHON-LONGUEVILLE-BARON**, Pauillac, Bordeaux 1985
334	£4.55	**COTES DU RHONE**, Domaine St Apollinaire 1988
339	£5.49	**PENFOLDS BIN 28 KALIMNA SHIRAZ** South Australia 1986
357	£3.95	**GAILLAC CEPAGE GAMAY**, Jean Cros, South-West 1989
361	£5.89	**BROUILLY**, E Loron, Beaujolais 1989
405	£7.99	**BAROLO RISERVA**, Borgogno, Piedmont 1982
432	£5.89	**RIOJA RESERVA**, Beronia 1982
449	£5.35	**CHATEAU DES COULINATS**, Ste Croix du Mont, Bordeaux, 1983
454	£7.50	**TOKAY ASZU 5 PUTTONYOS PUTTONYOS**, Tokaji 1981
488	£11.20	**SMITH WOODHOUSE LATE BOTTLED VINTAGE PORT (BOTTLED 1984)**, Douro 1979
491	£13.99	**WARRE'S QUINTA DA CAVADINHA**, Douro 1979
499	£1.99	**PETILLANT DE RAISIN (3%)**, Listel, Midi

CNL | Connollys

110 Edmund St, Birmingham, W Midlands B3 2ES (021 236 3837). Independent merchant whose wine selection is better than his poetry. **Opening Hours:** 9am-5.30pm Mon-Fri; 9.30am-1pm Sat. **Delivery:** free locally, nationally at cost. **Tastings:** occasional in-store plus popular tutored events. **Discounts:** 5% mixed case, larger orders negotiable.

Connolly's *Book of Bacchus* contains much of interest to the wine-lover in Birmingham's business quarter. Western Australian wines from Moss Wood and Cape Mentelle rub shoulders with a range of 1982 Domaine de la Romanée Conti Burgundies, and a recent introduction of individual domaine Rhône wines has proved popular. As to Connolly's poetry, we shall leave you to make up your own minds.
My brother-in-law, a motor car dealer,
Will only drink Chardonnay from William Wheeler,
Much to the chagrin of my dear little sister,
Whose particular favourite is from Buena Vista.

20	£14.95	**CHAMPAGNE PHILIPPONNAT BRUT ROSE**
23	£18.98	**CHAMPAGNE LAURENT PERRIER ROSE**
95	£10.00	**CLOUDY BAY CHARDONNAY, MARLBOROUGH** 1988
172	£5.46	**JOAO PIRES WHITE TABLE WINE**, Palmela 1988
174	£4.94	**BROWN BROTHERS LATE HARVEST ORANGE MUSCAT & FLORA**, N E Victoria 1988
194	£5.97	**DEINHARD HERITAGE SELECTION DEIDESHEIM**, Rheinpfalz 1987
299	£7.59	**CHATEAU RAMAGE LA BATISSE**, Haut-Médoc, Bordeaux 1985
308	£11.50	**PETALUMA COONAWARRA CABERNET/MERLOT** 1985
309	£11.73	**CHATEAU HAUT-BAGES-AVEROUS** (Château Lynch-Bages), Pauillac, Bordeaux 1986
314	£16.10	**TORRES GRAN CORONAS BLACK LABEL**, Penedés 1983
317	£19.40	**MONDAVI CABERNET SAUVIGNON RESERVE**, Napa Valley 1980
320	£18.50	**CHATEAU LYNCH-BAGES**, Pauillac, Bordeaux 1985
371	£11.10	**COLDSTREAM HILLS PINOT NOIR**, Yarra Valley 1988
499	£1.99	**PETILLANT DE RAISIN (3%)**, Listel, Midi

CWS | The Co-Op

Head Office: Fairhills Rd, Irlam, Manchester M30 8BD (061 834 1212). National organisation composed of several societies, not all necessarily stocking the same range of products. **Opening Hours:** variable. **Tastings:** occasionally in-store.

In previous issues of the *Guide* we have reported on the challenge facing Arabella Woodrow MW, wine buyer for the Co-op, in trying to introduce the concept of good wine to the independently-minded managers of nearly 2,500 co-ops. With every year, however, it becomes clearer that Dr Woodrow is beginning to win her fight. Co-op shelves now contain a range of wines that would not disgrace some far smarter shops - were it not for the awfulness of most of their labels.

41	£3.49	**ALSACE PINOT BLANC**, Cave Vinicole de Turckheim 1989
148	£2.69	**PIERRE CHAUMONT ANJOU BLANC**, Remy Pannier, Loire
197	£2.39	**LOHENGRIN RUDESHEIMER ROSENGARTEN**, Rudesheimer Weinkellerei, Nahe 1988
243	£2.39	**BULGARIAN COUNTRY WINE, MERLOT/GAMZA,** Suhindol
323	£2.59	**COTEAUX DU TRICASTIN**, Cellier de l'Enclave des Papes, Rhône

383	£2.49	**VALPOLICELLA CARISSA**, Pasqua, Veneto
480	£4.65	**CASSONS FINE OLD RUBY PORT**, Smith Woodhouse, Douro
496	£1.39	**GOLDENER OKTOBER LIGHT WHITE**, St Ursula Weinkellerei, Rheinhessen

C&B | Corney & Barrow

12 Helmet Row, London, EC1V 3QJ (071 251 4051). Established merchant with branches in London and Newmarket. **Opening Hours:** 9am-7pm Mon-Fri. **Delivery:** free within M25 for 2+ cases, free nationally for 3+ cases. **Tastings:** regularly in-store plus tutored events.

Corney & Barrow is a Janus of a company, with two quite different faces. On the one hand, there is the City firm from whom very lucky and faithful customers are occasionally allowed to buy a case or two of Pétrus; on the other, there is the shop in the louche environs of the Portobello Road that sells interesting bottles of Spanish wine, French country wine and Chardonnay and Cabernet Sauvignon from Simi, one of the best wineries in California. Actually, there is only one C&B list - it's just that it is taking rather a while to convert some of the firm's more pin-striped customers to the Simi-er side of life. Today, however, some of those same customers have even been seen to follow C&B's advice to chill their Sancerre Rouge.

3	£6.95	**YALUMBA ANGAS BRUT**, Barossa Valley
23	£18.50	**CHAMPAGNE LAURENT PERRIER ROSE**
28	£3.45	**VIN DE PAYS DES COTES DE GASCOGNE** Plaimont, South-West 1989
43	£4.69	**PINOT BIANCO**, Vigna al Monte, Puglia 1989
90	£8.74	**CHATEAU CONSTANTIN**, Graves, Bordeaux 1986
92	£9.39	**SIMI CHARDONNAY**, Sonoma 1985
95	£10.50	**CLOUDY BAY CHARDONNAY**, Marlborough 1988
312	£12.76	**SIMI CABERNET SAUVIGNON RESERVE**, Napa Valley 1981
418	£37.00	**SOLAIA**, Antinori, Tuscany 1986

CWM | Cornwall Wine Merchants

Chapel Rd, Tuckingmill, Camborne, Cornwall (0209 715765). Wholesaler selling to the public by the mixed case. **Delivery:** free within 75 miles, nationally at cost. **Tastings:** organised on request.

For some wine merchants, a price list is just that - a printed list of names and prices. For others, its production is a major publishing venture, involving designers, photographers and writers galore. Nick Richards has ploughed the middle course, making a list using what we imagine to be a fairly modest home computer, but taking the trouble to describe every wine, producer and region. And the wines are worth describing: two dozen well chosen Burgundies, a range of sparkling wines and Champagnes that includes the rare 1982 Piper Heidsieck Brut Sauvage, a set of affordably appealing Bordeaux such as Ramage la Batisse 1987 (at £7.29) and a strong range of Antipodeans.

22	£16.50	**CHAMPAGNE BRICOUT CARTE D'OR BRUT PRESTIGE**
24	£18.75	**CHAMPAGNE LOUIS ROEDERER BRUT PREMIER**
38	£4.29	**ALSACE TOKAY-PINOT GRIS**, Cave Vinicole de Turckheim 1988
134	£ 6.50	**NOBILOS SAUVIGNON BLANC**, Marlborough 1989
168	£15.00	**ALSACE GEWURZTRAMINER SELECTION DE GRAINS NOBLES**, Cave Vinicole de Turckheim 1988
187	£5.99	**ORLANDO ST HELGA RIESLING**, Barossa Valley 1986

267	£2.75	**VIN DE PAYS DE L'AUDE CABERNET SAUVIGNON**, Paul Boutinot, Midi 1987
276	£3.89	**CONCHA Y TORO MERLOT**, Maipo 1986
299	£8.50	**CHATEAU RAMAGE LA BATISSE**, Haut-Médoc, Bordeaux 1985
336	£4.99	**CROZES HERMITAGE**, Delas Freres, Rhône 1988
397	£4.99	**RECIOTO DELLA VALPOLICELLA**, Cantine Sociale di Soave, Veneto 1982
464	£27.50	**CHATEAU RIEUSSEC**, Sauternes, Bordeaux 1983
482	£5.45	**SMITH WOODHOUSE RUBY PORT**, Douro

CGW | Cote Green Wines Ltd.

45/47 Compstall Road, Marple Bridge, Stockport, Cheshire (061 462 0155). Independent family merchant. **Delivery:** free within 20 miles, nationally at cost. **Tastings:** regularly in-store plus tutored events. **Discounts:** 7% on mixed cases.

Following in the footsteps of Francis Murray, owner of the award-winning Barnes Wine Shop, Richard Suter, like Murray a former policeman, has turned his hobby into a very successful wine business. Suter's enthusiasm for the subject is evident throughout his list, with exhortations such as 'Come in and have a browse - there's lots more to look at' and tasting notes which make it perfectly clear that the wines listed are almost all his personal favourites. Cheshire has a good selection of 'smart' merchants; it needs a few more that are as friendly as Cote Green.

4	£5.32	**ASTI MARTINI**, Martini & Rossi, Piedmont
22	£17.31	**CHAMPAGNE BRICOUT CARTE D'OR BRUT PRESTIGE**
29	£3.47	**VIN DE PAYS DES COTES DE GASCOGNE**, Domaine de Perras, South-West 1989
41	£4.48	**ALSACE PINOT BLANC**, Cave Vinicole de Turckheim 1989
54	£7.19	**POUILLY LOCHE CHATEAU DE LOCHE**, Caves des Grands Crus Vinzelles, Burgundy 1987
80	£6.89	**WOLF BLASS BARREL-FERMENTED CHARDONNAY**, South Australia 1988
149	£2.99	**CHENIN BLANC**, E & J Gallo 1988
157	£3.17	**RETSINA OF ATTICA**, Kourtaki
220	£5.48	**KREUZNACHER KAPELLENPFAD WEISSBURGUNDER SPATLESE**, E Anheuser, Nahe 1986
233	£3.63	**WHITE GRENACHE**, E & J Gallo 1989
267	£2.89	**VIN DE PAYS DE L'AUDE CABERNET SAUVIGNON**, Paul Boutinot, Midi 1987
276	£3.99	**CONCHA Y TORO MERLOT**, Maipo 1986
299	£9.17	**CHATEAU RAMAGE LA BATISSE**, Haut-Médoc, Bordeaux 1985
331	£4.75	**RASTEAU COTES DU RHONE VILLAGES**, Caves des Vignerons de Rasteau 1988
414	£16.69	**TIGNANELLO**, Antinori, Tuscany 1985

COV | County Vintners

Unit 21, Whitebridge Estate, Stone, Staffs (0785 817229) Wine warehouse dealing by the mixed case. **Opening hours:** 9am-5.30pm Mon-Fri; 9am-1pm Sat. **Delivery:** free locally and around their Oxfordshire depot, nationally at cost. **Tastings:** regularly in-store.

Oxbridge graduates Francis Peel and Mark Eardley set up their business five years ago, selling mainly to the trade. They took over Whitebridge Wines in Stone in 1989 and are now looking to expand their sales to the public. Although they do stock a range from other countries, the list concentrates on the traditional areas of France and they have high hopes for their newly acquired range of Bergerac wines from Domaine du Gouyat. There are more exciting places to buy wine from - but not around here..

3	£5.99	**YALUMBA ANGAS BRUT**, Barossa Valley
36	£4.21	**JURANCON SEC VIGUERIE ROYALE**,Les Vignerons des Coteaux, South-West 1988
261	£5.99	**BODEGAS Y CAVAS DE WEINERT CABERNET SAUVIGNON**, Mendoza 1983
266	£2.76	**PLOVDIV CABERNET SAUVIGNON**, Bulgarian Vintners 1985
290	£6.75	**FIRESTONE CABERNET SAUVIGNON**, Santa Ynez 1986
353	£10.69	**ST JOSEPH CUVEE ANAIS DOMAINE DU CHENE**, Marc Rouvière, Rhône 1987
414	£14.95	**TIGNANELLO**, Antinori, Tuscany 1985
441	£3.49	**Morris Rutherglen Liqueur Muscat**

| **CUM** | **Cumbrian Cellar** |

1 St Andrews Square, Penrith, Cumbria CA11 7AN (0768 63664). Independent merchant with a taste for exotica. **Opening Hours:** 9am-5.30pm Mon-Sat. **Delivery:** free within Cumbria, nationally at cost. **Tastings:** occasionally in-store plus tutored events. **Discounts:** 5% on mixed case.

At about the time that this *Guide* will appear on the shelves, the Cumbrian Cellar will be ten years old. Happy birthday. Though the list is well-structured and attractive, there are no great speciality areas here, although not many other merchants stock Cypriot, Zimbabwean, Texan, Russian and Israeli wines - as well as copies of this *Guide*. Well worth a visit while you are in the Lake District - if only to pick up some delicious Bison Grass vodka.

24	£19.35	**CHAMPAGNE LOUIS ROEDERER BRUT PREMIER**
49	£6.90	**BABICH SEMILLON/CHARDONNAY**, Gisborne 1989
127	£5.25	**MUSCADET DE SEVRE ET MAINE SUR LIE**, G Bossard, Loire 1989
157	£3.45	**RETSINA OF ATTICA**, Kourtaki
177	£4.30	**BADEN DRY**, ZBW
194	£5.80	**DEINHARD HERITAGE SELECTION DEIDESHEIM**, Rheinpfalz 1987
255	£4.50	**MINERVOIS CHATEAU DE BLOMAC**, Midi 1988
276	£3.95	**CONCHA Y TORO MERLOT**, Maipo 1986
338	£5.55	**WYNNS COONAWARRA SHIRAZ** 1987
361	£6.20	**BROUILLY**, E Loron, Beaujolais 1989
471	£6.95	**AMONTILLADO TIO DIEGO**, Valdespino, Jerez
488	£10.90	**SMITH WOODHOUSE LATE BOTTLED VINTAGE PORT (BOTTLED 1984)**, Douro 1979
491	£14.60	**WARRE'S QUINTA DA CAVADINHA**, Douro 1979

| **D** | **Davisons** |

Head Office: 7 Aberdeen Rd, Croydon, Surrey CR0 1EQ (081 681 3222). London and Home Counties chain with 78 branches, allied to the Master Cellar warehouse (q.v.). **Opening Hours:** 10am-2pm & 5pm - 10pm Mon-Sat; 12-2pm & 7pm-9pm Sun. **Delivery** free locally, nationally at cost. **Tastings:** regularly in certain stores. **Discounts:** a hefty 8.5 % off mixed cases.

Regional Chain of the Year in the 1990 *Guide*, Davisons continues to succeed by maintaining the atmosphere of the 'little shop on the corner run by the nice couple'.

There are good Alsace wines from Hugel, a compact but classy German range and several vintage ports from the top houses. A browse among the claret section of the list reveals over 130 wines, including all the first growths and Pétrus, most of which are said to be available in all the shops (though we haven't noticed the Pétrus in our local branch). These are the shops to frequent if your shopping list includes Château Rieussec (five vintages are stocked), a magnum of Valpolicella, a four-pack of Fosters and a few packets of crisps..

3	£5.25	**YALUMBA ANGAS BRUT**, Barossa Valley
4	£5.95	**ASTI MARTINI**, Martini & Rossi, Piedmont
40	£4.75	**COOKS MARLBOROUGH SEMILLON** 1987
61	£11.25	**CHABLIS 1ER CRU VAILLONS**, E Defaix, Burgundy 1985
129	£5.25	**MONTANA SAUVIGNON BLANC**, Marlborough 1989
142	£7.95	**POUILLY BLANC FUME DOMAINE CHAILLOUX**, Châtelain, Loire 1987
160	£5.25	**ALSACE GEWURZTRAMINER**, Caves Coop des Viticulteurs d'Ingersheim 1987
172	£4.75	**JOAO PIRES WHITE TABLE WINE**, Palmela 1988
213	£4.95	**NIERSTEINER SPIEGELBERG KABINETT,** Guntrum, Rheinhessen 1988
250	£3.25	**COTEAUX DE MURVIEL DOMAINE DE LIMBARDIE**, Boukandoura & Hutin, Midi 1988
266	£2.79	**PLOVDIV CABERNET SAUVIGNON**, Bulgarian Vintners 1985
289	£7.25	**CHATEAU BEAUMONT**, Cru Bourgeois Médoc, Bordeaux 1986
292	£7.75	**ORLANDO ST HUGO CABERNET SAUVIGNON**, Coonawarra 1986
305	£10.25	**CHATEAU MAUCAILLOU**, Moulis, Bordeaux 1986
320	£19.50	**CHATEAU LYNCH-BAGES**, Pauillac, Bordeaux 1985
339	£6.49	**PENFOLDS BIN 28 KALIMNA SHIRAZ**, South Australia 1986
348	£5.75	**CHATEAUNEUF-DU-PAPE DOMAINE FONT DE MICHELLE**, Gonnet, Rhône 1985
358	£3.99	**GAMAY DE L'ARDECHE**, Georges Duboeuf, Rhône 1989
365	£7.95	**FLEURIE LA MADONE**, Georges Duboeuf, Beaujolais 1988
369	£10.25	**SANTENAY LE CHENAY**, Domaine Bernard Morey, Burgundy 1985
376	£15.25	**CHAMBOLLE MUSIGNY**, Domaine Mâchard de Gramont, Burgundy 1986
392	£4.65	**BARBERA D'ASTI COLLINA CROJA**, Castelvero, Piedmont 1988
464	£13.50	**CHATEAU RIEUSSEC**, Sauternes, Bordeaux 1983

DVY | Davy & Co Ltd

161-165 Greenwich High Road, London SE10 8JA (081 858 6014) . Independent merchant. **Opening Hours:** 10am-7pm Mon-Fri; 10am-5pm Sat. **Delivery:** nationally at cost. **Tastings:** regularly in-store plus tutored events.

A wonderfully English blend of ancient and modern, this is the company behind all those sawdust-floored wine bars with names like the 'Boot & Flogger', pints of port and tough tannic Englishman's claret. So much for the ancient. The 'modern' is increasingly evident in the listing of wines like the gloriously New World Stoneleigh Sauvignon Blanc and the Domaine de Limbardie wines from southern France. All in all, Davy's is rather like an endearing old gent who loves good modern jazz...

46	£4.90	**SOAVE CASTEGGIOLA**, G Rizzardi, Veneto 1987
74	£5.35	**RIOJA BLANCO SECO RESERVA**, CVNE 1985
81	£6.05	**STONELEIGH CHARDONNAY**, Marlborough 1988
95	£9.00	**CLOUDY BAY CHARDONNAY**, Marlborough 1988
161	£5.30	**ALSACE GEWURZTRAMINER DAMBACH**, Louis Gisselbrecht 1988
174	£4.05	**BROWN BROS LATE HARVEST ORANGE MUSCAT & FLORA**, N E Victoria 1988
250	£3.85	**COTEAUX DE MURVIEL DOMAINE DE LIMBARDIE**, Boukandoura & Hutin, Midi 1988
266	£2.75	**PLOVDIV CABERNET SAUVIGNON,** Bulgarian Vintners 1985
395	£4.95	**VALPOLICELLA CLASSICO VIGNETI MARA**, Cesari, Veneto 1987
398	£5.65	**FRANCIACORTA ROSSO**, Barone Pizzini Piomarta, Lombardy 1987
422	£3.90	**ALMANSA MARIUS TINTO RESERVA**, Bodegas Piqueras 1982
443	£9.55	**CAMPBELLS RUTHERGLEN MUSCAT**

ROD	Rodney Densem

Stapeley Bank, London Rd, Nantwich, Cheshire CW5 7JW (0270 623665). Independent merchant operating retail and wholesale. **Opening Hours:** 10am-6pm Mon, Tue; 9am-1pm Wed; 9am-6pm Thu-Sat. **Delivery:** free within 30 miles, nationally at cost. **Tastings:** regularly in-store plus tutored events. **Discounts:** 5% on mixed cases.

Rodney and Margie Densem have learned that one of the biggest problems facing any retailer is the smallness of the margin he can make on wholesale prices - so they have done the sensible thing of both cutting out the middle man (by buying directly) and of becoming middle men themselves (by acting as wholesalers). The combined result is to allow them to stock some 800 wines and to price them very reasonably.

4	£5.35	**ASTI MARTINI**, Martini & Rossi, Piedmont
6	£6.80	**CLAIRETTE DE DIE CUVEE IMPERIAL**, Union des Producteurs, Rhône
24	£18.75	**CHAMPAGNE LOUIS ROEDERER BRUT PREMIER**
73	£5.55	**LINDEMANS BIN 65 CHARDONNAY**, Murray River 1989
87	£7.79	PENFOLDS CHARDONNAY, South Australia 1988
174	£5.20	BROWN BROTHERS LATE HARVEST ORANGE MUSCAT & FLORA, N E Victoria 1988
236	£6.05	**TORRES CABERNET SAUVIGNON ROSE**, Curico 1989
294	£8.65	**ROSEMOUNT SHOW RESERVE COONAWARRA CABERNET SAUVIGNON** 1987
297	£8.65	**PENFOLDS BIN 389 SHIRAZ/CABERNET**, South Australia 1986
311	£11.99	**CHATEAU HAUT-MARBUZET**, St Estèphe, Bordeaux 1985
313	£11.99	**CHATEAU MOUTON-BARONNE-PHILIPPE**, Pauillac, Bordeaux 1986
379	£16.95	**VOSNE-ROMANEE LES MALCONSORTS**, Moillard, Burgundy 1986
387	£3.50	**MONTEPULCIANO D'ABRUZZO**, Tollo, Abruzzi 1987
444	£10.69	**BAILEYS FOUNDERS LIQUEUR MUSCAT**, Glenrowan
458	£16.45	**CHATEAU LAMOTHE-GUIGNARD**, Sauternes, Bordeaux 1986
489	£13.06	**HENRIQUES & HENRIQUES 10 YEAR OLD SERCIAL**, Madeira
490	£13.06	**HENRIQUES & HENRIQUES 10 YEAR OLD MALMSEY**, Madeira

PD	Peter Dominic

Head Office: Astra House, River Way,Harlow, Essex CM20 2DT (0279 26801). High Street chain with over 600 branches. **Opening Hours:** 9am-9pm Mon-Sat; 12-2pm & 7pm-9pm Sun at most stores. **Delivery:** free locally, nationally at cost. **Tastings:** regularly in-store. **Discounts:** 5% on case price.

While Thresher, Victoria Wine and Augustus Barnett all show signs of annual improvement, Peter Dominic have sometimes seemed to be floundering in the shallows. The list of successes in the 1990 Challenge, however, does provide some evidence that a broader range of good wines has fought its way through to the Peter Dominic shelves.

This chain has such potential (not to mention a fair few keen managers) that it would not take very much effort and commitment on the part of Grand Metropolitan, its owners, to make it a really strong contender.

4	£5.49	**ASTI MARTINI**, Martini & Rossi, Piedmont
28	£2.99	**VIN DE PAYS DES COTES DE GASCOGNE**, Plaimont, South-West 1989
73	£5.29	**LINDEMANS BIN 65 CHARDONNAY**, Murray River 1989
74	£5.45	**RIOJA BLANCO SECO RESERVA**, CVNE 1985
129	£5.15	**MONTANA SAUVIGNON BLANC**, Marlborough 1989
136	£5.99	**ADLER FELS SAUVIGNON BLANC**, Sonoma 1987

147	£2.49	**RAMADA ALMEIRIM BLANCO**
152	£4.15	**COOKS CHENIN BLANC**, Hawkes Bay 1987
174	£5.25	BROWN BROTHERS LATE HARVEST ORANGE MUSCAT & FLORA, N E Victoria 1988
195	£6.75	**THREE CHOIRS BACCHUS**, Gloucestershire 1989
206	£2.89	**KLUSSERATHER ST MICHAEL**, Zentrallkellerei Mosel-Saar-Ruwer 1986
266	£2.89	**PLOVDIV CABERNET SAUVIGNON**, Bulgarian Vintners 1985
276	£3.79	**CONCHA Y TORO MERLOT**, Maipo 1986
331	£3.99	**RASTEAU COTES DU RHONE VILLAGES**, Caves des Vignerons de Rasteau 1988
344	£6.75	**BOTOBOLAR ST GILBERT RED WINE**, Mudgee 1987
358	£3.49	**GAMAY DE L'ARDECHE**, Georges Duboeuf, Rhône 1989
401	£7.95	**CHIANTI CLASSICO RISERVA DUCALE**, Ruffino, Tuscany 1986
424	£4.49	**ROMEIRA GARRAFEIRA**, Cavas Velhas 1980
454	£7.50	**TOKAY ASZU 5 PUTTONYOS**, Tokaji 1981
497	£1.69	**LAMBRUSCO LIGHT (BLUSH WHITE)**, Giacobazzi, Emilia-Romagna
499	£1.89	**PETILLANT DE RAISIN (3%)**, Listel, Midi

DRI	**Drinksmart**

Bullhead St, Wigston, Leicester LE8 1P8 (0533 881122). Modern independent merchant in purpose-built premises. **Tastings:** regularly in-store and to outside groups on request. **Discounts:** on case purchases, many of which are six-bottle cases.

The name Drinksmart doesn't have quite the same resonance as Justerini & Brooks or even the Hungerford Wine Co. And Julian Twaites' assertion that his 18,000 sq ft shop-cum-warehouse is the 'largest drinks superstore in the UK' hardly sets traditional wine lovers' minds racing. But just take a look at these award winners; it's a selection many a less prosaically named merchant would be proud of.

Apart from these wines, and an extensive range of bottles from Eastern Europe, there's a large selection of port, claret and Burgundy. Twaites is such a forward-looking, value-oriented merchant that it's impossible not to wonder how much greater a reputation his firm might have if, like Superbrew, it changed its name....

4	£5.45	**ASTI MARTINI**, Martini & Rossi, Piedmont
52	£5.95	**HOUGHTON VERDELHO**, Swan Valley 1988
76	£6.19	**MONTROSE CHARDONNAY**, Mudgee 1989
77	£6.25	**KIES ESTATE SEMILLON/SAUVIGNON**, Barossa Valley 1988
86	£7.49	**MUSCADET DE SEVRE ET MAINE SUR LIE CHATEAU DE CHASSELOIR (OAK-AGED)**, Loire 1987
129	£4.79	**MONTANA SAUVIGNON BLANC**, Marlborough 1989
136	£6.99	**ADLER FELS SAUVIGNON BLANC**, Sonoma 1987
138	£6.99	HUNTERS SAUVIGNON BLANC, Marlborough 1989
159	£4.75	**TORRES GEWURZTRAMINER**, Curico 1988
174	£4.49	BROWN BROTHERS LATE HARVEST ORANGE MUSCAT & FLORA, N E Victoria 1988
177	£2.95	**BADEN DRY**, ZBW
229	£8.95	KREUZNACHER BRUCKES RIESLING AUSLESE, Schloss Plettenberg, Nahe 1985
233	£3.25	**WHITE GRENACHE**, E & J Gallo 1989
243	£2.15	**BULGARIAN COUNTRY WINE**, Merlot/Gamza, Suhindol
266	£2.69	**PLOVDIV CABERNET SAUVIGNON**, Bulgarian Vintners 1985
281	£4.79	CHATEAU TOUR MARTINES BORDEAUX SUPERIEUR 1983
284	£2.99	**SPECIAL RESERVE STAMBOLOVO MERLOT**, Bulgarian Vintners 1985
286	£5.99	**COLUMBIA CREST CABERNET SAUVIGNON**, Washington State 1985

288	£6.75	**PETER LEHMANN CABERNET SAUVIGNON**, Barossa Valley 1985
320	£27.95	CHATEAU LYNCH-BAGES, Pauillac, Bordeaux 1985
321	£29.25	CHATEAU GRUAUD-LAROSE (Cordier), St Julien, Bordeaux 1978
444	£10.95	BAILEYS FOUNDERS LIQUEUR MUSCAT, Glenrowan
452	£6.49	**PETER LEHMANN BOTRYTIS RIESLING**, Barossa Valley 1984
460	£15.75	CHATEAU RABAUD-PROMIS, Sauternes, Bordeaux 1986
474	£8.39	**DON LUIS AMONTILLADO**, Burdon, Jerez
476	£10.75	MATUSALEM OLOROSO MUY VIEJO, Gonzalez Byass, Jerez
478	£10.75	AMONTILLADO DEL DUQUE, Gonzalez Byass, Jerez
482	£5.89	**SMITH WOODHOUSE RUBY PORT**, Douro
488	£10.45	**SMITH WOODHOUSE LATE BOTTLED VINTAGE PORT (BOTTLED 1984)**, Douro 1979
491	£14.25	**WARRE'S QUINTA DA CAVADINHA**, Douro 1979
499	£1.89	**PETILLANT DE RAISIN (3%)**, Listel, Midi

DX | Drinkx plc

406-408 Merton Road, London SW18 5AD (081-877 0444) & Arch 85, Goding St, London SE11 5EZ (071 582 4540). Young independent company ready to take on the world. **Opening Hours:** 10am-8pm Mon-Sat; 12-3pm Sun. **Delivery:** free locally, nationally at cost. **Tastings:** regular in-store plus tutored events. **Discounts:** on large quantities.

'We merely hope that, like Demosthenes... you find in our list "a flagon of wine that I may soak my brain and get an ingenious idea."' Giles Clarke has had a number of ingenious ideas in his time: buying Majestic, selling his shares in Majestic a few years later for rather a lot of money and, he would argue, starting a curiously named business that stocks 'all of the beverage requirements of home and office'.

So, the Drinkx list includes Blackdown sparkling water, Cordier's Texan Sauvignon Blanc, Tyrer's Australian Chardonnay (from a winery that looks like Dr Who's Tardis), 1952 Krug, 1986 Peter Sichel Club Claret, and the 1985 Guigal Côte Rôtie 'La Landonne' for just £195 a bottle - typical boardroom fare... Would-be wine investors may be interested in Drinkx's (if that's the correct grammar) offer to manage their portfolios — along with around a million pounds worth of other people's cellars.

23	£18.49	**CHAMPAGNE LAURENT PERRIER ROSE**
24	£19.99	**CHAMPAGNE LOUIS ROEDERER BRUT PREMIER**
41	£3.99	**ALSACE PINOT BLANC**, Cave Vinicole de Turckheim 1989
95	£10.49	**CLOUDY BAY CHARDONNAY**, Marlborough 1988
107	£13.25	**CULLENS CHARDONNAY**, Margaret River 1987
106	£18.00	**LEEUWIN ESTATE CHARDONNAY**, Margaret River 1984
269	£2.99	**HOUSE CLARET**, Peter Sichel, Bordeaux
321	£26.25	**CHATEAU GRUAUD-LAROSE (CORDIER)**, St Julien, Bordeaux 1978
340	£5.99	**COTES DU RHONE**, Guigal 1986

GD | George Dutton & Son. See Willoughby's

EP | Eldridge Pope

Head Office: Weymouth Ave, Dorchester, Dorset, DT1 1QT (0305 251251). South of England chain with 13 shops including four Reynier Wine Libraries. **Opening Hours:** 9am-6pm Mon-Sat. **Delivery:**

free locally for one case and nationally for three cases. **Tastings:** regularly in-store plus tutored events. **Discounts:** 5% on mixed cases.

The firm that brought you Gundlach Bundschu and Grgich Hills from California and 11 different wines from Luxembourg has increased its list of Spanish wines this year from seven to nine. Rather endearingly, however, it resolutely bucks the trend by not building up its range of four Australians. Dorset wine lovers are lucky to have a local merchant that can offer such uncommercial wines as 1971 and 1976 Mosels, six different late-harvest Alsatians and sweet Loires dating back to 1947 (Moulin Touchais at £30), as well as an easy-reference vintage guide assessing the years whose wines are listed. Eldridge Pope also deserve credit for running an enthusiastic campaign to increase the sales of wines from their pubs.

23	£18.50	**CHAMPAGNE LAURENT PERRIER ROSE**
76	£5.99	**MONTROSE CHARDONNAY**, Mudgee 1989
150	£3.65	**VOUVRAY DEMI-SEC**, Les Caves des Viticulteurs, Loire 1988
216	£5.50	**SCHARZHOFBERGER KABINETT KESSELSTATT**, Mosel-Saar-Ruwer 1988
228	£7.22	**GRAACHER HIMMELREICH RIESLING SPATLESE**, F W Gymnasium, Mosel-Saar-Ruwer 1988
289	£6.50	**CHATEAU BEAUMONT**, Cru Bourgeois Médoc, Bordeaux 1986
319	£20.00	**CHATEAU PICHON-LONGUEVILLE-BARON**, Pauillac, Bordeaux 1985
320	£22.95	**CHATEAU LYNCH-BAGES**, Pauillac, Bordeaux 1985
321	£26.00	**CHATEAU GRUAUD-LAROSE (CORDIER)**, St Julien, Bordeaux 1978
387	£3.50	**MONTEPULCIANO D'ABRUZZO**, Tollo, Abruzzi 1987
417	£23.50	**BAROLO MONPRIVATO**, G Mascarello, Piedmont 1985
451	£5.99	**CHATEAU LA NERE**, Dulac & Seraphon, Loupiac, Bordeaux 1986
464	£27.50	**CHATEAU RIEUSSEC**, Sauternes, Bordeaux 1983

EBA | Ben Ellis & Assocs

The Harvesters, Lawrence Lane, Buckland, Betchworth, Surrey RH3 7BE (073784 2160). Independent mail-order firm selling by the case. **Delivery:** free locally, nationally at cost. **Tastings:** regularly in-store plus tutored events.

With a name that makes it sound like a firm of accountants, this is a very straight-down-the-line company with plenty of readily drinkable clarets from the early 1980s, serious Burgundies and the inevitable Cloudy Bay. The tasting expertise is provided by Mark Pardoe, a newly-qualified Master of Wine who outclassed all the other candidates to take the Madame Bollinger Award. And, yes, that particular Champagne does feature on the list, along with the George Goulet house fizz.

47	£5.26	**LUGANA**, Ca Dei Frati, Lombardy 1989
95	£9.53	**CLOUDY BAY CHARDONNAY**, Marlborough 1988
109	£11.31	**CHATEAU DE FIEUZAL**, Graves, Bordeaux 1986
138	£7.33	**HUNTERS SAUVIGNON BLANC**, Marlborough 1989
172	£4.86	**JOAO PIRES WHITE TABLE WINE**, Palmela 1988
319	£15.33	**CHATEAU PICHON-LONGUEVILLE-BARON**, Pauillac, Bordeaux 1985
373	£11.98	**AU BON CLIMAT PINOT NOIR** 1988
402	£5.99	**VINO NOBILE DI MONTEPULCIANO RISERVA**, Fattorio del Cerro, Tuscany 1985

EOO   Everton's of Ombersley

Worcester Rd, Ombersley, Nr Droitwich, Worcs WR9 0EW (0905 620282). 45-year-old family owned, centre-of-England chain with branches in Hagley, Ombersley, Pershore and Upton. **Opening Hours:** 9am-6pm Tue-Fri; 9am-5.30pm Sat; closed for lunch 1pm-2pm each day. **Tastings:** occasionally in-store plus tutored events.

Over the last half century, Don Everton has built up a very handy little chain, with a list that, apart from the award winners listed below, includes Antonin Rodet Burgundies, a good selection of Grande Marque Champagnes and a growing selection of well-chosen wines from the New World and, thank goodness, English vineyards. Droitwich has often featured among southerners' jokes about the barren wastes of the North. Everton's is the kind of company to prove them wrong.

4	£5.70	**ASTI MARTINI**, Martini & Rossi, Piedmont	
23	£19.50	**CHAMPAGNE LAURENT PERRIER ROSE**	
24	£19.29	**CHAMPAGNE LOUIS ROEDERER BRUT PREMIER**	
134	£6.89	**NOBILOS SAUVIGNON BLANC**, Marlborough 1989	
184	£4.71	**ASTLEY HUXELVANER**, Worcestershire 1989	
303	£10.30	**ROUGE HOMME COONAWARRA CABERNET SAUVIGNON** 1985	
317	£19.96	**MONDAVI CABERNET SAUVIGNON RESERVE**, Napa Valley 1980	
337	£5.35	**ROUGE HOMME SHIRAZ/CABERNET**, Coonawarra 1985	
359	£5.00	**BEAUJOLAIS-VILLAGES**, Georges Duboeuf 1989	
363	£5.70	**REGNIE CRISTAL**, Georges Duboeuf, Beaujolais 1989	
364	£6.16	**MORGON JEAN DESCOMBES**, Georges Duboeuf, Beaujolais 1989	
378	£15.98	**MONDAVI PINOT NOIR RESERVE**, Napa Valley 1986	
453	£8.00	**BONNEZEAUX**, Jean Godineau, Loire 1987	
493	£20.65	**QUINTA DO NOVAL 20 YEAR OLD TAWNY PORT**, Douro	

EVI   Evingtons

120 Evington Rd, Leicester, LE2 1HH (0533 542702). Independent merchant. **Opening Hours:** 9.30am-6pm Mon-Sat. **Delivery:** free locally, nationally at cost. **Tastings:** regularly in-store plus tutored events. **Discounts:** 5% on mixed cases.

Apart from the specialist offerings of 'fine and rare' Bordeaux and ports he has put together, Simon March has developed an enviable selection of Antipodean wines, including the rare, organic Botobolar red. Iberia is well covered too, as, with such wines as the excellent Château de Blomac, is southern France,.

4	£5.45	**ASTI MARTINI**, Martini & Rossi, Piedmont	
24	£19.25	**CHAMPAGNE LOUIS ROEDERER BRUT PREMIER**	
49	£5.98	**BABICH SEMILLON/CHARDONNAY**, Gisborne 1989	
74	£5.85	**RIOJA BLANCO SECO RESERVA**, CVNE 1985	
119	£4.29	**SAUMUR BLANC**, Caves des Vignerons de Saumur, Loire 1988	
172	£4.69	**JOAO PIRES WHITE TABLE WINE**, Palmela 1988	
174	£5.69	BROWN BROTHERS LATE HARVEST ORANGE MUSCAT & FLORA, N E Victoria 1988	
255	£4.09	**MINERVOIS CHATEAU DE BLOMAC**, Midi 1988	
277	£4.95	**SEAVIEW CABERNET SAUVIGNON**, South Australia 1985	
297	£8.85	**PENFOLDS BIN 389 SHIRAZ/CABERNET**, South Australia 1986	
336	£5.35	**CROZES HERMITAGE**, Delas Frères, Rhône 1988	
339	£6.19	**PENFOLDS BIN 28 KALIMNA SHIRAZ**, South Australia 1986	

341	£7.25	**VACQUEYRAS CUVEE DES TEMPLIERS**, Domaine le Clos de Cazeaux, Rhône1986
344	£7.30	**BOTOBOLAR ST GILBERT RED WINE**, Mudgee 1987
422	£4.49	**ALMANSA MARIUS TINTO RESERVA**, Bodegas Piqueras 1982
486	£9.25	**WARRE'S WARRIOR VINTAGE CHARACTER PORT**, Douro
487	£9.65	**COSSART GORDON 5 YEAR OLD BUAL**, Madeira
491	£14.95	**WARRE'S QUINTA DA CAVADINHA**, Douro 1979
499	£2.25	**PETILLANT DE RAISIN (3%)**, Listel, Midi

FAR   Farr Vintners

19 Sussex Street, Pimlico, London, SW1V 4RR (071 828 1960). Very up-market supplier of ancient wine. **Delivery:** nationally at cost. **Tastings:** tutored tastings and 'theme evenings'. **Discounts:** 5% on 10+ cases.

If you have a friend who's going to be 110 this year, Farr Vintners can supply you with a bottle of Lafite of his or her birth year; a 56 year-old might similarly appreciate a set of six bottles of 1935 port (at only £120 apiece). Old vintages are what this sometimes rather snooty company are about - and it does them well. If there are any more bottles of 'Thomas Jefferson' wine to be had, you'll doubtless be able to buy them from Farr.

AF   Alexr Findlater & Co. Ltd

Heveningham High House, Nr Halesworth, Suffolk IP19 0EA (0986 83 274) & Vauxhall Cellars, 72 Goding Street, London SE11 5AW (071 587 0982). Australian specialist selling by the case. **Opening Hours:** 9.30am-8pm Mon-Fri; 9.30am-6pm Sat. **Delivery:** free nationally for 3+ cases. **Tastings:** bottles opened regularly.

As last year's *Guide* arrived in the bookshops, Alexr Findlater folded his Abbey Road tent and moved to Vauxhall. Early rumours suggested that this Australian, Italian and German specialist had given up retailing wine completely. This was fortunately not the case, but would-be customers now have to buy by the dozen. Findlater's list is still impressive, even when one looks beyond the Australian range. There are no less than 18 Trocken and Halbtrocken German wines - including the rare, organic, oaky Dr Loosen 'barrique' Müller-Thurgau - and 20 examples of 1985 Bordeaux. And in the unlikely event that you can't find what you want on this list, Findlater says he will be delighted to obtain it for you — provided you buy an unbroken case.

98	£10.99	**GEOFF MERRILL CHARDONNAY**, McLaren Vale 1987
134	£6.45	**NOBILOS SAUVIGNON BLANC**, Marlborough 1989
144	£8.99	**MOUNT HURTLE SAUVIGNON BLANC**, McLaren Vale 1989
488	£11.20	**SMITH WOODHOUSE LATE BOTTLED VINTAGE PORT (BOTTLED 1984)**, Douro 1979

FDL   Findlater Mackie Todd

Findlater House, 22 Great Queen St, London WC2B 5BB (071 831 7701). Established merchant and mail order specialist. **Delivery:** free on UK mainland. **Tastings:** regularly in-store plus tutored events. **Discounts:** £1.15 per case for 3+ cases.

If you have been persuaded to buy wine from one of the offers that fall out of your Visa Card bills, you have possibly, like the Queen, become a customer of one of Britain's three largest mail-order merchants. Founded in 1823, Findlaters keeps a lowish profile but offers good ranges of Bordeaux and sherry, coupled with increasingly strong selections from Italy, Spain, and Germany, all of which benefited from the merging of the company's list with that of Henry Townsend, the merchant it took over late in 1988. The company's avowed policy we described last year of discouraging individual bottle purchases and encouraging case sales has evidently been so successful that, in early 1990, Findlater's closed its retail shop in Covent Garden.

401   £6.29   **CHIANTI CLASSICO RISERVA DUCALE**, Ruffino, Tuscany 1986

FW	Fleming's Wines

31 Forehill, Ely, Cambs CB7 4AA (0353 667753). Independent merchant. **Opening Hours:** 9.30am-6pm Mon, Wed-Sat. **Delivery:** free locally, nationally at cost. **Tastings:** regularly in-store plus tutored events.

Charlotte Fleming's experience at Oddbins and Moreno has clearly left her with an enduring love of good sherry; hers remains an address for anyone desperate for a bottle of great Gonzalez Byass Oloroso. But there are all sorts of other out-of-the-ordinary wines here, from obscure French country wines to Inniskillin's Canadian Chardonnay and Yarra Yering's extraordinary Australian Pinot Noir. Ms Fleming would appreciate your support in her attempts to promote English wines too...

29	£2.95	**VIN DE PAYS DES COTES DE GASCOGNE**, Domaine de Perras, South-West 1989
38	£4.50	**ALSACE TOKAY-PINOT GRIS**, Cave Vinicole de Turckheim 1988
56	£6.35	**LIBRARY COLLECTION CHARDONNAY**, Tiefenbrunner, Trentino-Alto Adige 1988
57	£8.30	**INNISKILLIN CHARDONNAY**, Niagara 1988
124	£5.35	**MUSCADET**, Bregeon, Loire 1988
163	£6.20	**ALSACE GEWURZTRAMINER**, Pierre Frick & Fils 1988
174	£4.75	**BROWN BROS LATE HARVEST ORANGE MUSCAT & FLORA**, N E Victoria 1988
196	£9.80	**ALSACE RIESLING GRAND CRU BRAND**, Cave Vinicole de Turckheim 1985
303	£8.75	**ROUGE HOMME COONAWARRA CABERNET SAUVIGNON** 1985
329	£3.80	**TRICASTIN DOMAINE DE RASPAIL**, J Jalifier, Rhône 1988
382	£26.95	**YARRA YERING PINOT NOIR**, Yarra Valley 1987
442	£7.50	**MUSCAT DE RIVESALTES**, Château de la Tuilerie, Midi 1988
454	£9.50	**TOKAY ASZU 5 PUTTONYOS**, Tokaji 1981
476	£10.50	**MATUSALEM OLOROSO MUY VIEJO**, Gonzalez Byass, Jerez
478	£10.50	**AMONTILLADO DEL DUQUE**, Gonzalez Byass, Jerez
496	£1.80	**GOLDENER OKTOBER LIGHT WHITE**, St Ursula Weinkellerei, Rheinhessen

FWC	Fulham Rd Wine Centre

899-901 Fulham Rd, London SW6 5HU (071 736 7009). Confident (and deservedly so) young merchant. **Opening Hours:** 10am-8pm Mon-Sat; 12-3pm Sun. **Delivery:** free locally, nationally at cost. **Tastings:** regularly in-store plus some of the best tutored events. **Discounts:** 5% off 12+ bottles.

Last year's London Wine Merchant of the Year, the Fulham Road Wine Centre has, if anything, improved on its previous performance. Apart from the airy, inviting shop, the friendly and genuinely interested staff (who have not only tasted the wines but also read their way through some of the antiquarian wine books that are for sale here), the Centre can also boast one of Britain's very best wine schools. Hardly surprisingly, they rarely have to look outside their own list when devising comparative tastings – we could put together three or four from just the recommendations listed here.

23	£18.50	**CHAMPAGNE LAURENT PERRIER ROSE**
24	£18.75	**CHAMPAGNE LOUIS ROEDERER BRUT PREMIER**
28	£2.79	**VINS DE PAYS DES COTES DE GASCOGNE**, Plaimont, South-West 1989
38	£4.50	**ALSACE TOKAY-PINOT GRIS**, Cave Vinicole de Turckheim 1988
41	£4.29	**ALSACE PINOT BLANC**, Cave Vinicole de Turckheim 1989
43	£4.69	**PINOT BIANCO**, Vigna al Monte, Puglia 1989
59	£8.99	**PINOT BIANCO**, Jermann, Friuli-Venezia Giulia 1988
70	£4.99	**VERDICCHIO CA'SAL DI SERRA**, Umani Ronchi, Marches 1986
95	£10.50	**CLOUDY BAY CHARDONNAY**, Marlborough 1988
101	£11.49	**MOUNTADAM CHARDONNAY**, High Eden Ridge 1989
103	£12.20	**VITA NOVA CHARDONNAY** 1988
104	£13.50	**VILLA MARIA BARRIQUE-FERMENTED CHARDONNAY**, Auckland 1987
105	£13.60	**TARRAWARRA CHARDONNAY**, Yarra Valley 1987
129	£4.99	**MONTANA SAUVIGNON BLANC**, Marlborough 1989
134	£6.45	**NOBILOS SAUVIGNON BLANC**, Marlborough 1989
136	£6.69	**ADLER FELS SAUVIGNON BLANC**, Sonoma 1987
137	£6.85	**POUILLY FUME VIEILLES VIGNES**, Caves de Pouilly sur Loire 1988
138	£6.95	**HUNTERS SAUVIGNON BLANC**, Marlborough 1989
167	£11.55	**ALSACE GEWURZTRAMINER GRAND CRU KESSLER**, Schlumberger 1985
174	£4.89	**BROWN BROTHERS LATE HARVEST ORANGE MUSCAT & FLORA**, N E Victoria 1988
193	£5.99	**OLD LUXTERS RESERVE**, Chiltern Valley Wines, Buckinghamshire 1989
194	£6.50	**DEINHARD HERITAGE SELECTION DEIDESHEIM**, Rheinpfalz 1987
242	£17.76	**PARKER VINEYARD BLUSH MACABEO/BASTARDO/VIOGNIER**, Randy Nacho, San Atogen Valley 1987
250	£3.50	**COTEAUX DE MURVIEL DOMAINE DE LIMBARDIE**, Boukandoura & Hutin, Midi 1988
260	£4.75	**FAUGERES CHATEAU LA LIQUIERE**, V Gaillard, Midi 1988
287	£6.49	**RAIMAT CABERNET SAUVIGNON**, Lerida 1985
303	£9.50	**ROUGE HOMME COONAWARRA CABERNET SAUVIGNON** 1985
308	£11.50	**PETALUMA COONAWARRA CABERNET/MERLOT** 1985
314	£15.00	**TORRES GRAN CORONAS BLACK LABEL**, Penedés 1983
315	£15.99	**WYNNS JOHN RIDDOCH CABERNET SAUVIGNON**, Coonawarra 1985
319	£22.95	**CHATEAU LYNCH-BAGES**, Pauillac, Bordeaux 1985
321	£26.00	**CHATEAU GRUAUD-LAROSE** (Cordier), St Julien, Bordeaux 1978
337	£5.25	**ROUGE HOMME SHIRAZ/CABERNET**, Coonawarra 1985
338	£5.49	**WYNNS COONAWARRA SHIRAZ** 1987
354	£10.75	**CORNAS**, Guy de Barjac, Rhône 1986
373	£11.75	**AU BON CLIMAT PINOT NOIR** 1988
378	£16.00	**MONDAVI PINOT NOIR RESERVE**, Napa Valley 1986
429	£4.99	**RAIMAT TEMPRANILLO**, Lerida 1987
434	£6.90	**RIOJA**, Bodegas Remelluri 1985
442	£7.99	**MUSCAT DE RIVESALTES**, Château de la Tuilerie, Midi 1988
450	£5.75	**DOMAINE DU NOBLE (DEJEAN PERE & FILS)**, Loupiac, Bordeaux 1986
464	£27.50	**CHATEAU RIEUSSEC**, Sauternes, Bordeaux 1983
472	£7.25	**DON ZOILO VERY OLD FINO**, Jerez
491	£13.99	**WARRE'S QUINTA DA CAVADINHA**, Douro 1979
499	£1.99	**PETILLANT DE RAISIN (3%)**, Listel, Midi

| FUL | Fullers |

South of England Wine Merchant of the Year

Head Office: Griffin Brewery, Chiswick Lane South, Chiswick, London W4 2QB (081 994 3691). Regional High Street chain with 59 shops, mainly in the Thames Valley. **Opening Hours:** 9am-9pm Mon-Sat; 12-2pm & 7pm-9pm Sun. **Delivery:** free locally. **Tastings:** regularly in-store plus tutored events.

If anyone had suggested that the Fullers of five years ago might even have been considered for an award like this, let alone win it, no one would have given the idea house room. But we have watched Mark Dally's wine buying effort over that period, and have been increasingly heartened by the way in which a small High Street chain has been transformed into a good place to look for wine.

Dally has been sensible in not being overly ambitious, and has been concentrating his attention on introducing new wines in the vital £4-£7 price bracket, and on educating Fullers' managers to a remarkably high degree. With chains like this on their doorstep, perhaps the Peter Dominics of this world might finally begin to get their act together too.

4	£5.35	**ASTI MARTINI**, Martini & Rossi, Piedmont
7	£6.25	**CREMANT DE BOURGOGNE ROSE**, Caves de Bailly, Burgundy 1987
23	£19.99	**CHAMPAGNE LAURENT PERRIER ROSE**
24	£17.49	**CHAMPAGNE LOUIS ROEDERER BRUT PREMIER**
28	£2.65	**VIN DE PAYS DES COTES DE GASCOGNE PLAIMONT**, South-West 1989
46	£4.55	**SOAVE CASTEGGIOLA**, G Rizzardi, Veneto 1987
70	£4.99	**VERDICCHIO CA'SAL DI SERRA**, Umani Ronchi, Marches 1986
95	£9.99	**CLOUDY BAY CHARDONNAY**, Marlborough 1988
117	£3.35	**ANJOU BLANC CHUPIN**, G Saget, Loire 1989
129	£4.99	**MONTANA SAUVIGNON BLANC**, Marlborough 1989
134	£6.75	**NOBILOS SAUVIGNON BLANC**, Marlborough 1989
174	£4.95	**BROWN BROS LATE HARVEST ORANGE MUSCAT & FLORA**, N E Victoria 1988
243	£2.29	**BULGARIAN COUNTRY WINE, MERLOT/GAMZA**, Suhindol
266	£2.55	**PLOVDIV CABERNET SAUVIGNON**, Bulgarian Vintners 1985
293	£7.65	**LE CARILLON DE L'ANGELUS** (Château l'Angélus), St Emilion, Bordeaux 1987
330	£3.99	**COTES DU RHONE**, Château du Grand Moulas 1988
337	£4.99	**ROUGE HOMME SHIRAZ/CABERNET**, Coonawarra 1985
414	£12.95	**TIGNANELLO**, Antinori, Tuscany 1985
439	£2.95	**MOSCATEL DE VALENCIA**, Vicente Gandia 1988
491	13.99	**WARRE'S QUINTA DA CAVADINHA**, Douro 1979

| G | Gateway |

Head Office: Hawkfield Business Park, Whitchurch Lane, Bristol, Avon BS14 0TJ (0272 359359). National supermarket chain with over 600 stores. **Opening Hours:** vary. **Tastings:** occasionally in-store.

We were surprised at Gateway's success in the 1989 Challenge. This year we knew what to expect — and were not disappointed. The keynote here is sensible, good value buying, whose fruits are most obvious in such wines as the very keenly priced German Kabinetts, in Gateway's own label Médoc, and in the Caves de Buxy Bourgogne Rouge. If you are used to driving straight past Gateway on your way to Sainsbury, Tesco or Waitrose, stop and take a look at its range. You might be as agreeably surprised as we once were.

4	£4.99	**ASTI MARTINI**, Martini & Rossi, Piedmont
118	£3.35	**MUSCADET**, Château de la Mouchetière, Loire 1989
129	£5.49	**MONTANA SAUVIGNON BLANC**, Marlborough 1989
203	£2.45	**ST JOHANNER ABTEY KABINETT**, Jakob Demmer, Rheinhessen 1988
204	£2.89	**NIERSTEINER SPIEGELBERG KABINETT**, P J Steffens, Rheinhessen 1988
205	£2.95	**BINGER ST ROCHUSKAPELLE SPATLESE**, Rheinberg Kellerei, Rheinhessen 1988
230	£2.25	**GATEWAY LAMBRUSCO ROSE**, Donelli Vini, Emilia-Romagna
231	£2.99	**PIEMONTELLO PINK**, Piedmont
243	£2.19	**BULGARIAN COUNTRY WINE, MERLOT/GAMZA**, Suhindol
274	£3.35	**GATEWAY MEDOC**, Les Chais Beaucairois, Bordeaux
280	£4.49	**WOLF BLASS RED LABEL**, Barossa Valley 1986
303	£9.50	**ROUGE HOMME COONAWARRA CABERNET SAUVIGNON** 1985
311	£10.95	**CHATEAU HAUT-MARBUZET**, St Estèphe, Bordeaux 1985
324	£2.59	**COTEAUX DU TRICASTIN**, Vignerons de l'Ardèche, Rhône 1989
367	£4.45	**BOURGOGNE PINOT NOIR**, Caves de Buxy, Burgundy 1987
491	£14.49	**WARRE'S QUINTA DA CAVADINHA**, Douro 1979

GON | Gauntleys of Nottingham

4 High St, Exchange Arcade, Nottingham NG1 2ET (0602 417973). Independent family merchant. **Opening Hours:** 7.30am-5.30pm Mon-Sat. **Delivery:** free locally, nationally at cost. **Tastings:** regularly in-store plus tutored events. **Discounts:** a colossal 10% on case purchases.

Two years ago, John Gauntley added a fine wine section to the tobacconist shop founded in 1880 by his great-grandfather. Since then he has embraced the subject of wine with all the fervour of a convert to a new cause. And, like all converts, he is eager to share his enthusiasm with others, singing the praises of such new additions to his list as the Martinborough Chardonnay 1988 and the Guigal Côte Rôtie 'Brune et Blonde' 1985. Smokers will be glad to know that Gauntleys still offers a good range of cigars; they might even have an empty cigar box or two for claret drinkers to sniff at...

23	£16.60	**CHAMPAGNE LAURENT PERRIER ROSE**
28	£3.25	**VIN DE PAYS DES COTES DE GASCOGNE**, Plaimont, South-West 1989
48	£5.10	**MACON-VINZELLES**, Caves des Grands Crus, Burgundy 1987
96	£11.20	**MARTINBOROUGH VINEYARDS CHARDONNAY**, Wairarapa 1988
101	£9.80	**MOUNTADAM CHARDONNAY**, High Eden Ridge 1989
108	£14.40	**ROSEMOUNT ROXBURGH CHARDONNAY**, Hunter Valley 1987
142	£8.10	**POUILLY BLANC FUME DOMAINE CHAILLOUX**, Châtelain, Loire 1987
143	£7.75	**RONGOPAI SAUVIGNON BLANC**, Waikato 1989
264	£11.00	**MAS DE DAUMAS GASSAC**, Vin de Pays de l'Hérault, South-West 1988
289	£6.30	**CHATEAU BEAUMONT**, Cru Bourgeois Médoc, Bordeaux 1986
303	£9.10	**ROUGE HOMME COONAWARRA CABERNET SAUVIGNON** 1985
311	£11.60	**CHATEAU HAUT-MARBUZET**, St Estèphe, Bordeaux 1985
337	£4.85	**ROUGE HOMME SHIRAZ/CABERNET**, Coonawarra 1985
338	£5.25	**WYNNS COONAWARRA SHIRAZ** 1987
345	£6.55	**BAILEYS BUNDARRA SHIRAZ**, Glenrowan 1986
349	£10.20	**RIDGE GEYSERVILLE ZINFANDEL**, Sonoma 1987
378	£9.90	**MONDAVI PINOT NOIR RESERVE**, Napa Valley 1986
380	£19.40	**VOSNE-ROMANEE 1ER CRU BEAUMONTS**, Daniel Rion, Burgundy 1986
428	£4.50	**QUINTA DE CAMARATE**, Fonseca, Azeitão 1985
436	£11.95	**RIOJA RESERVA 904**, La Rioja Alta 1976
437	£10.40	**TINTO PESQUERA**, Fernandez, Ribera del Duero 1986
443	£8.95	**CAMPBELLS RUTHERGLEN MUSCAT**

444	£10.75	BAILEYS FOUNDERS LIQUEUR MUSCAT, Glenrowan
476	£11.30	MATUSALEM OLOROSO MUY VIEJO, Gonzalez Byass, Jerez
478	£11.30	AMONTILLADO DEL DUQUE, Gonzalez Byass, Jerez
488	£11.60	SMITH WOODHOUSE LATE BOTTLED VINTAGE PORT (BOTTLED 1984), Douro 1979
491	£13.40	WARRE'S QUINTA DA CAVADINHA, Douro 1979

| **MG** | **Matthew Gloag Ltd** |

Bordeaux House, 33 Kinnoull Street, Perth PH1 5EU (0738 21101). Independent merchant since 1800. **Opening Hours:** 9am-5pm Mon-Fri. **Delivery:** free within Scotland, nationally at cost. **Tastings:** tutored events for customers club. **Discounts:** 5% discount for club members.

A glance at Matthew Gloag's letter-head tells you a great deal about this company. There's the Royal Warrant, and the picture of the small game bird familiar to drinkers of the firm's Famous Grouse whisky. At first sight, the pocket-sized list seems very like that letter-head: unashamedly old-fashioned, with wines like 'Gloag's Pintail Amontillado', Gloag's White Burgundy and a Tennyson quote from a 1908 Gloag wine list. But some of the wines listed are resolutely modern: Chateau Ste Michelle Fume Blanc from Washington State and St Helena Pinot Noir from New Zealand.

171	£4.05	MOSCATO D'ASTI, Viticoltoro dell'Acquesi, Piedmont 1989
172	£5.65	JOAO PIRES WHITE TABLE WINE, Palmela 1988
259	£4.75	COTEAUX D'AIX EN PROVENCE CHATEAU PIGOUDET GRANDE RESERVE 1985
320	£28.75	CHATEAU LYNCH-BAGES, Pauillac, Bordeaux 1985
340	£5.95	COTES DU RHONE, Guigal 1986
388	£4.25	BARBERA D'ASTI, Viticoltori dell'Acquesi, Piedmont 1988
421	£4.05	VINA ALBALI RESERVA, Felix Solis, Valdepeñas 1983

| **GH** | **Goedhuis & Co** |

101 Albert Bridge Rd, London SW11 4PF (071 223 6724). Independent City-style merchant. **Opening Hours:** 9am-6pm Mon-Fri. **Delivery:** free locally and nationally (depending on size of order). **Tastings:** occasionally in-store plus tutored events.

Johnny Goedhuis remains one of the London merchants whose name features in the Filofaxes of red-braced City wine drinkers who like to lay down a few cases of claret - and in the pocket books of a growing number of increasingly thirsty Japanese wine buyers. But, in the current era of conspicuous non-spending, Goedhuis has proved that he is just as good at supplying French wines for around a fiver a bottle.

28	£3.00	VIN DE PAYS DES COTES DE GASCOGNE Plaimont, South-West 1989
38	£5.40	ALSACE TOKAY-PINOT GRIS, Cave Vinicole de Turckheim 1988
61	£11.80	CHABLIS 1ER CRU VAILLONS, E Defaix, Burgundy 1985
132	£5.40	REUILLY, H Beurdin, Loire 1988
140	£7.35	SANCERRE CLOS DE LA CROIX AU GARDE, Domaine H Pelle, Loire 1990
239	£4.85	CHATEAU THIEULEY BORDEAUX CLAIRET 1989
278	£4.30	CHATEAU NICOT, Bordeaux 1986
328	£3.25	VIN DE PAYS DE L'AUDE DOMAINE PERRIERE, Jeanine Mercadier, Midi 1988

GHW | Grape Hive Wines

392a Chiswick High Rd, London W4 5TF (081 994 5673). Independent merchant. **Opening Hours:** 9am-10.30pm Mon-Sat; 12-3pm & 7pm-10pm Sun. **Delivery:** free within 6 miles. **Tastings:** occasionally in-store. **Discounts:** 5-10% on case purchases.

Mr Chadha and Mr Bhatti are an optimistic pair of wine merchants: 'The future for the High Street specialists is very bright, because of their flexibility and enthusiasm.' In their case, eight years' experience and that same enthusiasm have made for a range of 500 wines and the following list of award winners...

3	£5.89	**YALUMBA ANGAS BRUT,** Barossa Valley	
6	£7.79	**CLAIRETTE DE DIE CUVEE IMPERIAL,** Union des Producteurs, Rhône	
74	£4.99	**RIOJA BLANCO SECO RESERVA,** CVNE 1985	
108	£15.49	**ROSEMOUNT ROXBURGH CHARDONNAY,** Hunter Valley 1987	
174	£5.49	**BROWN BROTHERS LATE HARVEST ORANGE MUSCAT & FLORA,** N E Victoria 1988	
243	£2.39	**BULGARIAN COUNTRY WINE, MERLOT/GAMZA,** Suhindol	
254	£4.99	**CAHORS,** Les Côtes d'Olt, South-West 1986	
266	£2.69	**PLOVDIV CABERNET SAUVIGNON,** Bulgarian Vintners 1985	
267	£3.79	**VIN DE PAYS DE L'AUDE CABERNET SAUVIGNON,** Paul Boutinot, Midi 1987	
276	£4.29	**CONCHA Y TORO MERLOT,** Maipo 1986	
326	£2.99	**COTES DU VENTOUX,** Paul Boutinot, Rhône 1989	
331	£4.99	**RASTEAU COTES DU RHONE VILLAGES,** Caves des Vignerons de Rasteau 1988	
336	£6.99	**CROZES HERMITAGE,** Delas Frères, Rhône 1988	
363	£5.99	**REGNIE CRISTAL,** Georges Duboeuf, Beaujolais 1989	
364	£5.99	**MORGON JEAN DESCOMBES,** Georges Duboeuf, Beaujolais 1989	
366	£2.59	**MILION PINOT NOIR,** Navip, Vranje 1986	
387	£4.29	**MONTEPULCIANO D'ABRUZZO,** Tollo, Abruzzi 1987	
428	£5.29	**QUINTA DE CAMARATE,** Fonseca, Azeitão 1985	
471	£7.99	**AMONTILLADO TIO DIEGO,** Valdespino, Jerez	
472	£7.99	**DON ZOILO VERY OLD FINO,** Jerez	
499	£2.99	**PETILLANT DE RAISIN (3%),** Listel, Midi	

GI | Grape Ideas

3/5 Hythe Bridge St, Oxford, Oxon OX1 2EW (0865 791313) & Grape Ideas Fine Vintage Wine Warehouse, 2a Canfield Gardens, London SW1. Retail arm of wholesale operation. **Opening Hours:** Oxford 10am-7pm Mon-Sat; 11am-2pm Sun; London 10am-9pm Mon-Sat; 12-2pm Sun. **Delivery:** free locally, nationally at cost. **Tastings:** regularly in-store plus tutored events. **Discounts:** depending on quantity.

The special subject of this Oxford and north London retail/wholesale warehouse is undoubtedly South America, with 20 wines from Argentina and Chile. The more impressive wines on the list, however, come from the traditional countries of Europe, Australia and New Zealand. Burgundy in particular is well covered - with a good mixture of domaine and négociant wines - and the list of Bordeaux includes such sensible if unfashionable buys as 1984 Château Labégorce Zédé at £6.95, and the Portuguese selection features the rarely-seen Sogrape Méthode Champenoise.

20	£16.90	**CHAMPAGNE PHILIPPONNAT BRUT ROSE**
23	£18.85	**CHAMPAGNE LAURENT PERRIER ROSE**
24	£16.10	**CHAMPAGNE LOUIS ROEDERER BRUT PREMIER**

28	£2.79	**VIN DE PAYS DES COTES DE GASCOGNE**, Plaimont, South-West 1989
54	£6.60	**POUILLY LOCHE CHATEAU DE LOCHE**, Caves Grands Crus Vinzelles, Bugundy 1987
95	£9.95	**CLOUDY BAY CHARDONNAY**, Marlborough 1988
117	£3.45	**ANJOU BLANC CHUPIN**, G Saget, Loire 1989
152	£3.99	**COOKS CHENIN BLANC**, Hawkes Bay 1987
172	£3.99	**JOAO PIRES WHITE TABLE WINE**, Palmela 1988
314	£15.85	**TORRES GRAN CORONAS BLACK LABEL**, Penedés 1983
322	£28.00	**CHATEAU FIGEAC**, St Emilion Grand Cru, Bordeaux 1982
388	£3.75	BARBERA D'ASTI, Viticoltori dell'Acquesi, Piedmont 1988
438	£19.50	**FERREIRA BARCA VELHA**, Douro 1981
449	£3.75	**CHATEAU DES COULINATS**, Ste-Croix-du-Mont, Bordeaux 1983
464	£14.50	CHATEAU RIEUSSEC, Sauternes, Bordeaux 1983
491	£13.20	**WARRE'S QUINTA DA CAVADINHA**, Douro 1979
499	£1.99	**PETILLANT DE RAISIN (3%)**, Listel, Midi

GNW   Great Northern Wine Co

The Dark Arches, Leeds Canal Basin, Leeds, W Yorks LSD1 4BR (0532 461200). Independent merchant. **Opening Hours:** 9am-6.30pm Mon-Fri; 9am-5.30pm Sun. **Delivery:** free locally, nationally at cost. **Tastings:** regularly in-store plus tutored events. **Discounts:** wholesale price for 12 bottles.

Arguably one of the most fairly named merchants in the country, this is a young (four year-old) firm to which any British wine lover should make a detour - even if some southerners might find the prospect of those 'Dark Arches' beneath Leeds railway station a little daunting. The quality of the range of wines is clear from the award winners below, but there are several other specialities - including half bottles of Jura Vin de Paille, full bottles of 1976 Beerenauslese and Antinori's Vin Santo – and a constantly changing unlisted selection 'to allow us to sell rare, unusual and interesting wines'.

3	£4.99	**YALUMBA ANGAS BRUT**, Barossa Valley
47	£5.49	**LUGANA, CA DEI FRATI**, Lombardy 1989
51	£5.80	**PRELUDIO NO. 1**, Tenuta di Torrebianco, Puglia 1989
59	£8.99	**PINOT BIANCO**, Jermann, Friuli-Venezia Giulia 1988
68	£4.99	**BERGERAC SEC DOMAINE DE GRANDCHAMP**, Nick Ryman, South-West 1988
74	£5.49	RIOJA BLANCO SECO RESERVA, CVNE 1985
87	£7.79	PENFOLDS CHARDONNAY, South Australia 1988
92	£9.00	**SIMI CHARDONNAY**, Sonoma 1985
95	£10.50	**CLOUDY BAY CHARDONNAY**, Marlborough 1988
115	£16.99	**MEURSAULT**, Drouhin, Burgundy 1988
126	£4.50	**CHATEAU LA JAUBERTIE BERGERAC SEC**, Henry Ryman, South-West 1987
129	£4.99	MONTANA SAUVIGNON BLANC, Marlborough 1989
172	£4.49	**JOAO PIRES WHITE TABLE WINE**, Palmela 1988
175	£5.50	**QUADY ESSENSIA ORANGE MUSCAT** 1987
195	£6.75	**THREE CHOIRS BACCHUS**, Gloucestershire 1989
240	£4.60	**CHATEAU LA JAUBERTIE BERGERAC ROSE**, Henry Ryman, South-West 1987
262	£5.40	**CORBIERES CHATEAU DE LASTOURS (FUT DE CHENE)**, Midi 1985
294	£7.85	**ROSEMOUNT SHOW RESERVE COONAWARRA CABERNET SAUVIGNON** 1987
297	£8.49	**PENFOLDS BIN 389 SHIRAZ/CABERNET, SOUTH AUSTRALIA 1986**
299	£8.50	**CHATEAU RAMAGE LA BATISSE**, Haut-Médoc, Bordeaux 1985
316	£18.65	**PENFOLDS BIN 707 CABERNET SAUVIGNON**, South Australia 1986
331	£4.29	**RASTEAU COTES DU RHONE VILLAGES**, Caves des Vignerons de Rasteau 1988
339	£5.49	**PENFOLDS BIN 28 KALIMNA SHIRAZ**, South Australia 1986
442	£7.99	**MUSCAT DE RIVESALTES**, Château de la Tuilerie, Midi 1988
444	£10.95	BAILEYS FOUNDERS LIQUEUR MUSCAT, Glenrowan
472	£7.25	DON ZOILO VERY OLD FINO, Jerez

GRT | Great Western Wine

57 Walcot St, Bath, Avon BA1 3BN (0225 448428). Independent merchant selling by the case. **Opening Hours:** 10am-7pm Mon-Sat. **Delivery:** free within 10 miles, nationally at cost. **Tastings:** regularly in-store plus tutored events.

Confusingly sharing virtually the same name as the English specialist in Reading (*see below*) this friendly firm states that 'wines are always open to taste at the Bath Wine Centre', evoking irresistible images of a merchant specialising in Burgundies to sip at in the tub. In fact there are some wines from that region (including a 1985 Santenay Gravières from Domaine de la Pousse d'Or) that we would be delighted to sip in the bath or anywhere else for that matter. And we would be just as happy to indulge ourselves in the firm's excellent range of French country wines. Perhaps to avoid further confusion with its namesake, this Great Western restricts its English range to a pair from Pilton Manor.

23	£19.20	**CHAMPAGNE LAURENT PERRIER ROSE**	
28	£2.99	**VINS DE PAYS DES COTES DE GASCOGNE**, Plaimont, South-West 1989	
74	£5.70	**RIOJA BLANCO SECO RESERVA**, CVNE 1985	
78	£6.39	**MITCHELTON MARSANNE**, Goulburn Valley 1987	
80	£6.05	**WOLF BLASS BARREL-FERMENTED CHARDONNAY**, South Australia 1988	
83	£7.49	**MITCHELTON RESERVE CHARDONNAY**, Goulburn Valley 1988	
99	£11.45	**TREFETHEN CHARDONNAY**, Napa Valley 1986	
100	£11.45	**PETALUMA CHARDONNAY**, Adelaide Hills 1987	
106	£13.05	**LEEUWIN ESTATE CHARDONNAY**, Margaret River 1984	
188	£5.29	**PILTON MANOR DRY RESERVE**, Somerset 1987	
289	£8.29	**CHATEAU BEAUMONT**, Cru Bourgeois Médoc, Bordeaux 1986	
294	£7.75	**ROSEMOUNT SHOW RESERVE COONAWARRA CABERNET SAUVIGNON** 1987	
308	£11.45	**PETALUMA COONAWARRA CABERNET/ MERLOT** 1985	
311	£12.54	**CHATEAU HAUT-MARBUZET**, St Estèphe, Bordeaux 1985	
322	£26.39	**CHATEAU FIGEAC**, St Emilion Grand Cru, Bordeaux 1982	
336	£4.99	**CROZES HERMITAGE**, Delas Frères, Rhône 1988	
364	£6.79	**MORGON JEAN DESCOMBES**, Georges Duboeuf, Beaujolais 1989	
449	£5.46	**CHATEAU DES COULINATS**, Ste-Croix-du-Mont, Bordeaux 1983	
491	£13.99	**WARRE'S QUINTA DA CAVADINHA**, Douro 1979	

GWR | Great Western Wines

254 Kentwood Hill, Tilehurst, Reading RG3 6DP (0734 451958). English specialist. **Opening Hours:** Ring first to check: 24 hour answerphone. **Delivery:** free locally, nationally at cost. **Tastings:** regularly in-store plus tutored events. **Discounts:** 10% for case sales.

'We are a new company set up in the heart of the Thames Valley to specialise in quality English Wines...' Beat a path to this door; Great Western not only offers a stunning range of locally produced wines, including examples from some very obscure vineyards, but also manages to stock mature vintages, which demonstrate just how well these wines can age. In other countries, the idea of a specialist in local produce would not be unusual; in Britain, firms like Great Western need and deserve all our support.

179	£3.75	**WICKHAM VINEYARD MEDIUM DRY**, Hampshire 1988
183	£4.50	**NUTBOURNE MANOR HUXELREBE**, Sussex 1989
184	£4.50	**ASTLEY HUXELVANER**, Worcestershire 1989
188	£4.59	**PILTON MANOR DRY RESERVE**, Somerset 1987

190	£4.75	SHAWSGATE MULLER THURGAU, East Anglia 1989
195	£6.75	THREE CHOIRS BACCHUS, Gloucestershire 1989
211	£4.50	THAMES VALLEY VINEYARD SCHONBURGER MEDIUM, Berkshire 1989
214	£3.99	ASTLEY MADELEINE ANGEVINE, Worcestershire 1989
219	£5.25	LAMBERHURST KERNER, Kent 1986
456	£9.00	THAMES VALLEY VINEYARD BOTRYTIZED SCHEUREBE, Berkshire 1989

PTR	Peter Green

Joint Winner: Scottish Wine Merchant of the Year

37a/b Warrender Park Rd, Edinburgh EH9 1HJ (031 229 5925). Independent merchant who seems
to get almost everything right. **Opening Hours:** 9.30am-6.30pm Mon-Fri; 9.30am-6.30pm Sat.
Tastings: large annual tasting. **Discounts:** 5% on unbroken cases.

Another much-deserved prize for Michael Romer, a man who, as we said
when awarding him this same prize last year, has a hawk-like ability to
home in on good wines from just about anywhere in the world. We could
continue to wax lyrically for another paragraph or two, but need we say
more for the moment? Once equipped with your Peter Green list, you'll be
able to calculate for yourselves the quantity of drinking pleasure this firm
offers.

4	£5.25	ASTI MARTINI, Martini & Rossi, Piedmont
23	£20.65	CHAMPAGNE LAURENT PERRIER ROSE
24	£17.99	CHAMPAGNE LOUIS ROEDERER BRUT PREMIER
50	£5.99	SOAVE CLASSICO, Pieropan, Veneto 1989
51	£5.70	PRELUDIO NO. 1, Tenuta di Torrebianco, Puglia 1989
57	£6.65	INNISKILLIN CHARDONNAY, Niagara 1988
68	£4.99	BERGERAC SEC DOMAINE DE GRANDCHAMP, Nick Ryman, South-West 1988
70	£4.75	VERDICCHIO CA'SAL DI SERRA, Umani Ronchi, Marches 1986
80	£5.95	WOLF BLASS BARREL-FERMENTED CHARDONNAY, South Australia 1988
81	£5.99	STONELEIGH CHARDONNAY, Marlborough 1988
100	£11.65	PETALUMA CHARDONNAY, Adelaide Hills 1987
108	£14.60	ROSEMOUNT ROXBURGH CHARDONNAY, Hunter Valley 1987
127	£5.25	MUSCADET DE SEVRE ET MAINE SUR LIE, G Bossard, Loire 1989
129	£4.99	MONTANA SAUVIGNON BLANC, Marlborough 1989
134	£6.20	NOBILOS SAUVIGNON BLANC, Marlborough 1989
157	£2.99	RETSINA OF ATTICA, Kourtaki
166	£6.75	MARK WEST VINEYARDS GEWURZTRAMINER, Sonoma 1988
167	£10.85	ALSACE GEWURZTRAMINER GRAND CRU KESSLER, Schlumberger 1985
172	£4.75	JOAO PIRES WHITE TABLE WINE, Palmela 1988
236	£4.45	TORRES CABERNET SAUVIGNON ROSE, Curico 1989
243	£2.19	BULGARIAN COUNTRY WINE, MERLOT/GAMZA, Suhindol
264	£10.25	MAS DE DAUMAS GASSAC, Vin de Pays de l'Hérault, South-West 1988
289	£7.75	CHATEAU BEAUMONT, Cru Bourgeois Médoc, Bordeaux 1986
317	£20.99	MONDAVI CABERNET SAUVIGNON RESERVE, Napa Valley 1980
337	£4.95	ROUGE HOMME SHIRAZ/CABERNET, Coonawarra 1985
378	£11.99	MONDAVI PINOT NOIR RESERVE, Napa Valley 1986
393	£4.35	CORVO ROSSO, Sicily 1987
414	£14.45	TIGNANELLO, Antinori, Tuscany 1985
421	£3.89	VINA ALBALI RESERVA, Felix Solis, Valdepeñas 1983
432	£4.70	RIOJA RESERVA, Beronia 1982
435	£7.35	GRANDE ESCHOLA, Quinta do Cotto, Douro 1985
441	£7.75	MORRIS RUTHERGLEN LIQUEUR MUSCAT

454	£6.85	**TOKAY ASZU 5 PUTTONYOS,** Tokaji 1981
471	£7.35	**AMONTILLADO TIO DIEGO,** Valdespino, Jerez
475	£7.99	**DOS CORTADOS,** Williams & Humbert, Jerez
476	£9.75	MATUSALEM OLOROSO MUY VIEJO, Gonzalez Byass, Jerez
478	£9.75	**AMONTILLADO DEL DUQUE,** Gonzalez Byass, Jerez

GRN   Greens

47/51 Great Suffolk St, London SE1 0BS (071 633 0936). Very old gentleman of an independent merchant, selling by the case. **Delivery:** nationally at cost. **Tastings:** occasional plus tutored events. **Discounts:** negotiable.

For a genteel 203 -year- old like Greens, the last few years have been more than a little traumatic. First there was the short-livedperiod of ownership by Bibendum; then a marriage to Alastair Peebles' Oxford & Cambridge Fine Wine Co; then removal from the Royal Exchange shop to allow building work to be carried out, and lastly the departure of Alastair Peebles.

Under its new management, the aim is apparently to spread the range of styles and prices rather more widely than in the past. However, while the will may be there, it is easy to see why this process is taking place rather slowly; the boardrooms to whom Greens sells a major proportion of its wine are not traditionally places in which Californian, Australian or French country wines are drunk.

TGB   The Grog Blossom

48 King St, Royston, Herts SG8 9BA (0763 247201); 253 West End Lane, West Hampstead, London NW6 1XN; 66 Notting Hill Gate, London. Small independent chain. **Delivery:** free within 2 miles. **Tastings:** regularly in-store. **Discounts:** 5% on case sales.

These very Oddbins-like stores are giving the super-chain a run for its money on at least one London street. Paul O'Connor's three-link chain offers a well-chosen (if often changing) selection of wines, as well as some 50 malt whiskies and 200 beers. Grog Blossom owes its name, by the way, not to a pretty wild plant, but to what the OED describes as a 'pimple or redness on nose from intemperance'.

29	£3.29	**VIN DE PAYS DES COTES DE GASCOGNE,** Domaine de Perras, South-West 1989
267	£2.75	**VIN DE PAYS DE L'AUDE CABERNET SAUVIGNON,** Paul Boutinot, Midi 1987
472	£7.25	**DON ZOILO VERY OLD FINO,** Jerez

HFV   Harcourt Fine Wines

3 Harcourt Street, London W1 (071 723 7202). English specialist merchant. **Opening Hours:** 11.30am-6.30pm Tues-Fri; 10am-3pm Sat. **Delivery:** free locally, nationally at cost. **Tastings:** regularly in-store plus organised events. **Discounts:** 5% on case sales.

If you want to buy a bottle of English wine in London, this is the place to come. And although the list below doesn't show it, Harcourt also has a new range of German wines on offer. Neither country is an easy one to specialise in, and we applaud the resilience and adaptability of the owners. Until this year, this firm was known as the English Wine Shop; presumably, the new name may serve as less of a deterrent to Englishmen and women who'd rather drink bad foreign wine than even try a good example of winemaking from this country.

183	£5.25	**NUTBOURNE MANOR HUXELREBE,** Sussex 1989	
189	£5.05	**STAPLE ST JAMES MULLER-THURGAU,** Staple Vineyards, Kent 1989	
211	£4.65	**THAMES VALLEY VINEYARD SCHONBURGER MEDIUM,** Berkshire 1989	
456	£4.50	THAMES VALLEY VINEYARD BOTRYTIZED SCHEUREBE, Berkshire 1989	

GHS	Gerard Harris

2 Green End St, Aston Clinton, Aylesbury, Bucks HP22 5HP (0296 631041).Independent merchant. **Opening Hours:** 9.30am-8.00pm Tues-Sat. **Delivery:** free locally, nationally at cost. **Tastings:** occasionally in-store plus tutored tastings and dinners. **Discounts:** 10% on case sales.

The idea of running a single cellar that supplies a restaurant list and a retail shop seems so sensible that it is surprising that the Bell at Aston Clinton is one of the very few establishments to have hit on it. So, if you don't quite feel up to buying a bottle of Romanée-Conti La Tâche 1982 with your meal, you can buy one from the shop (for £61) and take it home with you. Elsewhere on the Bell Inn shelves, you could also find two vintages of the rare Cloudy Bay Cabernet Sauvignon-Merlot, an impressive set of 1982 Bordeaux and Dr Loosen's Erdener Praelat Riesling Auslese 1976 (for £17.12). And, even if your pocket doesn't stretch to a weekend at the Bell, you could always let your wine stay in its cellars - for just £3.75 per case per year.

3	£7.05	**YALUMBA ANGAS BRUT,** Barossa Valley
23	£19.95	**CHAMPAGNE LAURENT PERRIER ROSE**
24	£19.40	**CHAMPAGNE LOUIS ROEDERER BRUT PREMIER**
49	£5.75	**BABICH SEMILLON/CHARDONNAY,** Gisborne 1989
65	£5.20	**VIN DE PAYS DES COTES DE GASCOGNE DOMAINE DU TARIQUET CUVEE BOIS,** Grassa, South-West
74	£5.40	**RIOJA BLANCO SECO RESERVA,** CVNE 1985
86	£9.25	**MUSCADET DE SEVRE ET MAINE SUR LIE CHATEAU DE CHASSELOIR (OAK-AGED),** Loire 1987
95	£9.80	**CLOUDY BAY CHARDONNAY,** Marlborough 1988
172	£4.60	**JOAO PIRES WHITE TABLE WINE,** Palmela 1988
174	£4.65	BROWN BROTHERS LATE HARVEST ORANGE MUSCAT & FLORA, N E Victoria 1988
175	£9.70	**QUADY ESSENSIA ORANGE MUSCAT** 1987
236	£4.20	**TORRES CABERNET SAUVIGNON ROSE,** Curico 1989
263	£5.75	**MADIRAN, CHATEAU D'AYDIE,** South-West 1988
264	£9.90	MAS DE DAUMAS GASSAC, Vin de Pays de l'Hérault, South-West 1988
287	£5.70	**RAIMAT CABERNET SAUVIGNON,** Lerida 1985
290	£7.20	**FIRESTONE CABERNET SAUVIGNON,** Santa Ynez 1986
298	£9.00	**CHATEAU LA TOUR DE BY,** Haut-Médoc, Bordeaux 1986
321	£24.28	**CHATEAU GRUAUD-LAROSE** (Cordier), St Julien, Bordeaux 1978
371	£10.95	**COLDSTREAM HILLS PINOT NOIR,** Yarra Valley 1988
414	£14.99	TIGNANELLO, Antinori, Tuscany 1985
470	£4.85	**AMONTILLADO NAPOLEON,** Hidalgo, Jerez
472	£6.99	DON ZOILO VERY OLD FINO, Jerez

HPD	Harpenden Wines

68 High St, Harpenden, Herts AL5 2SP (0582 765605). Expanding independent merchant. **Opening Hours:** 10am-10pm Mon-Fri; 9am-10pm Sat; 12-3pm & 7pm-9pm Sun. **Delivery:** free locally, nationally at cost. **Tastings:** regularly in-store. **Discounts:** 5% mixed case, 7.5% unbroken case (not credit cards).

Experience gained importing and wholesaling French wines led Paul Beaton to set up a retail outlet in August 1987. Since then, although he remains loyal to France - and especially keen on Bordeaux - Beaton has trodden the now familiar paths to the vineyards of Australia and New Zealand. Retailing evidently suits him; a second Harpenden shop should open, in Watford, before the end of 1990.

4	£5.59	**ASTI MARTINI,** Martini & Rossi, Piedmont
83	£7.49	**MITCHELTON RESERVE CHARDONNAY,** Goulburn Valley 1988
95	£10.59	**CLOUDY BAY CHARDONNAY,** Marlborough 1988
129	£5.45	**MONTANA SAUVIGNON BLANC,** Marlborough 1989
174	£4.99	BROWN BROTHERS LATE HARVEST ORANGE MUSCAT & FLORA, N E Victoria 1988
311	£12.95	**CHATEAU HAUT-MARBUZET,** St Estèphe, Bordeaux 1985
320	£22.50	CHATEAU LYNCH-BAGES, Pauillac, Bordeaux 1985
449	£4.99	**CHATEAU DES COULINATS,** Ste-Croix-du-Mont, Bordeaux 1983
454	£7.50	**TOKAY ASZU 5 PUTTONYOS,** Tokaji 1981
499	£2.10	**PETILLANT DE RAISIN (3%),** Listel, Midi

HAR	Harrods Ltd

Knightsbridge, London SW1X 7XL (071 730 1234). Undeniably singular store with deluxe wine department. **Opening Hours:** 9am-6pm (7pm Wed) Mon-Sat. **Delivery:** free locally, nationally at cost. **Tastings:** regularly in-store plus occasional special events. **Discounts:** unbroken cases for the price of 11 bottles of most wines.

If Harrods haven't got it in stock, people used to say, they would get it in for you. Well, we suspect that even Harrods might have difficulty in obtaining such unobtainables as a case of 1989 Cloudy Bay Sauvignon Blanc, but the Knightsbridge store can offer that winery's Chardonnay - and an alternative Marlborough Sauvignon Blanc from Montana.

Harrods' customers are not supposed to question the premium they pay to carry their purchases home in those smart green bags. Is it a little *infra dig* of us to point out that the Matusalem Oloroso Muy Viejo from Gonzalez Byass sold by Harrods for £15.00 is available in branches of Oddbins at a mere £10.99?

24	£21.50	**CHAMPAGNE LOUIS ROEDERER BRUT PREMIER**
74	£6.50	**RIOJA BLANCO SECO RESERVA,** CVNE 1985
95	£11.00	**CLOUDY BAY CHARDONNAY,** Marlborough 1988
106	£14.50	**LEEUWIN ESTATE CHARDONNAY,** Margaret River 1984
112	£15.59	**CABREO LA PIETRA,** Ruffino, Tuscany 1986
129	£5.50	**MONTANA SAUVIGNON BLANC,** Marlborough 1989
167	£20.00	**ALSACE GEWURZTRAMINER GRAND CRU KESSLER,** Schlumberger 1985
174	£5.45	BROWN BROS LATE HARVEST ORANGE MUSCAT & FLORA, N E Victoria 1988
224	£8.25	**LAMBERHURST SCHONBURGER,** Kent 1988
287	£7.00	**RAIMAT CABERNET SAUVIGNON,** Lerida 1985
298	£8.85	**CHATEAU LA TOUR DE BY,** Haut-Médoc, Bordeaux 1986

299	£9.25	**CHATEAU RAMAGE LA BATISSE**, Haut-Médoc, Bordeaux 1985
308	£14.00	**PETALUMA COONAWARRA CABERNET/MERLOT** 1985
314	£16.75	**TORRES GRAN CORONAS BLACK LABEL**, Penedés 1983
403	£6.99	**TANCA FARRA**, Sella e Mosca, Sardinia 1984
436	£12.00	**RIOJA RESERVA 904**, La Rioja Alta 1976
437	£12.00	**TINTO PESQUERA**, Fernandez, Ribera del Duero 1986
454	£8.00	**TOKAY ASZU 5 PUTTONYOS**, Tokaji 1981
471	£8.40	**AMONTILLADO TIO DIEGO**, Valdespino, Jerez
476	£15.00	MATUSALEM OLOROSO MUY VIEJO, Gonzalez Byass, Jerez
477	£12.75	**SANDEMAN ROYAL AMBROSANTE**, Jerez
486	£9.00	**WARRE'S WARRIOR VINTAGE CHARACTER PORT**, Douro
491	£17.50	**WARRE'S QUINTA DA CAVADINHA**, Douro 1979

| **HV** | **Harveys of Bristol** |

Harvey House, 31 Denmark St, Bristol, Avon BS1 5DQ (0272 268882) & 27 Pall Mall, London SW1Y 4JH (071 839 4695). Reassuringly solid traditional merchant with large fortified wine interests. **Opening Hours:** 9am-4.45pm Mon-Fri; 9am-1pm Sat. **Delivery:** free locally, nationally at cost. **Tastings:** regularly in-store plus tutored events.

Harveys' most recent price list comes with a foreword by Roald Dahl describing the pleasure he has derived from the 'en primeur' 1982 and 1983 Bordeaux he bought himself in 1983 and 1984, dropping the name of 'my friend Bruno Prats at Cos d'Estournel', and encouraging Harveys' customers to follow his, Dahl's, example by laying in large quantities of the 1988s and 1989s. Harveys is certainly a good company from which to buy newborn claret but, as the most recent lists prove, this is increasingly a merchant that seeks to sell wines from further afield. As the list's introduction states, 'We went as far as tasting a wine from Peru...'

24	£18.55	**CHAMPAGNE LOUIS ROEDERER BRUT PREMIER**
95	£10.75	**CLOUDY BAY CHARDONNAY**, Marlborough 1988
132	£5.89	**REUILLY**, H Beurdin, Loire 1988
160	£5.23	**ALSACE GEWURZTRAMINER**, Caves Coop des Viticulteurs d'Ingersheim 1987
174	£5.56	**BROWN BROS LATE HARVEST ORANGE MUSCAT & FLORA**, N E Victoria 1988
223	£5.80	**SCHLOSS BOCKELHEIMER KUPFERGRUBE RIESLING**, Von Plettenberg, Nahe 1986
261	£4.36	**BODEGAS Y CAVAS DE WEINERT CABERNET SAUVIGNON**, Mendoza 1983
289	£7.84	**CHATEAU BEAUMONT**, Cru Bourgeois Médoc, Bordeaux 1986
354	£11.63	**CORNAS**, Guy de Barjac, Rhône 1986
381	£18.63	**CLOS VOUGEOT GRAND CRU**, Chateau de la Tour, Burgundy 1982
407	£9.45	**CASTELLO DI CAMIGLIANO ROSSO**, Tuscany 1986
426	£4.97	**DAO PORTA DOS CAVALEIROS RESERVA**, Caves São João 1983
431	£5.30	**LAR DE BARROS RESERVA**, Bodega Inviosa, Extremadura 1986

| **RHV** | **Richard Harvey Wines** |

Home Farm, Morden, Wareham, Dorset BH20 7DW (092945 224). Phone for details.

The mention of 'house wines' on the first page of Richard Harvey's list takes on an ironic note when one discovers that last year's West Country Merchant of the Year is running his business from his own house - in this case a farmhouse. This state of affairs is, we understand, the temporary consequence of Harvey having bought his company back from Coopers of Wessex, an Allied Lyons subsidiary that had purchased it the previous year.

Harvey's range, however, is as varied as ever, including as it does wines from some of France's more obscure regions, a growing range from Italy and Wake Court, a local Dorset wine. We look forward to seeing Richard Harvey re-established in new premises in the very near future.

HFW | **Haughton Fine Wines**

Chorley Green Lane, Chorley, Nantwich, Cheshire CW5 8JR (0270 74537). Friendly, hard-to-fault independent merchant with good organic selection. **Opening Hours:** 9.00am-5.30pm Mon-Fri; 9.00am-12.30pm Sat. **Delivery:** free within 25 miles, nationally at cost. **Tastings:** regular in-store plus tutored tastings and dinner events.

Last year's Northern Wine Merchant of the Year, Haughton Fine Wines is rapidly becoming one of the best known young wine companies in Britain. The secret of its success lies in Bruce and Judy Kendrick's mixture of professionalism and enthusiasm, both of which are clearly evident in the firm's ring-bound, pocket-book-sized list. Well written and laid out, it contains such useful information as the proportions of each grape variety used by each Bordeaux château, the way its wine is made and whether, as in the case of a fair number, that a particular wine is organic.

The range is as impressive as ever, seamlessly combining the best of the New World (with impeccable wines from Mountadam) with the best of the old: Bourgogne Irancy from Leon Bienvenue. Who could ask for anything more?

7	£7.29	**CREMANT DE BOURGOGNE ROSE**, Caves de Bailly, Burgundy 1987
48	£5.66	**MACON VINZELLES**, Caves des Grands Crus, Burgundy 1987
84	£6.82	**SCHINUS MOLLE CHARDONNAY**, Mornington Peninsula 1989
93	£9.77	**POUILLY FUISSE**, M Delorme, Burgundy 1985
96	£10.70	**MARTINBOROUGH VINEYARDS CHARDONNAY**, Wairarapa 1988
101	£10.99	**MOUNTADAM CHARDONNAY**, High Eden Ridge 1989
143	£8.42	**RONGOPAI SAUVIGNON BLANC**, Waikato 1989
155	£7.20	**MILLTON VINEYARDS BARREL-FERMENTED CHENIN BLANC**, Gisborne 1988
226	£6.50	**MILLTON VINEYARDS OPOU RIVER RIESLING**, Gisborne 1989
248	£3.42	**COTES DE GASCOGNE**, Domaine de Mathalin, South-West 1987
285	£5.62	**DAVID WYNN CABERNET**, High Eden Ridge 1986
332	£4.49	**COTES DE PROVENCE DOMAINE DU JAS D'ESCLANS**, Lorges-Lapouge 1986
341	£5.99	**VACQUEYRAS CUVEE DES TEMPLIERS**, Domaine Clos de Cazeaux, Rhône 1986
492	£15.02	**BANYULS GRAND CRU SELECT VIEUX**, L'Etoile, Midi 1969

HHC | **Haynes Hanson & Clarke**

17 Lettice St, London, SW6 4EH (071 736 7878) and 36 Kensington Church Street, London W8 4BX. Independent merchant with heavy Burgundian bent. **Opening Hours:** 9.30am-7.00pm Mon-Sat. **Delivery:** free within London, nationally at cost for under 5 cases. **Tastings:** regular in-store plus tutored and organised events. **Discounts:** 10% on unmixed cases.

Anthony Hanson has the gentlemanly good manners associated with the most traditional members of the British wine trade; unlike many of those members, however, he is extraordinarily down-to-earth when it comes to the subject of quality and value. So while they continue to sell Burgundy that tastes of consommé from négociants with whom they have been dealing since the 1066 vintage, Hanson is flying the flag for individual estate wines that taste of the grape from which they are made, whether they are from Burgundy, Bordeaux, the Loire or California.

Customers have the choice between buying by mail, squeezing themselves into the dolls-house-sized Kensington shop, or driving across to the Lettice Street warehouse. Whichever they choose, the service they receive will be, well, gentlemanly.

| 362 | £5.99 | **BROUILLY**, Andre Large, Beaujolais 1989 |

H&H   Hector & Honorez

The White House, 29 Hollow Lane, Ramsey, Cambs PE17 1DE (0487 710777).High-class independent merchant. **Delivery:** free locally, nationally at cost. **Tastings:** organised tutored tastings and events. **Discounts:** 5% on unmixed case sales.

Christian Honorez worked with Anthony Byrne (q.v.) before starting this company, and his experience there is very apparent in his Byrne-like concentration on a small and (in some cases) exclusive set of good producers. Apart from a range of vintage ports (including 1963 Warre), the list is restricted to France and Italy. The wines are well chosen and, within these limitations, nicely wide-ranging - from both colours of 1986 Givry and an oak-aged Pacherenc-du-Vic-Bilh to 1982 Château Lynch Bages.

74	£5.40	**RIOJA BLANCO SECO RESERVA**, CVNE 1985
124	£4.90	**MUSCADET**, Bregeon, Loire 1988
138	£7.99	**HUNTERS SAUVIGNON BLANC**, Marlborough 1989
164	£6.40	**ALSACE TOKAY-PINOT GRIS HERRENWEG**, Domaine Barmes-Buecher 1988

HW   Hedley Wright

The Country Wine Cellars, 10-11 Twyford Centre, London Rd, Bishops Stortford, Herts (0279 506512).Independent by-the-case merchant. **Opening Hours:** 10.00am-6.00pm Mon-Wed, Sat; 10.00am-8.00pm Thurs, Fri. **Delivery:** free within 25 miles, free nationally for 2 cases at mail order prices. **Tastings:** regular in-store plus tutored tastings and dinner events. **Discounts:** for members of the Hedley Wright 'Bonus Club'.

'Wishing you all a long hot summer, with some night time rain for our farming customers'. This comment from the Spring list, supports the rural image given by the 'Country Wine Cellars' address, of a nice, old fashioned, conservative backwoods merchant, In fact, however, Hedley Wright are anything but old fashioned, as was demonstrated by their their signing-up of the exclusive agency for Nogales/Montes, arguably the best winery in Chile, and by their introduction into Britain of the Wine Preserver (which they no longer stock however). Apart from the Chilean wines and good - if brief - lists of Burgundies,Bordeaux and German wines, Hedley Wright can also supply smoked , salmon, venison, olives and 'tracklements' - whatever they may be...

| 24 | £18.50 | **CHAMPAGNE LOUIS ROEDERER BRUT PREMIER** |

48	£6.20	**MACON-VINZELLES**, Caves des Grands Crus, Burgundy 1987
51	£5.80	**PRELUDIO NO. 1**, Tenuta di Torrebianco, Puglia 1989
55	£5.40	**CHARDONNAY DI S MICHELE VIGNETO ZARAOSTI**, Roberto Zeni, Trentino-Alto Adige 1989
85	£6.95	**JULIUS WILE CHARDONNAY** 1986
95	£9.20	**CLOUDY BAY CHARDONNAY**, Marlborough 1988
97	£9.99	**COLDSTREAM HILLS CHARDONNAY**, Yarra Valley 1988
122	£4.45	**SAUVIGNON DE TOURAINE DOMAINE DE LA PRESLE**, Jean-Marie Penet, Loire 1988
128	£5.20	**MUSCADET DE SEVRE ET MAINE**, Château de la Ragotière, Loire 1988
129	£4.99	**MONTANA SAUVIGNON BLANC**, Marlborough 1989
133	£6.39	**HILL-SMITH ESTATE SAUVIGNON BLANC**, Barossa Valley 1989
161	£5.25	**ALSACE GEWURZTRAMINER DAMBACH**, Louis Gisselbrecht 1988
270	£2.99	NOGALES CABERNET SAUVIGNON, Discover Wine, Curico Valley 1988
282	£4.99	**MONTES CABERNET SAUVIGNON**, Discover Wine, Curico Valley 1987
283	£4.95	**CHATEAU LA CLAVERIE** (Francois Thienpont), Côte de Francs, Bordeaux 1987
292	£6.75	**ORLANDO ST HUGO CABERNET SAUVIGNON**, Coonawarra 1986
314	£15.00	**TORRES GRAN CORONAS BLACK LABEL**, Penedés 1983
336	£5.75	**CROZES HERMITAGE**, Delas Frères, Rhône 1988
371	£9.99	**COLDSTREAM HILLS PINOT NOIR**, Yarra Valley 1988
395	£4.95	**VALPOLICELLA CLASSICO VIGNETI MARA**, Cesari, Veneto 1987
405	£7.40	**BAROLO RISERVA**, Borgogno, Piedmont 1982
414	£15.95	TIGNANELLO, Antinori, Tuscany 1985
464	£27.50	CHATEAU RIEUSSEC, Sauternes, Bordeaux 1983
471	£4.85	**AMONTILLADO TIO DIEGO**, Valdespino, Jerez
487	£8.95	**COSSART GORDON 5 YEAR OLD BUAL**, Madeira
488	£11.10	**SMITH WOODHOUSE LATE BOTTLED VINTAGE PORT (BOTTLED 1984)**, Douro 1979
491	£15.90	**WARRE'S QUINTA DA CAVADINHA**, Douro 1979

| **HEM** | The Hermitage |

124 Fortis Green Road, London N10 3DU (081 365 2122). Stylish new independent merchant. **Opening Hours:** 10.30am-8.00pm Tues-Sat; 12.00-2.30pm Sun. **Delivery:** free locally, nationally at cost. **Tastings:** organised theme events. **Discounts:** 5% on (mixed) case sales.

The concise, smart Hermitage list is exemplary. Gill Reynolds' experience at Adnams is very apparent in the way in which wines from all the right places have been chosen for all the right reasons. A good blend of Old and New World (with some especially juicy offerings from the latter) are complemented by a range of associated goodies: Taylor & Lake nut oils, a selection of corkscrews, a pewter Drip Stopper, basket bottle-carriers and wine glasses.

47	£5.75	**LUGANA**, Ca Dei Frati, Lombardy 1989
49	£5.75	**BABICH SEMILLON/CHARDONNAY**, Gisborne 1989
56	£7.25	**LIBRARY COLLECTION CHARDONNAY**, Tiefenbrunner, Trentino-Alto Adige 1988
74	£5.99	**RIOJA BLANCO SECO RESERVA**, CVNE 1985
95	£9.85	**CLOUDY BAY CHARDONNAY**, Marlborough 1988
122	£5.25	**SAUVIGNON DE TOURAINE DOMAINE DE LA PRESLE**, Jean-Marie Penet, Loire 1988
134	£6.45	**NOBILOS SAUVIGNON BLANC**, Marlborough 1989
138	£6.95	**HUNTERS SAUVIGNON BLANC**, Marlborough 1989
156	£8.75	**VOUVRAY DEMI-SEC CLOS DE BOURG**, Huet, Loire 1983
172	£4.99	**JOAO PIRES WHITE TABLE WINE**, Palmela 1988

174	£4.95	BROWN BROTHERS LATE HARVEST ORANGE MUSCAT & FLORA, N E Victoria 1988
175	£5.50	QUADY ESSENSIA ORANGE MUSCAT 1987
259	£4.99	COTEAUX D'AIX EN PROVENCE CHATEAU PIGOUDET GRANDE RESERVE, Midi 1985
290	£7.50	FIRESTONE CABERNET SAUVIGNON, Santa Ynez 1986
292	£7.35	ORLANDO ST HUGO CABERNET SAUVIGNON, Coonawarra 1986
303	£9.75	ROUGE HOMME COONAWARRA CABERNET SAUVIGNON 1985
322	£32.00	CHATEAU FIGEAC, St Emilion Grand Cru, Bordeaux 1982
340	£6.25	COTES DU RHONE, Guigal 1986
349	£10.99	RIDGE GEYSERVILLE ZINFANDEL, Sonoma 1987
367	£5.45	BOURGOGNE PINOT NOIR, Caves de Buxy, Burgundy 1987
378	£17.85	MONDAVI PINOT NOIR RESERVE, Napa Valley 1986
388	£3.65	BARBERA D'ASTI, Viticoltori dell'Acquesi, Piedmont 1988
390	£4.35	CABERNET DEL TRENTINO, Ca'Vit, Trentino-Alto Adige 1987
394	£3.99	QUATTRO VICARIATI, Ca'Vit, Trentino-Alto Adige 1986
409	£10.95	RECIOTO DELLA VALPOLICELLA, Allegrini, Veneto 1988
412	£12.50	CEPPARELLO, Isole e Olena, Tuscany 1986
417	£23.25	BAROLO MONPRIVATO, G Mascarello, Piedmont 1985
422	£3.65	ALMANSA MARIUS TINTO RESERVA, Bodegas Piqueras 1982
428	£4.99	QUINTA DE CAMARATE, Fonseca, Azeitao 1985
436	£12.50	RIOJA RESERVA 904, La Rioja Alta 1976
437	£10.50	TINTO PESQUERA, Fernandez, Ribera del Duero 1986
472	£3.99	DON ZOILO VERY OLD FINO, Jerez
482	£5.99	SMITH WOODHOUSE RUBY PORT, Douro

H&D   Hicks & Don Ltd

Park House, North Elmham, Dereham, Norfolk (036 281 571). Independent merchant selling by-the-case. **Opening Hours:** 9.00am-5.30pm Mon-Fri. **Delivery:** free nationally for orders over 3 cases. **Tastings:** organised/tutored events.

'We aim to take the risk out of wine buying'. The two Masters of Wine who run this East Anglian merchant are very good at achieving this aim, while taking the trouble, nevertheless, to seek out good wines other companies might bypass. So, apart from a long list of clarets (H&D are *en primeur* specialists) their list includes a Sauvignon de St Bris, a Gaillac Gamay, a dry German Pinot Gris, a 1986 white Vacqueyras, a 1979 red from Greece, and five English wines, including the Elmham Park made by Robin Don...

24	£20.74	CHAMPAGNE LOUIS ROEDERER BRUT PREMIER
28	£3.54	VINS DE PAYS DES COTES DE GASCOGNE, Plaimont, South-West 1989
47	£6.50	LUGANA, Ca Dei Frati, Lombardy 1989
101	£11.37	MOUNTADAM CHARDONNAY, High Eden Ridge 1989
195	£9.02	THREE CHOIRS BACCHUS, Gloucestershire 1989
276	£4.70	CONCHA Y TORO MERLOT, Maipo 1986
357	£5.93	GAILLAC CEPAGE GAMAY, Jean Cros, South-West 1989
445	£6.28	CHATEAU DES TOURS, Ste-Croix-du-Mont, Bordeaux 1986
487	£10.71	COSSART GORDON 5 YEAR OLD BUAL, Madeira
491	£13.99	WARRE'S QUINTA DA CAVADINHA, Douro 1979

HBV   High Breck Vintners

Spats Lane, Headley, Nr Bordon, Hants GU35 8SY (0428 713689). Independent merchant with a number of regional agents in the south and East Anglia. **Opening Hours:** 9.30am-6pm Mon-Fri;

9.30am-12 Sat. **Delivery:** free locally, nationally at cost.**Tastings:** regularly in-store plus organised tutored tastings.

Ever thought of buying your favourite wine merchant? That's what Howard Baveystock did in late 1989 when he purchased High Breck from Tom Johnson, the former advertising executive who had founded it in 1972. The emphasis here is on French estates whose wines are often unavailable elsewhere. (The rest of the world is represented by just five Germans and two Italians - and both of the latter come in 2-litre bottles.) Prices are generally very fair, and clearly pitched at people who expect value for their money.

126	£5.36	**CHATEAU LA JAUBERTIE BERGERAC SEC,** Henry Ryman, South-West 1987
165	£7.18	**ALSACE TOKAY-PINOT GRIS RESERVE PERSONELLE,** Wiederhirm 1988
240	£5.36	**CHATEAU LA JAUBERTIE BERGERAC ROSE,** Henry Ryman, South-West 1987
298	£8.24	**CHATEAU LA TOUR DE BY,** Haut-Médoc, Bordeaux 1986

GHL | **George Hill of Loughborough**

The Wine Shop, 59 Wards End, Loughborough, Leics LE11 3HB (0509 212717). Independent merchant. **Opening Hours:** 9am-6pm Mon-Sat. **Delivery:** free locally, nationally at cost. **Tastings:** tutored tastings plus organised events. **Discounts:** very good – 8-10% on case sales.

Yet another grocer-turned-wine merchant, this 81-year-old family firm deserves to be better known; its list features a surprising number of good wines in more mature vintages. So, there is the 1985 Mondavi Pinot Noir, the 1979 Jaboulet Châteauneuf 'Les Cèdres' and a 1985 Château de Moulin à Vent. We wonder whether the happy presence of these older wines has anything to do with Andrew Hill's occasionally odd views on vintages. His opinion that 1986 clarets are 'drinking before the 1985s' is nothing if not unconventional.

76	£5.83	**MONTROSE CHARDONNAY,** Mudgee 1989
134	£5.97	**NOBILOS SAUVIGNON BLANC,** Marlborough 1989
157	£2.47	**RETSINA OF ATTICA,** Kourtaki
213	£4.75	**NIERSTEINER SPIEGELBERG KABINETT,** Guntrum, Rheinhessen 1988
288	£6.23	**PETER LEHMANN CABERNET SAUVIGNON,** Barossa Valley 1985
314	£14.11	**TORRES GRAN CORONAS BLACK LABEL,** Penedés 1983
367	£5.42	**BOURGOGNE PINOT NOIR,** Caves de Buxy, Burgundy 1987
375	£14.73	**POMMARD CROIX BLANCHE,** Jacques Parent, Burgundy 1986
422	£3.76	**ALMANSA MARIUS TINTO RESERVA,** Bodegas Piqueras 1982
432	£5.36	**RIOJA RESERVA,** Beronia 1982
444	£9.26	**BAILEYS FOUNDERS LIQUEUR MUSCAT,** Glenrowan
449	£4.99	**CHATEAU DES COULINATS,** Ste-Croix-du-Mont, Bordeaux 1983
452	£5.98	**PETER LEHMANN BOTRYTIS RIESLING,** Barossa Valley 1984
476	£12.28	**MATUSALEM OLOROSO MUY VIEJO,** Gonzalez Byass, Jerez
478	£12.28	**AMONTILLADO DEL DUQUE,** Gonzalez Byass, Jerez
487	£6.67	**COSSART GORDON 5 YEAR OLD BUAL,** Madeira

JEH | **J E Hogg**

61 Cumberland St, Edinburgh, EH3 6RA (031 556 4025). Traditional independent family merchant. **Opening Hours:** 9am-1pm & 2.30pm-6pm Mon, Tue, Thu, Fri; 9am-1pm Wed, Sat. **Delivery:** free in Edinburgh, nationally at cost. **Tastings:** tutored tastings and organised events. **Discounts:** some case discounts.

Ask a canny Scottish wine drinker for the name of a good wine merchant, and there's a high chance he won't mention J E Hogg - for the simple reason that he'd rather keep this source of well chosen vinous bargains to himself. Hogg's list consists of two sheets of orange paper crammed with wines from all parts of the world with handwritten additions and deletions. Rare treats include a Hugel Alsace called 'Sporen' that every self-respecting Scots merchant ought to stock.

RHW Rodney Hogg Wines

52 High St, Higham Ferrers, Northants NN9 8BL (0933 317420). Independent merchant. **Opening Hours:** 9.30am-5.30pm Mon-Fri, but ring first to check. **Delivery:** free within 30 miles, nationally at cost, collection discount. **Tastings:** regularly in-store plus tutored tastings and organised events. **Discounts:** 2.5% for prompt payment.

Higham Ferrers sounds just like the kind of English village to which characters from a PG Wodehouse novel might motor down for a country house weekend. And, had Wodehouse been born a few decades later, he might well have been tempted to invent this wine merchant, running his business from his 200-year-old house. This is not to suggest that there is anything Wodehousian about Rodney Hogg. He and his business are decidedly unstuffy; there are few wines on his wide-ranging list that cost over £10, though a fair number taste as if they might.

HOL Holland Park Wine Co

12 Portland Rd, Holland Park, London W11 (071 221 9614). Independent merchant. **Opening Hours:** 10am-9pm Mon-Fri; 10am-6pm Sat. **Delivery:** free locally, nationally at cost. **Tastings:** regular in-store plus tutored events. **Discounts:** 5% case.

Formerly the Addison Avenue Wine Co, one of the countless Business Expansion Scheme launches that fell on hard times, we marked this firm's rebirth with a new entry in last year's *Guide*. The business is prospering, James Handford having laid down some rock-solid policy foundations: 'to stock some of the world's well-known greats and to introduce new wines of equal or better quality which represent better value'. Less conventionally, Handford is 'keen to introduce more wines from traditional regions'.

23	£18.49	**CHAMPAGNE LAURENT PERRIER ROSE**
24	£17.95	**CHAMPAGNE LOUIS ROEDERER BRUT PREMIER**
29	£3.29	**VIN DE PAYS DES COTES DE GASCOGNE**, Domaine de Perras, South-West 1989
38	£4.39	**ALSACE TOKAY-PINOT GRIS**, Cave Vinicole de Turckheim 1988
43	£4.49	**PINOT BIANCO**, Vigna al Monte, Puglia 1989
74	£5.95	**RIOJA BLANCO SECO RESERVA**, CVNE 1985
102	£10.75	**CRICHTON HALL CHARDONNAY** 1987
138	£7.25	**HUNTERS SAUVIGNON BLANC**, Marlborough 1989
166	£7.49	**MARK WEST VINEYARDS GEWURZTRAMINER**, Sonoma 1988
168	£9.95	ALSACE GEWURZTRAMINER SELECTION DE GRAINS NOBLES, Cave Vinicole de Turckheim 1988
174	£4.75	BROWN BROTHERS LATE HARVEST ORANGE MUSCAT & FLORA, N E Victoria 1988
264	£15.95	MAS DE DAUMAS GASSAC, Vin de Pays de l'Hérault, South-West 1988
299	£8.49	**CHATEAU RAMAGE LA BATISSE**, Haut-Médoc, Bordeaux 1985
319	£29.16	**CHATEAU PICHON-LONGUEVILLE-BARON**, Pauillac, Bordeaux 1985
320	£18.95	CHATEAU LYNCH-BAGES, Pauillac, Bordeaux 1985
331	£4.35	**RASTEAU COTES DU RHONE VILLAGES**, Caves des Vignerons de Rasteau 1988

371	£10.75	**COLDSTREAM HILLS PINOT NOIR**, Yarra Valley 1988
414	£16.95	TIGNANELLO, Antinori, Tuscany 1985
421	£3.35	**VINA ALBALI RESERVA**, Felix Solis, Valdepeñas 1983

| **HOP** | **Hopton Wines** |

Hopton Court, Cleobury Mortimer, Kidderminster, Worcs DY14 0HH (0299 270482) & Teme Street, Tenbury Wells. Expanding independent merchant selling by the case. **Opening Hours:** Hopton Court manned during office hours, Tenbury Wells shop open 9am-9pm Mon-Sat. **Delivery:** free within 50 miles, nationally at cost. **Tastings:** regularly in-store plus tutored events. **Discounts:** for quantity.

A small but growing company whose influence is gradually becoming apparent on the wine lists of a number of restaurants in and around Worcestershire. The Hopton range shows both care and knowledge, and this is nowhere more apparent than in the selections from Burgundy- and Spain, where enthusiasts who can withstand the temptation of the 1942 Castillo Ygay may indulge themselves in some of the few creditable examples of Valdepeñas and Navarra on the market. Beware though, when ordering, of a list that often indicates vintages as, for example, 1987/8: make sure you get the one you want.

57	£8.00	**INNISKILLIN CHARDONNAY**, Niagara 1988
58	£10.37	**MACON-CLESSE DOMAINE DE LA BON GRAN CUVEE TRADITION**, Jean Thevenet, Burgundy 1987
81	£6.33	**STONELEIGH CHARDONNAY**, Marlborough 1988
95	£14.47	**CLOUDY BAY CHARDONNAY**, Marlborough 1988
152	£3.84	**COOKS CHENIN BLANC**, Hawkes Bay 1987
175	£11.76	**QUADY ESSENSIA ORANGE MUSCAT** 1987
298	£9.98	**CHATEAU LA TOUR DE BY**, Haut-Médoc, Bordeaux 1986
314	£20.14	**TORRES GRAN CORONAS BLACK LABEL**, Penedés 1983
321	£34.21	**CHATEAU GRUAUD-LAROSE** (Cordier), St Julien, Bordeaux 1978

| **HUN** | **Hungerford Wine Co** |

---

128 High St, Hungerford, Berks RG17 0DL (0488 83238) & 24 High St, Hungerford, Berks RG17 0NF (0488 683238). Flamboyant Bordeaux buffs with restaurant 'The Galloping Crayfish'. **Opening Hours:** 9am-5.30pm Mon-Fri. **Delivery:** free locally, £10 for 1-5 cases nationally, 6+ cases free. **Tastings:** regularly in-store plus tutored events at the restaurant. **Discounts:** 5% unbroken case.

'Hi and welcome to our wine list'. The opening line sets the tone for Nick Davies's retail list - or rather the large folded sheet offering 'just a small selection of our stocks'. Hungerford seems to have given up putting out a 'proper' list for the moment, but it has made up for this by keeping in touch with its customers in other ways - including extraordinarily detailed *en primeur* offers (complete with a promise not to be undersold by any other merchant) and a telephone information service. Hungerford remains what it has always been- wacky; Davies is the only wine merchant we know to offer a range of outsize bottles of top claret, to advertise in *VIZ* and to have been described as a 'plonker' by the *Star*.

24	£17.50	**CHAMPAGNE LOUIS ROEDERER BRUT PREMIER**
82	£6.75	**WOLLUNDRY CHARDONNAY/SEMILLON**, Hunter Valley 1986
86	£4.50	**MUSCADET DE SEVRE ET MAINE SUR LIE CHATEAU DE CHASSELOIR (OAK-AGED)**, Loire 1987
101	£11.49	MOUNTADAM CHARDONNAY, High Eden Ridge 1989

109	£12.55	**CHATEAU DE FIEUZAL**, Graves, Bordeaux 1986
161	£5.00	**ALSACE GEWURZTRAMINER DAMBACH**, Louis Gisselbrecht 1988
172	£4.75	**JOAO PIRES WHITE TABLE WINE**, Palmela 1988
174	£4.40	**BROWN BROTHERS LATE HARVEST ORANGE MUSCAT & FLORA**, N E Victoria 1988
269	£3.65	**HOUSE CLARET**, Peter Sichel, Bordeaux
318	£19.50	**CHATEAU L'EVANGILE**, Pomerol, Bordeaux 1987
320	£19.17	**CHATEAU LYNCH-BAGES**, Pauillac, Bordeaux 1985
361	£5.45	**BROUILLY, E LORON**, Beaujolais 1989
499	£2.50	**PETILLANT DE RAISIN (3%)**, Listel, Midi

H&O   Hunter & Oliver

Astra House, Harlow CM20 2DT (0279 26801)
Secretive new chain of 70+ shops opened hurriedly and seemingly quite indiscriminately by Grand Met, inventor of Baileys Irish Cream and Piat d'Or, and owner of Peter Dominic (q.v.) and Bottoms Up (q.v.)

JOB   Jeroboams

51 Elizabeth St, London SW1W 9PP (071 823 5623) & 24 Bute Street London SW7 3EX. Up-market deli. **Opening Hours:** 9am-7pm Mon-Fri; 9am-6pm Sat. **Delivery:** free locally **Tastings:** occasional in-store. **Discounts:** 5% on case sales.

Cheese and wine may not always be as easily matched as is generally supposed, but good ranges of both live very happily together in this seductive shop. Be warned, though - any thoughts of going into Jeroboams merely to buy a single bottle of wine should be dismissed forthwith; you're almost certain to walk out with some olive oil, balsamic vinegar, honey, Brie or Cornish Yarg too...

| 486 | £7.99 | **WARRE'S WARRIOR VINTAGE CHARACTER PORT**, Douro |

J&B   Justerini & Brooks

61 St James St, London SW1A 1LZ (071 493 8721) & 39 George St, Edinburgh EH2 2HN (031 226 4202). Traditional merchant, a subsidiary of drinks giant IDV. **Opening Hours:** 9.00am-5.30pm Mon-Fri (-6.00pm in Edinburgh); 9.30am-1.00pm Sat (Edinburgh only). **Delivery:** free locally for over 2 cases, nationally for over 5 cases, otherwise at cost. **Tastings:** occasional public tastings, plus tutored and organised events. **Discounts:** upto £3 per case depending on quantity.

Justerini's apparently has very mixed feelings about guides such as this, imagining perhaps that any publication that lists and describes 180 different firms may drive wedges between traditional wine merchants (such as J&B) and their customers. Well, that's certainly not our intention: indeed, we very much approve of the traditionally cosy, faithful marriage between a customer and 'his wine merchant' - providing that that company can fulfil all of a wine drinker's needs, without dictating or confining his choices. Two or three years ago, this IDV subsidiary would only have filled that role for a very conservative kind of customer. Today, the range is far wider, extending from the inevitable en primeur first growths to a 16-page section of the list devoted exclusively to wines at under £5 a bottle. You still may not wish to commit yourself completely to J&B, but there's certainly scope here for a meaningful relationship.

| 436 | £10.65 | **RIOJA RESERVA 904,** La Rioja Alta 1976 |

| K&B | King & Barnes |

The Horsham Brewery, 18 Bishopric, Horsham, West Sussex RH12 1QP (0403 69344). Wine retailing arm of a country brewery. **Opening Hours:** 9.00am-6.00pm Mon-Sat. **Delivery:** free locally. **Tastings:** occasionally in-store (Saturdays), organised events, tutored tastings and dinners for 'Case and Cellar Club' members. **Discounts:** 5% on (mixed) cases.

'The wine side of King & Barnes has been quite quiet, but with the advent of more people drinking wine...we have built up a quality image and service.' Simon Deakin, this Sussex brewery's wine and spirits manager, clearly has ambitions for the future - and a list that already features a number of carefully selected, non-clichéed wines, ranging from the Roger Lavigne Saumur Champigny to the Hunter's Pinot Noir from New Zealand, the Kouros Nemea red from Greece and the Hogue Cellars Chardonnay from Washington State. Could King & Barnes be an Adnams in the making?

24	£17.20	**CHAMPAGNE LOUIS ROEDERER BRUT PREMIER**
122	£4.25	**SAUVIGNON DE TOURAINE DOMAINE DE LA PRESLE,** Jean-Marie Penet, Loire 1988
134	£6.35	**NOBILOS SAUVIGNON BLANC,** Marlborough 1989
138	£7.05	**HUNTERS SAUVIGNON BLANC,** Marlborough 1989
183	£4.60	**NUTBOURNE MANOR HUXELREBE,** Sussex 1989
261	£5.35	**BODEGAS Y CAVAS DE WEINERT CABERNET SAUVIGNON,** Mendoza 1983
262	£4.75	**CORBIERES CHATEAU DE LASTOURS (FUT DE CHENE),** Midi 1985
298	£6.65	**CHATEAU LA TOUR DE BY,** Haut-Médoc, Bordeaux 1986
442	£6.60	**MUSCAT DE RIVESALTES,** Château de la Tuilerie, Midi 1988
487	£8.35	**COSSART GORDON 5 YEAR OLD BUAL,** Madeira

| L&W | Lay & Wheeler |

6 Culver Street West, Colchester, Essex CO1 1JA (0206 764446) & The Wine Market, Gosbecks Road, Colchester, Essex . Essex's- and one of England's- finest. **Opening Hours:** 8.00am-8.00pm Mon-Sat (Wine Market); 8.30am-5.30pm Mon-Sat (Culver Street). **Delivery:** free locally and free nationally for over 2 cases. **Tastings:** regular in-store plus tutored tastings and organised events. **Discounts:** 1.5% on 4 case orders, 3% on 12 case orders.

What can anyone say about Lay & Wheeler that has not been said a thousand times before? This is quite simply one of the very finest wine merchants (city or country) in Britain, and one that is always among the front runners for any kind of prize. People who enjoy reading about wine as well as drinking it should also seek out a copy of the Lay & Wheeler list; apart from its vinous contents, it is a first class informative read. The following list of award winners speaks for itself.

6	£5.98	**CLAIRETTE DE DIE CUVEE IMPERIAL,** Union des Producteurs, Rhone
14	£12.20	**LAY & WHEELER CHAMPAGNE EXTRA QUALITY BRUT,** Duval Leroy
23	£19.35	**CHAMPAGNE LAURENT PERRIER ROSE**
24	£18.25	**CHAMPAGNE LOUIS ROEDERER BRUT PREMIER**
28	£3.15	**VIN DE PAYS DES COTES DE GASCOGNE** Plaimont, South-West 1989
81	£6.95	**STONELEIGH CHARDONNAY,** Marlborough 1988
82	£6.95	**WOLLUNDRY CHARDONNAY/SEMILLON,** Hunter Valley 1986
92	£8.95	**SIMI CHARDONNAY,** Sonoma 1985
95	£9.95	**CLOUDY BAY CHARDONNAY,** Marlborough 1988

96	£9.95	MARTINBOROUGH VINEYARDS CHARDONNAY, Wairarapa 1988
111	£14.95	PULIGNY MONTRACHET, DOMAINE CARILLON, Burgundy 1987
113	£16.25	MEURSAULT CLOS DU CROMIN, O Leflaive, Burgundy 1986
115	£16.99	MEURSAULT, Drouhin, Burgundy 1988
139	£7.30	SANCERRE, Henry Natter, Loire 1988
155	£7.20	MILLTON VINEYARDS BARREL-FERMENTED CHENIN BLANC, Gisborne 1988
167	£10.95	ALSACE GEWURZTRAMINER GRAND CRU KESSLER, Schlumberger 1985
174	£4.50	BROWN BROTHERS LATE HARVEST ORANGE MUSCAT & FLORA, N E Victoria 1988
190	£5.25	SHAWSGATE MULLER THURGAU, East Anglia 1989
191	£4.95	HENSCHKE RIESLING, Barossa Valley 1987
250	£3.55	COTEAUX DE MURVIEL DOMAINE DE LIMBARDIE, Boukandoura & Hutin, Midi 1988
278	£4.30	CHATEAU NICOT, Bordeaux 1986
296	£7.85	ST JULIEN, Anthony Barton, Bordeaux 1985
303	£8.95	ROUGE HOMME COONAWARRA CABERNET SAUVIGNON 1985
307	£9.95	LAKE'S FOLLY CABERNET SAUVIGNON, Hunter Valley 1987
310	£10.75	CYRIL HENSCHKE CABERNET SAUVIGNON, Henschke, Barossa Valley 1986
312	£12.55	SIMI CABERNET SAUVIGNON RESERVE, Napa Valley 1981
321	£26.00	CHATEAU GRUAUD-LAROSE (Cordier), St Julien, Bordeaux 1978
330	£3.85	COTES DU RHONE, Chateau du Grand Moulas 1988
340	£5.45	COTES DU RHONE, Guigal 1986
341	£5.75	VACQUEYRAS CUVEE DES TEMPLIERS, Domaine le Clos de Cazeaux, Rhône 1986
348	£7.75	CHATEAUNEUF-DU-PAPE DOMAINE FONT DE MICHELLE, Gonnet, Rhône 1985
354	£9.95	CORNAS, Guy de Barjac, Rhône 1986
370	£10.45	HICKINBOTHAM PINOT NOIR, Geelong 1988
393	£4.65	CORVO ROSSO, Sicily 1987
450	£6.20	DOMAINE DU NOBLE (Dejean Pere & Fils), Loupiac, Bordeaux 1986
458	£12.95	CHATEAU LAMOTHE-GUIGNARD, Sauternes, Bordeaux 1986
491	£14.25	WARRE'S QUINTA DA CAVADINHA, Douro 1979

LAY | Laytons

19-20 Midland Road, London NW1 2AD (071 388 5081 / 071 387 8235). Independent merchant allied to André Simon (q.v.). **Opening Hours:** 9.00am-7.00pm Mon-Sat. **Delivery:** free nationally for orders over £100. **Tastings:** regularly in-store and tutored tastings. **Discounts:** None.

Celebrating his 25th price list, Graham Chidgey recalls what he reckoned to be his firm's contribution to wine drinking in Britain over the last quarter of a century. The claims are large — that Laytons had 'revitalised the laying down of vintage port' and encouraged 'en primeur' buying. Just as significantly we would say has been Chidgey's support for individual estate Burgundies. This is the only price list published in 1990 to include a competition for cricket lovers.

346	£6.99	RYECROFT SHIRAZ, Mclaren Vale, 1986

LEA | Lea & Sandeman

301 Fulham Road, London SW10 9QH (071 376 4767). Independent merchant. **Opening Hours:** 9.30am-8.30pm Mon-Sat. **Delivery:** nationally at cost, free for orders over £100. **Tastings:** regularly in-store plus tutored tastings. **Discounts:** 5% on a case if collected.

It is highly appropriate that this company should have its *Guide* entry within a few lines of that for Laytons. The Lea & Sandeman shop is situated in the former Caves de la Madeleine (which belonged to Graham Chidgey) and Charles Lea previously worked for Laytons, too. The background shows; the range is broad, but very French-oriented: 'Wines from Elsewhere' make up a scant three of the list's 19 pages. There is some good value to be found, however, in wines like the 1985 red St Aubin at £7.00. There are excellent ports too; not from the firm that once belonged to Patrick Sandeman's family, but from the excellent house of Churchill Graham.

23	£18.95	**CHAMPAGNE LAURENT PERRIER ROSE**
114	£17.95	**YARRA YERING CHARDONNAY,** Yarra Valley 1987
131	£5.95	**QUINCY,** P & J Mardon, Loire 1988
296	£8.95	**ST JULIEN,** Anthony Barton, Bordeaux 1985
319	£14.95	**CHATEAU PICHON-LONGUEVILLE-BARON,** Pauillac, Bordeaux 1985
346	£6.99	**RYECROFT SHIRAZ,** McLaren Vale 1986
349	£9.50	**RIDGE GEYSERVILLE ZINFANDEL,** Sonoma 1987
377	£13.75	**CALERA JENSEN PINOT NOIR,** San Benito 1987
414	£17.95	**TIGNANELLO,** Antinori, Tuscany 1985
436	£11.50	**RIOJA RESERVA 904,** La Rioja Alta 1976
453	£7.45	**BONNEZEAUX,** Jean Godineau, Loire 1987
471	£7.25	**AMONTILLADO TIO DIEGO,** Valdespino, Jerez

LTW	The Littlewoods Organisation

Head office: J M Centre, Old Hall Street, Liverpool L70 1AB (051 235 2222). Underperforming and unprepossessing 91-branch national supermarket chain. **Opening Hours:** 9.00am-5.30pm Mon-Sat with local variations. **Tastings:** occasionally in-store. **Discounts:** 12 bottles for the price of 11.

Littlewoods says it has begun to take its wine department seriously. We have seen no evidence to support this claim and would suggest that the people who make it spend a little time looking at the shelves - and tasting the wine - of Spar and the Co-op.

1	£3.15	**MOSCATO SPUMANTE,** Santero, Piedmont
4	£5.45	**ASTI MARTINI,** Martini & Rossi, Piedmont
231	£2.89	**PIEMONTELLO PINK,** Piedmont

LWL	London Wine Ltd

Chelsea Wharf, 15 Lots Road, London SW10 (071 351 6856). Independent by-the-case merchant. **Opening Hours:** 9.00am-9.00pm Mon-Fri; 10.am-7.00pm Sat; 10.30am-5.30pm Sun. **Delivery:** free locally, nationally at cost. **Tastings:** regularly in-store and hope to introduce tutored tastings. **Discounts:** 5% on sales over £1,000. That's right, £1,000.

One of the capital's first genuine wine warehouses, London Wine has, for many years, been very much in the shadow of the Majestic store on the other side of the river. The London Wine list is still shorter than those of its bigger rival but, in quality terms, the competition between the two is hotter than ever in the past, thanks to wines like Duboeuf Beaujolais, Turckheim Alsace, Ca'Vit Italians, Calera Pinot Noir, Hunter's Sauvignon Blanc...

23	£19.95	**CHAMPAGNE LAURENT PERRIER ROSE**
38	£3.99	**ALSACE TOKAY-PINOT GRIS,** Cave Vinicole de Turckheim 1988
129	£4.79	**MONTANA SAUVIGNON BLANC,** Marlborough 1989
133	£5.95	**HILL-SMITH ESTATE SAUVIGNON BLANC,** Barossa Valley 1989
138	£6.90	**HUNTERS SAUVIGNON BLANC,** Marlborough 1989

284	£2.99	**SPECIAL RESERVE STAMBOLOVO MERLOT**, Bulgarian Vintners 1985
358	£3.49	**GAMAY DE L'ARDECHE**, Georges Duboeuf, Rhône 1989
359	£4.99	**BEAUJOLAIS-VILLAGES**, Georges Duboeuf 1989
390	£3.99	**CABERNET DEL TRENTINO**, Ca'Vit, Trentino-Alto Adige 1987
394	£4.99	**QUATTRO VICARIATI**, Ca'Vit, Trentino-Alto Adige 1986

LHV | Lorne House Vintners

Unit 5, Hewitts Industrial Estate, Cranleigh GU6 8LW (0483 271445). Independent merchant. **Opening Hours:** 9.00am-5.00pm Mon-Thurs; 9.00am-7.00pm Fri; 9.00am-1.00pm Sat. **Delivery:** free within 25 miles, nationally at cost. **Tastings:** regularly in-store plus tutored tastings. **Discounts:** 10% on pre-shipment orders.

'Lorne House Vintners has not really been successful with the New World...it is generally felt that, at the everyday end of the market, that is around say £4 per bottle, France still wins...' Many would agree with Dirk Collingwood, who describes his aim as being to 'offer wines of...depth with purposeful flavour, wines for enjoyment that grow on you as the bottle is slowly consumed and, last but not least, the wines must be affordable'. His rather homespun list achieves just this very effectively indeed.

MWW | Majestic Wine Warehouses

By the Case Merchant of the Year

421 Kings Rd, London SW6 4RN (071 731 3131). Benchmark by-the-case style: 46 warehouses in south & central England. **Opening Hours:** Mon - Sat 10am - 8pm Sun 10am - 6pm **Delivery:** free locally, nationally at cost. **Tastings:** regularly in-store.

Having apparently settled into life under its new owners, Majestic surprised everyone by undertaking an almost complete clear-out of its senior management. Quite what effect this will have on the company's future style and policy is unclear; we very much hope that Majestic will maintain the impetus and buying skill that earned it both last, and this, year's By the Case Award from the *Guide*. The length of the following list of award winners, and its variety, would alone have made Majestic a strong contender for any award - the consistently high quality of service and atmosphere makes this, as the phrase goes, the original and best of the wine warehouse genre.

3	£4.95	**YALUMBA ANGAS BRUT**, Barossa Valley
5	£4.99	**BRUT DE SAUMUR**, Caves des Vignerons de Saumur, Loire 1987
7	£6.75	**CREMANT DE BOURGOGNE ROSE**, Caves de Bailly, Burgundy 1987
11	£10.85	**CHAMPAGNE DE TELMONT BRUT**
19	£15.75	**CHAMPAGNE POL ROGER DEMI-SEC**
23	£19.95	**CHAMPAGNE LAURENT PERRIER ROSE**
24	£19.95	**CHAMPAGNE LOUIS ROEDERER BRUT PREMIER**
28	£2.39	**VIN DE PAYS DES COTES DE GASCOGNE**, Plaimont, South-West 1989
63	£4.50	**RIOJA BLANCO SECO MONTE REAL**, Bodegas Riojanas 1986
70	£4.99	**VERDICCHIO CA'SAL DI SERRA**, Umani Ronchi, Marches 1986
81	£6.99	**STONELEIGH CHARDONNAY**, Marlborough 1988
86	£7.49	**MUSCADET DE SEVRE ET MAINE SUR LIE CHATEAU DE CHASSELOIR (OAK-AGED)**, Loire 1987
90	£8.69	**CHATEAU CONSTANTIN**, Graves, Bordeaux 1986
95	£9.99	**CLOUDY BAY CHARDONNAY**, Marlborough 1988

108	£15.99	**ROSEMOUNT ROXBURGH CHARDONNAY**, Hunter Valley 1987
110	£14.79	**ZD CHARDONNAY**, Napa Valley 1987
117	£3.35	**ANJOU BLANC CHUPIN**, G Saget, Loire 1989
126	£4.49	**CHATEAU LA JAUBERTIE BERGERAC SEC**, Henry Ryman, South-West 1987
134	£6.75	**NOBILOS SAUVIGNON BLANC**, Marlborough 1989
151	£3.89	**COTEAUX DU LAYON ST-AUBIN DE LUIGNE**, Bancheraau, Loire 1988
152	£3.99	**COOKS CHENIN BLANC**, Hawkes Bay 1987
172	£4.25	**JOAO PIRES WHITE TABLE WINE**, Palmela 1988
175	£5.35	**QUADY ESSENSIA ORANGE MUSCAT** 1987
182	£4.15	**ALSACE RIESLING**, Seltz 1988
188	£4.99	**PILTON MANOR DRY RESERVE**, Somerset 1987
216	£4.99	**SCHARZHOFBERGER KABINETT KESSELSTATT**, Mosel-Saar-Ruwer 1988
218	£4.99	**GAU-BISCHOFSHEIMER KELLERSBERG RIESLING SPATLESE**, Kellerstaat
229	£7.95	**KREUZNACHER BRUCKES RIESLING AUSLESE**, Schloss Plettenberg, Nahe 1985
239	£4.29	**CHATEAU THIEULEY BORDEAUX CLAIRET** 1989
243	£2.25	**BULGARIAN COUNTRY WINE**, Merlot/Gamza, Suhindol
245	£2.59	**DOMAINE DES LENTHERIC GRENACHE MERLOT** Lentheric Père et Fils, Midi 1988
246	£2.89	**CABARDES**, Château Ventenac, Midi 1989
251	£3.89	**CORBIERES**, Château du Luc, Midi 1988
252	£3.75	**COTES DE BERGERAC PETITE BORIE**, M Sadoux, South-West 1987
266	£2.59	**PLOVDIV CABERNET SAUVIGNON**, Bulgarian Vintners 1985
269	£2.99	**HOUSE CLARET**, Peter Sichel, Bordeaux
284	£5.29	**SPECIAL RESERVE STAMBOLOVO MERLOT**, Bulgarian Vintners 1985
291	£6.99	**ALLANDALE CABERNET SAUVIGNON**, Hunter Valley 1986
294	£7.69	**ROSEMOUNT SHOW RESERVE COONAWARRA CABERNET SAUVIGNON** 1987
297	£8.49	**PENFOLDS BIN 389 SHIRAZ/CABERNET**, South Australia 1986
308	£10.95	**PETALUMA COONAWARRA CABERNET/MERLOT** 1985
309	£10.95	**CHATEAU HAUT-BAGES-AVEROUS** (Château Lynch-Bages), Pauillac, Bordeaux 1986
316	£16.99	**PENFOLDS BIN 707 CABERNET SAUVIGNON**, South Australia 1986
326	£2.99	**COTES DU VENTOUX**, Paul Boutinot, Rhône 1989
339	£5.25	**PENFOLDS BIN 28 KALIMNA SHIRAZ**, South Australia 1986
367	£4.95	**BOURGOGNE PINOT NOIR**, Caves de Buxy, Burgundy 1987
387	£2.49	**MONTEPULCIANO D'ABRUZZO**, Tollo, Abruzzi 1987
414	£14.95	**TIGNANELLO**, Antinori, Tuscany 1985
424	£4.99	**QUINTA DE CAMARATE**, Fonseca, Azeitão 1985
443	£9.95	**CAMPBELLS RUTHERGLEN MUSCAT**
445	£2.35	**CHATEAU DES TOURS**, Ste-Croix-du-Mont, Bordeaux 1986
460	£19.99	**CHATEAU RABAUD-PROMIS**, Sauternes, Bordeaux 1986
482	£4.59	**SMITH WOODHOUSE RUBY PORT**, Douro
491	£14.95	**WARRE'S QUINTA DA CAVADINHA**, Douro 1979

M&S | Marks & Spencer

Head office: St Michael House, 57 Baker St, London W1A 1DN (071 935 4422). Up-market supermarket chain beloved by the thirtysomethings. **Opening Hours**: Many (most London) branches open until 8.00pm Mon-Fri, 9,00am-6.00pm Sat. **Delivery**: nationally at cost. **Tastings**: none. **Discounts**: 12 bottles for the price of 11.

On the wine front, M&S is a little like an English tennis player. Everyone wants it to do well, and it keeps on showing promise, but there still isn't quite enough stamina and commitment to take it into the final against a player of the class of Sainsbury or Tesco. Far too many chances are grabbed - and thrown away. One of the best examples of this frustrating inconsistency is the set of white Bordeaux, launched to wide applause, which virtually disappeared from the shelves within months of their first appearance.

There are good wines here, and at lower prices than in the past; we are particularly pleased to see the good new French country wines. The buying team has shown its tasting skills in two of the most difficult of styles, Champagne and low-alcohol, but trick shots alone do not win a match.

2	£3.25	ST MICHAEL BLUSH FRIZZANTE
18	£14.99	ST MICHAEL ROSE CHAMPAGNE DE ST GALL, Union Champagne
21	£15.99	ST MICHAEL VINTAGE CHAMPAGNE DE ST GALL, Union Champagne 1985
28	£2.79	VIN DE PAYS DES COTES DE GASCOGNE, Plaimont, South-West 1989
66	£4.99	ST MICHAEL AUSTRALIAN CHARDONNAY, Basedows, Barossa Valley 1988
186	£4.95	ST MICHAEL ENGLISH WINE, (Carr Taylor Vineyard), Kent
234	£3.49	ST MICHAEL FRENCH COUNTRY ROSE, Georges Duboeuf
237	£4.50	ST MICHAEL CALIFORNIA BLUSH, The Christian Brothers
268	£2.99	ST MICHAEL GRAPE SELECTION MERLOT, Vin de Pays de l'Aude, Foncalieu l'Aude, Midi
273	£3.29	ST MICHAEL CLARET, Gallaire, Bordeaux 1986
333	£4.50	ST MICHAEL AUSTRALIAN CABERNET/SHIRAZ, Penfolds, South Australia 1987
356	£2.99	ST MICHAEL GRAPE SELECTION GAMAY, Vin de Pays de l'Ardèche, Rhône
386	£2.99	CANTINA SETTESOLI ROSSO, Sicily 1987
466	£2.99	ST MICHAEL FINO SHERRY, Williams & Humbert, Jerez
469	£4.29	ST MICHAEL RICH CREAM SHERRY (Harveys) Jerez
498	£1.69	ST MICHAEL SPARKLING APERITIF BLUSH, Klosterhof

MC | The Master Cellar

7 Aberdeen Road, Croydon, Surrey (081 686 9989). Wine warehouse sibling of the Davisons chain, situated at the HQ of their parent, JTDavies. **Opening Hours:** 10.00am-8.00pm Tues-Fri; 10.00am-6.00pm Sat, Sun. **Delivery:** free locally, nationally at cost. **Tastings:** regularly in-store plus tutored and organised events. **Discounts:** for orders over 10 cases.

This Croydon wine warehouse has all of the virtues of the Davisons chain's smaller shops - but a wider range of older wines. Prices are extraordinarily competitive too, thanks to the JT Davies policy of buying wine to lay down for subsequent sale.

3	£4.80	YALUMBA ANGAS BRUT, Barossa Valley
4	£5.45	ASTI MARTINI, MARTINI & ROSSI, Piedmont
24	£16.40	CHAMPAGNE LOUIS ROEDERER BRUT PREMIER
28	£2.70	VIN DE PAYS DES COTES DE GASCOGNE, Plaimont, South-West 1989
40	£4.30	COOKS MARLBOROUGH SEMILLON 1987
75	£6.35	FIRESTONE CHARDONNAY, Santa Ynez 1987
129	£4.80	MONTANA SAUVIGNON BLANC, Marlborough 1989
142	£7.25	POUILLY BLANC FUME DOMAINE CHAILLOUX, Châtelain, Loire 1987
149	£2.95	CHENIN BLANC, E & J Gallo 1988
152	£4.30	COOKS CHENIN BLANC, Hawkes Bay 1987
159	£4.75	TORRES GEWURZTRAMINER, Curico 1988
160	£4.80	ALSACE GEWURZTRAMINER, Caves Coop des Viticulteurs d'Ingersheim 1987
174	£4.75	BROWN BROTHERS LATE HARVEST ORANGE MUSCAT & FLORA, N E Victoria 1988
213	£4.50	NIERSTEINER SPIEGELBERG KABINETT, Guntrum, Rheinhessen 1988
233	£2.95	WHITE GRENACHE, E & J Gallo 1989
236	£4.75	TORRES CABERNET SAUVIGNON ROSE, Curico 1989
250	£2.95	COTEAUX DE MURVIEL DOMAINE DE LIMBARDIE, Boukandoura & Hutin, Midi 1988
289	£6.60	CHATEAU BEAUMONT, Cru Bourgeois Médoc, Bordeaux 1986
290	£6.35	FIRESTONE CABERNET SAUVIGNON, Santa Ynez 1986

292	£6.95	**ORLANDO ST HUGO CABERNET SAUVIGNON**, Coonawarra 1986
314	£16.50	**TORRES GRAN CORONAS BLACK LABEL**, Penedés 1983
320	£17.30	CHATEAU LYNCH-BAGES, Pauillac, Bordeaux 1985
339	£5.49	**PENFOLDS BIN 28 KALIMNA SHIRAZ**, South Australia 1986
348	£7.25	**CHATEAUNEUF-DU-PAPE DOMAINE FONT DE MICHELLE**, Gonnet, Rhône 1985
365	£7.25	**FLEURIE LA MADONE**, Georges Duboeuf, Beaujolais 1988
369	£9.35	**SANTENAY LE CHENAY**, Domaine Bernard Morey, Burgundy 1985
414	£16.40	**TIGNANELLO**, Antinori, Tuscany 1985
430	£5.35	**RIOJA CRIANZA**, Navajas 1985
431	£5.30	**LAR DE BARROS RESERVA**, Bodega Inviosa, Extremadura 1986
437	£12.95	**TINTO PESQUERA**, Fernandez, Ribera del Duero 1986
464	£14.20	CHATEAU RIEUSSEC, Sauternes, Bordeaux 1983
472	£6.25	**DON ZOILO VERY OLD FINO**, Jerez
473	£6.25	**DON ZOILO MANZANILLA**, Sanlucar de Barrameda
482	£5.20	**SMITH WOODHOUSE RUBY PORT**, Douro

MCL | McLeods

Bridge Street, Louth, Lincs LN11 0DR (0507 601094). Probably the only wine merchant selling 'Mariner' bottled gas and offering a dry-cleaning service in the world. **Opening Hours:** 10.00am-8.30pm every day (normal licensing hours). **Delivery:** free locally. **Tastings:** wines occasionally open for sampling. **Discounts:** 5% for case orders, 10% for over 2 cases.

Steeple-spotters who find their way to Louth's 15th century St James's Church (England's highest) should make time to stop in at the small Georgian shop that lies in its shadow. McLeod's offers the local populace a keenly-priced range of wines, cheeses and 'ethnic foods' that is a lot less conservative than some of the good burghers might be used to. To encourage experimentation, the company urges its customers to 'club together' and take advantage of case discounts; it also offers free glass loan and - a thoughtful touch- free loan of an ice bucket.

73	£5.27	**LINDEMANS BIN 65 CHARDONNAY**, Murray River 1989
233	£3.40	**WHITE GRENACHE**, E & J Gallo 1989
313	£15.87	**CHATEAU MOUTON-BARONNE-PHILIPPE**, Pauillac, Bordeaux 1986
364	£5.75	**MORGON JEAN DESCOMBES**, Georges Duboeuf, Beaujolais 1989
365	£8.70	**FLEURIE LA MADONE**, Georges Duboeuf, Beaujolais 1988

MM | Michael Menzel

297-299 Eccleshall Rd, Sheffield, South Yorks S11 8NX (0742 683557). Realistic but not unimaginative independent merchant. **Opening Hours:** 10.00am-9.00pm Mon-Sat; 12.00-2.00pm & 7.00pm-9.00pm Sun. **Delivery:** free in Sheffield, nationally at cost. **Tastings:** none. **Discounts:** available on certain cases.

'We do not wish to expand as the quality of our service would suffer... As the competition has been getting hotter in the last few years, we tend to have moved upmarket.' All credit to Michael Menzel for acknowledging the realities of the market (we get very bored with merchants decrying the supermarkets), and for putting together a truly excellent list. Burgundy is clearly a fascination (with a long selection from Drouhin and Faiveley) but Rhônes are carefully picked too, as are a wide variety of often quite quirky wines. This, for example, is the place to come for a Blauer Portugieser from

Germany, or the ultra-traditional 1975 Pira Barolo. Prices are very fair.

4	£5.20	ASTI MARTINI, Martini & Rossi, Piedmont
19	£15.50	CHAMPAGNE POL ROGER DEMI-SEC
20	£14.99	CHAMPAGNE PHILIPPONNAT BRUT ROSE
23	£18.98	CHAMPAGNE LAURENT PERRIER ROSE
24	£18.65	CHAMPAGNE LOUIS ROEDERER BRUT PREMIER
25	£18.85	CHAMPAGNE LANSON BRUT 1979
46	£5.75	SOAVE CASTEGGIOLA, G Rizzardi, Veneto 1987
74	£5.98	RIOJA BLANCO SECO RESERVA, CVNE 1985
80	£6.75	WOLF BLASS BARREL-FERMENTED CHARDONNAY, South Australia 1988
81	£6.95	STONELEIGH CHARDONNAY, Marlborough 1988
104	£14.50	VILLA MARIA BARRIQUE-FERMENTED CHARDONNAY, Auckland 1987
115	£18.95	MEURSAULT, Drouhin, Burgundy 1988
134	£7.55	NOBILOS SAUVIGNON BLANC, Marlborough 1989
157	£2.85	RETSINA OF ATTICA, Kourtaki
174	£5.45	BROWN BROTHERS LATE HARVEST ORANGE MUSCAT & FLORA, N E Victoria 1988
177	£4.35	BADEN DRY, ZBW
194	£6.35	DEINHARD HERITAGE SELECTION DEIDESHEIM, Rheinpfalz 1987
195	£6.75	THREE CHOIRS BACCHUS, Gloucestershire 1989
276	£3.90	CONCHA Y TORO MERLOT, Maipo 1986
313	£11.55	CHATEAU MOUTON-BARONNE-PHILIPPE, Pauillac, Bordeaux 1986
314	£15.00	TORRES GRAN CORONAS BLACK LABEL, Penedes 1983
317	£18.95	MONDAVI CABERNET SAUVIGNON RESERVE, Napa Valley 1980
322	£34.95	CHATEAU FIGEAC, St Emilion Grand Cru, Bordeaux 1982
338	£5.98	WYNNS COONAWARRA SHIRAZ 1987
340	£5.80	COTES DU RHONE, Guigal 1986
393	£4.98	CORVO ROSSO, Sicily 1987
399	£6.30	CAMPO FIORIN, Masi, Veneto 1985
402	£6.30	VINO NOBILE DI MONTEPULCIANO RISERVA, Fattorio del Cerro, Tuscany 1985
414	£18.50	TIGNANELLO, Antinori, Tuscany 1985
472	£7.25	DON ZOILO VERY OLD FINO, Jerez
473	£7.98	DON ZOILO MANZANILLA, Sanlucar de Barrameda
475	£9.99	DOS CORTADOS, Williams & Humbert, Jerez
476	£13.75	MATUSALEM OLOROSO MUY VIEJO, Gonzalez Byass, Jerez
478	£13.75	AMONTILLADO DEL DUQUE, Gonzalez Byass, Jerez
493	£22.50	QUINTA DO NOVAL 20 YEAR OLD TAWNY PORT, Douro

MIL	Millevini

3 Middlewood Road, High Lane, Stockport, Cheshire (0663 64366). Mail order Italian specialist; no shop, though orders may be collected. **Delivery:** free within 20 miles, nationally at cost, 3% collection discount. **Tasting:** for outside clubs on request. **Discounts:** 4% on orders over 3 cases.

Finally, after a prolonged sojourn in the desert of public apathy towards Italian wine, Richard Lever is beginning to look as though he's in the right place at the right time. Millevini is not Britain's very best Italian specialist, but it is one of the best.

55	£7.42	CHARDONNAY DI S MICHELE VIGNETO ZARAOSTI, Roberto Zeni, Trentino-Alto Adige 1989
59	£8.35	PINOT BIANCO, JERMANN, Friuli-Venezia Giulia 1988
70	£4.93	VERDICCHIO CA'SAL DI SERRA, Umani Ronchi, Marches 1986
402	£7.87	VINO NOBILE DI MONTEPULCIANO RISERVA, Fattorio del Cerro, Tuscany 1985
403	£7.98	TANCA FARRA, Sella e Mosca, Sardinia 1984

MTL	Mitchells Wine Merchants

354 Meadowhead, Sheffield, S.Yorkshire S8 74J (0742 745587/740311). Expanding independent family merchant with 3 branches in Sheffield. **Opening Hours:** 8.30am-10.00pm Mon-Sat; 12.00 noon-3.00pm Sun. **Delivery:** free within 10 miles, nationally at cost. **Tastings:** regularly in-store plus tutored tastings with more organised events planned. **Discounts:** 10% on unbroken cases, 5% on mixed cases.

Run by 'two Yorkshire lads who love their wines but still enjoy a pint', Mitchells is a family business that was begun 55 years ago as a butchers and for some while was known as the 'Beef and Beer' shop. Today, having cast off the wholesaling arm, the firm is a serious retailer with a good, broad range of wines (of which the following are representative) and a selection of beers that includes Coopers Bib Barrel from Australia and Mexico's Simpatico. There's no beef nowadays- not even Torres Gran Sangre de Toro.

4	£4.85	**ASTI MARTINI**, Martini & Rossi, Piedmont
5	£6.95	**BRUT DE SAUMUR**, Caves des Vignerons de Saumur, Loire 1987
19	£16.45	**CHAMPAGNE POL ROGER DEMI-SEC**
25	£19.45	**CHAMPAGNE LANSON BRUT 1979**
129	£3.99	**MONTANA SAUVIGNON BLANC**, Marlborough 1989
177	£3.25	**BADEN DRY**, ZBW
203	£3.19	**ST JOHANNER ABTEYKABINETT**, Jacob Demmer, Rheinhessen 1988
213	£3.95	**NIERSTEINER SPIEGELBERG KABINETT**, Guntrum, Rheinhessen 1988
231	£2.95	**PIEMONTELLO PINK**, Piedmont
311	£11.95	**CHATEAU HAUT-MARBUZET**, St Estèphe, Bordeaux 1985
313	£11.99	**CHATEAU MOUTON-BARONNE-PHILIPPE**, Pauillac, Bordeaux 1985
320	£25.95	**CHATEAU LYNCH-BAGES**, Pauillac, Bordeaux 1985
321	£24.95	**CHATEAU GRUAUD-LAROSE** (Cordier), St Julien, Bordeaux 1978
363	£6.35	**REGNIE CRISTAL**, Georges Duboeuf, Beaujolais 1989
364	£6.95	**MORGON JEAN DESCOMBES**, Georges Duboeuf, Beaujolais 1989
379	£16.95	**VOSNE-ROMANEE LES MALCONSORTS**, Moillard, Burgundy 1986
391	£4.29	**TEROLDEGO ROTALIANO**, Gaierhof, Trentino-Alto Adige 1988
401	£5.69	**CHIANTI CLASSICO RISERVA DUCALE**, Ruffino, Tuscany 1986
432	£5.95	**RIOJA RESERVA**, Beronia 1982
433	£5.45	**RIOJA RESERVA ALBINA**, Bodegas Riojanas 1984
476	£9.25	**MATUSALEM OLOROSO MUY VIEJO**, Gonzalez Byass, Jerez
478	£9.25	**AMONTILLADO DEL DUQUE**, Gonzalez Byass, Jerez
482	£5.45	**SMITH WOODHOUSE RUBY PORT**, Douro
499	£2.49	**PETILLANT DE RAISIN (3%)**, Listel, Midi

MOR	Moreno Wines

2 Norfolk Place, London W2 1QN (071 723 6897) & 11 Marylands Road, London W9 2DU. Independent Spanish specialist. **Opening Hours:** 9.30am-8.00pm Mon-Fri; 10.00am-8.00pm Sat. **Delivery:** free locally and nationally for orders over 3 cases. **Tastings:** monthly club meetings. **Discounts:** on mixed cases.

Sometimes Manuel Moreno must wish he had been born with Italian rather than Spanish blood; Italian wines are simply so much more interesting than most Iberians - a fact that, to judge by recent import statistics, is fully appreciated by British wine drinkers. But Moreno perseveres - with wines from Spain, Portugal and now South America, constantly striving to match Iberian style and quality with the demands of the British consumer. While outstanding young Spanish wines are still rare, Moreno can offer some gorgeous old ones, including such delights as Ygay 1942.

63	£4.95	**RIOJA BLANCO SECO MONTE REAL**, Bodegas Riojanas 1986
74	£5.35	**RIOJA BLANCO SECO RESERVA**, CVNE 1985
172	£4.85	**JOAO PIRES WHITE TABLE WINE**, Palmela 1988
243	£2.45	**BULGARIAN COUNTRY WINE, MERLOT/GAMZA**, Suhindol
314	£15.59	**TORRES GRAN CORONAS BLACK LABEL**, Penedés 1983
424	£4.39	**ROMEIRA GARRAFEIRA**, Cavas Velhas 1980
430	£4.99	**RIOJA CRIANZA**, Navajas 1985
431	£5.19	**LAR DE BARROS RESERVA**, Bodega Inviosa, Extremadura 1986
433	£6.15	**RIOJA RESERVA ALBINA**, Bodegas Riojanas 1984
436	£11.99	**RIOJA RESERVA 904**, La Rioja Alta 1976
476	£13.89	MATUSALEM OLOROSO MUY VIEJO, Gonzalez Byass, Jerez
478	£13.89	**AMONTILLADO DEL DUQUE**, Gonzalez Byass, Jerez

M&V   Morris & Verdin

28 Churton St, London SW1V 2LP (071 630 8888). Serious- but not too serious- independent merchant. **Opening Hours:** 9.30am-5.30pm Mon-Fri; 10.00am-5.00pm Sat. **Delivery:** free locally, nationally at cost. **Tastings:** occasionally in-store. **Discounts:** negotiable.

Jasper Morris MW is generally thought of in the wine trade as a specialist in Burgundy, the region about which he recently wrote a very good book. A look at the Morris & Verdin shelves - and at the award winners listed below - reveals a much broader range of vinous interests. Lovers of traditional French wines will particularly appreciate the style of Morris's Californian offerings, all of which are made in a decidedly Gallic style.

23	£18.00	**CHAMPAGNE LAURENT PERRIER ROSE**
24	£17.60	**CHAMPAGNE LOUIS ROEDERER BRUT PREMIER**
28	£2.90	**VIN DE PAYS DES COTES DE GASCOGNE** Plaimont, South-West 1989
95	£9.90	**CLOUDY BAY CHARDONNAY**, Marlborough 1988
103	£12.20	**VITA NOVA CHARDONNAY** 1988
250	£3.30	COTEAUX DE MURVIEL DOMAINE DE LIMBARDIE, Boukandoura & Hutin, Mid1988
351	£9.10	**QUPE SYRAH** 1988
373	£11.50	AU BON CLIMAT PINOT NOIR 1988
380	£18.60	**VOSNE-ROMANEE 1ER CRU BEAUMONTS**, Daniel Rion, Burgundy 1986

MRS   Wm Morrison Supermarkets Ltd

41, Industrial Estate, Wakefield N Yorks WF2 0XF (0274 497421). Yorkshire-based supermarket chain. **Opening Hours:** 8.30am-6.00pm Mon-Wed & Sat; 8.30am-8.00pm Thu, Fri. **Delivery:** none. **Tastings:** occasional.

This underrated chain has made extraordinary leaps in quality over the last few years, under the guiding hand of wine buyer Nick Wakefield. Particular credit is due to Wakefield for introducing his customers to unusual, not to say esoteric, wines such as the Quady Essensia from California and the extraordinary Morris Liqueur Muscat from Australia. In-store tastings are a welcome development for any supermarket, too.

74	£5.49	**RIOJA BLANCO SECO RESERVA**, CVNE 1985
80	£6.55	**WOLF BLASS BARREL-FERMENTED CHARDONNAY**, South Australia 1988
129	£4.99	**MONTANA SAUVIGNON BLANC**, Marlborough 1989
149	£3.29	**CHENIN BLANC**, E & J Gallo 1988

157	£2.99	RETSINA OF ATTICA, Kourtaki
161	£5.25	ALSACE GEWURZTRAMINER DAMBACH, Louis Gisselbrecht 1988
175	£5.50	QUADY ESSENSIA ORANGE MUSCAT 1987
231	£2.89	PIEMONTELLO PINK, Piedmont
391	£4.29	TEROLDEGO ROTALIANO, Gaierhof, Trentino-Alto Adige 1988
401	£6.29	CHIANTI CLASSICO RISERVA DUCALE, Ruffino, Tuscany 1986
413	£15.69	CABREO IL BORGO, Ruffino, Tuscany 1986
430	£5.19	RIOJA CRIANZA, Navajas 1985
441	£7.50	MORRIS RUTHERGLEN LIQUEUR MUSCAT
447	£4.59	CHATEAU DE BERBEC, Premieres Côtes de Bordeaux 1987
496	£1.59	GOLDENER OKTOBER LIGHT WHITE, St Ursula Weinkellerei, Rheinhessen
499	£1.99	PETILLANT DE RAISIN (3%), Listel, Midi

| LNR | Le Nez Rouge Wine Club |

12 Brewery Road, London N7 9NH (071 609 4711) & The Birches Industrial Estate, East Grinstead, Sussex RH19 1XZ. Mail-order club for Francophiles, now with retail outlets. **Opening Hours:** 9.00am-5.30pm Mon-Fri; 10.00am-2.00pm Sat. **Delivery:** free within London or within 20 miles of East Grinstead. **Tastings:** bottles regularly open for sampling, tutored tastings and organised events. **Discounts:** £2.00 per case on wines collected.

Last year, the purchase of Sussex wholesaler K F Butler made for an expansion of the list and, more importantly, the opening of a second 'Club Shop' in Butler's East Grinstead warehouse. However, the Le Nez Rouge style established by Joseph Berkmann remains unchanged: heaps of single estate French wines (particularly Burgundy), tons of Duboeuf Beaujolais, a surprisingly wide set of individual Muscadets from Sauvion, truly mouth watering Bordeaux from the 1980s and 1970s and some undervalued Antipodeans.

28	£3.13	VINS DE PAYS DES COTES DE GASCOGNE, Plaimont, South-West 1989
241	£4.60	ROSE DE PROVENCE CARTE NOIRE, Les Maitres Vignerons 1989
263	£5.87	MADIRAN, CHATEAU D'AYDIE, South-West 1988
283	£4.95	CHATEAU LA CLAVERIE (Francois Thienpont), Côte de Francs, Bordeaux 1987
289	£6.03	CHATEAU BEAUMONT, Cru Bourgeois Medoc, Bordeaux 1986
322	£26.66	CHATEAU FIGEAC, St Emilion Grand Cru, Bordeaux 1982
358	£3.99	GAMAY DE L'ARDECHE, Georges Duboeuf, Rhône 1989
359	£4.68	BEAUJOLAIS-VILLAGES, Georges Duboeuf 1989
363	£5.99	REGNIE CRISTAL, Georges Duboeuf, Beaujolais 1989
364	£5.89	MORGON JEAN DESCOMBES, Georges Duboeuf, Beaujolais 1989
365	£6.89	FLEURIE LA MADONE, Georges Duboeuf, Beaujolais 1988
374	£14.31	NUITS ST GEORGES, Alain Michelot, Burgundy 1986

| JN | James Nicholson Wine Merchants |

27a Lillyleagh St, Crossgar, Co. Down, N Ireland (0396 830091). New outlet for established import & wholesale business. **Opening Hours:** 10.00am-7.00pm Mon-Thurs; 10.00am-8.00pm Fri; 10.00am-6.00pm Sat. **Delivery:** free nationally. **Tastings:** regularly in-store plus tutored tastings and organised events. **Discounts:** 10% (approx) per case.

The first Ulster merchant to make its way into the *Guide*, James Nicholson provides further evidence that anyone who imagines this part of the UK to be culturally deprived ought to think again. Tim Mondavi tutored the firm's tasting of his wines, as did Pierre Dourthe of Château Maucaillou. The list is not long, but the wines on it, all of good - often excellent - provenance, each have a very good reason to be there.

| 51 | £5.80 | **PRELUDIO NO. 1,** Tenuta di Torrebianco, Puglia 1989 |

| **NIC** | **Nicolas** |

157 Great Portland St, London W1N 5FP (071 436 9636). 5-branch London chain. **Opening Hours:** 9am - 9pm Mon-Sat; 12 - 3pm & 7pm - 9pm Sun. **Delivery:** free within 1 mile, nationally at cost. **Tastings:** regularly in-store, tutored tastings. **Discounts:** 5% on mixed cases.

Formerly Buckinghams, this small London chain was bought by Nicolas and transformed into an English-accented version of the French giant's home-territory operation. Both the UK staff and the French management have learned a great deal from the experience - it is said to have deterred Nicolas from buying Augustus Barnett - but there was little difficulty in introducing Nicolas' habitual French profit margin. Whatever its name, this was and is still a very pricy place to buy what is admittedly a generally good range of wines.

3	£7.25	**YALUMBA ANGAS BRUT,** Barossa Valley
23	£19.56	**CHAMPAGNE LAURENT PERRIER ROSE**
24	£17.99	**CHAMPAGNE LOUIS ROEDERER BRUT PREMIER**
31	£3.99	**CENTENARY SEMILLON** 1987
115	£18.50	**MEURSAULT, DROUHIN,** Burgundy 1988
157	£2.99	**RETSINA OF ATTICA,** Kourtaki
174	£4.95	**BROWN BROTHERS LATE HARVEST ORANGE MUSCAT & FLORA,** N E Victoria 1988
175	£7.00	**QUADY ESSENSIA ORANGE MUSCAT** 1987
177	£4.00	**BADEN DRY,** ZBW
437	£12.95	**TINTO PESQUERA,** Fernandez, Ribera del Duero 1986
491	£16.95	**WARRE'S QUINTA DA CAVADINHA,** Douro 1979

| **RN** | **Rex Norris** |

50 Queens Rd, Haywards Heath, W Sussex RH16 1EE (0444 454756). Independent merchant with a constantly changing selection. **Opening Hours:** 9am-5.30pm Mon,Tues,Thurs; 9am-1pm Wed; 9am-7.30pm Fri; 9am-4.30pm Sat. **Delivery:** free within 5 miles. **Tastings:** wines regularly open for sampling plus occasional in-store tastings. **Discounts:** 10% on cases, 7% for not using your credit card.

'We have been in business for 13 years and hope to continue, as long as the new business rate allows us to operate profitably...' The slightly worried note is one that will strike a chord with a great many other independent wine merchants. If the rates did make life too difficult for Rex Norris, Sussex wine drinkers would lose a great source of all sorts of fairly-priced French, Antipodean, Italian and Spanish bottles, many of which are bought in by Rex Norris in quantities too small to make them worth printing them on a regular list.

| 86 | £5.59 | **MUSCADET DE SEVRE ET MAINE SUR LIE CHATEAU DE CHASSELOIR (OAK-AGED),** Loire 1987 |
| 129 | £5.09 | **MONTANA SAUVIGNON BLANC,** Marlborough 1989 |

134	£6.55	**NOBILOS SAUVIGNON BLANC,** Marlborough 1989
292	£7.45	**ORLANDO ST HUGO CABERNET SAUVIGNON,** Coonawarra 1986
357	£4.29	**GAILLAC CEPAGE GAMAY,** Jean Cros, South-West 1989
408	£9.80	**PRUNAIO,** Landini, Tuscany 1986

OD	Oddbins

Wine Merchant of the Year

Head Office, 31-33 Weir Rd, Durnsford Industrial Estate, Wimbledon, London SW19 8UG (081 879 1199). 144-branch heavyweight champion of the High Street. **Opening Hours:** Mon - Sat 9am - 9pm Sun 12 - 3pm 7pm - 9pm **Delivery:** free locally. **Tastings:** regularly in-store plus organised events. **Discounts:** 5% on cases and a '7 for the price of 6' offer on all Champagnes.

When we asked our panel of judges to vote on the 1991 *Sunday Telegraph Good Wine Guide* Merchant of the Year, 12 unhesitatingly named Oddbins as their first choice. Among their comments were: 'They still pick the best wines'; 'It's where I do my wine buying'; 'To be fair, it has to be them for the sheer quality of wines and staff'; 'They honestly have no competition - not with the number of their outlets and the level of friendly expertise'; 'There really is no contest'. Their verdict confirmed by the results of the *WINE Magazine* International Challenge. The following list represents only a third of the Oddbins award winners.

3	£4.99	**YALUMBA ANGAS BRUT,** Barossa Valley
4	£5.45	**ASTI MARTINI,** Martini & Rossi, Piedmont
6	£5.99	**CLAIRETTE DE DIE CUVEE IMPERIAL,** Union des Producteurs, Rhône
8	£7.99	**VOUVRAY BRUT,** Huet, Loire
9	£9.49	**WILSONS PINOT NOIR/CHARDONNAY,** Adelaide Hills
22	£13.99	**CHAMPAGNE BRICOUT CARTE D'OR BRUT PRESTIGE**
23	£19.49	**CHAMPAGNE LAURENT PERRIER ROSE**
37	£3.99	**HARDY'S BIRD SERIES CHARDONNAY,** South Australia 1989
38	£3.99	**ALSACE TOKAY-PINOT GRIS,** Cave Vinicole de Turckheim 1988
41	£3.79	**ALSACE PINOT BLANC,** Cave Vinicole de Turckheim 1989
44	£4.69	**MACON-LUGNY,** Eugene Blanc, Burgundy 1988
62	£3.69	**KILLAWARRA CHARDONNAY,** South Australia 1989
69	£4.49	**HARDY'S NOTTAGE HILL SEMILLON,** South Australia 1989
69	£4.99	**CHATEAU ROQUEFORT CUVEE PRESTIGE,** Bordeaux 1988
70	£4.99	**VERDICCHIO CA'SAL DI SERRA,** Umani Ronchi, Marches 1986
73	£4.99	**LINDEMANS BIN 65 CHARDONNAY,** Murray River 1989
74	£5.49	**RIOJA BLANCO SECO RESERVA,** CVNE 1985
80	£5.99	**WOLF BLASS BARREL-FERMENTED CHARDONNAY,** South Australia 1988
84	£6.49	**SCHINUS MOLLE CHARDONNAY,** Mornington Peninsula 1989
87	£6.99	**PENFOLDS CHARDONNAY,** South Australia 1988
88	£6.99	**CHATEAU COUHINS-LURTON,** Graves, Lurton, Bordeaux 1987
97	£9.99	**COLDSTREAM HILLS CHARDONNAY,** Yarra Valley 1988
101	£9.99	**MOUNTADAM CHARDONNAY,** High Eden Ridge 1989
108	£14.99	**ROSEMOUNT ROXBURGH CHARDONNAY,** Hunter Valley 1987
115	£15.99	**MEURSAULT,** Drouhin, Burgundy 1988
129	£4.75	**MONTANA SAUVIGNON BLANC,** Marlborough 1989
136	£6.69	**ADLER FELS SAUVIGNON BLANC,** Sonoma 1987
140	£6.99	**SANCERRE CLOS DE LA CROIX AU GARDE,** Domaine H Pelle, Loire 1989
154	£4.99	**JURANCON MOELLEUX CUVEE THIBAULT (BARRIQUE-AGED),** Domaine de Bellegarde, South-West 1988
157	£2.79	**RETSINA OF ATTICA,** Kourtaki

169	£3.35	**TOLLEY'S PEDARE LATE HARVEST MUSCAT BLANC A PETITS GRAINS**, Barossa Valley 1988
172	£3.99	**JOAO PIRES WHITE TABLE WINE**, Palmela 1988
174	£4.49	**BROWN BROS LATE HARVEST ORANGE MUSCAT & FLORA**, N E Victoria 1988
177	£2.79	**BADEN DRY**, ZBW
180	£3.99	**VILLA SACHSEN TROCKEN**, Rheingau 1988
181	£3.49	**SEAVIEW RHINE RIESLING**, South East Australia 1987
185	£4.89	**FREINSHEIMER GOLDBERG RIESLING TROCKEN KABINETT**, Lingenfelder, Rheinpfalz 1987
187	£4.99	**ORLANDO ST HELGA RIESLING, BAROSSA VALLEY** 1986
196	£7.99	**ALSACE RIESLING GRAND CRU BRAND**, Cave Vinicole de Turckheim 1985
217	£4.99	**KIONA LATE PICKED RIESLING**, Washington State 1988
227	£6.99	**RUPPERTSBERGER GEISBOHL RIESLING SPATLESE**, Dr Burklin-Wolf, Rheinpfalz 1985
235	£3.59	**FRONTON CHATEAU BELLEVUE ROSE**, South-West 1988
249	£3.49	**COTES DU ROUSSILLON**, Château de Jau, Midi 1987
257	£4.49	**GROSSKARLBACHER OSTERBERG DORNFELDER**, Lingenfelder, Rheinpfalz 1989
263	£5.69	**MADIRAN**, Château d'Aydie, South-West 1988
264	£8.99	**MAS DE DAUMAS GASSAC**, Vin de Pays de l'Hérault, South-West 1988
266	£2.69	**PLOVDIV CABERNET SAUVIGNON**, Bulgarian Vintners 1985
270	£3.19	**NOGALES CABERNET SAUVIGNON**, Discover Wine, Curico Valley 1988
275	£3.49	**SANDEMAN CLARET**, Bordeaux 1986
277	£3.99	**SEAVIEW CABERNET SAUVIGNON**, South Australia 1985
284	£5.19	**SPECIAL RESERVE STAMBOLOVO MERLOT**, Bulgarian Vintners 1985
285	£4.99	**DAVID WYNN CABERNET**, High Eden Ridge 1986
286	£5.49	**COLUMBIA CREST CABERNET SAUVIGNON**, Washington State 1985
292	£7.25	**ORLANDO ST HUGO CABERNET SAUVIGNON**, Coonawarra 1986
297	£7.69	**PENFOLDS BIN 389 SHIRAZ/CABERNET**, South Australia 1986
313	£11.99	**CHATEAU MOUTON-BARONNE-PHILIPPE**, Pauillac, Bordeaux 1986
314	£16.99	**TORRES GRAN CORONAS BLACK LABEL**, Penedés 1983
316	£16.99	**PENFOLDS BIN 707 CABERNET SAUVIGNON**, South Australia 1986
323	£2.79	**COTEAUX DU TRICASTIN**, Cellier de l'Enclave des Papes, Rhône
339	£4.99	**PENFOLDS BIN 28 KALIMNA SHIRAZ**, South Australia 1986
340	£5.39	**COTES DU RHONE**, Guigal 1986
349	£8.99	**RIDGE GEYSERVILLE ZINFANDEL**, Sonoma 1987
351	£9.99	**QUPE SYRAH** 1988
355	£14.99	**PENFOLDS MAGILL ESTATE**, South Australia 1986
366	£2.69	**MILION PINOT NOIR**, Navip, Vranje 1986
371	£9.99	**COLDSTREAM HILLS PINOT NOIR**, Yarra Valley 1988
380	£18.99	**VOSNE-ROMANEE 1ER CRU BEAUMONTS**, Daniel Rion, Burgundy 1986
389	£3.59	**BARDOLINO**, Fraterna Portalupi, Veneto 1988
410	£9.99	**MON PRA**, Conterno e Fantino, Piedmont 1987
411	£11.99	**BAROLO RISERVA, GIACOMO CONTERNO**, Piedmont 1983
416	£19.99	**BARBARESCO**, Gaja, Piedmont 1986
419	£2.65	**CASTILLO DE ALHAMBRA**, Vinicola de Castilla, La Mancha 1989
423	£3.99	**MEIA PIPA**, Joao Pires, Palmela 1987
429	£4.99	**RAIMAT TEMPRANILLO**, Lerida 1987
432	£5.89	**RIOJA RESERVA**, Beronia 1982
435	£6.99	**GRANDE ESCHOLA**, Quinta do Cotto, Douro 1985
437	£9.99	**TINTO PESQUERA**, Fernandez, Ribera del Duero 1986
440	£3.99	**SAMOS NECTAR 10 YEAR OLD**, Cooperatives Vinicoles de Samos
441	£7.25	**MORRIS RUTHERGLEN LIQUEUR MUSCAT**
448	£3.99	**MONTANA LATE HARVEST RHINE RIESLING**, Marlborough 1987
454	£5.99	**TOKAY ASZU 5 PUTTONYOS**, Tokaji 1981
455	£8.99	**KIONA ICE WINE RIESLING**, Washington State 1987
460	£14.99	**CHATEAU RABAUD-PROMIS**, Sauternes, Bordeaux 1986

461	£7.49	**RECIOTO DI SOAVE DEI CAPITELLE**, Anselmi, Veneto 1987
462	£7.99	**TORCOLATO**, Maculan, Veneto 1986
464	£13.99	**CHATEAU RIEUSSEC**, Sauternes, Bordeaux 1983
474	£4.99	**DON LUIS AMONTILLADO**, Burdon, Jerez
476	£10.99	**MATUSALEM OLOROSO MUY VIEJO**, Gonzalez Byass, Jerez
478	£10.99	**AMONTILLADO DEL DUQUE**, Gonzalez Byass, Jerez
491	£14.99	**WARRE'S QUINTA DA CAVADINHA**, Douro 1979
496	£1.39	**GOLDENER OKTOBER LIGHT WHITE**, St Ursula Weinkellerei, Rheinhessen
499	£1.85	**PETILLANT DE RAISIN (3%)**, Listel, Midi

| **OBC** | **The Old Butcher's Wine Cellar** |

High St, Cookham-on-Thames, Berks SL6 9SQ (0628 810605). Retail outlet for large wholesale operation. **Opening Hours:** 10.00am-7.00pm Mon-Sat. **Delivery:** free locally, nationally at cost. **Tastings:** regularly in-store, plus tutored events.

This young (1988) Cookham shop clearly benefits from being the retail arm of wholesalers Stratford's Wine Shippers, and thus having access to that firm's agencies in Europe and the New World. The list features some 500 wines, including some petit château clarets that are unavailable elsewhere, as well as the wonderful Old Luxters Reserve from Chiltern Valley vineyards.

23	£19.49	**CHAMPAGNE LAURENT PERRIER ROSE**
24	£17.90	**CHAMPAGNE LOUIS ROEDERER BRUT PREMIER**
28	£3.49	**VIN DE PAYS DES COTES DE GASCOGNE**, Plaimont, South-West 1989
76	£5.99	**MONTROSE CHARDONNAY**, Mudgee 1989
131	£6.99	**QUINCY**, P & J Mardon, Loire 1988
134	£6.80	**NOBILOS SAUVIGNON BLANC**, Marlborough 1989
145	£8.75	**POUILLY FUME BUISSON MENARD**, Didier Dagueneau, Loire 1988
193	£6.45	**OLD LUXTERS RESERVE**, Chiltern Valley Wines, Buckinghamshire 1989
288	£4.95	**PETER LEHMANN CABERNET SAUVIGNON**, Barossa Valley 1985
299	£7.49	**CHATEAU RAMAGE LA BATISSE**, Haut-Médoc, Bordeaux 1985
334	£5.75	**COTES DU RHONE**, Domaine St Apollinaire 1988
340	£5.99	**COTES DU RHONE**, Guigal 1986
381	£32.50	**CLOS VOUGEOT GRAND CRU**, Château de la Tour, Burgundy 1982
452	£6.85	**PETER LEHMANN BOTRYTIS RIESLING**, Barossa Valley 1984

| **OLS** | **The Old St Wine Co** |

309 Old St, London EC1V 6LE (071 729 1768). Traditional City merchant. **Opening Hours:** 10.00am-7.00pm Mon-Fri; 11.00am-2.00pm Sat. **Delivery:** free within 18 miles, free nationally for orders over 4 cases. **Tastings:** tutored tastings and events, plus regular in-store tastings.

The Old Street list invites customers to 'call in to our treasure trove of rare, interesting and unusual wines'. To accept the invitation is to be offered a fairly brief but generally carefully selected list of almost exclusively French wines, including such relative affordables as Château Latour 1977 (at 28.00) and Château Lynch Bages 1981 (at 22.90). The Old Street address is also the place to find The Nearly Private Wine Club, which holds good tutored tastings and dinners in aid of children's charities.

| 8 | £7.99 | **VOUVRAY BRUT**, Huet, Loire |

71	£5.00	MINERVOIS, DOMAINE DE LA TOUR BOISEE VIEILLI EN FUT DE CHENE, Jean Louis Poudou, Midi
156	£8.30	VOUVRAY DEMI-SEC CLOS DE BOURG, Huet, Loire 1983
182	£4.15	ALSACE RIESLING, Seltz 1988
256	£4.35	CORBIERES, CHATEAU HELENE VIEILLI EN FUT DE CHENE, Marie-Hélène Gau, Midi 1985
289	£6.50	CHATEAU BEAUMONT, Cru Bourgeois Médoc, Bordeaux 1986
453	£6.99	BONNEZEAUX, Jean Godineau, Loire 1987
464	£27.50	CHATEAU RIEUSSEC, Sauternes, Bordeaux 1983
471	£6.99	AMONTILLADO TIO DIEGO, Valdespino, Jerez

ORG | Organic Wine Co

PO Box 81, High Wycombe, Bucks, HP13 5QN (0494 446557).Independent merchant specialising in organic wine, but only if it tastes good. **Opening Hours:** 9.00am-5.30pm Mon-Fri; 9.00am-1.00pm Sat. **Delivery:** free within 10 miles, nationally at cost. **Tastings:** regular tastings at various locations. **Discounts:** negociable.

If your image of organic wine merchants was of skinny, bearded creatures wearing leather sandals and pullovers made out of porridge, go and meet Tony Mason, a man who believes in the business of selling healthy wine. The Organic Wine Co's association with Europe's biggest organic distributor has helped Mason to put together a list that includes creditable organic wines from just about everywhere - from New Zealand to Transdanubia. And taking over West Heath Wines' mail order operation has helped him to sell them. If you like jazz, you may have already met Mr Mason - in his mobile 'Organic Bar' with which he attends festivals around the country.

155	£7.20	MILLTON VINEYARDS BARREL-FERMENTED CHENIN BLANC, Gisborne 1988
226	£6.50	MILLTON VINEYARDS OPOU RIVER RIESLING, Gisborne 1989
300	£8.65	CHATEAU DE PUY (ROBERT AMOREAU), Bordeaux Supérieur 1982

P | Parfrements

68 Cecily Rd, Cheylesmore Rd, West Midlands CV3 5LA (0203 503646). One-man wholesale/retail business. **Opening Hours:** n/a - orders taken by telephone. **Delivery:** free nationally. **Tastings:** tutored tastings and organised events. **Discounts:** 2.5% for payment with order, 10% on orders over 10 cases.

Gerald Gregory is one of Britain's surprisingly numerous band of one-man-band, enthusiastic wine merchants. His business has been built up steadily through one-to-one contact with Midlands-based wine lovers who trust Gregory to direct them towards wines he has found that they are often unlikely to encounter elsewhere. Good value wines from France remain the focus of interest, but the New World is beginning to attract greater attention

| 367 | £6.15 | BOURGOGNE PINOT NOIR, Caves de Buxy, 1987 |

THP | Thos Peatling

Head office: Westgate House, Bury St Edmunds, Suffolk IP33 1QT (0284 755948).East of England chain with 34 branches, of which the newest is the Peatlings Wine Centre (formerly Ostlers),

Clerkenwell Road, London EC1. **Opening Hours:** varied. **Delivery:** free locally, nationally at cost for orders under 5 cases. **Tastings:** regularly in-store plus tutored tastings and organised events. **Discounts:** 5% on cases.

Thos Peatling 'may be traditional but are far from boring'. The description by Tony Keys, whose Ostlers wine shop was bought by Thos Peatling last year, seems to be a fair one. This East Anglian (in the widest sense of the term) merchant still honours the tradition of bottling some of its own claret, but competes with the most go-ahead firms in the country in its keenness to stock the newest and best from such countries as Australia and New Zealand, for which the Ostlers premises (now the Peatlings Wine Centre) will be a showcase. The range is excellent (including 140 Burgundies), as is the informatively readable wine list.

4	£5.99	**ASTI MARTINI**, Martini & Rossi, Piedmont	
24	£18.25	**CHAMPAGNE LOUIS ROEDERER BRUT PREMIER**	
31	£4.15	**CENTENARY SEMILLON** 1987	
53	£6.49	**SEPPELTS CHARDONNAY**, South-East Australia 1989	
68	£5.09	**BERGERAC SEC DOMAINE DE GRANDCHAMP**, Nick Ryman, South-West 1988	
73	£5.29	**LINDEMANS BIN 65 CHARDONNAY**, Murray River 1989	
77	£6.29	**KIES ESTATE SEMILLON/SAUVIGNON**, Barossa Valley 1988	
80	£6.19	**WOLF BLASS BARREL-FERMENTED CHARDONNAY**, South Australia 1988	
87	£7.79	**PENFOLDS CHARDONNAY**, South Australia 1988	
88	£7.99	**CHATEAU COUHINS-LURTON**, Graves, Lurton, Bordeaux 1987	
97	£10.99	**COLDSTREAM HILLS CHARDONNAY**, Yarra Valley 1988	
100	£11.69	**PETALUMA CHARDONNAY**, Adelaide Hills 1987	
101	£12.15	MOUNTADAM CHARDONNAY, High Eden Ridge 1989	
105	£14.99	**TARRAWARRA CHARDONNAY**, Yarra Valley 1987	
107	£14.39	**CULLENS CHARDONNAY**, Margaret River 1987	
109	£11.49	**CHATEAU DE FIEUZAL**, Graves, Bordeaux 1986	
138	£6.99	**HUNTERS SAUVIGNON BLANC**, Marlborough 1989	
149	£2.99	**CHENIN BLANC**, E & J Gallo 1988	
161	£5.25	**ALSACE GEWURZTRAMINER DAMBACH**, Louis Gisselbrecht 1988	
162	£5.99	**ALSACE AUXERROIS MOENCHREBEN RORSCHWIHR**, Rolly Gassmann 1987	
174	£4.55	**BROWN BROS LATE HARVEST ORANGE MUSCAT & FLORA**, N E Victoria 1988	
175	£5.75	**QUADY ESSENSIA ORANGE MUSCAT** 1987	
233	£2.99	**WHITE GRENACHE**, E & J Gallo 1989	
277	£4.29	**SEAVIEW CABERNET SAUVIGNON**, South Australia 1985	
295	£7.99	**CHATEAU SOCIANDO MALLET**, Haut-Médoc, Bordeaux 1986	
297	£8.49	**PENFOLDS BIN 389 SHIRAZ/CABERNET**, South Australia 1986	
298	£8.50	**CHATEAU LA TOUR DE BY**, Haut-Médoc, Bordeaux 1986	
313	£11.59	**CHATEAU MOUTON-BARONNE-PHILIPPE**, Pauillac, Bordeaux 1986	
314	£15.00	**TORRES GRAN CORONAS BLACK LABEL**, Penedés 1983	
315	£13.99	**WYNNS JOHN RIDDOCH CABERNET SAUVIGNON**, Coonawarra 1985	
319	£21.49	**CHATEAU PICHON-LONGUEVILLE-BARON**, Pauillac, Bordeaux 1985	
321	£26.15	**CHATEAU GRUAUD-LAROSE** (Cordier), St Julien, Bordeaux 1978	
354	£10.75	**CORNAS**, Guy de Barjac, Rhône 1986	
361	£5.85	**BROUILLY**, E Loron, Beaujolais 1989	
371	£10.99	**COLDSTREAM HILLS PINOT NOIR**, Yarra Valley 1988	
372	£11.15	**SAVIGNY-LES-BEAUNE 1ER CRU LES LAVIERES**, Domaine Chandon de Briailles, Burgundy 1986	
389	£3.99	**BARDOLINO**, Fraterna Portalupi, Veneto 1988	
436	£10.65	**RIOJA RESERVA 904**, La Rioja Alta 1976	
444	£11.99	**BAILEYS FOUNDERS LIQUEUR MUSCAT**, Glenrowan	
460	£14.90	**CHATEAU RABAUD-PROMIS**, Sauternes, Bordeaux 1986	
476	£11.15	**MATUSALEM OLOROSO MUY VIEJO**, Gonzalez Byass, Jerez	
478	£11.15	**AMONTILLADO DEL DUQUE**, Gonzalez Byass, Jerez	

491	£16.39	**WARRE'S QUINTA DA CAVADINHA**, Douro 1979
494	£28.99	**WARRE'S FINE OLD PORT**, Douro
99	£1.99	**PETILLANT DE RAISIN (3%)**, Listel, Midi

CPW | Christopher Piper Wines

1 Silver St, Ottery St Mary, Devon EX11 1D. (0404 814139). Jolly independent merchant with passion for Burgundy and Beaujolais. **Opening Hours:** 8.30am-6.30pm Mon-Fri; 9.30am-5pm Sat. **Delivery:** Free locally, also nationally for 6+ cases. **Tastings:** regularly in-store plus tutored events on request. **Discounts:** 5% on (mixed) cases, 10% on orders over 3 cases.

A brief look at the wine list from this popular merchant will show why he is held in such high regard. It manages to combine a wealth of information with enthusiasm and good sense. The selection is mainly French but there are also full ranges from CVNE, Mondavi, Brown Brothers and Louis Guntrum and over 100 wines in half-bottles. Chris Piper and his partner John Earle also do an occasional double act on wine weekends at the Thurlestone Hotel, where Chris's exuberance is nicely matched by John's laconic wit.

69	£8.20	**CHATEAU ROQUEFORT CUVEE PRESTIGE**, Bordeaux 1988
74	£5.45	**RIOJA BLANCO SECO RESERVA**, CVNE 1985
80	£6.10	**WOLF BLASS BARREL-FERMENTED CHARDONNAY**, South Australia 1988
96	£10.46	**MARTINBOROUGH VINEYARDS CHARDONNAY**, Wairarapa 1988
120	£5.47	**SAUMUR BLANC CHATEAU DE VILLENEUVE**, Robert Chevalier, Loire 1988
122	£4.72	**SAUVIGNON DE TOURAINE DOMAINE DE LA PRESLE**, Jean-Marie Penet, Loire 1988
174	£4.44	**BROWN BROTHERS LATE HARVEST ORANGE MUSCAT & FLORA**, N E Victoria 1988
177	£3.58	**BADEN DRY**, ZBW
213	£4.61	**NIERSTEINER SPIEGELBERG KABINETT**, Guntrum, Rheinhessen 1988
241	£4.99	**ROSE DE PROVENCE CARTE NOIRE**, Les Maitres Vignerons 1989
322	£30.37	**CHATEAU FIGEAC**, St Emilion Grand Cru, Bordeaux 1982
367	£5.20	**BOURGOGNE PINOT NOIR**, Caves de Buxy, Burgundy 1987
387	£2.99	**MONTEPULCIANO D'ABRUZZO**, Tollo, Abruzzi 1987
399	£5.23	**CAMPO FIORIN**, Masi, Veneto 1985
451	£6.99	**CHATEAU LA NERE**, Dulac & Seraphon, Loupiac, Bordeaux 1986
462	£14.79	**TORCOLATO**, Maculan, Veneto 1986
487	£9.57	**COSSART GORDON 5 YEAR OLD BUAL**, Madeira
491	£14.33	**WARRE'S QUINTA DA CAVADINHA**, Douro 1979

TP | Terry Platt Wines

Ferndale Rd, Llandudno Junction, Gwynned LL31 9NT (0492 592971). Wholesale/retail merchant selling by the case. **Opening Hours:** 8.30am-5.30pm Mon-Fri. **Delivery:** free locally, nationally at cost. **Tastings:** wines occasionally open for sampling. **Discounts:** none.

Since the emphasis switched from retailing to wholesaling, there are now no Terry Platt shops, but the firm still sells by the mixed case and indeed makes customers' lives more interesting by offering them attractively priced tasting cases of newly listed wines, ranging from fine Bordeaux to such New World stars as New Zealand's Hunters wines and the Hogues from Washington State.

| 4 | £5.64 | **ASTI MARTINI**, Martini & Rossi, Piedmont |

24	£18.64	**CHAMPAGNE LOUIS ROEDERER BRUT PREMIER**
61	£11.97	**CHABLIS 1ER CRU VAILLONS,** E Defaix, Burgundy 1985
75	£6.88	**FIRESTONE CHARDONNAY,** Santa Ynez 1987
89	£9.21	**CHATEAU LA LOUVIERE,** Graves, Bordeaux 1986
138	£7.46	**HUNTERS SAUVIGNON BLANC,** Marlborough 1989
290	£6.83	**FIRESTONE CABERNET SAUVIGNON,** Santa Ynez 1986
378	£16.07	**MONDAVI PINOT NOIR RESERVE,** Napa Valley 1986

| POW | Portland Wine Company (formerly SuperBrew) |

16 North Parade, Sale Moor Manchester M33 3JS (061 962 8752). Recently re-christened (but still super) independent merchant. **Opening Hours:**10.00am-10.00pm Mon-Sat; 12.00-2.00pm & 7.00pm-9.30pm Sun. **Delivery:** free within 20 miles. **Tastings:** regular in-store plus tutored tastings. **Discounts:** 5% on case sales.

Blind tastings are a great leveller - as much of wine merchants as of wines. So, while one or two double- or triple-barrelled City-style merchants were able to claim a dozen or so award winners from the 1990 WINE Magazine International Challenge, the unprepossessing-sounding Superbrew managed no less than 111, of which we have room to list a mere 40 or so. Under its new name - The Portland Wine Company - this is a company to watch.

3	£5.75	**YALUMBA ANGAS BRUT,** Barossa Valley
4	£5.19	**ASTI MARTINI, MARTINI & ROSSI,** Piedmont
29	£3.19	**VIN DE PAYS DES COTES DE GASCOGNE,** Domaine de Perras, South-West 1989
38	£4.49	**ALSACE TOKAY-PINOT GRIS,** Cave Vinicole de Turckheim 1988
40	£4.29	**COOKS MARLBOROUGH SEMILLON** 1987
41	£3.99	ALSACE PINOT BLANC, Cave Vinicole de Turckheim 1989
56	£6.75	**LIBRARY COLLECTION CHARDONNAY,** Tiefenbrunner, Trentino-Alto Adige 1988
74	£5.49	**RIOJA BLANCO SECO RESERVA,** CVNE 1985
75	£6.35	**FIRESTONE CHARDONNAY,** Santa Ynez 1987
80	£6.55	**WOLF BLASS BARREL-FERMENTED CHARDONNAY,** South Australia 1988
81	£4.69	**STONELEIGH CHARDONNAY,** Marlborough 1988
100	£10.89	**PETALUMA CHARDONNAY,** Adelaide Hills 1987
101	£9.95	MOUNTADAM CHARDONNAY, High Eden Ridge 1989
119	£3.99	**SAUMUR BLANC,** Caves des Vignerons de Saumur, Loire 1988
129	£4.69	**MONTANA SAUVIGNON BLANC,** Marlborough 1989
133	£5.99	**HILL-SMITH ESTATE SAUVIGNON BLANC,** Barossa Valley 1989
135	£6.69	**COOPERS CREEK SAUVIGNON BLANC,** Marlborough 1989
143	£8.50	**RONGOPAI SAUVIGNON BLANC,** Waikato 1989
152	£3.89	**COOKS CHENIN BLANC,** Hawkes Bay 1987
215	£4.95	**SICHEL RIESLING KABINETT,** Rheinpfalz 1988
233	£3.39	**WHITE GRENACHE,** E & J Gallo 1989
236	£4.59	**TORRES CABERNET SAUVIGNON ROSE,** Curico 1989
243	£2.39	**BULGARIAN COUNTRY WINE, MERLOT/GAMZA,** Suhindol
251	£3.19	**CORBIERES,** Château du Luc, Midi 1988
259	£4.69	COTEAUX D'AIX EN PROVENCE CHATEAU PIGOUDET GRANDE RESERVE , Midi 1985
262	£4.99	**CORBIERES** Château de Lastours (Fut de Chene), Midi 1985
266	£2.75	**PLOVDIV CABERNET SAUVIGNON,** Bulgarian Vintners 1985
267	£2.79	**VIN DE PAYS DE L'AUDE CABERNET SAUVIGNON,** Paul Boutinot, Midi 1987
280	£4.49	**WOLF BLASS RED LABEL,** Barossa Valley 1986
284	£5.49	**SPECIAL RESERVE STAMBOLOVO MERLOT,** Bulgarian Vintners 1985
298	£8.49	**CHATEAU LA TOUR DE BY,** Haut-Médoc, Bordeaux 1986
299	£8.49	**CHATEAU RAMAGE LA BATISSE,** Haut-Médoc, Bordeaux 1985

309	£10.99	**CHATEAU HAUT-BAGES-AVEROUS** (Château Lynch-Bages), Pauillac, Bordeaux 1986
320	£20.45	CHATEAU LYNCH-BAGES, Pauillac, Bordeaux 1985
358	£3.99	**GAMAY DE L'ARDECHE**, Georges Duboeuf, Rhône 1989
363	£5.99	**REGNIE CRISTAL**, Georges Duboeuf, Beaujolais 1989
364	£6.49	**MORGON JEAN DESCOMBES**, Georges Duboeuf, Beaujolais 1989
393	£4.49	**CORVO ROSSO**, Sicily 1987
428	£4.69	**QUINTA DE CAMARATE**, Fonseca, Azeitão 1985
459	£11.49	**SICHEL BEERENAUSLESE DEIDESHEIMER HOFSTUCK**, Rheinpfalz 1988
464	29.79	CHATEAU RIEUSSEC, Sauternes, Bordeaux 1983
477	10.99	**SANDEMAN ROYAL AMBROSANTE**, Jerez

| **AR** | **Arthur Rackhams** |

Head Office: 5 High Rd, Byfleet, Weybridge, Surrey KT14 7QF (09323 51585). 14 branch London and Surrey chain with associated stores: Viticulteur, 391 Kings Road, London SW10, The Vintner, 66 Kensington Church Street, London W8, and Wineland, Upper Richmond Road, London SW15.Also a mail order club, The Vintner. **Opening Hours**: 10am - 6pm and 10am-10pm **Delivery**: free nationally for orders over 5 cases. **Tastings**: weekly in-store plus tutored and organised events including the annual 'Vintner Festival'. **Discounts**: for club members

After launching the Vintner Wine Club and the 'Viticulteur' agency, shop and range devoted to single estate wines from France, James Rackham has broadened his horizons to introduce British wine drinkers to the wines of Spain, through his 'Bodega' selections. Sadly, like Viticulteur, this range is let down by the quality of far too many of its wines. The Arthur Rackhams shops and The Vintner have good staff, do offer reasonable ranges, and an excellent spread of Champagnes, but they still seem to be less impressive than they were a few years ago when this chain won an award from the *Guide*..

| **RAE** | **Raeburn Fine Wine & Foods** |

Joint Winner: Scottish Wine Merchant of the Year.

23 Comely Bank Rd, Edinburgh, EH4 1DS (031 332 5166). Grocery store with an ace fine wine merchant attached. **Opening Hours**: Mon - Sat 9am - 7pm. **Delivery**: free locally, nationally at cost. **Tastings**: tutored tastings and organised events. **Discounts**: 2.5% on a mixed case, 5% on unmixed cases.

Someday soon, somebody will have to make a film about Zubair Mahomed; it will be called 'My Beautiful Grocer' and will depict the way in which a young man whose parents ran a small grocery shop decided to turn it into one of the best wine merchants in the country. At first he built up his list following the recommendations that appeared in magazines like *WINE*. Very soon, however, he began importing wines directly from individual estates, and selling them both in the shop (which is still a grocers) and to local restaurateurs, proving in the process that his own taste buds were every bit as good as those of the magazine panels. The small shop is packed with all sorts of high-class wines, many of them available in quantities too small for us to list here. But almost anything you find on the Raeburn shelves should be worth buying - including the packets of biscuits and soap powder that still rub shoulders with the wines.

8	£8.50	VOUVRAY BRUT, Huet, Loire
16	£13.95	CHAMPAGNE CUVEE DE RESERVE, H Billiot
127	£4.95	MUSCADET DE SEVRE ET MAINE SUR LIE, G Bossard, Loire 1989
156	£7.80	VOUVRAY DEMI-SEC CLOS DE BOURG, Huet, Loire 1983
314	£13.95	TORRES GRAN CORONAS BLACK LABEL, Penedés 1983
460	£11.95	CHATEAU RABAUD-PROMIS, Sauternes, Bordeaux 1986
476	£9.99	MATUSALEM OLOROSO MUY VIEJO, Gonzalez Byass, Jerez
478	£9.95	AMONTILLADO DEL DUQUE, Gonzalez Byass, Jerez

RAV | Ravensbourne Wine Co

13 Bell House, 49 Greenwich High Rd London SE10 8JL (081 692 9655). Independent merchant selling by the case. **Opening Hours:** 9am-5pm Mon-Fri; 10am-2pm Sat. **Delivery:** free locally, nationally at cost. **Tastings:** regular tutored events. **Discounts:** variable.

'Our bespoke consultancy service is here to give you peace of mind', says the very-hard-to-read Ravensbourne list, going on to state that the company is a supplier to 'Parties...Exhibitions, Conferences, Boardrooms, Arbours...' We wondered a bit about the arbours (might they have meant 'Harbours'?), but could easily understand why party-givers and other kinds of customer would want to buy wine here. The two ex-Oddbins employees who founded Ravensbourne have put together a good range, with an accent on French country, Italian and organic wines.

23	£17.99	CHAMPAGNE LAURENT PERRIER ROSE
24	£18.79	CHAMPAGNE LOUIS ROEDERER BRUT PREMIER
46	£5.15	SOAVE CASTEGGIOLA, G Rizzardi, Veneto 1987
76	£6.09	MONTROSE CHARDONNAY, Mudgee 1989
127	£4.90	MUSCADET DE SEVRE ET MAINE SUR LIE, G Bossard, Loire 1989
129	£4.99	MONTANA SAUVIGNON BLANC, Marlborough 1989
172	£5.05	JOAO PIRES WHITE TABLE WINE, Palmela 1988
210	£4.25	BIDDENDEN MULLER-THURGAU, Kent 1989
243	£2.29	BULGARIAN COUNTRY WINE, MERLOT/GAMZA, Suhindol
266	£2.55	PLOVDIV CABERNET SAUVIGNON, Bulgarian Vintners 1985
276	£3.79	CONCHA Y TORO MERLOT, Maipo 1986
284	£2.99	SPECIAL RESERVE STAMBOLOVO MERLOT, Bulgarian Vintners 1985
288	£6.49	PETER LEHMANN CABERNET SAUVIGNON, Barossa Valley 1985
332	£3.99	COTES DE PROVENCE DOMAINE DU JAS D'ESCLANS, Lorges-Lapouge 1986
334	£4.99	COTES DU RHONE, Domaine St Apollinaire 1988
344	£6.79	BOTOBOLAR ST GILBERT RED WINE, Mudgee 1987
345	£6.65	BAILEYS BUNDARRA SHIRAZ, Glenrowan 1986
367	£4.55	BOURGOGNE PINOT NOIR, Caves de Buxy, Burgundy 1987
401	£6.39	CHIANTI CLASSICO RISERVA DUCALE, Ruffino, Tuscany 1986
444	£10.99	BAILEYS FOUNDERS LIQUEUR MUSCAT, Glenrowan
452	£6.23	PETER LEHMANN BOTRYTIS RIESLING, Barossa Valley 1984
499	£2.09	PETILLANT DE RAISIN (3%), Listel, Midi

RD | Reid Wines

The Mill, Marsh Lane, Hallatrow, Nr Bristol BS18 5EB (0761 52645) & Unit 2, Block 3, Vestry Trading Estate, Otford Road, Sevenoaks. Delightfully unique independent merchant. **Opening Hours:** telephone first if visiting Hallatrow; Sevenoaks 10am-6pm Mon-Fri; 10am-1pm Sat. **Delivery:** free locally, nationally at cost. **Tastings:** regularly in-store plus tutored events. **Discounts:** 5% on orders over £250 at Sevenoaks only.

'We sell to anybody who can afford to buy; that encompasses people from Lands End to John O'Groats. We will continue to expand as long as we can enjoy selling and sampling. Oh, I nearly forgot - and eating.' Bill Baker (the most expansive and - in his own girth - expanded wine merchant in Britain) runs a very different kind of wine business. This is where you can buy glorious older wines from just about everywhere, including Heitz Martha's Vineyard 1975 (£30) and 1972 Hermitage La Chapelle (£77.50) of which the always entertainingly annotated list makes a typical Reids comment: 'Isn't it absurd how the prices of La Chapelle have gone through the roof? We could not recommend anyone to buy this wine, despite the fact that it is very good.' Discover Reids soon; it could change your drinking life.

REW	La Reserva Wines

Unit 6, Spring Grove Mills, Manchester Rd, Linthwaite, Huddersfield HD7 5QG (0484 846732). Independent merchant specializing in Spanish wines. **Opening Hours:** 9.30am-5.30pm Mon-Sat. **Delivery:** free locally, nationally at cost. **Tastings:** regularly in-store plus tutored events. **Discounts:** 10% on mixed case.

Besides being the home of the Sair Inn, one of the best pubs in the world, Linthwaite (pronounced Linfit) also contains a converted mill which houses potters, a fabric warehouse and La Reserva, probably the best place to buy Spanish wines outside London. But it's not just a place to ramble among the Riojas. There are also good ranges of Italian, Australian and New Zealand wines plus a fine wine section containing dusty bottles of classed growth clarets, Vega Sicilia and 1975 Torres Black Label.

RES	La Reserve

56 Walton St, London SW3 1RB (071 589 2020). Independent merchant with 3 shops in London and two associated London outlets, Le Picoleur and Le Sac à Vin. **Opening Hours:** 9.30am-8pm Mon-Fri; 9.30am-6pm Sat. **Delivery:** free locally, nationally at cost. **Tastings:** regular programme of tastings held at the Ski Club of Great Britain. **Discounts:** 5% on case.

Along with La Vigneronne, La Reserve has cornered a large chunk of the market in 'smart' wine shops. Its branches, including the Walton Street shop opposite one of Prince Charles's favourite restaurants, offer a range of 'serious' wine, from the Sunday Claret (£4.50) to a 1934 Richebourg from Bourée (£86.50) and, for that really special occasion, 1961 Krug (£150). Regular tutored tastings include such topics as 'Which is the best château in St Julien?' and 'Dom Pérignon Vertical'.

Under new ownership since late 1988, however, La Reserve and, more particularly, its two associate shops, Le Picoleur and Le Sac à Vin, is making a greater effort to supply more everyday wines at (relatively) closer to everyday prices.

98	£10.99	GEOFF MERRILL CHARDONNAY, McLaren Vale 1987
144	£8.99	MOUNT HURTLE SAUVIGNON BLANC, McLaren Vale 1989
418	£37.00	SOLAIA, Antinori, Tuscany 1986
489	£13.06	HENRIQUES & HENRIQUES 10 YEAR OLD SERCIAL, Madeira
490	£13.06	HENRIQUES & HENRIQUES 10 YEAR OLD MALMSEY, Madeira

Reynier Wine Libraries

At Trinity Square London EC3; Upper Tachbrook St, London SW1; Little Castle Stret, Exeter and Frog Lane, Bristol.

A mini-chain of wine bars/shops that belongs to Eldridge Pope (q.v.) and sells wines from the Eldridge Pope list.

WRB	Wm Robbs

48 Fore St, Hexham, Northumberland NE46 (0434 606083) & Robbs at Tynedale, Hexham, Northumberland (0434 607788). Supermarket with enthusiastic wine department which has its own wine club **Opening Hours:** 9.00am-5.00pm Mon-Thu; 9.00am-7.00pm Fri; 9.00am-5.30pm Sat. **Delivery:** free locally. **Tastings:** regular in-store tastings. **Discounts:** 5-15% depending on quantity.

Hexham is a fairly quiet place of an evening, so it is perhaps unsurprising that Robbs' Fine Wine Club tastings after dusk every Tuesday have proved to be so popular. But the wines must have had something to do with it too. We'd be tempted to sniff and sip our way through the following selection even if there was a long list of alternative entertainments.

4	£4.95	**ASTI MARTINI,** Martini & Rossi, Piedmont
28	£3.65	**VIN DE PAYS DES COTES DE GASCOGNE** Plaimont, South-West 1989
74	£5.59	**RIOJA BLANCO SECO RESERVA,** CVNE 1985
75	£9.25	**FIRESTONE CHARDONNAY,** Santa Ynez 1987
80	£6.35	**WOLF BLASS BARREL-FERMENTED CHARDONNAY,** South Australia 1988
83	£8.19	**MITCHELTON RESERVE CHARDONNAY,** Goulburn Valley 1988
87	£10.99	PENFOLDS CHARDONNAY, South Australia 1988
129	£5.09	**MONTANA SAUVIGNON BLANC,** Marlborough 1989
133	£6.49	**HILL-SMITH ESTATE SAUVIGNON BLANC,** Barossa Valley 1989
149	£3.39	**CHENIN BLANC,** E & J Gallo 1988
231	£2.99	PIEMONTELLO PINK, Piedmont
233	£3.39	**WHITE GRENACHE,** E & J Gallo 1989
275	£3.65	**SANDEMAN CLARET,** Bordeaux 1986
277	£6.29	**SEAVIEW CABERNET SAUVIGNON,** South Australia 1985
297	£11.35	**PENFOLDS BIN 389 SHIRAZ/CABERNET,** South Australia 1986
311	£12.99	**CHATEAU HAUT-MARBUZET,** St Estèphe, Bordeaux 1985
316	£24.90	**PENFOLDS BIN 707 CABERNET SAUVIGNON,** South Australia 1986
339	£7.95	**PENFOLDS BIN 28 KALIMNA SHIRAZ,** South Australia 1986
355	£15.95	**PENFOLDS MAGILL ESTATE,** South Australia 1986
358	£4.35	**GAMAY DE L'ARDECHE,** Georges Duboeuf, Rhône 1989
359	£6.49	**BEAUJOLAIS-VILLAGES,** Georges Duboeuf 1989
363	£7.35	**REGNIE CRISTAL,** Georges Duboeuf, Beaujolais 1989
364	£7.85	**MORGON JEAN DESCOMBES,** Georges Duboeuf, Beaujolais 1989
386	£3.09	**CANTINA SETTESOLI ROSSO,** Sicily 1987
393	£5.19	**CORVO ROSSO,** Sicily 1987
449	£6.29	**CHATEAU DES COULINATS,** Ste-Croix-du-Mont, Bordeaux 1983
477	£10.49	**SANDEMAN ROYAL AMBROSANTE,** Jerez

RTW	The Rose Tree Wine Co.

15 Sutton Parade, Cheltenham, Glos GL50 2AE (0242 583732). Independent merchant. **Opening Hours:** 9am-7pm Mon-Fri; 9am-6pm Sat. **Delivery:** free locally, nationally at cost. **Tastings:** regularly in-store plus tutored events. **Discounts:** 5% on mixed cases.

The Rose Tree list has one annoying habit we thought had disappeared from retailers' lists, of quoting prices exclusive of VAT — which makes the whole range at first glance seem 15% cheaper than it really is. The wines that are listed are a good selection, though, a broad range of single-estate wines, a spread of ready-to-drink 1987 clarets and a few Californians that don't appear on everybody else's shelves. We were interested by the reason given for stocking Chateau Musar: 'because ... no serious wine merchant can be without it'.

R&I	Russell & McIver Ltd

The Rectory, St Mary-at-Hill, London EC3R 8EE (071 283 3575). City merchants offering more than first meets the eye. **Opening Hours:** 9am-5.30pm Mon-Fri. **Delivery:** free locally for 1 case and nationally for 5+ cases. **Tastings:** regularly in-store plus tutored events. **Discounts:** negotiable.

Any company that claims to incorporate 'Simon the Cellarer Ltd' has to make one curious - and there is plenty to look at in what proves to be a less Cityish list than those of some of its neighbours. Value for money and affordability are clearly considerations here, as is evinced by the selection of petit château Bordeaux and the presence of a Liebfraumilch ('We feel that we have one of the best...Drink the current vintage'). Burgundy, the Loire, Alsace and Germany are well covered, but the New World, like Italy, remains relatively undiscovered.

454	£7.50	**TOKAY ASZU 5 PUTTONYOS**, Tokaji 1981

SAF	Safeway

Head Office: Argyll House, Millington Rd, Hayes, Middx UB3 4HY (081 756 2149). Increasingly green and upmarket national chain with 288 stores. **Opening Hours:** 8am-8pm Mon-Thu; 8am-9pm Fri; 8am-7pm Sat. **Tastings:** regularly in-store plus tutored events.

'Everything you want from a store...' If, like a growing number of people, you want organic food and wine, Safeway must be top of your list of places to shop. Other chains have taken an interest in organic wine; Safeway is the sponsor of the annual Organic Wine Fair and, in its buying, has committed itself to the tricky task of putting together an organic range that offers the same value and is of the same standard as the rest of the wines on its shelves.

Those wines are a pretty impressive lot too, particularly when they are compared to the Safeway range of three or four years ago. The chain still has a little distance to cover before it can truly claim to have caught up with the range and quality offered by Tesco and Sainsbury, but it is chasing hard.

1	£3.15	**SAFEWAY MOSCATO SPUMANTE**, Santero, Piedmont
4	£5.09	**ASTI MARTINI**, Martini & Rossi, Piedmont
118	£3.55	**MUSCADET**, Chateau de la Mouchètiere, Loire 1989
137	£6.85	**POUILLY FUME VIEILLES VIGNES**, Caves de Pouilly sur Loire 1988
141	£6.89	**SANCERRE DOMAINE DES P'TITS PERRIERS**, A Vatan, Loire 1988
150	£3.65	**VOUVRAY DEMI-SEC**, Les Caves des Viticulteurs, Loire 1988
178	£3.89	**WEISSER BURGUNDER DRY**, Rietburg, Rheinpfalz 1986
207	£3.45	**SAFEWAY GEWURZTRAMINER**, St Georg's Weinkellerei, Rheinpfalz
231	£2.95	**PIEMONTELLO PINK**, Piedmont
233	£2.99	**WHITE GRENACHE**, E & J Gallo 1989

266	£2.59	**PLOVDIV CABERNET SAUVIGNON,** Bulgarian Vintners 1985
327	£3.09	**COTES DU RHONE,** Château Joanny, Rhône 1988
335	£4.49	**FETZER LAKE COUNTY ZINFANDEL** 1986
366	£2.29	**MILION PINOT NOIR,** Navip, Vranje 1986
420	£2.75	**DON DARIAS VINO DE MESA,** Bodegas Vitorianas, Alto Ebro
447	£4.45	**CHATEAU DE BERBEC,** Premieres Côtes de Bordeaux 1987
499	£1.99	**PETILLANT DE RAISIN (3%),** Listel, Midi

JS	J Sainsbury plc

Supermarket Wine Merchant of the Year

Head Office: Stamford House, Stamford St, London SE1 9LL (071 921 6000). The 288-branch supermarket most others would like to be. **Opening Hours:** 8.30am-8pm Mon-Thu; 8.30am-9pm Fri; 8.30am-6pm Sat.

'We have customers, Sainsbury's has converts...' The comment by an executive from a rival chain says everything that needs to be said about the supermarket that has become Britain's biggest wine retailer. Sainsbury's skill has been to go out looking for high-quality wines, whatever their price and provenance. The very idea of an own-label Washington State Sauvignon Blanc would never have struck most other wine merchants - and any who might have thought of it would have dismissed any such wine out of hand as unsaleable. But then, those other merchants wouldn't have been selling to converts - people who trust Sainsbury to give them good, interesting, flavoursome, good-value wine. The rest of Britain's wine merchants, and a fair few wine producers, should erect a symbolic monument to Sainsbury, the company that has unarguably done more than anyone else to introduce the British to wine in general - and to the world of flavours that lies beyond Liebfraumilch and Piat d'Or.

7	£4.05	**CREMANT DE BOURGOGNE ROSE,** Caves de Bailly, Burgundy 1987
12	£11.45	**SAINSBURY'S ROSE CHAMPAGNE**
24	£16.95	**CHAMPAGNE LOUIS ROEDERER BRUT PREMIER**
25	£14.95	**CHAMPAGNE LANSON BRUT** 1979
27	£2.69	**SAINSBURY'S VIN DE PAYS DES COTES DE GASCOGNE,** Domaine Bordes, South-West 1989
68	£4.95	**BERGERAC SEC DOMAINE DE GRANDCHAMP,** Nick Ryman, South-West 1988
70	£4.75	**VERDICCHIO CA'SAL DI SERRA,** Umani Ronchi, Marches 1986
75	£6.75	**FIRESTONE CHARDONNAY,** Santa Ynez 1987
78	£6.39	**MITCHELTON MARSANNE,** Goulburn Valley 1987
123	£4.49	**SAINSBURY'S WASHINGTON STATE SAUVIGNON BLANC,**Columbia Crest 1987
157	£2.19	**RETSINA OF ATTICA,** Kourtaki
172	£4.25	**JOAO PIRES WHITE TABLE WINE,** Palmela 1988
176	£2.65	**SAINSBURY'S TROCKEN,** Rheinhessen
198	£2.39	**SAINSBURY'S MOSELLE,** Mosel-Saar-Ruwer
199	£2.55	**SAINSBURY'S MORIO-MUSKAT,**Rheinpfalz
209	£3.99	**SAINSBURY'S AUSLESE,** Rheinpfalz 1988
221	£5.75	**FORSTER JESUITENGARTEN RIESLING KABINETT,** Dr Burklin-Wolf, Rheinpfalz 1988
225	£5.75	**WEHLENER SONNENUHR RIESLING KABINETT,** Dr Loosen, Mosel-Saar-Ruwer 1988
232	£3.19	**SAINSBURY'S COTES DU LUBERON ROSE,** Domaine de Panisse, Rhône 1989
233	£2.98	**WHITE GRENACHE,** E & J Gallo 1989
272	£3.19	**CHATEAU LA TUQUE,** Bordeaux 1988

292	£7.50	**ORLANDO ST HUGO CABERNET SAUVIGNON**, Coonawarra 1986
305	£9.95	**CHATEAU MAUCAILLOU**, Moulis, Bordeaux 1986
325	£2.65	**SAINSBURY'S COTES DU RHONE**
334	£4.75	**COTES DU RHONE**, Domaine St Apollinaire 1988
380	£15.25	**VOSNE-ROMANEE 1ER CRU BEAUMONTS**, Daniel Rion, Burgundy 1986
384	£2.79	**SAINSBURY'S CANNONAU DEL PARTEOLLA**, Sardinia 1987
385	£2.89	**SAINSBURY'S DOLCETTO D'ACQUI**, Piedmont 1988
414	£13.75	**TIGNANELLO**, Antinori, Tuscany 1985
419	£2.69	**CASTILLO DE ALHAMBRA**, Vinicola de Castilla, La Mancha 1989
424	£3.95	**ROMEIRA GARRAFEIRA**, Cavas Velhas 1980
425	£4.45	**QUINTA DA BACALHOA**, Palmela 1987
446	£4.25	**BOUVIER TROCKENBEERENAUSLESE**, Alexander Unger, Burgenland 1983
465	£2.95	**SAINSBURY'S AGED AMONTILLADO**, Jerez
467	£3.29	**SAINSBURY'S OLOROSO**, Jerez
481	£4.79	**SAINSBURY'S RUBY PORT**, Douro
495	£1.49	**SAINSBURY'S MOSCATINO**

| **SAN** | **Sandiway Wine Co.** |

2 School Way, Sandiway, Cheshire CW8 2NH (0606 882101). Down-to-earth independent merchant. **Opening Hours:** 9am-10pm (with lunch and tea breaks) Mon, Tue, Thu-Sat; 9am-1pm Wed; 11am-2pm & 7pm-10pm Sun. **Delivery:** free locally. **Tastings:** occasionally in-store plus tutored events. **Discounts:** 5% on mixed cases.

'16 years ago, we were a very ordinary scruffy corner off-licence. We have steadily improved since then and are now arguably the best scruffy corner off-licence in Cheshire.' After ploughing our way through the piles of self-important claims to wine-selling greatness, we were refreshed by Graham Wharmby's self-deprecation. Almost as refreshed as we might be by almost any of the wines from his crowded village grocers-cum-wine merchant. From Palmer 1959 to Juras from Bailley and Lastours Corbières, this is great wine-buying territory. There is no list yet, because 'regular changes make the production of a full one more of a liability than a sales aid' but their range of award-winners below should give you some idea of the kind of wine you might find.

4	£5.39	**ASTI MARTINI**, Martini & Rossi, Piedmont
29	£3.29	**VIN DE PAYS DES COTES DE GASCOGNE**, Domaine de Perras, South-West 1989
38	£4.29	**ALSACE TOKAY-PINOT GRIS**, Cave Vinicole de Turckheim 1988
41	£4.49	**ALSACE PINOT BLANC**, Cave Vinicole de Turckheim 1989
77	£6.25	**KIES ESTATE SEMILLON/SAUVIGNON**, Barossa Valley 1988
92	£12.00	**SIMI CHARDONNAY**, Sonoma 1985
95	£9.89	**CLOUDY BAY CHARDONNAY**, Marlborough 1988
108	£13.00	**ROSEMOUNT ROXBURGH CHARDONNAY**, Hunter Valley 1987
134	£6.25	**NOBILOS SAUVIGNON BLANC**, Marlborough 1989
138	£6.95	**HUNTERS SAUVIGNON BLANC**, Marlborough 1989
266	£2.54	**PLOVDIV CABERNET SAUVIGNON**, Bulgarian Vintners 1985
267	£2.76	**VIN DE PAYS DE L'AUDE CABERNET SAUVIGNON**, Paul Boutinot, Midi 1987
294	£7.85	**ROSEMOUNT SHOW RESERVE COONAWARRA CABERNET SAUVIGNON** 1987
331	£4.69	**RASTEAU COTES DU RHONE VILLAGES**, Caves des Vignerons de Rasteau 1988
337	£5.17	**ROUGE HOMME SHIRAZ/CABERNET**, Coonawarra 1985
499	£2.09	**PETILLANT DE RAISIN (3%)**, Listel, Midi

SEB   Sebastopol Wines

Sebastopol Barn, London Rd, Blewbury, Oxon OX11 9HB. (0235 850471). Independent merchant offering good value for money. **Opening Hours:** 10.30am-5.30pm Mon-Sat. **Delivery:** free locally, nationally at cost. **Tastings:** regularly in-store plus tutored events. **Discounts:** 5% on unbroken cases.

'We haven't ventured into new areas yet' was the comment from Sebastopol last year, implying that the introduction of wines from Australia, California and New Zealand to a predominantly French regional list was on the cards. Now, indeed, Sebastopol customers can enliven their drinking with comparative tastings of, say, Rhônes and Penfolds Shirazes, picked from a very tempting range. And all of the wines should be in perfect condition as 'fanatic consideration is given to storage in the barn at controlled temperature'.

23	£19.67	**CHAMPAGNE LAURENT PERRIER ROSE**
87	£8.20	**PENFOLDS CHARDONNAY**, South Australia 1988
95	£10.95	**CLOUDY BAY CHARDONNAY**, Marlborough 1988
120	£3.99	**SAUMUR BLANC CHATEAU DE VILLENEUVE**, Robert Chevalier, Loire 1988
122	£3.88	**SAUVIGNON DE TOURAINE DOMAINE DE LA PRESLE**, Jean-Marie Penet, Loire 1988
124	£3.90	**MUSCADET**, Bregeon, Loire 1988
264	£10.99	**MAS DE DAUMAS GASSAC**, Vin de Pays de l'Hérault, South-West 1988
269	£3.67	**HOUSE CLARET**, Peter Sichel, Bordeaux
297	£8.26	**PENFOLDS BIN 389 SHIRAZ/CABERNET**, South Australia 1986
306	£10.56	**CHATEAU HAUT-BAGES-LIBERAL**, Pauillac, Bordeaux 1986
339	£5.94	**PENFOLDS BIN 28 KALIMNA SHIRAZ**, South Australia 1986
343	£6.75	**CROZES HERMITAGE**, Alain Graillot, Rhône 1986
349	£10.81	**RIDGE GEYSERVILLE ZINFANDEL**, Sonoma 1987
437	£10.61	**TINTO PESQUERA**, Fernandez, Ribera del Duero 1986
464	£25.40	**CHATEAU RIEUSSEC**, Sauternes, Bordeaux 1983

SK   Seckford Wines

2 Betts Ave, Martlesham Heath, Ipswich, Suffolk IP5 7RH (0473 626072). Independent merchant with particularly good range of fine old wine. **Opening Hours:** 10am-6pm Mon-Fri. **Delivery:** by arrangement. **Tastings:** events throughout the year.

Seckford's current Fine Wine List features such delights as cases of 1986 Romanée-Conti Montrachet (£4,500) and 1945 Dows (a snip at £1,695). We'd love to know whether wines like these are ever sold to the same people who buy the Plaimont Colombard (£2.46 per bottle) or even the Château le Bon Pasteur 1983 (£11.85). We certainly hope so, because even the loftiest of palates would find plenty to enjoy for less than a £7 a bottle from this slim but broad-ranging list.

95	£9.95	**CLOUDY BAY CHARDONNAY**, Marlborough 1988
129	£4.99	**MONTANA SAUVIGNON BLANC**, Marlborough 1989
134	£6.50	**NOBILOS SAUVIGNON BLANC**, Marlborough 1989
174	£4.50	**BROWN BROTHERS LATE HARVEST ORANGE MUSCAT & FLORA**, N E Victoria 1988
264	£9.95	**MAS DE DAUMAS GASSAC**, Vin de Pays de l'Hérault, South-West 1988
320	£16.95	**CHATEAU LYNCH-BAGES**, Pauillac, Bordeaux 1985
337	£5.20	**ROUGE HOMME SHIRAZ/CABERNET**, Coonawarra 1985

340	£5.40	**COTES DU RHONE**, Guigal 1986
441	£7.40	MORRIS RUTHERGLEN LIQUEUR MUSCAT
448	£5.40	**MONTANA LATE HARVEST RHINE RIESLING**, Marlborough 1987

SEL | Selfridges

400 Oxford St, London W1A 1AB (071 629 1234). Department store with very active wine section. **Opening Hours:** 9.30am-6pm Mon-Wed, Fri, Sat; 9.30am-8pm Thu. **Delivery:** free locally, nationally at cost. **Tastings:** regularly in-store plus tutored events. **Discounts:** on some cases.

With no disrespect to Harrods, Selfridges actually does have the best wine selection of any London department store. And its prices are rather closer to the ones you might expect to pay elsewhere. If there's a wine you are looking for that you can't find on anybody else's list, call Selfridges.

23	£20.95	**CHAMPAGNE LAURENT PERRIER ROSE**
24	£19.50	**CHAMPAGNE LOUIS ROEDERER BRUT PREMIER**
68	£5.35	**BERGERAC SEC DOMAINE DE GRANDCHAMP**, Nick Ryman, South-West 1988
81	£6.45	**STONELEIGH CHARDONNAY**, Marlborough 1988
89	£11.50	**CHATEAU LA LOUVIERE**, Graves, Bordeaux 1986
102	£11.95	**CRICHTON HALL CHARDONNAY** 1987
134	£6.25	**NOBILOS SAUVIGNON BLANC**, Marlborough 1989
149	£3.50	**CHENIN BLANC**, E & J Gallo 1988
174	£5.25	**BROWN BROTHERS LATE HARVEST ORANGE MUSCAT & FLORA**, N E Victoria 1988
183	£4.50	**NUTBOURNE MANOR HUXELREBE**, Sussex 1989
233	£3.50	**WHITE GRENACHE**, E & J Gallo 1989
365	£8.50	**FLEURIE LA MADONE**, Georges Duboeuf, Beaujolais 1988
399	£5.95	**CAMPO FIORIN**, Masi, Veneto 1985
414	£13.75	**TIGNANELLO**, Antinori, Tuscany 1985
422	£4.25	**ALMANSA MARIUS TINTO RESERVA**, Bodegas Piqueras 1982
436	£12.75	**RIOJA RESERVA 904**, La Rioja Alta 1976
437	£10.95	**TINTO PESQUERA**, Fernandez, Ribera del Duero 1986
454	£7.10	**TOKAY ASZU 5 PUTTONYOS**, Tokaji 1981
472	£7.75	DON ZOILO VERY OLD FINO, Jerez
473	£7.75	**DON ZOILO MANZANILLA**, Sanlúcar de Barrameda
476	£13.74	MATUSALEM OLOROSO MUY VIEJO, Gonzalez Byass, Jerez
477	£11.63	**SANDEMAN ROYAL AMBROSANTE**, Jerez
486	£9.50	**WARRE'S WARRIOR VINTAGE CHARACTER PORT**, Douro
499	£1.95	**PETILLANT DE RAISIN (3%)**, Listel, Midi

SHV | Sherborne Vintners

The Old Vicarage, Leigh, Sherborne, Dorset DT9 6HL (0935 873033). One-man-band with good Iberian selection. **Opening Hours:** 9.00am-7.00pm Mon-Sat. **Delivery:** free within 20 miles, nationally at cost. **Tastings:** wines occasionally open for tasting, organised customers' club events.

Ian Sinnott still describes his company as a Spanish specialist (it once formed part of the Spanish-specialist Sherston franchise), but, as the following list of award winners makes very clear, the Sherborne net trawls far more widely than that. This mostly mail-order company could supply the most adventurous of wine drinkers with just about every style they might want. Running the company must be pretty hard work, though; in answer to our questions about staff training, he noted two words: 'no staff'.

23	£20.88	**CHAMPAGNE LAURENT PERRIER ROSE**	
38	£4.31	**ALSACE TOKAY-PINOT GRIS,** Cave Vinicole de Turckheim 1988	
56	£6.53	**LIBRARY COLLECTION CHARDONNAY,** Tiefenbrunner, Trentino-Alto Adige 1988	
97	£10.03	**COLDSTREAM HILLS CHARDONNAY,** Yarra Valley 1988	
98	£10.96	**GEOFF MERRILL CHARDONNAY,** McLaren Vale 1987	
105	£13.53	**TARRAWARRA CHARDONNAY,** Yarra Valley 1987	
119	£3.85	**SAUMUR BLANC,** Caves des Vignerons de Saumur, Loire 1988	
133	£5.95	**HILL-SMITH ESTATE SAUVIGNON BLANC,** Barossa Valley 1989	
135	£6.41	**COOPERS CREEK SAUVIGNON BLANC,** Marlborough 1989	
144	£8.86	**MOUNT HURTLE SAUVIGNON BLANC,** McLaren Vale 1989	
172	£4.66	**JOAO PIRES WHITE TABLE WINE,** Palmela 1988	
215	£4.66	**SICHEL RIESLING KABINETT,** Rheinpfalz 1988	
250	£4.08	**COTEAUX DE MURVIEL DOMAINE DE LIMBARDIE,** Boukandoura & Hutin, Midi 1988	
260	£4.90	**FAUGERES CHATEAU LA LIQUIERE,** V Gaillard, Midi 1988	
284	£3.26	**SPECIAL RESERVE STAMBOLOVO MERLOT,** Bulgarian Vintners 1985	
303	£9.21	**ROUGE HOMME COONAWARRA CABERNET SAUVIGNON** 1985	
337	£4.66	**ROUGE HOMME SHIRAZ/CABERNET,** Coonawarra 1985	
349	£7.93	**RIDGE GEYSERVILLE ZINFANDEL,** Sonoma 1987	
358	£3.96	**GAMAY DE L'ARDECHE,** Georges Duboeuf, Rhône 1989	
359	£4.08	**BEAUJOLAIS-VILLAGES,** Georges Duboeuf 1989	
371	£10.03	**COLDSTREAM HILLS PINOT NOIR,** Yarra Valley 1988	
390	£3.96	**CABERNET DEL TRENTINO,** Ca'Vit, Trentino-Alto Adige 1987	
394	£5.25	**QUATTRO VICARIATI,** Ca'Vit, Trentino-Alto Adige 1986	
427	£4.55	**DUERO,** Bodegas Peñalba 1985	
431	£4.45	**LAR DE BARROS RESERVA,** Bodega Inviosa, Extremadura 1986	
434	£7.11	**RIOJA,** Bodegas Remelluri 1985	
436	£11.48	**RIOJA RESERVA 904,** La Rioja Alta 1976	
459	£11.31	**SICHEL BEERENAUSLESE, DEIDESHEIMER HOFSTUCK,** Rheinpfalz 1988	
474	£8.86	**DON LUIS AMONTILLADO,** Burdon, Jerez	
475	£8.05	**DOS CORTADOS,** Williams & Humbert, Jerez	
476	£12.83	**MATUSALEM OLOROSO MUY VIEJO,** Gonzalez Byass, Jerez	
478	£12.83	**AMONTILLADO DEL DUQUE,** Gonzalez Byass, Jerez	
489	£13.06	**HENRIQUES & HENRIQUES 10 YEAR OLD SERCIAL,** Madeira	
490	£13.06	**HENRIQUES & HENRIQUES 10 YEAR OLD MALMSEY,** Madeira	

AS	André Simon Ltd

14 Davies St, London W1Y 1LJ (071 499 9144); 50 Elizabeth Street, London SW1 & 21 Motcomb Street, London SW1. Small up-market traditional chain providing well-sited shopfronts for Laytons (q.v.) wines; the two companies are closely linked. **Opening Hours:** 9.30am - 7.00pm Mon-Fri; 9.30am-1.00pm Sat. **Delivery:** free within London, nationally at cost. **Tastings:** occasionally in-store plus tutored tastings and organised events. **Discounts:** none.

One can almost hear Graham Chidgey, the *eminence plutôt grise* behind both Laytons and André Simon, saying the words that appear in the most recent list: 'For several years our German selection was on the decline, a reflection more of the general apathy of the consumers to these than to any negligence on our behalf...we are delighted to recommend a selection of some truly stunning wines - do not be put off because the wines are German - PLEASE!' Apart from these, the wood-panelled shops can also provide 'Jolly Good Claret', wines from the Newton winery in California and some great Deutz Champagne.

346	£6.99	**RYECROFT SHIRAZ,** McLaren Vale 1986	

SV   Smedley Vintners

Rectory Cottage, Luton, Beds LU2 8LU (046 276 214). Sensible independent merchant run by a Master of Wine. **Opening Hours:** 8.30am-9pm Mon-Fri (and by appointment at weekends). **Delivery:** free within 50 miles **Tastings:** regularly in-store plus tutored events. **Discounts:** available on unbroken cases.

'You may not necessarily recognise the name/region, but the wines are worth the experiment.' This message to Derek Smedley's customers came as part of a warning about price rises largely caused by the weakness of the pound, but it was very indicative of this merchant's keenness on value-for-money wines. So, this is the place to come for bottles from regions like the Coteaux des Baronnies and the Côtes de Thongue as well as some very well-chosen clarets. The German selection is sparse, but Italy is well covered and the New World selection includes the hard-to-find wines of Plantagenet.

23	£16.62	**CHAMPAGNE LAURENT PERRIER ROSE**	
206	£3.52	**KLUSSERATHER ST MICHAEL,** Zentrallkellerei Mosel-Saar-Ruwer 1986	
250	£3.56	**COTEAUX DE MURVIEL DOMAINE DE LIMBARDIE,** Boukandoura & Hutin, Midi 1988	
260	£4.60	**FAUGERES CHATEAU LA LIQUIERE,** V Gaillard, Midi 1988	
282	£4.60	**MONTES CABERNET SAUVIGNON,** Discover Wine, Curico Valley 1987	
290	£6.10	**FIRESTONE CABERNET SAUVIGNON,** Santa Ynez 1986	
298	£6.30	**CHATEAU LA TOUR DE BY,** Haut-Medoc, Bordeaux 1986	
359	£5.28	**BEAUJOLAIS-VILLAGES,** Georges Duboeuf 1989	
414	£12.66	**TIGNANELLO,** Antinori, Tuscany 1985	
434	£6.38	**RIOJA,** Bodegas Remelluri 1985	
487	£7.80	**COSSART GORDON 5 YEAR OLD BUAL,** Madeira	

SPR   Spar (UK) Ltd

Head Office: 32-40 Headstone Drive, Harrow, Middx HA3 5QT (081 863 5511). 2,000-branch national chain of independent grocers and supermarkets. **Opening Hours:** '8 till late'. **Tastings:** occasional in-store tastings. **Discounts:** depends on the individual retailer.

Philippa Carr, wine buyer for Spar, is married to Peter Carr of Augustus Barnett; both could have chosen rather less challenging - and potentially far less rewarding - jobs. While Peter has been persuading his bosses at Bass to take wine seriously, Philippa has quietly begun to introduce serious wine to a chain of some 2,000 individually run grocers. The quality of the wines she has chosen and of the list used to promote them deserves enormous credit. There are the inevitable Anjou Rosés and Soaves, of course, but alongside these there are the *Guide's* White Wine of the Year and a Cannonau del Parteolla. Watch this space.

41	£3.99	**ALSACE PINOT BLANC,** Cave Vinicole de Turckheim 1989
267	£2.55	**VIN DE PAYS DE L'AUDE CABERNET SAUVIGNON,** Paul Boutinot, Midi 1987
292	£7.59	**ORLANDO ST HUGO CABERNET SAUVIGNON,** Coonawarra 1986
367	£5.19	**BOURGOGNE PINOT NOIR,** Caves de Buxy, Burgundy 1987
388	£3.59	**BARBERA D'ASTI,** Viticoltori dell'Acquesi, Piedmont 1988
400	£5.35	**CABERNET RISERVA,** Lageder, Trentino-Alto Adige 1986
447	£4.49	**CHATEAU DE BERBEC,** Premières Côtes de Bordeaux 1987

SAS | St Albans Sherston Wine Co

97 Victoria St, St Albans, Herts AL1 3TJ (0727 58841). Enthusiastic independent merchant.
Opening Hours: Tues - Thurs 11.30am - 7pm Fri 11.30am - 8pm Sat 9.30am - 6pm. **Delivery:** free locally, nationally at cost. **Tastings:** regularly in-store and tutored tastings plus organised events. **Discounts:** 5% on (mixed) cases, 7.5% for Sherston Wine Club members.

This now independent remnant of the old Sherston Wine consortium still has the hallmark of that organisation: a longish list of Spanish wines. It was not, however, these wines that featured most strongly among its award winners at the Challenge; these more often came from France, Italy and Australia. If you would like to taste before you buy, turn up on a Friday or Saturday when Ernest Jacoby always has a few bottles open for customers.

41	£4.75	ALSACE PINOT BLANC,	Cave Vinicole de Turckheim 1989
142	£8.95	POUILLY BLANC FUME DOMAINE CHAILLOUX,	Châtelain, Loire 1987
241	£4.99	ROSE DE PROVENCE CARTE NOIRE,	Les Maitres Vignerons 1989
262	£5.95	CORBIERES CHATEAU DE LASTOURS (FUT DE CHENE),	Midi 1985
297	£8.99	PENFOLDS BIN 389 SHIRAZ/CABERNET,	South Australia 1986
311	£12.95	CHATEAU HAUT-MARBUZET,	St Estèphe, Bordeaux 1985
339	£5.35	PENFOLDS BIN 28 KALIMNA SHIRAZ,	South Australia 1986
359	£5.35	BEAUJOLAIS-VILLAGES,	Georges Duboeuf 1989
363	£5.99	REGNIE CRISTAL,	Georges Duboeuf, Beaujolais 1989
389	£3.99	BARDOLINO,	Fraterna Portalupi, Veneto 1988
414	£17.95	TIGNANELLO,	Antinori, Tuscany 1985
431	£5.95	LAR DE BARROS RESERVA,	Bodega Inviosa, Extremadura 1986
436	£11.75	RIOJA RESERVA 904,	La Rioja Alta 1976
499	£2.19	PETILLANT DE RAISIN (3%),	Listel, Midi

FSW | Frank E Stainton

3 Berrys Yard, Finkle St, Kendal, Cumbria LA9 4AB (0539 31886). Invigorated independent merchant. **Opening Hours:** 8.30am-6pm Mon-Sat. **Delivery:** free nationally for orders over £50. **Tastings:** wines regularly open for sampling, tutored tastings and organised events. **Discounts:** 5% for cash payment on a (mixed) case.

Frank Stainton used to have something of a reputation for providing a good conservative range of wines for the conservative wine drinkers of Cumbria. Those wines are still listed (the clarets include 1978 Haut-Brion and 1975 Mouton-Rothschild, and there are some first class Drouhin Burgundies) but there are some radical innovations, such as the range of eight different New Zealand wines and around 20 Australians. An opportunity to carry home something tasty from Kendal apart from the mintcake.

3	£5.95	YALUMBA ANGAS BRUT,	Barossa Valley
4	£5.45	ASTI MARTINI,	Martini & Rossi, Piedmont
24	£19.40	CHAMPAGNE LOUIS ROEDERER BRUT PREMIER	
49	£5.80	BABICH SEMILLON/CHARDONNAY,	Gisborne 1989
70	£4.99	VERDICCHIO CA'SAL DI SERRA,	Umani Ronchi, Marches 1986
97	£11.10	COLDSTREAM HILLS CHARDONNAY,	Yarra Valley 1988
118	£3.45	MUSCADET,	Château de la Mouchetière, Loire 1989
174	£4.80	BROWN BROTHERS LATE HARVEST ORANGE MUSCAT & FLORA,	N E Victoria 1988
213	£4.75	NIERSTEINER SPIEGELBERG KABINETT,	Guntrum, Rheinhessen 1988
314	£15.00	TORRES GRAN CORONAS BLACK LABEL,	Penedés 1983

349	£8.15	RIDGE GEYSERVILLE ZINFANDEL, Sonoma 1987
359	£5.85	BEAUJOLAIS-VILLAGES, Georges Duboeuf 1989
364	£6.75	MORGON JEAN DESCOMBES, Georges Duboeuf, Beaujolais 1989
371	£11.10	COLDSTREAM HILLS PINOT NOIR, Yarra Valley 1988
454	£7.50	TOKAY ASZU 5 PUTTONYOS, Tokaji 1981
464	£27.50	CHATEAU RIEUSSEC, Sauternes, Bordeaux 1983
491	£15.15	WARRE'S QUINTA DA CAVADINHA, Douro 1979

| SOB | Stones of Belgravia |

6 Pont St, London, SW1R 9EL(071 235 1612) & Stones of Chelsea Harbour, Unit M29, Chelsea Garden Market, London SW10 (071 823 3720). Independent merchant selling wine where the money is. **Opening Hours:** 8.30am-8.30pm Mon-Sat. **Delivery:** free locally, nationally at cost. **Tastings:** occasionally in-store.

If we had been asked to name which wine company we expected to see open a shop in the new Chelsea Harbour development, we would almost certainly have guessed it to be Stones. Like the Harbour's property dealers, Stones aims to sell to people who don't spend too much time comparing prices - customers who are ready to pay a little (sometimes more than a little) extra for quality and convenience.

The range doesn't need to be adventurous but is good, and it's worth mentioning that it does currently include older vintages of Château la Jaubertie that you won't find anywhere else.

| SUM | Summerlee Wines |

Summerlee Wine Centre, 64 High St, Earls Barton, Northants NN6 0JG (0604 810488). Quality conscious merchant majoring on Germany. **Opening Hours:** 9am-1pm Mon; 9am-1pm & 2pm-5.30pm Tues-Fri. **Delivery:** free in Oxford, Cambridge and London, nationally at cost. **Tastings:** regular in-store tastings plus organised events.

Germany's quality-conscious winemakers have needed every friend they could find in recent years - friends like Freddy Price, whose list states: 'We do not list Liebfraumilch, or indeed any cheap Rhein wines, but we can supply these on demand...' Apart from fine German estate wines (including examples from the Nahe and Franconia), Summerlee offers good, if brief selections from Bordeaux, the rest of France, Italy, Australia and New Zealand. And if by any chance you need brilliant photographs of any of these areas, Janet Price, Freddy's wife, can offer a a range from her portfolio.

24	£18.32	CHAMPAGNE LOUIS ROEDERER BRUT PREMIER
289	£6.84	CHATEAU BEAUMONT, Cru Bourgeois Médoc, Bordeaux 1986
320	£22.17	CHATEAU LYNCH-BAGES, Pauillac, Bordeaux 1985
336	£5.10	CROZES HERMITAGE, Delas Frères, Rhône 1988
445	£3.38	CHATEAU DES TOURS, Ste-Croix-du-Mont, Bordeaux 1986
461	£11.24	RECIOTO DI SOAVE DEI CAPITELLE, Anselmi, Veneto 1987
491	£14.09	WARRE'S QUINTA DA CAVADINHA, Douro 1979

| WC | The Sunday Times Wine Club |

New Aquitaine House, Paddock Rd, Reading, Berks RG4 0JY (0734 481711). Mail-order only wine-club. **Delivery:** free nationally for orders over £50. **Tastings:** tutored and organised events.

It is worth being a member of the *Sunday Times* Wine Club for at least one reason; its annual London Vintage Festival is the next best thing to a French or Italian wine fair - a real international event. The Festival also gives you a good chance to taste your way through at least part of the range. There are some real treats to be found here, but the quality of the range is far from consistent and prices are rarely low. Incidentally, if you are not a club-joiner by inclination, you can find most of the Wine Club wines in the Bordeaux Direct shops that are dotted around the outside of London.

Superbrew

The inelegant title from which the excellent Portland Wine Co (q.v.) has just changed its name.

T&W | T&W Wines

51 King Street, Thetford, Norfolk IP24 2AU (0842 765646). Independent merchant running vinous old folks' home. **Opening Hours:** 9.30-5.30 Mon-Fri; 9.30am-2.30pm Sat. **Delivery:** free locally, and nationally for 4+ cases. **Tastings:** occasionally in-store.

T&W's is one of the most tantalising and potentially frustrating lists we have seen. Tantalising because it is packed with wines ranging from Château Chalon, Montagne St Emilion 1955 (£27.50) to Beaune, Dr Barolet 1929 (£100) and Lafite 1919 (£375); frustrating, because alongside each of these, and alongside the list of current vintages, there is an indication of the number of bottles T&W have in stock. All too often, this figure is very small. Still, the list is so long, and it includes such, unexpected items – for example, a wealth of Californian wines (including a 1950 Louis Martini, a snip at £50) - that you're sure to find something you like.

282   £4.95   MONTES CABERNET SAUVIGNON, Discover Wine, Curico Valley 1987

TAN | Tanners

Centre of England Wine Merchant of the Year

Head office and main shop:26 Wyle Cop, Shrewsbury, Shropshire SY1 1XD (0743 232400). Model country wine merchant with 6 branches around the Welsh borders. **Opening Hours:** 9am - 5.30pm Mon-Sat. **Delivery:** free locally for orders over 1 case and nationally for orders over £75. **Tastings:** occasionally in-store plus regular tutored events. **Discounts:** available on quantities over 6 cases.

Tanners does it again, winning this prize for the second year running. And like all good winners, Tanners appears to beat the competition with relatively little apparent effort. This, one feels, is a company that simply gets on with the job of buying and selling good wine. There are some revealing lines in the current list: 'Wine is an agricultural product and has no need of big cities. We buy direct as far as possible...and use a Shropshire transporter to do most of our European collections...With low overheads, costs are kept to a minimum.' This is an attitude that appeals as much to us as it doubtless does to Tanners' many rural customers. The list is long and varied; the wines are of high quality and the prices are reasonable. Eminently prize-worthy.

4	£5.22	**ASTI MARTINI**, Martini & Rossi, Piedmont
23	£20.08	**CHAMPAGNE LAURENT PERRIER ROSE**
24	£18.18	**CHAMPAGNE LOUIS ROEDERER BRUT PREMIER**
28	£3.21	**VIN DE PAYS DES COTES DE GASCOGNE** Plaimont, South-West 1989
55	£6.57	**CHARDONNAY DI S MICHELE VIGNETO ZARAOSTI**, Roberto Zeni, Trentino-Alto Adige 1989
58	£6.36	**MACON-CLESSE DOMAINE DE LA BON GRAN CUVEE TRADITION**, Jean Thevenet, Burgundy 1987
70	£4.30	**VERDICCHIO CA'SAL DI SERRA**, Umani Ronchi, Marches 1986
88	£8.60	**CHATEAU COUHINS-LURTON**, Graves, Bordeaux 1987
95	£10.63	**CLOUDY BAY CHARDONNAY**, Marlborough 1988
114	£16.61	**YARRA YERING CHARDONNAY**, Yarra Valley 1987
129	£5.13	**MONTANA SAUVIGNON BLANC**, Marlborough 1989
152	£4.36	**COOKS CHENIN BLANC**, Hawkes Bay 1987
174	£5.08	**BROWN BROTHERS LATE HARVEST ORANGE MUSCAT & FLORA**, N E Victoria 1988
184	£4.75	**ASTLEY HUXELVANER**, Worcestershire 1989
194	£6.03	**DEINHARD HERITAGE SELECTION DEIDESHEIM**, Rheinpfalz 1987
214	£4.75	**ASTLEY MADELEINE ANGEVINE**, Worcestershire 1989
228	£7.29	**GRAACHER HIMMELREICH RIESLING SPATLESE**, F W Gymnasium, Mosel-Saar-Ruwer 1988
244	£3.11	**BOTRYS RED**, Botrys SA, Nemea
250	£3.40	**COTEAUX DE MURVIEL DOMAINE DE LIMBARDIE**, Boukandoura & Hutin, Midi 1988
264	£10.29	**MAS DE DAUMAS GASSAC**, Vin de Pays de l'Hérault, South-West 1988
269	£3.67	**HOUSE CLARET**, Peter Sichel, Bordeaux
276	£4.26	**CONCHA Y TORO MERLOT**, Maipo 1986
284	£3.52	**SPECIAL RESERVE STAMBOLOVO MERLOT**, Bulgarian Vintners 1985
314	£16.68	**TORRES GRAN CORONAS BLACK LABEL**, Penedés 1983
330	£3.97	**COTES DU RHONE**, Château du Grand Moulas 1988
354	£9.78	**CORNAS**, Guy de Barjac, Rhône 1986
393	£5.83	**CORVO ROSSO**, Sicily 1987
404	£7.87	**DOLCETTO D'ALBA COSCINA FRANCIA**, Conterno, Piedmont 1985
405	£8.14	**BAROLO RISERVA**, Borgogno, Piedmont 1982
414	£17.23	**TIGNANELLO**, Antinori, Tuscany 1985
422	£3.86	**ALMANSA MARIUS TINTO RESERVA**, Bodegas Piqueras 1982
428	£4.93	**QUINTA DE CAMARATE**, Fonseca, Azeitão 1985
434	£6.84	**RIOJA**, Bodegas Remelluri 1985
435	£7.73	**GRANDE ESCHOLA**, Quinta do Cotto, Douro 1985
437	£11.29	**TINTO PESQUERA**, Fernandez, Ribera del Duero 1986
439	£3.35	**MOSCATEL DE VALENCIA**, Vicente Gandia 1988
440	£6.04	**SAMOS NECTAR 10 YEAR OLD**, Cooperatives Vinicoles de Samos
454	£7.39	**TOKAY ASZU 5 PUTTONYOS**, Tokaji 1981
479	£4.32	**MAVRODAPHNE**, Botrys SA, Patras
499	£2.08	**PETILLANT DE RAISIN (3%)**, Listel, Midi

TO	Tesco

Head Office: Tesco House, Delamere Rd, Cheshunt, Herts EN8 9SL (0992 32222). Vigorously vinous supermarket chain with 360 branches nationwide. **Opening Hours:** varied. **Tastings:** regularly in-store.

Britain's wine drinkers are divided into two groups: those who cannot imagine buying a decent bottle of wine from Tesco, and those who have tasted bottles from the current range. Judging by the company's commercial success and by the steady expansion of its wine department, it is the second group that is growing; even some of the most traditional members of the wine trade now acknowledge that the Tesco and Sainsbury wine ranges compete both neck-and-neck with each other and with some of the best merchants in the country.

The motor that drives Tesco is the enthusiasm of a buying team that is ready to take risks by buying an extraordinarily wide range of wines - from good Vin de Pays made in the most obscure regions of France and own-label Australian Chardonnay to a long list of well-chosen German and Italian wines and ultimate quality Gonzalez Byass sherry.

4	£4.99	**ASTI MARTINI**, Martini & Rossi, Piedmont
10	£10.09	**CHAMPAGNE FORGET-BRIMONT 1ER CRU**
24	£21.00	**CHAMPAGNE LOUIS ROEDERER BRUT PREMIER**
34	£3.55	**CHARDONNAY, WILHELM WALCH TERMENO**, Trentino-Alto Adige 1989
35	£4.05	**TESCO AUSTRALIAN CHARDONNAY**
47	£4.45	**LUGANA, CA DEI FRATI**, Lombardy 1989
65	£4.29	**VIN DE PAYS DES COTES DE GASCOGNE DOMAINE DU TARIQUET CUVEE BOIS**, Grassa, South-West
81	£6.59	**STONELEIGH CHARDONNAY**, Marlborough 1988
119	£2.99	**SAUMUR BLANC**, Caves des Vignerons de Saumur, Loire 1988
125	£4.29	**VOUVRAY**, Chevalier de Moncontour, Loire
129	£4.85	**MONTANA SAUVIGNON BLANC**, Marlborough 1989
152	£3.79	**COOKS CHENIN BLANC**, Hawkes Bay 1987
158	£3.95	**TESCO ALSACE GEWURZTRAMINER**, Kuen 1988
170	£3.79	**VIN DE PAYS D'OC LES TERRES FINES CEPAGE MUSCAT**, Delta Domaines, Midi 1987
177	£2.55	**BADEN DRY**, ZBW
178	£3.59	**WEISSER BURGUNDER DRY**, Rietburg, Rheinpfalz 1986
200	£2.59	**TESCO BERNKASTELER KURFURSTLAY**, Moselland, Mosel-Saar-Ruwer
201	£2.69	**NAHE MEDIUM DRY MULLER THURGAU**, Nahe Winzer-Kellerein EG
202	£2.69	**RHEINPFALZ MEDIUM DRY SILVANER**, Deutsches Weintor
208	£3.99	**TESCO STEINWEILER KLOSTER-LIEBFRAUENBERG SPATLESE**, Deutsches Weintor, Rheinpfalz
212	£4.69	**BINGER SCHARLACHBERG DRY RIESLING KABINETT**, Villa Sachsen, Rhein hessen 1986
231	£2.95	PIEMONTELLO PINK, Piedmont
233	£3.19	**WHITE GRENACHE**, E & J Gallo 1989
335	£4.65	**FETZER LAKE COUNTY ZINFANDEL** 1986
350	£9.39	**COTE ROTIE**, Michel Bernard, Rhône 1986
352	£10.39	**HERMITAGE**, Cecile Mussel, Rhône 1985
372	£11.48	**SAVIGNY-LES-BEAUNE 1ER CRU LES LAVIERES**, Domaine Chandon de Briailles, Burgundy 1986
397	£4.99	**RECIOTO DELLA VALPOLICELLA**, Cantine Sociale di Soave, Veneto 1982
420	£2.35	**DON DARIAS VINO DE MESA**, Bodegas Vitorianas, Alto Ebro
439	£2.69	**MOSCATEL DE VALENCIA**, Vicente Gandia 1988
468	£4.29	**TESCO FINEST OLOROSO SECO**, Sanchez Romate, Jerez
476	£10.75	MATUSALEM OLOROSO MUY VIEJO, Gonzalez Byass, Jerez
483	£6.29	**TESCO LATE BOTTLED VINTAGE PORT (BOTTLED 1989)**, Smith Woodhouse, Douro 1984
496	£1.49	**GOLDENER OKTOBER LIGHT WHITE**, St Ursula Weinkellerei, Rheinhessen
499	£1.99	**PETILLANT DE RAISIN (3%)**, Listel, Midi

TH	Thresher

Head Office: Sefton House, 42 Church Rd, Welwyn Garden City, Herts AL8 6PJ (0707 328244).

Rapidly improving High Street chain with 968 branches nationwide. **Opening Hours:** 10am - 10.30pm (some regional variations). **Delivery:** free locally. **Tastings:** occasionally in-store. **Discounts:** vary with the amount spent plus selected promotions.

Once one of the most somnolent of the slumbering giants of the High Street, Thresher is growing ever more wakeful. Now run in tandem with its bright new off-shoot, The Wine Rack (q.v.), this huge chain is finally benefiting from some really skilled and increasingly adventurous wine buying, including, during the summer of 1990, one of the best sets of Alsace wines to be offered by any merchant. A greater range is being introduced to a larger number of shops; even so, knowing which ones sell which wines, and remembering to look at the sign telling you that this (good) outlet is a Thresher Wine Shop and not a (less well-stocked) Thresher Off-Licence can still be frustrating. But take the trouble to look; the Wine Shops really have become rewarding places to buy wine.

4	£5.59	ASTI MARTINI, Martini & Rossi, Piedmont
7	£6.75	CREMANT DE BOURGOGNE ROSE, Caves de Bailly, Burgundy 1987
24	£19.29	CHAMPAGNE LOUIS ROEDERER BRUT PREMIER
32	£3.79	CHATEAU DE LA ROUERGUE BARTHE, Bordeaux 1989
38	£4.29	ALSACE TOKAY-PINOT GRIS, Cave Vinicole de Turckheim 1988
39	£3.99	HILL-SMITH PIGGOT HILL SEMILLON, South Australia 1988
41	£3.95	ALSACE PINOT BLANC, Cave Vinicole de Turckheim 1989
65	£4.59	VIN DE PAYS DES COTES DE GASCOGNE DOMAINE DU TARIQUET CUVEE BOIS, Grassa, South-West
67	£4.99	CHATEAU BONNET RESERVE DU CHATEAU (OAK AGED), Entre-Deux-Mers, Lurton, Bordeaux 1988
81	£6.99	STONELEIGH CHARDONNAY, Marlborough 1988
87	£6.99	PENFOLDS CHARDONNAY, South Australia 1988
89	£7.99	CHATEAU LA LOUVIERE, Graves, Lurton, Bordeaux 1988
108	£14.99	ROSEMOUNT ROXBURGH CHARDONNAY, Hunter Valley 1987
116	£2.99	DOMAINE DE MONTMARIN SAUVIGNON, Vin de Pays des Cotes de Thongue, South-West 1989
121	£3.99	TATACHILLA HILL CHENIN BLANC, McLaren Vale 1988
129	£4.99	MONTANA SAUVIGNON BLANC, Marlborough 1989
130	£4.99	SAUVIGNON DE ST BRIS DOMAINE DU RELAIS DE POSTE, Luc Sorin, Burgundy 1989
145	£10.00	POUILLY FUME BUISSON MENARD, Didier Dagueneau, Loire 1988
146	£22.95	POUILLY FUME SILEX, Didier Dagueneau, Loire 1988
157	£2.85	RETSINA OF ATTICA, Kourtaki
172	£4.39	JOAO PIRES WHITE TABLE WINE, Palmela 1988
174	£4.89	BROWN BROTHERS LATE HARVEST ORANGE MUSCAT & FLORA, N E Victoria 1988
231	£3.29	PIEMONTELLO PINK, Piedmont
233	£3.39	WHITE GRENACHE, E & J Gallo 1989
239	£4.59	CHATEAU THIEULEY BORDEAUX CLAIRET 1989
266	£2.69	PLOVDIV CABERNET SAUVIGNON, Bulgarian Vintners 1985
287	£6.49	RAIMAT CABERNET SAUVIGNON, Lerida 1985
290	£7.15	FIRESTONE CABERNET SAUVIGNON, Santa Ynez 1986
294	£7.85	ROSEMOUNT SHOW RESERVE COONAWARRA CABERNET SAUVIGNON 1987
297	£7.69	PENFOLDS BIN 389 SHIRAZ/CABERNET, South Australia 1986
299	£7.59	CHATEAU RAMAGE LA BATISSE, Haut-Médoc, Bordeaux 1985
301	£8.49	DOMAINE DE MARTIALIS (Château Clos Fourtet), St Emilion, Bordeaux 1986
309	£12.75	CHATEAU HAUT-BAGES-AVEROUS (Château Lynch-Bages), Pauillac, Bordeaux 1986
320	£29.95	CHATEAU LYNCH-BAGES, Pauillac, Bordeaux 1985
338	£5.75	WYNNS COONAWARRA SHIRAZ 1987

339	£4.49	**PENFOLDS BIN 28 KALIMNA SHIRAZ**, South Australia 1986
359	£5.49	**BEAUJOLAIS-VILLAGES**, Georges Duboeuf 1989
364	£6.75	**MORGON JEAN DESCOMBES**, Georges Duboeuf, Beaujolais 1989
367	£5.35	**BOURGOGNE PINOT NOIR**, Caves de Buxy, Burgundy 1987
393	£4.65	**CORVO ROSSO**, Sicily 1987
396	£4.99	**NEBBIOLO DELLE LANGHE**, Berutti, Piedmont 1985
414	£15.25	**TIGNANELLO**, Antinori, Tuscany 1985
420	£2.95	**DON DARIAS VINO DE MESA**, Bodegas Vitorianas, Alto Ebro
429	£4.99	**RAIMAT TEMPRANILLO**, Lerida 1987
447	£4.59	**CHATEAU DE BERBEC**, Premieres Côtes de Bordeaux 1987
457	£4.99	**CHATEAU LE DRAGON**, Calvet, Bordeaux 1987
478	£11.50	**AMONTILLADO DEL DUQUE**, Gonzalez Byass, Jerez
491	£14.79	**WARRE'S QUINTA DA CAVADINHA**, Douro 1979
497	£1.69	**LAMBRUSCO LIGHT (BLUSH WHITE)**, Giacobazzi, Emilia-Romagna
499	£1.99	**PETILLANT DE RAISIN (3%)**, Listel, Midi
500	£1.99	**GRANTS OF ST JAMES MONTEVERDI ROSSO (3%)**, Piedmont

---

| UBC | The Ubiquitous Chip |

12 Ashton Lane, Glasgow, G12 8SJ (041 334 7109). Excellent Independent merchant and restaurant. **Opening Hours:** 12-10pm Mon-Fri; 10am-10pm Sat. **Delivery:** free locally, nationally at cost. **Tastings:** regular tutored events. **Discounts:** 5% off (mixed) cases.

The cultural capital of the north may not have as many good wine retailers as Edinburgh but with this, the merchant arm of one of the city's favourite restaurants, the Glaswegians have no reason to envy their neighbours on the other side of the country. The range of sparkling wines is extraordinary - but then, so are the lists of Bordeaux, Burgundies and Australians. The name, by the way, came from the Arnold Wesker play, *Chips with Everything* - and though, strictly speaking, you'll do your wine buying from 'The Chip Wine Shop', we've found their initially startling name has become a habit.

8	£7.50	**VOUVRAY BRUT**, Huet, Loire
74	£4.95	**RIOJA BLANCO SECO RESERVA**, CVNE 1985
75	£6.85	**FIRESTONE CHARDONNAY**, Santa Ynez 1987
90	£8.55	**CHATEAU CONSTANTIN**, Graves, Bordeaux 1986
95	£11.25	**CLOUDY BAY CHARDONNAY**, Marlborough 1988
172	£4.80	**JOAO PIRES WHITE TABLE WINE**, Palmela 1988
174	£5.30	**BROWN BROTHERS LATE HARVEST ORANGE MUSCAT & FLORA**, N E Victoria 1988
264	£10.99	**MAS DE DAUMAS GASSAC**, Vin de Pays de l'Hérault, South-West 1988
290	£6.30	**FIRESTONE CABERNET SAUVIGNON**, Santa Ynez 1986
292	£7.25	**ORLANDO ST HUGO CABERNET SAUVIGNON**, Coonawarra 1986
302	£8.95	**CHATEAU CARONNE-SAINTE-GEMME**, Haut-Médoc, Bordeaux 1982
303	£5.70	**ROUGE HOMME COONAWARRA CABERNET SAUVIGNON** 1985
317	£21.05	**MONDAVI CABERNET SAUVIGNON RESERVE**, Napa Valley 1980
357	£3.95	**GAILLAC CEPAGE GAMAY**, Jean Cros, South-West 1989
365	£6.90	**FLEURIE LA MADONE**, Georges Duboeuf, Beaujolais 1988
414	£17.35	**TIGNANELLO**, Antinori, Tuscany 1985
422	£3.45	**ALMANSA MARIUS TINTO RESERVA**, Bodegas Piqueras 1982
428	£4.99	**QUINTA DE CAMARATE**, Fonseca, Azeitão 1985
436	£9.90	**RIOJA RESERVA 904**, La Rioja Alta 1976
437	£10.95	**TINTO PESQUERA**, Fernandez, Ribera del Duero 1986
441	£7.90	**MORRIS RUTHERGLEN LIQUEUR MUSCAT**

U	Unwins

Head Office: Birchwood House, Victoria Rd, Dartford, Kent DA1 5AJ (0322 72711). Unassuming 305-branch chain in the South of England. **Opening Hours:** 10am-10pm Mon - Sat; 12-2pm & 7pm-9.30pm Sun. **Delivery:** free locally, nationally at cost. **Tastings:** occasionally in-store plus tutored events. **Discounts:** 10% off mixed cases for table wines and 5% for sparkling wines.

Of all Britain's larger High Street chains, this family-owned firm arguably cares the most about the knowledge of its staff. Nobody gets to manage one of the company's shops without undergoing some very heavy-duty training. The service they can offer is a cut above the High Street norm - but the wines they find themselves selling in those shops are an unwieldy mix of the excellent (at the top of the range), unusual and the dull.

If only this likeable chain would give its buyer the freedom to pursue the single-minded direction of, say, Davisons' Michael Davies or Fullers' Mark Dally, it could take 305 High Streets by storm.

4	£5.49	**ASTI MARTINI,** Martini & Rossi, Piedmont
23	£19.49	**CHAMPAGNE LAURENT PERRIER ROSE**
24	£17.49	**CHAMPAGNE LOUIS ROEDERER BRUT PREMIER**
26	£2.49	**VIN DE PAYS D'OC,** Les Chais Beaucairois, Midi
41	£4.09	**ALSACE PINOT BLANC,** Cave Vinicole de Turckheim 1989
65	£4.99	**VIN DE PAYS DES COTES DE GASCOGNE DOMAINE DU TARIQUET CUVEE BOIS,** Grassa, South-West
129	£4.99	**MONTANA SAUVIGNON BLANC,** Marlborough 1989
149	£3.59	**CHENIN BLANC,** E & J Gallo 1988
157	£3.19	**RETSINA OF ATTICA,** Kourtaki
233	£3.59	**WHITE GRENACHE,** E & J Gallo 1989
253	£4.29	**FITOU CHATEAU DE SEGUR,** Producteurs de Mont Tauch, Midi 1987
254	£3.35	**CAHORS,** Les Côtes d'Olt, South-West 1986
276	£3.99	**CONCHA Y TORO MERLOT,** Maipo 1986
298	£7.99	**CHATEAU LA TOUR DE BY,** Haut-Médoc, Bordeaux 1986
313	£17.99	**CHATEAU MOUTON-BARONNE-PHILIPPE,** Pauillac, Bordeaux 1986
319	£26.00	**CHATEAU PICHON-LONGUEVILLE-BARON,** Pauillac, Bordeaux 1985
320	£24.50	**CHATEAU LYNCH-BAGES,** Pauillac, Bordeaux 1985
322	£31.50	**CHATEAU FIGEAC,** St Emilion Grand Cru, Bordeaux 1982
361	£5.69	**BROUILLY,** E Loron, Beaujolais 1989
393	£4.69	**CORVO ROSSO,** Sicily 1987
482	£6.19	**SMITH WOODHOUSE RUBY PORT,** Douro
497	£1.19	**LAMBRUSCO LIGHT (BLUSH WHITE),** Giacobazzi, Emilia-Romagna

UC	The Upper Crust

3-4 Bishopsmead Parade, East Horsley, Surrey KT24 6RT (04865 3280). Astonishingly good independent merchant. **Opening Hours:** 9am-9pm Mon-Sat; 12-2pm & 7pm-9pm Sun. **Delivery:** free within 30 miles, nationally at cost. **Tastings:** regularly in-store plus tutored events. **Discounts:** 5% on case purchases for cash or cheque.

Last year's South of England Wine Merchant and Independent Merchant of the Year, the Upper Crust is still an astonishingly good place to go shopping for wine. Barry Ralph's keenness to find new wines and share his discoveries with others brims over from every page of his tightly-packed list. His comment on Mlle Monthélie-Douhairet's 1985 Monthélie is typical: 'Don't miss out on this bargain - made by a nonagenarian (well, a lady who's in her nineties anyway). This must be her medicine of life.'

7	£7.50	**CREMANT DE BOURGOGNE ROSE**, Caves de Bailly, Burgundy 1987
22	£19.95	**CHAMPAGNE BRICOUT CARTE D'OR BRUT PRESTIGE**
24	£18.00	**CHAMPAGNE LOUIS ROEDERER BRUT PREMIER**
29	£3.50	**VIN DE PAYS DES COTES DE GASCOGNE**, Domaine de Perras, South-West 1989
38	£4.60	**ALSACE TOKAY-PINOT GRIS**, Cave Vinicole de Turckheim 1988
41	£4.25	ALSACE PINOT BLANC, Cave Vinicole de Turckheim 1989
42	£4.75	**ALSACE SYLVANER HEIMBOURG**, Cave Vinicole de Turckheim 1987
47	£5.85	**LUGANA**, Ca Dei Frati, Lombardy 1989
49	£5.85	**BABICH SEMILLON/CHARDONNAY**, Gisborne 1989
50	£5.95	SOAVE CLASSICO, Pieropan, Veneto 1989
53	£5.99	**SEPPELTS CHARDONNAY**, South-East Australia 1989
61	£11.75	**CHABLIS 1ER CRU VAILLONS**, E Defaix, Burgundy 1985
70	£5.00	**VERDICCHIO CA'SAL DI SERRA**, Umani Ronchi, Marches 1986
74	£5.75	**RIOJA BLANCO SECO RESERVA**, CVNE 1985
75	£6.79	**FIRESTONE CHARDONNAY**, Santa Ynez 1987
81	£6.75	**STONELEIGH CHARDONNAY**, Marlborough 1988
85	£7.45	**JULIUS WILE CHARDONNAY** 1986
86	£9.25	**MUSCADET DE SEVRE ET MAINE SUR LIE CHATEAU DE CHASSELOIR (OAK-AGED)**, Loire 1987
98	£12.00	**GEOFF MERRILL CHARDONNAY**, McLaren Vale 1987
107	£14.25	**CULLENS CHARDONNAY**, Margaret River 1987
108	£14.75	**ROSEMOUNT ROXBURGH CHARDONNAY**, Hunter Valley 1987
109	£18.75	CHATEAU DE FIEUZAL, Graves, Bordeaux 1986
117	£3.65	**ANJOU BLANC CHUPIN**, G Saget, Loire 1989
121	£4.50	**TATACHILLA HILL CHENIN BLANC**, McLaren Vale 1988
129	£4.95	**MONTANA SAUVIGNON BLANC**, Marlborough 1989
134	£6.49	**NOBILOS SAUVIGNON BLANC**, Marlborough 1989
138	£6.95	HUNTERS SAUVIGNON BLANC, Marlborough 1989
144	£7.50	**MOUNT HURTLE SAUVIGNON BLANC**, McLaren Vale 1989
159	£4.25	**TORRES GEWURZTRAMINER**, Curico 1988
167	£12.75	**ALSACE GEWURZTRAMINER GRAND CRU KESSLER**, Schlumberger 1985
168	£18.79	ALSACE GEWURZTRAMINER SELECTION DE GRAINS NOBLES, Cave Vinicole de Turckheim 1988
171	£4.65	**MOSCATO D'ASTI**, Viticoltoro dell'Acquesi, Piedmont 1989
174	£4.95	BROWN BROTHERS LATE HARVEST ORANGE MUSCAT AND FLORA, N E Victoria 1988
175	£5.65	**QUADY ESSENSIA ORANGE MUSCAT** 1987
192	£6.89	**ALSACE RIESLING RESERVE**, Schlumberger 1986
196	£10.88	**ALSACE RIESLING GRAND CRU BRAND**, Cave Vinicole de Turckheim 1985
224	£5.69	**LAMBERHURST SCHONBURGER**, Kent 1988
225	£7.29	**WEHLENER SONNENUHR RIESLING KABINETT**, Dr Loosen, Mosel-Saar-Ruwer 1988
236	£4.66	**TORRES CABERNET SAUVIGNON ROSE**, Curico 1989
238	£4.50	**TOURAINE CABERNET ROSE**, Dorothy & Thierry Michaud, Loire 1989
250	£3.45	COTEAUX DE MURVIEL DOMAINE DE LIMBARDIE, Boukandoura & Hutin, Midi 1988
262	£5.45	**CORBIERES CHATEAU DE LASTOURS (FUT DE CHENE)**, Midi 1985
267	£2.75	**VIN DE PAYS DE L'AUDE CABERNET SAUVIGNON**, Paul Boutinot, Midi 1987
288	£6.95	**PETER LEHMANN CABERNET SAUVIGNON**, Barossa Valley 1985
294	£7.75	**ROSEMOUNT SHOW RESERVE COONAWARRA CABERNET SAUVIGNON** 1987
298	£8.95	**CHATEAU LA TOUR DE BY**, Haut-Médoc, Bordeaux 1986
299	£9.25	**CHATEAU RAMAGE LA BATISSE**, Haut-Médoc, Bordeaux 1985
301	£10.25	**DOMAINE DE MARTIALIS** (Château Clos Fourtet), St Emilion, Bordeaux 1986
303	£9.99	**ROUGE HOMME COONAWARRA CABERNET SAUVIGNON** 1985
311	£12.65	**CHATEAU HAUT-MARBUZET**, St Estèphe, Bordeaux 1985
314	£14.75	**TORRES GRAN CORONAS BLACK LABEL**, Penedés 1983
331	£4.50	**RASTEAU COTES DU RHONE VILLAGES**, Caves des Vignerons de Rasteau 1988
378	£9.75	**MONDAVI PINOT NOIR RESERVE**, Napa Valley 1986

380	£22.45	**VOSNE-ROMANEE 1ER CRU BEAUMONTS**, Daniel Rion, Burgundy 1986
388	£3.65	BARBERA D'ASTI, Viticoltori dell'Acquesi, Piedmont 1988
393	£4.85	**CORVO ROSSO**, Sicily 1987
409	£10.70	RECIOTO DELLA VALPOLICELLA, Allegrini, Veneto 1988
412	£12.25	**CEPPARELLO**, Isole e Olena, Tuscany 1986
414	£17.25	TIGNANELLO, Antinori, Tuscany 1985
415	£15.25	**BRUNELLO DI MONTALCINO MONTOSOLI**, Altesino, Tuscany 1985
417	£23.79	**BAROLO MONPRIVATO**, G Mascarello, Piedmont 1985
418	£38.00	**SOLAIA**, Antinori, Tuscany 1986
443	£9.40	**CAMPBELLS RUTHERGLEN MUSCAT**
444	£9.25	BAILEYS FOUNDERS LIQUEUR MUSCAT, Glenrowan
449	£5.50	**CHATEAU DES COULINATS**, Ste-Croix-du-Mont, Bordeaux 1983
472	£6.89	DON ZOILO VERY OLD FINO, Jerez
474	£8.89	**DON LUIS AMONTILLADO**, Burdon, Jerez
476	£12.89	MATUSALEM OLOROSO MUY VIEJO, Gonzalez Byass, Jerez
477	£10.25	**SANDEMAN ROYAL AMBROSANTE**, Jerez
478	£12.89	**AMONTILLADO DEL DUQUE**, Gonzalez Byass, Jerez
487	£10.25	**COSSART GORDON 5 YEAR OLD BUAL**, Madeira

V&C | Valvona & Crolla Ltd

Specialist Wine Merchant of the Year

19 Elm Row, Edinburgh, EH7 4AA (031 556 6066). Italian specialists. **Opening Hours:** 8.30am-6pm Mon-Sat. **Delivery:** free nationally. **Tastings:** regular tutored events. **Discounts:** 5% on mixed cases.

Is it any coincidence that two Italian specialists - Winecellars and Valvona & Crolla - were given top awards by our judges this year? Scotland, curiously enough, is great Lambrusco-drinking country (especially on Saturday nights); Valvona & Crolla deserves the credit for turning a growing number of Scots into drinkers of 'real' Italian wine, through its list and through its weekly tastings. They do sell Lambrusco - the sweet Saturday night variety and the dry version drunk in Italy - as well as just about every other kind of Italian wine anyone has ever heard of. And just to remind you that wine isn't the only thing bottled at many Italian estates, there are also fine olive oils from such familiar names as Frescobaldi and Lungarotti.

4	£4.89	**ASTI MARTINI**, Martini & Rossi, Piedmont
23	£17.89	**CHAMPAGNE LAURENT PERRIER ROSE**
55	£5.89	**CHARDONNAY DI S MICHELE VIGNETO ZARAOSTI**, Roberto Zeni, Trentino-Alto Adige 1989
59	£9.29	**PINOT BIANCO**, Jermann, Friuli-Venezia Giulia 1988
112	£15.59	**CABREO LA PIETRA**, Ruffino, Tuscany 1986
386	£2.79	**CANTINA SETTESOLI ROSSO**, Sicily 1987
387	£3.89	**MONTEPULCIANO D'ABRUZZO**, Tollo, Abruzzi 1987
389	£3.89	**BARDOLINO**, Fraterna Portalupi, Veneto 1988
391	£4.79	TEROLDEGO ROTALIANO, Gaierhof, Trentino-Alto Adige 1988
393	£4.39	**CORVO ROSSO**, Sicily 1987
399	£6.29	**CAMPO FIORIN**, Masi, Veneto 1985
400	£6.69	**CABERNET RISERVA**, Lageder, Trentino-Alto Adige 1986
401	£6.29	**CHIANTI CLASSICO RISERVA DUCALE**, Ruffino, Tuscany 1986
403	£5.69	**TANCA FARRA**, Sella e Mosca, Sardinia 1984
404	£6.99	**DOLCETTO D'ALBA COSCINA FRANCIA**, Conterno, Piedmont 1985
405	£7.99	**BAROLO RISERVA**, Borgogno, Piedmont 1982

406	£8.99	**ROSSO CONERO RISERVA BARRIQUE**, Mecvini, Marches 1987
409	£9.89	**RECIOTO DELLA VALPOLICELLA**, Allegrini, Veneto 1988
410	£11.49	MON PRA, Conterno e Fantino, Piedmont 1987
411	£12.89	**BAROLO RISERVA**, Giacomo Conterno, Piedmont 1983
412	£12.89	**CEPPARELLO**, Isole e Olena, Tuscany 1986
413	£15.69	**CABREO IL BORGO**, Ruffino, Tuscany 1986
416	£21.89	BARBARESCO, Gaja, Piedmont 1986
418	£36.00	**SOLAIA**, Antinori, Tuscany 1986
414	£16.59	TIGNANELLO, Antinori, Tuscany 1985
461	£14.89	**RECIOTO DI SOAVE DEI CAPITELLE**, Anselmi, Veneto 1987

| HVW | Helen Verdcourt |

Spring Cottage, Kimbers Lane, Maidenhead, Berks SL6 2QP (0628 25577). Very independent merchant. **Opening Hours:** telephone first to check. **Delivery:** free within 40 miles, nationally at cost. **Tastings:** regular tutored tastings.

Join the Helen Verdcourt Fan Club. Of all Britain's one-man (or, in this case, woman)-band merchants, few can claim such avid supporters than Ms Verdcourt. The secret of her success lies in choosing good wines and working really hard to introduce them to her customers through lists and tastings. Every year, while the customers of all sorts of 'smart' merchants miss out on getting hold of the strictly-rationed Cloudy Bay Sauvignon Blanc, Helen Verdcourt's fans can congratulate themselves on buying from a merchant who has not only ensured a sufficiency for them, but also a gorgeous alternative in the shape of the Hunters winery version of this variety.

29	£3.29	**VIN DE PAYS DES COTES DE GASCOGNE**, Domaine de Perras, South-West 1989
38	£4.45	**ALSACE TOKAY-PINOT GRIS**, Cave Vinicole de Turckheim 1988
41	£4.10	ALSACE PINOT BLANC, Cave Vinicole de Turckheim 1989
42	£4.50	**ALSACE SYLVANER HEIMBOURG**, Cave Vinicole de Turckheim 1987
70	£4.75	**VERDICCHIO CA'SAL DI SERRA**, Umani Ronchi, Marches 1986
74	£5.85	**RIOJA BLANCO SECO RESERVA**, CVNE 1985
95	£9.10	**CLOUDY BAY CHARDONNAY**, Marlborough 1988
104	£9.80	**VILLA MARIA BARRIQUE-FERMENTED CHARDONNAY**, Auckland 1987
135	£6.55	**COOPERS CREEK SAUVIGNON BLANC**, Marlborough 1989
138	£6.95	**HUNTERS SAUVIGNON BLANC**, Marlborough 1989
171	£3.95	**MOSCATO D'ASTI**, Viticoltoro dell'Acquesi, Piedmont 1989
172	£3.95	**JOAO PIRES WHITE TABLE WINE**, Palmela 1988
264	£12.60	MAS DE DAUMAS GASSAC, Vin de Pays de l'Hérault, South-West 1988
267	£2.75	**VIN DE PAYS DE L'AUDE CABERNET SAUVIGNON**, Paul Boutinot, Midi 1987
299	£8.25	**CHATEAU RAMAGE LA BATISSE**, Haut-Médoc, Bordeaux 1985
311	£11.90	**CHATEAU HAUT-MARBUZET**, St Estèphe, Bordeaux 1985
331	£4.29	**RASTEAU COTES DU RHONE VILLAGES**, Caves des Vignerons de Rasteau 1988
340	£5.25	**COTES DU RHONE**, Guigal 1986
359	£4.95	**BEAUJOLAIS-VILLAGES**, Georges Duboeuf 1989
388	£3.50	BARBERA D'ASTI, Viticoltori dell'Acquesi, Piedmont 1988
414	£15.85	TIGNANELLO, Antinori, Tuscany 1985

VW	Victoria Wine

Head Office: Brook House, Chertsey Rd, Woking, Surrey GU21 5BE2 (0483 715066). Vastly improved High Street chain with 900 branches nationwide. **Opening Hours:** varied - often 'till late}. **Delivery:** nationally at cost. **Tastings:** occasionally in-store.

Regular readers of the *Guide* may recall the year-by-year account of managing director Alan Smith's efforts to turn this ship around 180 degrees from the mediocre direction in which it was heading when he took it over. Under Smith, two new chains - South of the Bordeaux and Gare du Vin - were opened, but then closed, as it was decided that it made more sense to concentrate on building up Victoria Wine itself.

Like Thresher, its closest competitor, Victoria Wine has thrown itself into improving the quality of its range, casting out the often poor existing own-label wines and replacing them with far more interesting examples. Among these featured one of the most commendable gestures by any merchant during 1990: a Brazilian Cabernet, sold partly in aid of the Rain Forest appeal - and partly because it was very pleasant wine.

Like Thresher too, Victoria Wine still frustrates wine drinkers by having different ranges in different shops, but the best stores are already beginning to give Oddbins the competition it needs.

4	£5.39	**ASTI MARTINI**, Martini & Rossi, Piedmont
24	£18.99	**CHAMPAGNE LOUIS ROEDERER BRUT PREMIER**
28	£2.79	**VIN DE PAYS DES COTES DE GASCOGNE** Plaimont, South-West 1989
30	£3.29	**COTEAUX DE PIERREVERT LA BLAQUE**, Midi 1989
31	£3.29	**CENTENARY SEMILLON** 1987
37	£3.99	**HARDY'S BIRD SERIES CHARDONNAY**, South Australia 1989
38	£4.19	**ALSACE TOKAY-PINOT GRIS**, Cave Vinicole de Turckheim 1988
52	£6.30	**HOUGHTON VERDELHO**, Swan Valley 1988
53	£5.49	**SEPPELTS CHARDONNAY**, South-East Australia 1989
70	£4.59	**VERDICCHIO CA'SAL DI SERRA**, Umani Ronchi, Marches 1986
80	£6.25	**WOLF BLASS BARREL-FERMENTED CHARDONNAY**, South Australia 1988
126	£4.39	**CHATEAU LA JAUBERTIE BERGERAC SEC**, Henry Ryman, South-West 1987
129	£4.99	**MONTANA SAUVIGNON BLANC**, Marlborough 1989
157	£2.59	**RETSINA OF ATTICA**, Kourtaki
172	£4.99	**JOAO PIRES WHITE TABLE WINE**, Palmela 1988
174	£4.89	**BROWN BROTHERS LATE HARVEST ORANGE MUSCAT & FLORA**, N E Victoria 1988
192	£5.39	**ALSACE RIESLING RESERVE**, Schlumberger 1986
222	£5.69	**SERRIGER HEILIGENBORN RIESLING SPATLESE**, Staatliche Weinbaudomanen Trier, Mosel-Saar-Rüwer 1983
231	£2.99	**PIEMONTELLO PINK**, Piedmont
233	£3.19	**WHITE GRENACHE**, E & J Gallo 1989
240	£4.60	**CHATEAU LA JAUBERTIE BERGERAC ROSE**, Henry Ryman, South-West 1987
243	£2.39	**BULGARIAN COUNTRY WINE, MERLOT/GAMZA,** Suhindol
287	£5.99	**RAIMAT CABERNET SAUVIGNON**, Lerida 1985
309	£11.49	**CHATEAU HAUT-BAGES-AVEROUS** (Château Lynch-Bages), Pauillac, Bordeaux 1986
319	£29.10	**CHATEAU PICHON-LONGUEVILLE-BARON**, Pauillac, Bordeaux 1985
320	£14.95	**CHATEAU LYNCH-BAGES**, Pauillac, Bordeaux 1985
322	£32.10	**CHATEAU FIGEAC**, St Emilion Grand Cru, Bordeaux 1982
338	£4.99	**WYNNS COONAWARRA SHIRAZ** 1987
342	£5.99	**ST JOSEPH MEDAILLE D'ARGENT**, St Désirat, Rhône 1986
368	£6.99	**TREFETHEN PINOT NOIR**, Napa Valley 1984
414	£14.69	**TIGNANELLO**, Antinori, Tuscany 1985
454	£7.89	**TOKAY ASZU 5 PUTTONYOS**, Tokaji 1981

457	£9.99	**CHATEAU LE DRAGON**, Calvet, Bordeaux 1987
488	£11.49	**SMITH WOODHOUSE LATE BOTTLED VINTAGE PORT (BOTTLED 1984)**, Douro 1979
496	£1.59	**GOLDENER OKTOBER LIGHT WHITE**, St Ursula Weinkellerei, Rheinhessen
499	£1.99	**PETILLANT DE RAISIN (3%)**, Listel, Midi
500	£1.99	**GRANTS OF ST JAMES MONTEVERDI ROSSO (3%)**, Piedmont

---

| **LV** | **La Vigneronne** |

105 Old Brompton Rd, London SW7 3LE (071 589 6113). Independent merchant famous for fine and old wines. **Opening Hours:**10am-9pm Mon-Sat; 12-2pm Sun. **Delivery:** free within 5 miles, nationally at cost. **Tastings:** occasionally in-store plus tutored events and dinners.

Ask a wine lover in Canada where he buys some of his best bottles, and there's a good chance that he will give you the name of this Kensington shop. In Canada, all wine sales are controlled by local state monopolies, so any overseas store that can (and does) dispatch a range of old 'Fine and Rare' and obscure modern wines this far is bound to achieve star status. Even in the freer wine-selling climate of the British Isles, La Vigneronne performs a similar role: if there's a good wine you can't find anywhere else, this is a very good place to look. And if you want good, down-to-earth wine advice, Liz Berry MW is pretty unbeatable.

431	£5.30	**LAR DE BARROS RESERVA**, Bodega Inviosa, Extremadura 1986
477	£10.99	**SANDEMAN ROYAL AMBROSANTE**, Jerez
489	£13.06	**HENRIQUES & HENRIQUES 10 YEAR OLD SERCIAL**, Madeira
490	£13.06	**HENRIQUES & HENRIQUES 10 YEAR OLD MALMSEY**, Madeira

---

| **VER** | **Vinceremos Ltd.** |

Unit 10, Ashley Industrial Estate, Wakefield Road, Ossett WF5 9JD (0924 276 393). Organic specialist operating as a co-operative. **Opening Hours:** 9.15am-5pm Mon-Fri; 10am-4pm Sat. **Delivery:** free within 25 miles of Leeds and free nationally for 5+ cases. **Tastings:** regular tutored events. **Discounts:** negotiable.

To the best of our knowledge, Vinceremos is the only wine merchant that describes itself as a 'registered workers' co-operative', though the description might partially apply to Waitrose. Jerry Lockspeiser's firm is unusual in other ways. It is one of the very few in Britain to specialise almost exclusively in (mostly high quality) organic wines, offering mixed cases as an inducement to customers to taste the healthy difference. They could, for example, be compared with Vinceremos's rather less impressive non-organic Flame Lily whites from Zimbabwe and Tacama wines from Peru, which feature as part of the firm's commitment to offering right-on exotica - Nicaraguan rum, for example, is also available.

76	£5.50	**MONTROSE CHARDONNAY**, Mudgee 1989
127	£4.45	**MUSCADET DE SEVRE ET MAINE SUR LIE**, G Bossard, Loire 1989
155	£7.20	**MILLTON VINEYARDS BARREL-FERMENTED CHENIN BLANC**, Gisborne 1988
163	£6.50	**ALSACE GEWURZTRAMINER**, Pierre Frick & Fils 1988
226	£6.50	**MILLTON VINEYARDS OPOU RIVER RIESLING**, Gisborne 1989
288	£5.99	**PETER LEHMANN CABERNET SAUVIGNON**, Barossa Valley 1985
332	£3.95	**COTES DE PROVENCE DOMAINE DU JAS D'ESCLANS**, Lorges-Lapouge 1986
345	£6.20	**BAILEYS BUNDARRA SHIRAZ**, Glenrowan 1986

444	£10.15	BAILEYS FOUNDERS LIQUEUR MUSCAT, Glenrowan	
452	£5.75	PETER LEHMANN BOTRYTIS RIESLING, Barossa Valley 1984	

VR	Vintage Roots

25 Manchester Rd, Reading, Berks, RG1 3QE (0734 662569). **Opening Hours:** Telephone first to check. **Delivery:** free within 30 miles, nationally at cost. **Tastings:** tutored events organised for outside clubs. **Discounts:** £1.50 per case for collection.

If you are allergic to sulphur dioxide, or you're a strict vegetarian who worries about the way a wine may have been fined (with egg whites, for example, or fish intestines or, very rarely, ox blood), this is your kind of merchant. All of Vintage Roots' wines are genuinely organic, some are free of added sulphur and a few are guaranteed to be made without recourse to any kind of animal matter. Far more importantly, though, to would-be organic wine drinkers who have been disappointed by some of the ones they have tried, Vintage Roots' wines actually taste good. Whether as the firm's list bravely claims, headaches you get from drinking non-organic are really 'likely' to disappear' is slightly more questionable.

127	£4.25	MUSCADET DE SEVRE ET MAINE SUR LIE, G Bossard, Loire 1989	
155	£7.25	MILLTON VINEYARDS BARREL-FERMENTED CHENIN BLANC, Gisborne 1988	
226	£6.95	MILLTON VINEYARDS OPOU RIVER RIESLING, Gisborne 1989	
264	£9.99	MAS DE DAUMAS GASSAC, Vin de Pays de l'Hérault, South-West 1988	
334	£4.30	COTES DU RHONE, Domaine St Apollinaire 1988	
344	£5.99	BOTOBOLAR ST GILBERT RED WINE, Mudgee 1987	

V	The Vintner

The trading name of the Arthur Rackham mail-order club (head office: Winefare House, 5 High Road, Byfleet, Weybridge, Surrey KT14 7QF (0923 515 85) and also of their specialist shop at 66 Kensington Church Street, London W8 4BY (071 229 2629). See Arthur Rackhams

W	Waitrose Ltd

Head Office: Doncastle Rd, South Industrial Area, Bracknell, Berks RG12 4YA (0344 424680). Up-market but slightly reclusive supermarket chain with 90 branches in the South of England and Midlands. **Opening Hours:** 9am-6pm Mon, Tues; 9am-8pm Wed, Thu; 8.30am-9pm Fri; 8.30am-5.30pm Sat. **Discounts:** 5% on unbroken cases or orders over £100.

The policy of this chain's founders apparently forbids it to enter competitions of any kind. Thus, we regret to say, none of Waitrose's exclusive wines were tasted at this year's Challenge. The following list is of award winners that are stocked by the chain, but which were submitted by other companies. The Waitrose range is both commendable and generally reliable but, as we said last year, it is far less exciting than it ought - and used - to be. Comparison between this chain's selection and that of Booths, the similarly up-market north-of-England supermarket chain, is very revealing. Waitrose's mostly southern customers could do well to head a little further up the M1.

4	£5.25	ASTI MARTINI, Martini & Rossi, Piedmont	
7	£5.85	CREMANT DE BOURGOGNE ROSE, Caves de Bailly, Burgundy 1987	
32	£3.35	CHATEAU DE LA ROUERGUE BARTHE, Bordeaux 1989	

34	£4.55	**CHARDONNAY**, Wilhelm Walch Termeno, Trentino-Alto Adige 1989
74	£5.65	**RIOJA BLANCO SECO RESERVA**, CVNE 1985
78	£5.95	**MITCHELTON MARSANNE**, Goulburn Valley 1987
83	£4.95	**MITCHELTON RESERVE CHARDONNAY**, Goulburn Valley 1988
157	£2.45	**RETSINA OF ATTICA**, Kourtaki
222	£5.95	**SERRIGER HEILIGENBORN RIESLING SPATLESE**, Staatliche Weinbaudomanen Trier, Mosel-Saar-Rüwer 1983
366	£2.45	**MILION PINOT NOIR**, Navip, Vranje 1986
367	£4.45	**BOURGOGNE PINOT NOIR**, Caves de Buxy, Burgundy 1987
391	£3.95	**TEROLDEGO ROTALIANO**, Gaierhof, Trentino-Alto Adige 1988
447	£3.95	**CHATEAU DE BERBEC**, Premieres Côtes de Bordeaux 1987
496	£1.59	**GOLDENER OKTOBER LIGHT WHITE**, St Ursula Weinkellerei, Rheinhessen

---

WAW	**Waterloo Wine Co.**

59-61 Lant St, Borough London SE1 1QN (071 403 7967). Independent merchant. **Opening Hours:** 10am-6.30pm Mon-Fri; 10am-5.30pm Sat. **Delivery:** Free locally; nationally at cost. **Tastings:** monthly in-store and for groups by arrangement.

Though Waterloo's shop/warehouse premises are in Lant St, their offices are just around the corner in the charmingly appropriately-named Vine Yard. And both premises are but a cork's throw away from the venue for the 1990 *Wine Magazine* Challenge, where tasters spent an exhausting week doling out awards to, among 2,000 other wines, a healthy selection from the Waterloo range. The list below reflects two specialities at Waterloo - Antipodeans and French country wines, areas which if anything have been expanded this year.

Last year Paul Tutton took us to task for complaining that some of his listed wines lacked producers' names. We admit that we were mistaken - but wouldn't it be simpler to print them next to the wines rather than on the preceding page?

4	£4.95	**ASTI MARTINI**, Martini & Rossi, Piedmont
17	£13.75	**CHAMPAGNE MARTEL MILLESIME** 1985
37	£4.11	**HARDY'S BIRD SERIES CHARDONNAY**, South Australia 1989
71	£5.00	**MINERVOIS, DOMAINE DE LA TOUR BOISEE VIEILLI EN FUT DE CHENE**, Jean Louis Poudou, Midi
81	£6.07	**STONELEIGH CHARDONNAY**, Marlborough 1988
95	£9.17	**CLOUDY BAY CHARDONNAY**, Marlborough 1988
98	£10.07	**GEOFF MERRILL CHARDONNAY**, McLaren Vale 1987
129	£4.49	**MONTANA SAUVIGNON BLANC**, Marlborough 1989
144	£8.47	**MOUNT HURTLE SAUVIGNON BLANC**, McLaren Vale 1989
182	£4.31	**ALSACE RIESLING**, Seltz 1988
256	£4.35	**CORBIERES, CHATEAU HELENE VIEILLI EN FUT DE CHENE**, Marie-Hélène Gau, Midi 1985
277	£4.15	**SEAVIEW CABERNET SAUVIGNON**, South Australia 1985
289	£6.00	**CHATEAU BEAUMONT**, Cru Bourgeois Médoc, Bordeaux 1986
303	£8.00	**ROUGE HOMME COONAWARRA CABERNET SAUVIGNON** 1985
316	£16.75	**PENFOLDS BIN 707 CABERNET SAUVIGNON**, South Australia 1986
337	£4.67	**ROUGE HOMME SHIRAZ/CABERNET**, Coonawarra 1985
355	£15.29	**PENFOLDS MAGILL ESTATE**, South Australia 1986
436	£9.49	**RIOJA RESERVA 904**, La Rioja Alta 1976
437	£9.61	**TINTO PESQUERA**, Fernandez, Ribera del Duero 1986
453	£6.19	**BONNEZEAUX**, Jean Godineau, Loire 1987

WAC | Waters of Coventry

29 High St, Coventry, Warks CU1 5QS (0203 226657).Retail arm of wholesale merchant. **Opening Hours:**9.30am-5.30pm Mon-Fri; 9.30am-3pm Sat. **Delivery:** free within 20 miles for 1 case and nationally for 5+ cases. **Tastings:** regularly in-store. **Discounts:** negotiable.

As it approaches its 200th birthday, Waters of Coventry is steadily developing its list, based on the wholesale selection it offers to local hotels and restaurants, Robert Caldicott clearly knows his customers; although single-page list includes such delights as Lynch Bages 1985 and good value Côte Chalonnaise wines from Derain, it is also well stocked with 'Big Bottle Italian; wines and 'Litrevin' French Table Wine'. A place in which to pick and choose.

| 276 | £4.31 | **CONCHA Y TORO MERLOT**, Maipo 1986 |
| 320 | £22.30 | **CHATEAU LYNCH-BAGES**, Pauillac, Bordeaux 1985 |

WES | Wessex Wines

197 St Andrews Rd, Bridport, Dorset DT6 3BT (0308 23400).Good-value independent merchant. **Opening Hours:** 8.30am-9.30pm Mon-Sat. **Delivery:** free within 20 miles with collection discount. **Tastings:** regularly in-store plus tutored events. **Discounts:** 5% on 6 bottles of the same wine.

There are very few merchants in Britain who sell Canadian wine, and fewer still who sell Zimbabwean wine as well. Michael Farmer and his wife have put together a successful little business concentrating largely on inexpensive wines, particularly from some of the less well-known regions of France.

57	£7.25	**INNISKILLIN CHARDONNAY**, Niagara 1988
70	£3.78	**VERDICCHIO CA'SAL DI SERRA**, Umani Ronchi, Marches 1986
134	£6.06	**NOBILOS SAUVIGNON BLANC**, Marlborough 1989
188	£5.20	**PILTON MANOR DRY RESERVE**, Somerset 1987
243	£2.56	**BULGARIAN COUNTRY WINE, MERLOT/GAMZA**,Suhindol
266	£2.86	**PLOVDIV CABERNET SAUVIGNON**, Bulgarian Vintners 1985
281	£4.59	**CHATEAU TOUR MARTINES BORDEAUX SUPERIEUR 1983**
390	£4.40	**CABERNET DEL TRENTINO**, Ca'Vit, Trentino-Alto Adige 1987

WOC | Whitesides of Clitheroe

Shawbridge St, Clitheroe, Lancs BB7 1NA (0200 22281). The Clitheroe phenomenon part two (see D. Byrne) **Opening Hours:** 9.30am - 5.30pm Mon-Sat . **Delivery:** free within 50 miles, nationally at cost. **Tastings:** regularly in-store plus tutored events. **Discounts:** 5% on unbroken cases.

The second of Clitheroe's astonishing pair of top-class wine merchants, Whitesides shares D Byrne's skill at choosing wines - and apparent lack of interest in such unnecessary luxuries as smart wine lists. Were it not for the medals from last year's WINE Challenge on the cover, this could easily be the catalogue of a firm selling bar accessories. The way the wines are listed is just as Spartan; there's no room here for such niceties as pen-portraits of wines or producers. Presumably this former tobacconist's customers have no need of this kind of blandishment to buy; they trust the Whitesides' buying team to supply them with the kind of delicious award winners we have listed here.

4	£4.95	**ASTI MARTINI**, Martini & Rossi, Piedmont
24	£18.35	**CHAMPAGNE LOUIS ROEDERER BRUT PREMIER**
40	£4.09	**COOKS MARLBOROUGH SEMILLON** 1987
49	£5.45	**BABICH SEMILLON/CHARDONNAY**, Gisborne 1989
73	£4.99	**LINDEMANS BIN 65 CHARDONNAY**, Murray River 1989
80	£5.75	**WOLF BLASS BARREL-FERMENTED CHARDONNAY**, South Australia 1988
87	£7.95	**PENFOLDS CHARDONNAY**, South Australia 1988
108	£13.99	**ROSEMOUNT ROXBURGH CHARDONNAY**, Hunter Valley 1987
127	£4.25	**MUSCADET DE SEVRE ET MAINE SUR LIE**, G Bossard, Loire 1989
129	£4.75	**MONTANA SAUVIGNON BLANC**, Marlborough 1989
139	£6.79	**SANCERRE**, Henry Natter, Loire 1988
174	£4.45	**BROWN BROTHERS LATE HARVEST ORANGE MUSCAT & FLORA**, N E Victoria 1988
175	£5.45	**QUADY ESSENSIA ORANGE MUSCAT** 1987
231	£2.95	**PIEMONTELLO PINK**, Piedmont
247	£3.35	**VRANAC**, Slovin, Montenegro 1986
290	£6.55	**FIRESTONE CABERNET SAUVIGNON**, Santa Ynez 1986
292	£7.79	**ORLANDO ST HUGO CABERNET SAUVIGNON**, Coonawarra 1986
297	£7.99	**PENFOLDS BIN 389 SHIRAZ/CABERNET**, South Australia 1986
303	£8.19	**ROUGE HOMME COONAWARRA CABERNET SAUVIGNON** 1985
314	£14.85	**TORRES GRAN CORONAS BLACK LABEL**, Penedés 1983
316	£18.60	**PENFOLDS BIN 707 CABERNET SAUVIGNON**, South Australia 1986
317	£18.85	**MONDAVI CABERNET SAUVIGNON RESERVE**, Napa Valley 1980
339	£5.59	**PENFOLDS BIN 28 KALIMNA SHIRAZ**, South Australia 1986
355	£16.85	**PENFOLDS MAGILL ESTATE**, South Australia 1986
358	£3.79	**GAMAY DE L'ARDECHE**, Georges Duboeuf, Rhône 1989
359	£5.35	**BEAUJOLAIS-VILLAGES**, Georges Duboeuf 1989
362	5.65	**BROUILLY**, Andre Large, Beaujolais 1989
364	6.65	**MORGON JEAN DESCOMBES**, Georges Duboeuf, Beaujolais 1989
365	7.35	**FLEURIE LA MADONE**, Georges Duboeuf, Beaujolais 1988
378	9.25	**MONDAVI PINOT NOIR RESERVE**, Napa Valley 1986
444	8.59	**BAILEYS FOUNDERS LIQUEUR MUSCAT**, Glenrowan
491	13.75	**WARRE'S QUINTA DA CAVADINHA**, Douro 1979
493	19.99	**QUINTA DO NOVAL 20 YEAR OLD TAWNY PORT**, Douro

WID | Widcombe Wines

12 Widcombe Parade, Blaveton St, Bath BA2 4JT (0225 429624). Independent merchant. **Tastings:** occasionally in-store. **Discounts:** 5% on case sales.

David Cox is apologetic about his failure to produce a printed list for his customers; 'frequent changes in stock' apparently make the production of any such publication impracticable. These 'frequent changes' are emblematic of an enthusiasm that has led Mr Cox to include a large range of organic wines, as well as examples from Luxembourg, Algeria, China and India amongst his stock. His buying, however, is not indiscriminate - magpie that he is, he has been tempted by the brilliance of the wines listed below.

74	£5.47	**RIOJA BLANCO SECO RESERVA**, CVNE 1985
98	£10.62	**GEOFF MERRILL CHARDONNAY**, McLaren Vale 1987
134	£6.26	**NOBILOS SAUVIGNON BLANC**, Marlborough 1989
144	£8.54	**MOUNT HURTLE SAUVIGNON BLANC**, McLaren Vale 1989
149	£3.42	**CHENIN BLANC**, E & J Gallo 1988
172	£5.06	**JOAO PIRES WHITE TABLE WINE**, Palmela 1988
233	£3.42	**WHITE GRENACHE**, E & J Gallo 1989

243	£2.49	**BULGARIAN COUNTRY WINE, MERLOT/GAMZA,** Suhindol
259	£4.75	COTEAUX D'AIX EN PROVENCE CHATEAU PIGOUDET GRANDE RESERVE, Midi 1985
262	£5.16	**CORBIERES CHATEAU DE LASTOURS (FUT DE CHENE),** Midi 1985
284	£3.28	**SPECIAL RESERVE STAMBOLOVO MERLOT,** Bulgarian Vintners 1985
300	£8.65	**CHATEAU DE PUY** (Robert Amoreau), Bordeaux Supérieur 1982
442	£4.02	**MUSCAT DE RIVESALTES,** Château de la Tuilerie, Midi 1988
486	£7.99	**WARRE'S WARRIOR VINTAGE CHARACTER PORT,** Douro

| **WIL** | **Willoughbys of Manchester** |

Head Office: PO Box 2, Greengate, Middleton Junction Manchester M24 2AX (061 834 0641). Small chain with 3 shops in Manchester, Oldham and Wilmslow with associated outlets George Dutton & Sons in Chester and Thomas Baty & Sons in Liverpool. **Opening Hours** 9am-5.30pm Mon-Fri; 9am-5pm Sat. **Delivery:** free locally, nationally at cost. **Tastings:** regularly in-store plus tutored events. **Discounts:** 5% on case sales, 10% for 10+ cases.

The correct name for this firm is the resounding 'The Willoughbys Group of Fine Wine Companies' because Willoughbys itself is only one of the 'group' that also includes George Dutton of Chester and Thomas Baty of Liverpool. All share the same, extensive list of good, if rather conservatively chosen, wines. Bordeaux, Champagne and England are among the most favoured regions; the New World remains somewhat undiscovered. Even so, these are the kind of pleasant, well-stocked, well staffed shops that ought to be found in every town in Britain.

195	£6.75	**THREE CHOIRS BACCHUS,** Gloucestershire 1989
375	£16.95	**POMMARD CROIX BLANCHE,** Jacques Parent, Burgundy 1986
454	£7.50	**TOKAY ASZU 5 PUTTONYOS,** Tokaji 1981
473	£7.25	**DON ZOILO MANZANILLA,** Sanlúcar de Barrameda

| **WDW** | **Windrush Wines** |

The Barracks, Cecily Hill, Cirencester, Glos GL7 2EF (0285 650466) & 3 Market Place, Cirencester (0285 657807). Independent Burgundophile merchant. **Opening Hours:** 9am-6pm Mon-Sat. **Delivery:** free nationally. **Tastings:** regularly in-store plus tutored events.

Mark Savage introduced a new aspect to wine merchanting this year, with the launch of a vinous property scheme, offering not only vineyards and wineries for sale in various parts of the world, but providing a back-up consultancy service for the buyers. Few such pieces of property come up for sale very often in Burgundy, one of Savage's favourite regions, but he could probably find you a few acres in Germany, California or Oregon, all favourite sources of some of his wines.

58	£7.62	**MACON-CLESSE DOMAINE DE LA BON GRAN CUVEE TRADITION,** Jean Thevenet, Burgundy 1987
111	£14.85	**PULIGNY MONTRACHET,** Domaine Carillon, Burgundy 1987
343	£6.61	**CROZES HERMITAGE,** Alain Graillot, Rhône 1988

WBM | Wine Byre Merchants

Burnside, Cupar, Fife KY15 4BH (0334 53215). Independent merchant - a runaway success? **Opening Hours:** 10.30am-6pm Tue-Thu; 10.30am-7pm Fri, Sat. **Delivery:** free within 40 miles, nationally at cost. **Tastings:** regular tutored events. **Discounts:** 5% on mixed cases.

Lance Sharpus-Jones's decision to run away from London to the less frenzied countryside of Fife has provided the inhabitants of this part of Scotland with a source of really top-class wine to sip after a hard day on the links at St Andrews. And Burnside residents who need an excuse to pop down to the Wine Byre can always claim to be going to do some photocopying - another service Sharpus-Jones cheerfully offers.

5	£5.99	**BRUT DE SAUMUR**, Caves des Vignerons de Saumur, Loire 1987	
57	£6.45	**INNISKILLIN CHARDONNAY**, Niagara 1988	
73	£5.39	**LINDEMANS BIN 65 CHARDONNAY**, Murray River 1989	
95	£9.85	**CLOUDY BAY CHARDONNAY**, Marlborough 1988	
108	£14.95	**ROSEMOUNT ROXBURGH CHARDONNAY**, Hunter Valley 1987	
119	£5.99	**SAUMUR BLANC**, Caves des Vignerons de Saumur, Loire 1988	
133	£5.99	**HILL-SMITH ESTATE SAUVIGNON BLANC**, Barossa Valley 1989	
138	£7.99	**HUNTERS SAUVIGNON BLANC**, Marlborough 1989	
174	£4.95	**BROWN BROTHERS LATE HARVEST ORANGE MUSCAT & FLORA**, N E Victoria 1988	
269	£3.39	**HOUSE CLARET**, Peter Sichel, Bordeaux	
289	£6.49	**CHATEAU BEAUMONT**, Cru Bourgeois Médoc, Bordeaux 1986	
303	£4.95	**ROUGE HOMME COONAWARRA CABERNET SAUVIGNON** 1985	
311	£11.85	**CHATEAU HAUT-MARBUZET**, St Estèphe, Bordeaux 1985	
330	£3.99	**COTES DU RHONE**, Château du Grand Moulas 1988	

WCE | Winecellars

Independent Wine Merchant of the Year

153-155 Wandsworth High St, London SW18 (081 871 3979) & The Market, 213-215 Upper Street, London N1 (071 359 5386). Brilliant all-round merchant with heavy Italian bias. **Opening Hours:** 10.30am-8.30pm Mon-Fri; 10.30am-8pm Sat. **Delivery:** free within M25, nationally at cost. **Tastings:** wines always open plus regular tutored events and dinners.

Winecellars was in the running for three separate prizes this year: London Wine Merchant, Specialist Merchant and this, our highest accolade for an independent merchant, which it carried off after very little debate. In the few years since they first arrived in Wandsworth, Masters of Wine David Gleave and Nick Belfrage and their team have created an almost instant success story. At first, though, Winecellars' reputation was almost exclusively based around its phenomenal list of Italian wines (is there another wine merchant in the world *both* of whose buyers have written award-winning books on the same subject?).

More recently, customers have discovered that the ability to choose good Chianti and Gattinara in no way disables the facility to buy great Burgundy and Californian Syrah. Today, Winecellars is quite simply a magical place to buy any kind of wine.

7	£7.29	**CREMANT DE BOURGOGNE ROSE**, Caves de Bailly, Burgundy 1987
22	£16.55	**CHAMPAGNE BRICOUT CARTE D'OR BRUT PRESTIGE**
24	£18.55	**CHAMPAGNE LOUIS ROEDERER BRUT PREMIER**

29	£3.29	**VIN DE PAYS DES COTES DE GASCOGNE**, Domaine de Perras, South-West 1989
38	£4.65	**ALSACE TOKAY-PINOT GRIS**, Cave Vinicole de Turckheim 1988
41	£4.25	**ALSACE PINOT BLANC**, Cave Vinicole de Turckheim 1989
47	£5.69	**LUGANA**, Ca Dei Frati, Lombardy 1989
50	£5.55	**SOAVE CLASSICO**, Pieropan, Veneto 1989
95	£9.95	**CLOUDY BAY CHARDONNAY**, Marlborough 1988
108	£14.79	**ROSEMOUNT ROXBURGH CHARDONNAY**, Hunter Valley 1987
111	£15.95	**PULIGNY MONTRACHET**, Domaine Carillon, Burgundy 1987
132	£5.89	**REUILLY**, H Beurdin, Loire 1988
171	£3.09	**MOSCATO D'ASTI**, Viticoltore dell'Acquesi, Piedmont 1989
267	£3.09	**VIN DE PAYS DE L'AUDE CABERNET SAUVIGNON**, Paul Boutinot, Midi 1987
292	£7.55	**ORLANDO ST HUGO CABERNET SAUVIGNON**, Coonawarra 1986
299	£8.79	**CHATEAU RAMAGE LA BATISSE**, Haut-Médoc, Bordeaux 1985
351	£9.95	**QUPE SYRAH** 1988
357	£4.49	**GAILLAC CEPAGE GAMAY**, Jean Cros, South-West 1989
362	£6.25	**BROUILLY**, Andre Large, Beaujolais 1989
373	£11.95	**AU BON CLIMAT PINOT NOIR** 1988
377	£15.69	**CALERA JENSEN PINOT NOIR**, San Benito 1987
388	£3.55	**BARBERA D'ASTI**, Viticoltori dell'Acquesi, Piedmont 1988
400	£5.75	**CABERNET RISERVA**, Lageder, Trentino-Alto Adige 1986
409	£10.29	**RECIOTO DELLA VALPOLICELLA**, Allegrini, Veneto 1988
412	£12.65	**CEPPARELLO**, Isole e Olena, Tuscany 1986
414	£16.75	**TIGNANELLO**, Antinori, Tuscany 1985
415	£17.80	**BRUNELLO DI MONTALCINO MONTOSOLI**, Altesino, Tuscany 1985
417	£23.55	**BAROLO MONPRIVATO**, G Mascarello, Piedmont 1985
428	£4.79	**QUINTA DE CAMARATE**, Fonseca, Azeitão 1985
440	£4.65	**SAMOS NECTAR 10 YEAR OLD**, Cooperatives Vinicoles de Samos
441	£7.25	**MORRIS RUTHERGLEN LIQUEUR MUSCAT**
447	£5.19	**CHATEAU DE BERBEC**, Premières Côtes de Bordeaux 1987
461	£8.55	**RECIOTO DI SOAVE DEI CAPITELLE**, Anselmi, Veneto 1987
462	£8.89	**TORCOLATO**, Maculan, Veneto 1986
487	£6.65	**COSSART GORDON 5 YEAR OLD BUAL**, Madeira

WE | The Wine Emporium

7 Devon Place, Haymarket, Edinburgh EH12 5HG (031 346 111). Independent wine warehouse selling by the case. **Opening Hours:** 10am-8pm Mon-Fri; 10am-7pm Sat. **Delivery:** free within 50 miles of Edinburgh. **Tastings:** regularly in-store plus tutored events. **Discounts:** negotiable for large orders.

Edinburgh's answer to Majestic - though with a less extensive and less dazzling range of wines. But value is generally good and there are some impressive buys amongst them, including the award winner listed below.

| 402 | £6.50 | **VINO NOBILE DI MONTEPULCIANO RISERVA**, Fattoria del Cerra, Tuscany, 1985 |

WFP | Wines from Paris

The Vaults, 4 Giles St, Leith, Edinburgh EH6 6DJ (031 554 2652). Independent merchant selling by the case. **Opening Hours:** 10am-6pm Mon-Sat. **Delivery:** free on Scottish mainland, nationally at cost. **Tastings:** wines always available for tasting plus regular tutored events. **Discounts:** available.

Judith Paris has a rare skill among wine merchants - knowing how to blow her own trumpet and to blow it well. Every wine drinker in Edinburgh must by now have seen her pink and blue logo, and most must have tasted at least a few of the nicely varied and generally classy wines she stocks.

7	£7.50	**CREMANT DE BOURGOGNE ROSE**, Caves de Bailly, Burgundy 1987
49	£6.25	**BABICH SEMILLON/CHARDONNAY**, Gisborne 1989
84	£6.99	**SCHINUS MOLLE CHARDONNAY**, Mornington Peninsula 1989
114	£16.59	**YARRA YERING CHARDONNAY**, Yarra Valley 1987
117	£3.45	**ANJOU BLANC CHUPIN**, G Saget, Loire 1989
126	£4.75	**CHATEAU LA JAUBERTIE BERGERAC SEC**, Henry Ryman, South-West 1987
172	£4.35	**JOAO PIRES WHITE TABLE WINE**, Palmela 1988
240	£4.75	**CHATEAU LA JAUBERTIE BERGERAC ROSE**, Henry Ryman, South-West 1987
264	£10.75	**MAS DE DAUMAS GASSAC**, Vin de Pays de l'Hérault, South-West 1988
314	£15.00	**TORRES GRAN CORONAS BLACK LABEL**, Penedés 1983
373	£11.75	**AU BON CLIMAT PINOT NOIR** 1988
382	£26.56	**YARRA YERING PINOT NOIR**, Yarra Valley 1987
399	£6.95	**CAMPO FIORIN**, Masi, Veneto 1985
441	£7.50	**MORRIS RUTHERGLEN LIQUEUR MUSCAT**

WGA | Wine Growers Association

430 High Rd, Willesden, London NW10 2HA (081 451 0981). Mail-order Italian specialists. **Delivery:** included in price on UK mainland for 6+ cases. **Discounts:** available.

Once there were several wine shops that went by this rather odd name; today, however, it is the mail-order operation of Trust House Forte's wholesale specialist, Italian Wine Agencies, and thus a cousin of the Winery (q.v.) and Les Amis du Vin (q.v.). The range of Italian wines has always been exceptional - taking up 12 pages of the 26-page list - but the selection of wines from Bordeaux and California are good too, and a new range of estate wines from Burgundy and the south now improve what was a patchy and very négociant-dominated set of wines.

3	£6.25	**YALUMBA ANGAS BRUT**, Barossa Valley
55	£6.50	**CHARDONNAY DI S MICHELE VIGNETO ZARAOSTI**, Roberto Zeni, Trentino-Alto Adige 1989
402	£8.10	**VINO NOBILE DI MONTEPULCIANO RISERVA**, Fattorio del Cerro, Tuscany 1985
403	£6.99	**TANCA FARRA**, Sella e Mosca, Sardinia 1984
405	£9.20	**BAROLO RISERVA**, Borgogno, Piedmont 1982
407	£9.45	**CASTELLO DI CAMIGLIANO ROSSO**, Tuscany 1986
410	£10.55	**MON PRA**, Conterno e Fantino, 1987 Piedmont

WH | The Wine House

10 Stafford Rd, Wallington, Surrey SM6 9AD (081 669 6661). Independent country merchant with strong Iberian range. **Opening Hours:** 10am-6pm Tue-Sat; 12-2pm Sun. **Delivery:** free locally, nationally at cost. **Tastings:** regularly in-store pus tutored events. **Discounts:** 10% on mixed cases for members of customers' club, 'The Wine Circle'.

Like St Albans Sherston (q.v.), The Wine House began life as part of the Sherston consortium. The Iberian roots of the Sherston operation are still evident in the nine pages of its list that are devoted to Spanish wines. These include such rarities as Priorato and Ampurdán. The following award-winners confirm that the rest of the world is very effectively covered as well.

43	£4.75	**PINOT BIANCO**, Vigna al Monte, Puglia 1989
74	£5.55	**RIOJA BLANCO SECO RESERVA**, CVNE 1985
76	£6.50	**MONTROSE CHARDONNAY**, Mudgee 1989
80	£6.20	**WOLF BLASS BARREL-FERMENTED CHARDONNAY**, South Australia 1988
81	£6.90	**STONELEIGH CHARDONNAY**, Marlborough 1988
86	£8.25	**MUSCADET DE SEVRE ET MAINE SUR LIE CHATEAU DE CHASSELOIR (OAK-AGED)**, Loire 1987
106	£13.45	**LEEUWIN ESTATE CHARDONNAY**, Margaret River 1984
108	£14.99	**ROSEMOUNT ROXBURGH CHARDONNAY**, Hunter Valley 1987
134	£6.95	**NOBILOS SAUVIGNON BLANC**, Marlborough 1989
138	£6.99	**HUNTERS SAUVIGNON BLANC**, Marlborough 1989
175	£5.95	**QUADY ESSENSIA ORANGE MUSCAT** 1987
250	£3.99	**COTEAUX DE MURVIEL DOMAINE DE LIMBARDIE**, Boukandoura & Hutin, Midi 1988
288	£5.99	**PETER LEHMANN CABERNET SAUVIGNON**, Barossa Valley 1985
294	£7.85	**ROSEMOUNT SHOW RESERVE COONAWARRA CABERNET SAUVIGNON** 1987
296	£9.25	**ST JULIEN**, Anthony Barton, Bordeaux 1985
298	£7.50	**CHATEAU LA TOUR DE BY**, Haut-Médoc, Bordeaux 1986
302	£8.75	**CHATEAU CARONNE-SAINTE-GEMME**, Haut-Médoc, Bordeaux 1982
303	£9.95	**ROUGE HOMME COONAWARRA CABERNET SAUVIGNON** 1985
308	£11.75	**PETALUMA COONAWARRA CABERNET/MERLOT** 1985
309	£10.95	**CHATEAU HAUT-BAGES-AVEROUS** (Château Lynch-Bages), Pauillac, Bordeaux 1986
314	£16.99	**TORRES GRAN CORONAS BLACK LABEL**, Penedés 1983
320	£22.00	**CHATEAU LYNCH-BAGES**, Pauillac, Bordeaux 1985
322	£34.50	**CHATEAU FIGEAC**, St Emilion Grand Cru, Bordeaux 1982
366	£2.65	**MILION PINOT NOIR**, Navip, Vranje 1986
395	£4.99	**VALPOLICELLA CLASSICO VIGNETI MARA**, Cesari, Veneto 1987
399	£5.60	**CAMPO FIORIN**, Masi, Veneto 1985
408	£9.80	**PRUNAIO**, Landini, Tuscany 1986
414	£15.75	**TIGNANELLO**, Antinori, Tuscany 1985
422	£4.45	**ALMANSA MARIUS TINTO RESERVA**, Bodegas Piqueras 1982
427	£5.20	**DUERO**, Bodegas Peñalba 1985
428	£4.99	**QUINTA DE CAMARATE**, Fonseca, Azeitão 1985
432	£5.35	**RIOJA RESERVA**, Beronia 1982
434	£7.80	**RIOJA**, Bodegas Remelluri 1985
435	£7.65	**GRANDE ESCHOLA**, Quinta do Cotto, Douro 1985
436	£12.95	**RIOJA RESERVA 904**, La Rioja Alta 1976
442	£7.69	**MUSCAT DE RIVESALTES**, Château de la Tuilerie, Midi 1988
476	£9.95	**MATUSALEM OLOROSO MUY VIEJO**, Gonzalez Byass, Jerez
478	£9.95	**AMONTILLADO DEL DUQUE**, Gonzalez Byass, Jerez
486	£6.99	**WARRE'S WARRIOR VINTAGE CHARACTER PORT**, Douro

| **TWR** | **The Wine Rack** |

Joint Winner: Regional Chain Wine Merchant of the Year

Head Office: 23-25 Midland Rd, Thrapston, Kettering, Northants NN14 4JS (08012 3154). 28-branch chain of 'up-market Thresher' shops in the South-East. **Opening Hours:** 10am-10.30pm Mon-Sat for most stores. **Delivery:** free locally. **Tastings:** regularly in-store plus tutored events. **Discounts:** available for large orders.

Despite some very sniffy comments from one or two of its competitors, the Wine Rack chain has, in a remarkably short time, carved itself a nice little niche in the market, thanks to an unsuspected readiness on the part of

Thresher to commit themselves to quality wine retailing. The range - as this list indicates - is very impressive, the shops have been attractively designed and the staff are as enthusiastic and well chosen as the wines. The efforts of wine buyer Kim Tidy and former Oddbins marketing man Tim Waters appear to be paying quality dividends. If chains like this can be proved to be profitable, perhaps other brewers will be prepared to relinquish their obsession with beer and fags. We look forward to seeing this year's Regional ChainWine Merchant of the Year develop into a national chain that can really give Oddbins a run for its money.

4	£5.59	**ASTI MARTINI**, Martini & Rossi, Piedmont	
7	£6.79	**CREMANT DE BOURGOGNE ROSE**, Caves de Bailly, Burgundy 1987	
23	£19.99	**CHAMPAGNE LAURENT PERRIER ROSE**	
24	£19.29	**CHAMPAGNE LOUIS ROEDERER BRUT PREMIER**	
25	£42.50	**CHAMPAGNE LANSON BRUT** 1979 (magnum)	
32	£3.79	**CHATEAU DE LA ROUERGUE BARTHE**, Bordeaux 1989	
38	£4.29	**ALSACE TOKAY-PINOT GRIS**, Cave Vinicole de Turckheim 1988	
39	£3.99	**HILL-SMITH PIGGOT HILL SEMILLON**, South Australia 1988	
41	£3.95	ALSACE PINOT BLANC, Cave Vinicole de Turckheim 1989	
54	£6.19	**POUILLY LOCHE CHATEAU DE LOCHE**, Caves des Grands Crus Vinzelles, Burgundy 1987	
65	£4.59	**VIN DE PAYS DES COTES DE GASCOGNE DOMAINE DU TARIQUET CUVEE BOIS**, Grassa, South-West	
67	£4.99	**CHATEAU BONNET RESERVE DU CHATEAU (OAK AGED)**, Entre-Deux-Mers, Lurton, Bordeaux 1988	
81	£6.89	**STONELEIGH CHARDONNAY**, Marlborough 1988	
85	£7.20	**JULIUS WILE CHARDONNAY** 1986	
87	£6.99	PENFOLDS CHARDONNAY, South Australia 1988	
89	£7.99	**CHATEAU LA LOUVIERE**, Graves, Bordeaux 1986	
95	£9.99	**CLOUDY BAY CHARDONNAY**, Marlborough 1988	
97	£11.29	**COLDSTREAM HILLS CHARDONNAY**, Yarra Valley 1988	
99	£11.29	**TREFETHEN CHARDONNAY**, Napa Valley 1986	
108	£15.99	**ROSEMOUNT ROXBURGH CHARDONNAY**, Hunter Valley 1987	
116	£2.99	**DOMAINE DE MONTMARIN SAUVIGNON**, Vin de Pays des Côtes de Thongue, South-West 1989	
121	£3.99	**TATACHILLA HILL CHENIN BLANC**, McLaren Vale 1988	
129	£4.99	**MONTANA SAUVIGNON BLANC**, Marlborough 1989	
130	£4.99	**SAUVIGNON DE ST BRIS DOMAINE DU RELAIS DE POSTE**, Luc Sorin, Burgundy 1989	
145	£10.95	**POUILLY FUME BUISSON MENARD**, Didier Dagueneau, Loire 1988	
146	22.95	POUILLY FUME SILEX, Didier Dagueneau, Loire 1988	
157	£2.79	**RETSINA OF ATTICA**, Kourtaki	
172	£4.39	**JOAO PIRES WHITE TABLE WINE**, Palmela 1988	
174	£4.89	BROWN BROS LATE HARVEST ORANGE MUSCAT & FLORA, N E Victoria 1988	
231	£3.29	PIEMONTELLO PINK, Piedmont	
239	£4.59	**CHATEAU THIEULEY BORDEAUX CLAIRET** 1989	
262	£5.69	**CORBIERES CHATEAU DE LASTOURS (FUT DE CHENE)**, Midi 1985	
266	£2.79	**PLOVDIV CABERNET SAUVIGNON**, Bulgarian Vintners 1985	
287	£6.49	**RAIMAT CABERNET SAUVIGNON**, Lerida 1985	
290	£6.99	**FIRESTONE CABERNET SAUVIGNON**, Santa Ynez 1986	
297	£7.99	**PENFOLDS BIN 389 SHIRAZ/CABERNET**, South Australia 1986	
299	£7.59	**CHATEAU RAMAGE LA BATISSE**, Haut-Médoc, Bordeaux 1985	
301	£8.49	**DOMAINE DE MARTIALIS** (Château Clos Fourtet), St Emilion, Bordeaux 1986	
309	£12.75	**CHATEAU HAUT-BAGES-AVEROUS** (Château Lynch-Bages), Pauillac, Bordeaux 1986	
320	£29.95	CHATEAU LYNCH-BAGES, Pauillac, Bordeaux 1985	
338	£5.60	**WYNNS COONAWARRA SHIRAZ** 1987	

339	£4.49	**PENFOLDS BIN 28 KALIMNA SHIRAZ**, South Australia 1986	
359	£4.79	**BEAUJOLAIS-VILLAGES**, Georges Duboeuf 1989	
364	£6.79	**MORGON JEAN DESCOMBES**, Georges Duboeuf, Beaujolais 1989	
367	£5.39	BOURGOGNE PINOT NOIR, Caves de Buxy, Burgundy 1987	
371	£11.29	**COLDSTREAM HILLS PINOT NOIR**, Yarra Valley 1988	
393	£4.59	**CORVO ROSSO**, Sicily 1987	
396	£4.99	**NEBB IOLO DELLE LANGHE**, Berutti, Piedmont 1985	
414	£15.25	TIGNANELLO, Antinori, Tuscany 1985	
420	£2.89	**DON DARIAS VINO DE MESA**, Bodegas Vitorianas, Alto Ebro	
429	£4.99	**RAIMAT TEMPRANILLO**, Lerida 1987	
438	£16.99	**FERREIRA BARCA VELHA**, Douro 1981	
447	£4.59	**CHATEAU DE BERBEC**, Premières Côtes de Bordeaux 1987	
457	£5.29	**CHATEAU LE DRAGON**, Calvet, Bordeaux 1987	
476	£10.99	MATUSALEM OLOROSO MUY VIEJO, Gonzalez Byass, Jerez	
478	£10.99	**AMONTILLADO DEL DUQUE**, Gonzalez Byass, Jerez	
487	£8.99	**COSSART GORDON 5 YEAR OLD BUAL**, Madeira	
491	£14.79	**WARRE'S QUINTA DA CAVADINHA**, Douro 1979	
497	£1.69	**LAMBRUSCO LIGHT (BLUSH WHITE)**, Giacobazzi, Emilia-Romagna	
499	£1.99	**PETILLANT DE RAISIN (3%)**, Listel, Midi	

WIN	**The Winery**

4 Clifton Rd, London W9 1SS (071 286 6475). Pretty shop packed with wines from California-import supremo Geoffrey Roberts. **Opening Hours:**10.30am-8.30pm Mon-Fri; 10am-6.30pm Sat. **Delivery.** free in London and nationally for 2+ cases, otherwise as cost. **Tastings:** occasionally in-store. **Discounts:** negotiable.

Last year's Specialist Wine Merchant of the Year, this retail extension of the Les Amis du Vin wine club still stands alone as a centre of pilgrimage for anyone who wants to taste their way through the best of the Napa Valley and Sonoma. The Californian strength is derived from the firm's association with Geoffrey Roberts Associates, UK importers for almost all the top wineries in that state. But, as the following list makes clear, Australia (with wines from Petaluma, Rothbury and Yalumba) is another strength; there are good examples of Frescobaldi Chiantis too.

3	£5.25	**YALUMBA ANGAS BRUT**, Barossa Valley	
75	£6.35	**FIRESTONE CHARDONNAY**, Santa Ynez 1987	
99	£11.29	**TREFETHEN CHARDONNAY**, Napa Valley 1986	
100	£11.35	**PETALUMA CHARDONNAY**, Adelaide Hills 1987	
166	£7.50	**MARK WEST VINEYARDS GEWURZTRAMINER**, Sonoma 1988	
290	£6.55	**FIRESTONE CABERNET SAUVIGNON**, Santa Ynez 1986	
308	£11.50	**PETALUMA COONAWARRA CABERNET/MERLOT** 1985	
317	£18.95	**MONDAVI CABERNET SAUVIGNON RESERVE**, Napa Valley 1980	
335	£4.59	**FETZER LAKE COUNTY ZINFANDEL** 1986	
349	£8.29	**RIDGE GEYSERVILLE ZINFANDEL**, Sonoma 1987	
368	£8.50	**TREFETHEN PINOT NOIR**, Napa Valley 1984	
377	£15.50	**CALERA JENSEN PINOT NOIR**, San Benito 1987	
378	£16.00	**MONDAVI PINOT NOIR RESERVE**, Napa Valley 1986	
484	£6.99	**YALUMBA CLOCKTOWER TAWNY**, Barossa Valley	

WSO	**The Wine Society**

Gunnels Wood Rd, Stevenage, Herts SG1 2BG (0438 741177). Independent wine club, owned by its members and selling mail order, by-the-case. **Delivery:** included in price. **Tastings:** regular club events. **Discounts:** £2 per case for 5 +cases; collection discount.

Still by far the most genuine wine-selling wine club of them all -because it's the only one that really belongs to its members - the Wine Society is now also the biggest wine-cellaring wine club - by virtue of its brand-new, tempera-ture-controlled storage facility, the largest of its kind in Europe. The reason for its success lies partly in the almost unconscious sense of belonging shared by its members, many of whom inherited or were given their shares, and partly in the subtle way in which the Society has added a wide range of 'modern' wines to the traditional Bordeaux, Burgundies and ports for which it is perhaps still best known. This rounding-out of the range has given a fillip to the Society's consistent performance - helping it to come within a whisker of winning this year's 'By the Case' award .

15	£16.90	THE SOCIETY'S CHAMPAGNE, Alfred Gratien
24	£19.95	CHAMPAGNE LOUIS ROEDERER BRUT PREMIER
55	£8.95	CHARDONNAY DI S MICHELE VIGNETO ZARAOSTI, Roberto Zeni, Trentino-Alto Adige 1989
88	£9.95	CHATEAU COUHINS-LURTON, Graves, Lurton, Bordeaux 1987
99	£10.65	TREFETHEN CHARDONNAY, Napa Valley 1986
156	£7.90	VOUVRAY DEMI-SEC CLOS DE BOURG, Huet, Loire 1983
239	£4.90	CHATEAU THIEULEY BORDEAUX CLAIRET 1989
250	£3.45	COTEAUX DE MURVIEL DOMAINE DE LIMBARDIE, Boukandoura & Hutin, Midi 1988
302	£9.45	CHATEAU CARONNE-SAINTE-GEMME, Haut-Médoc, Bordeaux 1982
303	£10.95	ROUGE HOMME COONAWARRA CABERNET SAUVIGNON 1985
354	£10.90	CORNAS, Guy de Barjac, Rhône 1986
390	£3.25	CABERNET DEL TRENTINO, Ca'Vit, Trentino-Alto Adige 1987
417	£24.50	BAROLO MONPRIVATO, G Mascarello, Piedmont 1985
426	£4.65	DAO PORTA DOS CAVALEIROS RESERVA, Caves São João 1983
454	£8.25	TOKAY ASZU 5 PUTTONYOS, Tokaji 1981
471	£6.99	AMONTILLADO TIO DIEGO, Valdespino, Jerez
485	£7.95	THE SOCIETY'S CRUSTED PORT, Douro

WOI | Wines of Interest / Burlington Wines

46 Burlington Rd, Ipswich, Suffolk IP1 2HS (0473 215752). Infpendent merchant, selling by the case and, as Burlington Wines, by the bottle **Opening Hours:** 9am-6pm Mon-Fri; 9am-1pm Sat. **Delivery:** free locally, nationally at cost. **Tastings:** regularly in-store plus tutored events. **Discounts:** 5% on orders over 6 cases.

You can understand Tim Voelcker's dilemma. Ought he to call his company 'Burlington Wines' and attract all those London buyers who'll imagine his offices to be in the Burlington Arcade? Or ought he to call it 'Wines of Interest', a name that really does describe this merchant very well. In the end, Mr Voelcker has chosen to keep both hats. His 'interesting wines' range from 1981 Corton Languettes from Michel Voarick (£9.25), to a Collioure 1983 from Dr Parce (£9.75) and Dom Hermano Garrafeira 1980 from the Ribatejo in Portugal (£4.45) while the list touches Burlington base with classy favourites like the Tignanello and Roederer included below.

24	£17.99	CHAMPAGNE LOUIS ROEDERER BRUT PREMIER
29	£2.85	VIN DE PAYS DES COTES DE GASCOGNE, Domaine de Perras, South-West 1989
139	£6.75	SANCERRE, Henry Natter, Loire 1988
174	£4.79	BROWN BROTHERS LATE HARVEST ORANGE MUSCAT & FLORA, N E Victoria 1988
284	£5.50	SPECIAL RESERVE STAMBOLOVO MERLOT, Bulgarian Vintners 1985
292	£7.50	ORLANDO ST HUGO CABERNET SAUVIGNON, Coonawarra 1986
414	£14.95	TIGNANELLO, Antinori, Tuscany 1985

437	£10.85	**TINTO PESQUERA**, Fernandez, Ribera del Duero 1986
454	£5.95	**TOKAY ASZU 5 PUTTONYOS**, Tokaji 1981
478	£13.50	**AMONTILLADO DEL DUQUE**, Gonzalez Byass, Jerez
487	£8.95	**COSSART GORDON 5 YEAR OLD BUAL**, Madeira

| WIZ | Wizard Wine Warehouses |

Head Office: 226 Purley Way, Croydon, Surrey CRO 4XG (081 686 5703). 12-outlet South London wine warehouse chain selling by the case and bottle. **Opening Hours:** 10am - 8pm every day. **Delivery** £4 per case on orders costing less than £50; £2 for orders worth £50-100; free for orders over £100.**Tastings:** regularly in-store plus tutored events. **Discounts:** Unspilt cases are 'cheaper'; 5% discount on 10 or more unspilt cases.

Tony Mason, the man behind Wizard, was a founder of Majestic and thus one of the inventors of the wine warehouse. At Wizard, the chain he founded after leaving Majestic, he has created a set of stores where you can always be sure of finding some kind of bargain - as well as some wines whose presence seems entirely due to their cheapness. Sensible wine drinkers visit Wizard often , but they buy with care - and in half the stores they may do so by the bottle.

| 43 | £4.69 | **PINOT BIANCO**, Vigna al Monte, Puglia 1989 |
| 129 | £4.99 | **MONTANA SAUVIGNON BLANC**, Marlborough 1989 |

| WRW | The Wright Wine Co |

The Old Smithy, Raikes Rd, Skipton, N Yorks BD23 1MP (0756 4175). Unpretentious and affable independent merchant. **Opening Hours:** 9am-6pm Mon-Sat. **Delivery:** free within 35 miles, nationally at cost. **Tastings:** regularly in-store plus tutored events. **Discounts:** 5% on mixed case.

'The wine trade once was a noble profession and still should be. There are too many jumping on the bandwagon to make a quick buck and in so doing, have given the trade a bad name'. Bob Wright's list looks even more 'unsmart' than those of D Byrne and Whitesides but, like those companies, he makes up in quality and quantity what he lacks in frippery.

37	£5.20	**HARDY'S BIRD SERIES CHARDONNAY**, South Australia 1989
49	£5.95	**BABICH SEMILLON/CHARDONNAY**, Gisborne 1989
80	£6.30	**WOLF BLASS BARREL-FERMENTED CHARDONNAY**, South Australia 1988
174	£5.10	**BROWN BROTHERS LATE HARVEST ORANGE MUSCAT & FLORA**, N E Victoria 1988
175	£10.60	**QUADY ESSENSIA ORANGE MUSCAT** 1987
213	£5.35	**NIERSTEINER SPIEGELBERG KABINETT**, Guntrum, Rheinhessen 1988
303	£10.25	**ROUGE HOMME COONAWARRA CABERNET SAUVIGNON** 1985
311	£11.99	**CHATEAU HAUT-MARBUZET**, St Estèphe, Bordeaux 1985
314	£15.30	**TORRES GRAN CORONAS BLACK LABEL**, Penedés 1983
337	£5.25	**ROUGE HOMME SHIRAZ/CABERNET**, Coonawarra 1985
428	£5.20	**QUINTA DE CAMARATE**, Fonseca, Azeitao 1985
454	£9.20	**TOKAY ASZU 5 PUTTONYOS**, Tokaji 1981
493	£21.90	**QUINTA DO NOVAL 20 YEAR OLD TAWNY PORT**, Douro

| WWI | Woodhouse Wines |

The Brewery, Blandford Forum, Dorset DT11 9LS (0258 52141). Wine-selling arm of the Hall &

Woodhouse Brewery. **Delivery:** free within 80 miles, nationally at cost. **Tastings:** regularly held on the premises. **Discounts:** 5% for collection.

Angus Avery's range of wines is almost precisely what you might expect from a country merchant who tries to keep up with the times. Apart from the range of Bordeaux and Burgundies (including some fairly-priced, un-fashionable 1984s from both regions), there are half a dozen Bulgarians and around 14 wines each from Spain, Italy and Australia. There is little that is eye-catchingly original here, but much that is soundly commendable.

95	£9.85	**CLOUDY BAY CHARDONNAY**, Marlborough 1988
149	£3.30	**CHENIN BLANC**, E & J Gallo 1988
172	£4.85	**JOAO PIRES WHITE TABLE WINE**, Palmela 1988
233	£3.30	**WHITE GRENACHE**, E & J Gallo 1989
287	£6.05	**RAIMAT CABERNET SAUVIGNON**, Lerida 1985
450	£5.34	**DOMAINE DU NOBLE (DEJEAN PERE & FILS)**, Loupiac, Bordeaux 1986
470	£4.10	**AMONTILLADO NAPOLEON**, Hidalgo, Jerez
482	£6.36	**SMITH WOODHOUSE RUBY PORT**, Douro

PWY | Peter Wylie Fine Wines

Plymtree Manor, Plymtree, Cullompton, Devon, EXE15 2LE (088 47 555). Independent merchant specialising in fine old wines **Opening Hours:** 9am-6pm Mon-Fri; 9am-3pm Sat but ring first to check. **Delivery:** free within central London, nationally at cost.

Margaux 1950? Langoa-Barton 1925? Lafite 1914? Brane-Cantenac 1890? All of these, and a great many more like them, appeared in Peter Wylie's May 1990 list - at prices ranging from £90 for the Margaux to £440 for the Lafite. If you think this an outrageous amount to pay for a bottle of wine, just stop and think about the cost of a ticket to Covent Garden, or of dinner for two at Le Gavroche. What you are buying in each of these instances is memories. Mr Wylie is one of the best sources of vinous souvenirs in the world.

YAP | Yapp Bros

The Old Brewery, Water St, Mere, Wilts BA12 6QY (0747 860423). Rhône and Loire specialist. **Opening Hours:** 9am-5pm Mon-Fri; 9am-1pm Sat. **Delivery:** free within 50 miles, nationally at cost. **Tastings:** regularly in-store plus tutored events. **Discounts:** for quantity and collection.

Former dentist Robin Yapp deserves to be made a freeman of at least three French *departements*, in recognition of his almost single-minded devotion to the wines of the Loire and Rhône and, perhaps more specifically, the men and women who make them. A careful reading of the Yapp list and a few mixed cases provide the ideal introductory course to both regions. And when you've learned about those, you could follow Yapp into his new areas of enthusiasm: top class wines from Australia and California.

| 343 | £6.95 | **CROZES HERMITAGE**, Alain Graillot, Rhône 1988 |
| 347 | £6.50 | BREZEME CUVEE EUGENE DE MONTICAULT, Jean-Marie Lombard, Rhône 1985 |

YFW | Yorkshire Fine Wines

Sweethills, Nun Monkton, York, N. Yorks YO5 8ET (0423 330131). Independent merchant., 12 bottle sales only - angled towards the trade, but personal customers welcome. **Opening Hours:**

9.30am-5.30pm Mon-Fri. **Delivery:** free nationally for 5+ cases.**Tastings:** regularly in-store plus tutored events. **Discounts:** on 3+ cases, plus 4% for payment within 7 days.

Do you want to buy a Ponzi Pinot Noir from Oregon? A Pulham St Mary Rivaner from Norfolk? A rosé Burgundy from the Domaine de la Pousse d'Or? A Hamilton Russell Chardonnay from South Africa? Yorkshire Fine Wines is nothing if not aptly named. The range of wines offered by this wholesaler is one of the most impressive in the country. YFW operates from offices rather than a shop, but one can nevertheless browse by proxy, thanks to the satisfyingly fat, beautifully produced wine list, which includes articles by wine writers and merchants. Remember though, that since this is a trade list, VAT has not been included in the prices.

83	**£6.99**	**MITCHELTON RESERVE CHARDONNAY**, Goulburn Valley 1988	
138	**£6.95**	**HUNTERS SAUVIGNON BLANC**, Marlborough 1989	
436	**£10.65**	**RIOJA RESERVA 904**, La Rioja Alta 1976	

A-Z

HOW TO READ THE ENTRIES

Aglianico del Vulture (BASILICATA)[1] Full-bodied, best-known and best DOC red from this region, made from a grape used by the ancient Greeks **79 81 82** 85 88[2] £££[3] Fratelli d'Angelo 85[4] (WCE, L&W)[5]

1 Words that appear in SMALL CAPITALS have their own entry elsewhere in the A-Z.
2 Only those vintages that are good have been listed. The years that appear in bold are ready to drink.
3 Price guide: £ = under £3, ££ = £3-5, £££ = £5-8, ££££ = £8-12, £££££ = £12 and over.
4 This is a recommended example of the wine. Where possible we recommend one of the Guide's 500 wines, in which case it will appear as a number, for example 179.
5 Stockists — for an explanation of merchants' codes, see page 16. If the merchant is not featured in the Guide, its telephone number will appear.

Abboccato (Italy) Semi-dry

Abocado (Spain) Semi-dry

Abfüller/Abfüllung (Germany) Bottler/bottled by

Abruzzi (Italy) Wine region on the eastern coast. Often indifferent TREBBIANO whites. Finer MONTEPULCIANO reds **82 83** 85 88 89 £-££ 387

AC (France) See APPELLATION CONTROLEE

Acetic acid The main constituent of vinegar, this volatile acid (CH_3COOH) features in tiny proportions in all wines. In excess (as a result of careless winemaking) it can turn wine to vinegar.

Acidity Essential natural, balancing component (usually TARTARIC) which gives freshness. In hotter countries (and sometimes in cooler ones) it may be added by the winemaker

Aconcagua Valley (CHILE) Central valley region noted for its CABERNET SAUVIGNON

Adega (Portugal) Winery — equivalent to Spanish BODEGA

Adelaide Hills (Australia) Cool, high-altitude vineyard region, producing top-class RIESLING, but now also growing more fashionable varieties **84 85 86** 87 88 £££-£££££ 9

Aglianico del Vulture (BASILICATA) Full-bodied, best-known and best DOC red from this region, made from a grape used by the ancient Greeks **79 81 82** 85 88 £££ Fratelli d'Angelo 85 (WCE, L&W)

Agricola vitivinicola (Italy) Wine estate

Aguja (LEON) So-called 'needle' wines which owe their slight SPRITZ to the addition of ripe grapes to the fermented wine

Ahr (Germany) Northernmost ANBAUGEBIET, producing light red wines little seen in the UK

Aix-en-Provence (Coteaux d') (S France) Pleasant floral whites and dry rosés, and up-and-coming reds using BORDEAUX and RHONE varieties. A recent AC **80 81 82** 83 85 86 88 89 ££-£££ 259

Albana di Romagna (Italy) Unutterably dull white wine which, for political reasons, was made Italy's first white DOCG, thus making a mockery of the whole Italian system of denominations

Albariño (Spain) Spain's name for the Portuguese ALVARINHO. Produces often dull wine in GALICIA 87 88 £££ Martin Codax (A&A Wines 0483 2746660)

Aleatico (S Italy) Red grape producing sweet, Muscatty, sometimes fortified wines. Gives name to DOCs A. di PUGLIA and A. di Gradoli

Alella (Spain) DO district of CATALONIA, producing better whites than reds **85 86** 87 ££ Marqués de Alella (TAN)

Algeria Formerly a source of coarse, robust reds used to bolster French wine. Reds and rosés from the hilly regions are the most acceptable 85 86 87 88 £-££ Red Infuriator (PD)

Aligoté (BURGUNDY) The region's lesser white grape, making dry, sometimes sharp white wine traditionally mixed with cassis to make KIR. Also grown in the USSR where they think a lot of it 86 87 88 89 ££-£££ Aligoté de Bouzeron 88 (ADN) Bourgogne Aligoté 88 (M&S)

Almacenista (JEREZ) Fine, old, unblended sherry from a single SOLERA ££-£££££ Lustau Almacenista Oloroso (MWW)

Aloxe-Corton (BURGUNDY) COTE DE BEAUNE commune producing slow-maturing reds (including the GRAND CRU Corton) and whites (including Corton Charlemagne). Invariably pricy; variably great 78 79 83 85 87 88 89 £££££ Olivier Leflaive 86 (L&W)

Alsace (NE France) Dry (and occasionally sweeter) whites and pale reds pitched in style between France and Germany and named after grape varieties 83 85 86 87 88 89 £-£££££ 38 41 42 158 160 161 165 167 168 182 192 196

Alto Adige (NE Italy) A.k.a. ITALIAN TYROL and SUD TIROL. DOC for a range of exciting, mainly white, wines, often from Germanic grape varieties by lederhosened German dialect-speaking producers. The few reds — made from the LAGREIN and VERNATSCH — are light and fruity 86 87 88 89 £-££££ Cabernet Riserva, Lageder (AB)

Alvarinho (Portugal) White grape, at its best in VINHO VERDE blends and in the DO Alvarinho de Monção

Amabile (Italy) Semi-sweet

Amador County (California) Region noted for quality ZINFANDEL

Amaro (Italy) Bitter

Amarone (VENETO) Also 'bitter', used particularly to describe RECIOTOS

Amontillado (JEREZ) Literally 'like MONTILLA'. In Britain, medium-sweet sherry; in Spain, dry, nutty wine ££-££££ 465 470 471 474 478

Amoroso (JEREZ) Sweet sherry style devised for the British ££-££££ Sandemans Amoroso (OD)

Amtliche Prüfungsnummer (Germany) Official identification number relating to quality. Appears on all QbA/QmP wines

Anbaugebiet (Germany) Term for eleven large wine regions (eg RHEINGAU). QbA and QmP wines must have their ANBAUGEBIET

Ancenis (Coteaux d') (LOIRE) Light reds and deep pinks from the CABERNET FRANC and GAMAY, and MUSCADET-style whites 87 88 ££ J.Guidon 87 (YAP)

Anjou (LOIRE) Many dry and DEMI-SEC whites, mostly from the CHENIN BLANC. Usually awful rosé but good light claretty CABERNET reds

85 86 87 88 89 £-££££ 117 148

Annata (Italy) Vintage

Año (Spain) Year: preceded by a figure — eg 5 — indicates the wine's age at the time of bottling. Banned by the EC since 1986

AOC (France) See APPELLATION CONTROLEE

AP (Germany) Abbreviation for AMTLICHE PRUFUNGSNUMMER

Appellation Contrôlée(AC/AOC) (France) Designation for 'top quality' wine: guarantees origin, grape varieties and method of production — but not necessarily quality of winemaking

Apremont (E France) Floral, slightly PETILLANT white from skiing country 86 87 88 ££ Les Rocailles P.Boniface (THP UC)

Apulia (Italy) See PUGLIA

Arbois (E France) Light red PINOT NOIRS and dry whites from the JURA, most notably VIN JAUNE £££ Ch d'Arlay 85 (JS)

Ardèche (Coteaux de l') (RHONE) Light country reds, mainly from the SYRAH, and CHARDONNAY made by Burgundians who cannot get enough at home... 85 89 88 89 £-££ 356 358

Asciutto (Italy) Dry

Asenovgrad (BULGARIA) Demarcated northern wine region. Reds from CABERNET SAUVIGNON, MERLOT and MAVRUD 83 85 ££ Asenovgrad Mavrud 83 (MWW)

Assemblage (France) The art of blending wine from different grape varieties in a CUVEE. Associated with BORDEAUX and CHAMPAGNE

Asti (PIEDMONT) Town famous for sparkling SPUMANTE, lighter MOSCATO D'ASTI and red BARBERA D'ASTI 4 171

Astringent Makes the mouth pucker up. Mostly associated with young red wine. See TANNIN

Aszu (HUNGARY) The sweet 'syrup' made from 'nobly rotten' grapes (see BOTRYTIS) used to sweeten TOKAY 79 81 ££-££££ Hungarian State Cellars (MWW THP ADN)

Aubance (Coteaux de l') (LOIRE) Light wines (often semi-sweet) grown on the banks of a Loire tributary 87 88 ££

Aude (Vin de Pays de l') (SW France) Prolific *département* producing much ordinary red, white and rosé. Contains a couple of VDQS reds and rosés 86 87 88 £ 267, 268, 328

Ausbruch (AUSTRIA) Term for wines sweeter than German BEERE-NAUSLESEN but less sweet than TROCKENBEERENAUSLESEN

Auslese (Germany) Sweet wine from selected, ripe grapes usually affected by BOTRYTIS. Third rung on the QMP ladder

Austria Home of tangy, dry white GRUNER VELTLINER, usually drunk within a year of the harvest; of light, fresh PINOT NOIRS and other, sweet Germanic-style whites, including good value dessert styles 81 83 85 87 88 ££-£££ 446

Auxerrois (LUXEMBOURG) Local name for the PINOT GRIS — and the fresh, clean wine it makes here ££ 162

Auxey-Duresses (BURGUNDY) Best known for buttery rich whites but produces greater quantities of raspberryish reds. A slow developer 78 79 83 85 86 87 88 89 £££ Labouré Roi 86 (SAF,M&S)

Avelsbach (MOSEL-SAAR-RUWER) RUWER village producing delicate, light-bodied wines 83 85 86 87 88 89 £££ Avelsbacher Altenberg Riesling 85 Hohe Domkirche (L&W)

Avize (CHAMPAGNE) Fine white grape village

Ay (CHAMPAGNE) Ancient regional capital, growing mainly black grapes 79 82 83 85 88 89 ££££-£££££ Ayala (MWW)

Ayl (MOSEL-SAAR-RUWER) Distinguished SAAR village producing steely wines 73 85 86 87 88 89 ££ Ayler Kupp Riesling 88 (MWW)

Azienda (Italy) Estate

Bacchus White grape, a MULLER-THURGAU x RIESLING cross, making light, flowery wine. Grown in Germany and also England 195

Bad Durkheim (RHEINPFALZ) Chief Rheinpfalz town and source of some of the region's finest whites. Small production of reds **83 85** 87 88 89 ££-£££££ Durkheimer Schenkenbohl Winzergen Bad Durkheim 85 (EP)

Bad Kreuznach (NAHE) Chief and finest wine town of the region, giving its name to the entire lower Nahe **83 85** 87 88 89 ££-£££££ Kreuznacher Kronenberg - Zentralkellerei, Nahe 87 (L&W)

Badacsony (HUNGARY) Wine region particularly renowned for good, full-flavoured whites

Baden (Germany) Southernmost ANBAUGEBIET, largely represented by the huge ZBW cooperative. Wines are among the ripest, fullest and driest in Germany. Rarely classy, but can stand up well to food **83 85** 86 88 89 ££-£££££ 177

Baga (Portugal) One of the country's best, spicily fruity grape varieties — used in BAIRRADA

Bairrada (Portugal) DO wine region south of Oporto, producing dull whites and good value reds, often from the BAGA 75 78 80 83 85 £-£££ 426

Balance Harmony of fruitiness, ACIDITY, alcohol and TANNIN.Balance can develop with age but should also be evident in youth

Balaton (HUNGARY) Wine region producing fair quality reds and whites

Ban de vendange (France) Officially sanctioned harvest date

Bandol (PROVENCE) AOC red and rosé. MOURVEDRE reds are particularly good and spicy. They repay keeping **83 85** 86 87 88 89 £££ Mas de la Rouvière 85 (YAP)

Banyuls (PROVENCE) France's answer to port. Fortified, GRENACHE-based VIN DOUX NATUREL **85 86** 88 ££-£££ 492

Barbaresco (PIEDMONT) DOCG red from the NEBBIOLO grape, with spicy fruit, depth and complexity. Approachable earlier (three to five years) than neighbouring BAROLO **78 82** 85 86 88 89 ££-£££££ 416

Barbera (PIEDMONT) Grape making fruity, spicy, characterful wine (eg B. d'Alba and B.d'Asti), usually with robust acidity. Now grown in California **82 83** 85 86 88 89 ££-££££ 392 388

Bardolino (VENETO) Light and unusually approachable for a traditional DOC Italian red, refreshing with a hint of bitter cherries. Best drunk young **86 87 88** £-£££ 389

Barolo (PIEDMONT) Noblest of DOCG reds, undrinkably dry and tannic when young, but from a good producer and year, can last and develop extraordinary complexity **71 78 80 82** 85 88 89 ££-£££££ 405 411 417

Barossa Valley (Australia) Established wine region north-east of Adelaide, famous for traditional SHIRAZ, 'ports' and RIESLINGS which age to oily richness. CHARDONNAY and CABERNET are now taking over **85 86 87 88** ££-££££ 3 66 77 169 187 191 280 288 310 452 484

Barrique French barrel, particularly in BORDEAUX, holding 225 litres. Term used in Italy to denote barrel ageing 154

Barsac (BORDEAUX) AC neighbour of SAUTERNES, with similar, though not quite so rich, SAUVIGNON/SEMILLON dessert wines 75 76 80 81 83 86 88 89 £££-£££££ Ch Rieussec 83 (WSO)

Basilicata (Italy) Southern wine region chiefly known for AGLIANICO DEL VULTURE and some improving VINI DA TAVOLA 83 85 £-£££ Aglianico del Vulture 85 D'Angelo (WCE)

Bastardo Red grape used widely in port and previously in MADEIRA where there are a few wonderful bottles left. Shakespeare refers to a wine called 'Brown Bastard'

Bâtard-Montrachet (BURGUNDY) Biscuity-rich white GRAND CRU of

CHASSAGNE and PULIGNY MONTRACHET, very fine. Very expensive
78 79 81 82 83 85 86 87 88 89 £££££ Domaine Leflaive 86 (ADN L&W)

Baux-en-Provence (Coteaux des) (S France) Inexpensive, fruity reds,
whites and rosés of improving quality
85 86 88 89 £-£££ Terres Blanches Rosé 89 (WCE)

Beaujolais (BURGUNDY) Light, fruity red from the GAMAY, good chilled
and for early drinking; B.-Villages is better and one of the ten CRUS
better still, taking on pronounced Burgundian characteristics with
age. See B.-VILLAGES, MORGON, CHENAS, BROUILLY, COTE DE BROUILLY,
JULIENAS, MOULIN A VENT, FLEURIE, REGNIE, ST AMOUR, CHIROUBLES
83 85 87 88 89 £-££££ 360

Beaujolais Blanc (BURGUNDY) From the CHARDONNAY, rarely seen under
this name. Commonly sold as ST VERAN 84 85 86 87 88 (M&S)

Beaujolais-Villages (BURGUNDY) From the north of the region, fuller
flavoured and slightly more alcoholic than plain BEAUJOLAIS though
not necessarily from one of the named 'CRU' villages
85 86 87 88 89 £-£££ 359

Beaumes de Venise (RHONE) Sweet, grapy, fortified VIN DOUX NATUREL
from the MUSCAT which are just beginning to make
their appearance in the UK (White) 85 86 87 88 Dom de Coyeux 86
(TH,M&S) (Red) 85 86 88 89 Sainsbury's Beaumes de Venise (JS)

Beaune (BURGUNDY) Reliable commune for soft, raspberry and rose-petal
PINOT NOIR. The walled city is the site of the famous HOSPICES charity
auction. Also (very rare) whites 78 80 82 83 85 88 89 £££-££££ Beaune
Clos des Ursules 1986, Louis Jadot (VW)

Beerenauslese (Germany) Fourth stage in the QMP scale; sweet, luscious
wines from selected ripe grapes (*beeren*), hopefully affected by
BOTRYTIS 76 79 83 85 88 89 ££££-£££££ 459

Bellet (PROVENCE) Tiny AC behind Nice, producing good red, white and
rosé from local grapes including the ROLLE, the Braquet and the Folle
Noir. (Excessively) pricy and rarely seen in the UK
83 85 87 88 £££-££££ Ch de Crémat 87 (YAP)

Bentonite Clay used as a clarifying agent which attracts and absorbs
impurities. Popular as a non animal-derived FINING material

Bereich (Germany) Vineyard area, subdivision of an ANBAUGEBIET. On its
own indicates simple QBA wine, eg NIERSTEINER — finer wines are
followed by the name of a GROSSLAGE subsection and then, better, an
individual vineyard

Bergerac (BORDEAUX/SW) Lighter, often good value alternative to
everyday claret or dry white. Fine sweet MONBAZILLAC
85 86 87 88 89 £-£££ 68 126 240 252 271

Bernkastel (MOSEL-SAAR-RUWER) Town and vineyard area on the
MITTELMOSEL making some of the finest RIESLING (including the
famous Bernkasteler Doktor) and (sadly) a lake of poor quality cheap
wine
76 79 83 85 86 88 89 ££-£££££ 200

Bianco di Custoza (VENETO) Widely exported DOC, a reliable, crisp,
light white from a blend of grapes. A better alternative to most basic
SOAVE 88 89 £-££ Bianco di Custoza, Fraterni Portalupi 88 (WCE)

Bingen Village giving its name to a RHEINHESSEN BEREICH which includes
a number of well-known GROSSLAGEN 76 83 85 88 89 £-£££ 205 212

Biscuity Flavour of biscuits (eg Digestive or Rich Tea) often associated
with the CHARDONNAY grape, particularly in CHAMPAGNE and top-class
mature BURGUNDY, or with the yeast which fermented the wine

Black Muscat Grown chiefly as a table grape, also produces very
mediocre wine — apart from at the Quady winery in California
Quady Elysium Black Muscat 88 (MWW GHS UC)

Blanc de Noirs White (or pink) wine made from black grapes
££££-£££££ Schramsberg (WIN)

Blanc de Blancs White wine, usually sparkling, made solely from white
grapes. In CHAMPAGNE, denotes 100 per cent CHARDONNAY
ChampagneComte de Dampierre (BEN)

Blanquette de Limoux (MIDI) METHODE CHAMPENOISE sparkler, at its best
appley, crisp and clean. Takes on a yeasty, earthy flavour with age
££-£££ Aimery NV (W)

Blauburgunder (AUSTRIA) The PINOT NOIR, making light, sharp reds

Blauer Portugieser Red grape used in Germany and particularly
Austria for light, pale wine

Blaye (Côtes de/Premières Côtes de) (BORDEAUX) Reasonable Blayais
whites and sturdy AC reds. Premières Côtes are better
81 82 83 85 86 88 89 £-£££ 63 261

Bodega (Spain) Winery or wine cellar; producer

Body Usually used as 'full-bodied', meaning a wine with mouth-filling
flavours and probably a fairly high alcohol content

Bommes (BORDEAUX) SAUTERNES COMMUNE and village containing several
PREMIERS CRUS 75 76 79 80 81 83 86 88 89 ££££-£££££ Ch Lafaurie-
Peyraguey 77 (SAF,HUN)

Bonnezeaux (LOIRE) Delicious, sweet whites produced from the CHENIN
BLANC. They last for ever 75 76 83 85 88 89 ££-£££££ 453

Bordeaux (France) Largest quality wine region in France, producing
reds from CABERNET SAUVIGNON, CABERNET FRANC and MERLOT, and dry
and sweet whites from (principally) blends of SEMILLON and
SAUVIGNON
2 67 69 72 88 89 90 239 281 289 295 298 300 306 269 272-275 278 279 283 293
296 299 301 302 305 309 311 318 320 321 322 447 449 450 451 457 458 464

Botrytis *Botrytis cinerea*, a fungoid infection that attacks and shrivels
grapes, evaporating their water and concentrating their sweetness.
Vital to SAUTERNES and the finer German and Austrian sweet wines

Bottle-fermented Commonly found on the labels of US sparkling wines
to indicate the METHODE CHAMPENOISE, gaining wider currency.
Beware though, it can indicate inferior 'transfer method' wines

Bouquet Overall smell, often made up of several separate aromas

Bourg (Côtes de) (BORDEAUX) Inexpensive, fast-maturing, everyday AC
reds with solid fruit; lesser whites 81 82 83 85 86 88 89 £-£££ 156

Bourgueil (LOIRE) Red AC in the TOURAINE area, producing crisp, grassy
100 per cent CABERNET FRANC wines
83 85 86 88 89 ££-£££ Bourgueil Prestige, Sélection Vieilles Vignes, Jacques
Morin 87 (Professional Wine Services 0222 384445)

Bouzeron (BURGUNDY) Village in the CÔTE CHALONNAISE, principally
known for ALIGOTE
85 86 87 88 89 ££-£££ Aubert de Villaine 87 (ADN)

Bouzy Rouge (CHAMPAGNE) Sideline of a black grape village: an often
thin-bodied, rare and overpriced red wine
85 88 ££££-£££££ Georges Vesselle 86 (Jeroboams 071 225 2232)

Braquet (MIDI) Grape variety used in BELLET

Brauneberg (MOSEL-SAAR-RUWER) Village best known in UK for the Juffer
vineyard Brauneberger Juffer Riesling Auslese 88, Weingut H.Kraebs (QMP
Wines 0206 561 766)

Bricco Manzoni (PIEDMONT) Non-DOC red blend of NEBBIOLO and
BARBERA grapes, round and fruity. Drinkable young
79 82 83 85 86 88 89 £££-£££££ Roche dei Manzoni 85 (ADN,BD)

British Wine 'Made' wine from diluted grape concentrate bought in
from a number of countries. Avoid it. ENGLISH wine is the real stuff
— produced from grapes grown in England

Brouilly (BURGUNDY) Largest of the BEAUJOLAIS CRUS producing pure, fruity GAMAY   83 85 87 88 89   ££-££££ 361 362

Brunello di Montalcino Prestigious DOCG red from a SANGIOVESE clone, needs at least five years to develop complex and intense fruit and flavour.   77 81 82 83 85 88   £££-£££££ 415

Brut Dry, particularly of CHAMPAGNE and sparkling wines. *Brut nature/ sauvage/zéro* are even drier   5 8 11 14 20 22 24 25

Bual MADEIRA grape producing a soft, nutty wine, good with cheese   487

Bucelas (Portugal) DO area near Lisbon, best known for intensely coloured yet delicate, aromatic white wines. Rare in Britain

Bugey (E France) SAVOIE district producing a variety of wines, including white ROUSSETTE DE BUGEY from the grape of that name

Bulgaria Country inexorably conquering, one by one, the 'noble' grapes thanks to massive state-aided technology and advice from California. Reliable source of consistent, good value CABERNET SAUVIGNON and MERLOT and making (slower) progress with SAUVIGNON and CHARDONNAY. MAVRUD is the traditional red variety
81 83 84 85 86 87   £-££ 243

Burgenland (AUSTRIA) Wine region bordering HUNGARY, climatically ideal source of fine, sweet AUSLESEN and BEERENAUSLESEN   446

Buttery The rich, fat smell often found in good CHARDONNAY. Sometimes found in wine which has been left on its LEES

Buzbag (TURKEY) Rich, dry red wine which, sadly, is rarely well made and often oxidised

Buzet (Côtes de) (BORDEAUX) AC region adjoining BORDEAUX, producing light claretty reds, and whites from the SAUVIGNON
81 82 83 85 86 88 89   £-££ Sainsbury's Buzet (JS)

Cabernet d'Anjou/de Saumur (LOIRE) Light, fresh, grassy, blackcurranty rosés, typical of their grape, the CABERNET FRANC
83 85 86 87 88 89   £-££ Cabernet de Saumur, Cave des Vignerons de Saumur (TO)

Cabernet Franc Red grape, the CABERNET SAUVIGNON's younger brother. Produces simpler, blackcurranty wines, particularly in the LOIRE and Italy, but plays a more sophisticated role in BORDEAUX, especially in ST EMILION

Cabernet Sauvignon The great red grape of BORDEAUX, where it is blended with MERLOT. The most successful red VARIETAL, grown in every reasonably warm winemaking country   236 238 261 266 267 270 277 282 285-88 290-92 294 297 303 307 310 312 315-17 333 337 400

Cadillac (BORDEAUX) Known for sweet whites (not quite as sweet or fine as SAUTERNES) for drinking young and well-chilled
£-£££ Ch Lardiley 85 (EP)

Cahors (SW France) 'Rustic' BORDEAUX-like reds produced mainly from the local TANNAT and the Cot (MALBEC), full-flavoured and still quite full-bodied, though have lightened recently
82 83 85 86 88 89   £-£££ Dom du Gaudou (ADN)

Cairanne Named COTE DU RHONE village for powerful, sound reds
78 79 82 83 85 88 89   £££ Côtes du Rhône Villages, Cairanne 87, N Thompson (LAY)

Calabria (Italy) The 'toe' of the boot, making little-seen Gaglioppo reds and Greco whites   ££ Librandi (under the 'Ciro' brand) (V&C,WGA)

Campania (Italy) Region surrounding Naples, best known for TAURASI, LACRYMA CHRISTI and GRECO DI TUFO

Cannonau Heady, robust DOC red from SARDINIA
82 83 84 85 86 88   £-££ Tenute Sella & Mosca 84 (WGA)

Canon Fronsac Small AC bordering on POMEROL for sound attractive reds from some good-value PETIT CHATEAUX

78 79 81 82 83 85 86 88 89 ££-£££ Ch de Gazin 82 (L&W) Ch Mazeris (L&W)

Cantenac (BORDEAUX) HAUT MEDOC COMMUNE containing a number of top CHATEAUX including Palmer
    78 79 81 82 83 85 86 88 89 ££-£££££ St Michael Margaux 87 (M&S)

Cantina (Sociale) (Italy) Winery cooperative

Capsule On a wine bottle, the lead or plastic sheath covering the cork

Carbonic Maceration See MACERATION CARBONIQUE

Carcavelos (Portugal) Sweet, usually disappointing fortified wines from a region close to Lisbon. Rare in Britain

Carignan Prolific red grape making usually dull, coarse wine for blending, and classier fare in CORBIERES and FITOU
    £-££ 251 256 262 260

Cariñena (Spain) Important DO of Aragon for rustic reds, high in alcohol. Also some whites
    75 79 82 83 85 88 £-££ Don Mendo, Monte Ducay

Carmignano (TUSCANY) Exciting alternative to CHIANTI, in the same style but with the addition of CABERNET grapes 75 79 82 83 85 88 £££-££££
    Villa di Capezzana 1985 (WCE PD UC) 1986 (WCE TAN UBC)

Carneros (California) Small, cool, high-quality region shared between the NAPA and SONOMA VALLEYS, and producing top-class CHARDONNAY and PINOT NOIR 85 86 87 88 £££-££££ Acacia Pinot Noir (LV) Cuvaison
    Chardonnay 86 (BWS) Saintsbury Pinot Noir/Chardonnay (HHC)

Casa vinicola (Italy) Firm buying and vinifying grapes

Casa (Italy, Spain, Portugal) Firm (company)

Cassis (PROVENCE) Rare, spicy white made from UGNI BLANC, CLAIRETTE and MARSANNE Clos Ste Magdeleine 86 (Francois Sack) (YAP)

Cat's pee Describes the tangy smell often found in typical — and frequently delicious — MULLER-THURGAU and SAUVIGNON

Cava (Spain) Sparkling wine produced by the METHODE CHAMPENOISE, traditionally distinctively 'earthy' but now much improved
    ££-£££ Codorniu Chardonnay (BIC)

Cave (France) Cellar

Cave Cooperative (France) Cooperative winery

Cépage (France) Grape variety

Cerasuolo (ABRUZZI) A pink wine from the MONTEPULCIANO grape, greatly benefiting from newer, cool fermentation techniques
    £££ Valentini 85 (WCE)

Cérons (BORDEAUX) Bordering on SAUTERNES with similar, less fine, but cheaper wines ££ The Society's Cérons (WSO)

Chablis (BURGUNDY) Often overpriced and overrated white, but a truly fine example still has that steely, European finesse that New World CHARDONNAYS have trouble capturing
    78 79 81 85 86 87 88 89 ££-£££££ 60 61

Chai (France) Cellar/winery

Chalonnais/Côte Chalonnaise (BURGUNDY) Increasingly sought-after source of lesser-known, less complex BURGUNDIES — GIVRY, MONTAGNY, RULLY and MERCUREY. Potentially (rather than actually) good value 84 85 86 87 88 89 £-££££ 361

Chambolle-Musigny (BURGUNDY) One of the finest red wine COMMUNES, producing rich, fragrant, deeply flavoured wines. Le Musigny is the GRAND CRU **78 80 83** 85 86 88 89 £££-££££ 376

Champagne (France) In the north-east of France, source of the finest and greatest (and jealously guarded) sparkling wines, from the PINOT NOIR, PINOT MEUNIER and CHARDONNAY grape ££££-£££££ 10-25

Chaptalisation The legal (in some regions) addition of sugar during fermentation to boost a wine's alcohol content

Chardonnay The great white grape of BURGUNDY, CHAMPAGNE and now

the New World. Versatile, classy and as capable of fresh simple charm in Bulgaria as of buttery, hazelnutty richness in MEURSAULT
9 34 35 37 49 53 54 55 56 57 62 66 73 75 76 79 80 81 83 82 84 85 87 91 92 94-100 102-108

Charmat The inventor of the CUVE CLOSE method of producing cheaper sparkling wines

Charta (Germany) Syndicate of RHEINGAU producers using an arch as a symbol to indicate their new dry (TROCKEN) styles

Chassagne-Montrachet (BURGUNDY) COTE DE BEAUNE COMMUNE making grassy, biscuity, fresh yet rich whites and mid-weight, wild fruit reds. Pricy but recommended
78 79 81 83 85 86 88 89 £££-£££££ 'Morgeot', Henri Germain 85 (ADN)

Chasselas Widely grown, prolific white grape making light, often dull fruity wine principally in Switzerland, eastern France and Germany

Château (usually BORDEAUX) Literally 'castle'; practically, vineyard or wine estate

Châteauneuf-du-Pape (RHONE) Traditionally, the best reds (rich and spicy) and whites (rich and floral) from the southern Rhône valley
78 79 80 81 83 85 86 88 89 £££-£££££ 348

Château-Chalon (E France) Speciality JURA AC for a VIN JAUNE of good keeping quality

Château-Grillet (RHONE) Tiny, pricy property, region and APPELLATION producing great VIOGNIER white
86 87 88 £££££ Chateâu-Grillet 1987, 1988 (YAP)

Chef de culture (France) Vineyard manager

Chénas (BURGUNDY) One of the ten BEAUJOLAIS CRUS, the least well-known but worth seeking out 83 85 88 89 £££ Jean-Georges 89 (AF)

Chêne (France) Oak, as in 'FUTS DE CHENE' — oak barrels

Chenin Blanc The white grape of the LOIRE, neutral and with high acidity; can produce anything from bone dry to very sweet, long-lived wines with characteristic honeyed taste. Also grown with success in S Africa, USA and Australia. See VOUVRAY, QUARTS DE CHAUMES, BONNEZEAUX, SAUMUR 121 149 152 155

Cheverny (LOIRE) Light, floral VDQS whites from the SAUVIGNON and CHENIN BLANC
86 87 88 89 £-££ Sauvignon de Cheverny 87, Francois Cazin (L&W)

Chianti (CLASSICO, PUTTO) (TUSCANY) Famous red DOCG, round and extrovert, but of variable quality. The cockerel or cherub insignia of the Classico or Putto growers should indicate a finer wine
79 81 82 83 85 88 ££-££££ 401

Chiaretto (LOMBARDY) Recommendable light red and rosé wines from around Lake Garda £-££ Portalupi 88 (WCE)

Chile Rising (if often old-fashioned) source of CABERNET SAUVIGNON, SAUVIGNON/SEMILLON whites and some experimental CHARDONNAY
81 82 83 84 85 86 88 £-£££ 33 236 270 282

Chinon (LOIRE) CABERNET FRANC-based reds, rosés and whites, light and grassy when young. From a hot summer, reds can age for up to ten years 83 85 86 88 89 ££-£££ Raffault 88 (L&W)

Chiroubles (BURGUNDY) One of the ten BEAUJOLAIS CRUS, drinks best when young and full of almost *nouveau*-style fruit
83 85 87 88 89 £££ Dom Chaysson 'Les Fargues' 87 (L&W)

Chorey-lès-Beaune (BURGUNDY) Modest, warm reds once sold as COTE DE BEAUNE VILLAGES, now beginning to be appreciated
78 80 83 85 86 88 89 £££ Tollot-Beaut 86 (L&W)

Chusclan (RHONE) Named village of COTES DU RHONE with perhaps the best rosé of the area ££ Chusclan Rosé 89, Les Vignerons de Chusclan (BD)

Cinsaut/Cinsault Prolific hot climate fruity red grape with high acidity, often blended with GRENACHE. One of the thirteen permitted varieties of CHATEAUNEUF-DU-PAPE and also in the blend of Château Musar in the Lebanon

Cissac (BORDEAUX) HAUT-MEDOC village close to ST ESTEPHE, producing similar though lesser wines
78 79 81 82 83 85 86 88 89 £££-££££ Chairman's Claret 83 (EP)

Clairette de Die (RHONE) Pleasant, if dull, sparkling wine. The Cuvée Tradition made with MUSCAT is far better; grapy and fresh — like a top-class French ASTI SPUMANTE £££ Archard Vincent (YAP)

Clairette Dull workhorse white grape of southern France

Clare Valley (Australia) Well-established region producing high quality Rieslings which age well. (Look for Tim Knappstein, Lindemans Watervale)

Clarete (Spain) Term for light red wine, frowned on by the EC

Classico (Italy) May only be used on a central, historic area of a DOC, eg CHIANTI CLASSICO, VALPOLICELLA Classico 50 395 401

Climat (BURGUNDY) An individual vineyard

Clos (France) Literally, a walled vineyard — and often a finer wine

Colares (Portugal) DO region near Lisbon for heavy, tannic red wines. The vines are grown in deep sand. Surprisingly hard to find in the UK — even from specialists ££-£££ Chitas Garrafeira 57 (SEL)

Colheita (Portugal) Harvest or vintage

Colle/colli (Italy) Hill/hills

Colli Berici (VENETO) DOC for red and white — promising CABERNETS

Colle Orientali del Friuli (Friuli-Venezia Giulia) Excellent clean, fresh, lively whites from near the Yugoslav border
86 87 88 89 £££ Pinot Grigio Volpe Pasini 87 (WCE)

Colombard White grape grown in SW France principally for distillation into Armagnac, but sometimes blended with UGNI BLANC to make a crisp dry wine. Also planted in Australia and USA, where it is known as 'French Colombard'
£ VdP des Cotes de Gascogne 89 (Grassa) widely available

Commandaria (Cyprus) Traditional, rich, dessert wine with concentrated raisiny fruit £-££ Commandaria St John (WOC)

Commune (France) Small demarcated plot of land named after its principal town or village. Equivalent to an English parish

Condrieu (RHONE) Fabulous, pricy white from the VIOGNIER grape — old-fashioned, full, rich, aromatic wine
84 85 86 87 88 £££££ Guigal 86 (OD) Georges Verny 87 (LNR)

Consejo Regulador (Spain) Spain's administrative body for the enforcement of the DO laws

Consorzio (Italy) Syndicate of producers, often using their own seal of quality

Coonawarra (Australia) Important, southerly and cool climate wine area of South Australia, famed for excellent RIESLINGS, minty CABERNET SAUVIGNON and, more recently, CHARDONNAY
(Red) 82 84 85 86 87 88 (White) 84 86 87 88 ££-£££££ 292 294 303 315

Corbières Highly successful everyday drinking red, of variable quality but at its best full, fruity country wine 85 86 88 89 £-££ 251 156 262

Corked Unpleasant, musty smell, caused by fungus attacking cork

Cornas (RHONE) Dark red from the SYRAH grape, hugely tannic when young but good value for tucking away
76 78 79 82 83 85 88 89 ££££ 354

Corsica (France) Mediterranean island making robust reds, whites and rosés, often high in alcohol
82 83 85 86 88 ££ Les Producteurs Sica Uval (SOB) Domaine Peraldi (BC,WC)

Cosecha (Spain) Harvest or vintage

Costières du Gard (SW France) Good, fruity country reds, lesser-seen whites and rosés Ch St Vincent Costières du Gard 85 (WCE)

Cot The red grape of CAHORS and the LOIRE, also the MALBEC of BORDEAUX £-££ Touraine Cépage Cot 85, Marc Michaud (UC)

Côte de Beaune (Villages) A geographical distinction; with Villages on a label, indicates red wines from one or more of the villages in the Côte de Beaune. Confusingly, wine labelled simply 'Côte de Beaune' comes from a small area around Beaune itself. These (red and white) wines are rare 78 79 83 85 88 89

Côte de Brouilly (BURGUNDY) One of the ten BEAUJOLAIS CRUS; distinct from BROUILLY and often finer. Floral and ripely fruity; will keep for a year or two 83 85 87 88 89 £££ Ch Thivin (ADN) Duboeuf 88/9 (LNR)

Côte de Nuits (BURGUNDY) Northern, and principally 'red' end of the COTE D'OR Cote de Nuits Villages 85, Laboure-Roi (SAF)

Côte des Blancs (CHAMPAGNE) Principal CHARDONNAY-growing area Le Mesnil Blanc de Blancs NV (FWL,RAE,BI)

Côte d'Or (BURGUNDY) Geographical designation for the central, finest slopes running down the region, encompassing the COTE DE NUITS and COTE DE BEAUNE

Côte Rôtie (RHONE) Massive, powerful SYRAH reds from the northern Rhône, very fine, need at least six (better ten) years 76 78 79 82 83 85 88 89 ££££-£££££ 350

Coteaux Champenois (CHAMPAGNE) APPELLATION for the still wine of the area, thin and light 79 82 83 85 88 89 £££££ A.Bonnet (CDV)

Côtes de Provence Improving, good value fruity rosés and whites, and ripe spicy reds 85 86 87 88 89 £-£££ Dom de St Baillou 85, Dom Cuvee de Roudai 86 (BI)

Côtes du Rhône (Villages) Large APPELLATION for warm, fruity, spicy reds both medium and full-bodied, and full spicy reds. Villages, particularly if named, are finer and very good value 83 85 86 87 88 89 £-£££ 327 330 332 334-340

Cotesti (ROMANIA) Easterly vineyards growing some French varieties

Côte(s), Coteaux (France) Hillsides, slopes — prefixed to, e.g. Beaune indicates finer wine

Cotnari (ROMANIA) Traditional white dessert wine, of good repute

Coulure Vine disorder caused by adverse climatic conditions, causing grapes to shrivel and fall

Cream sherry Popular style produced by sweetening an OLOROSO ££-£££ Valdespino (OLS) Benito (CWS)

Crémant (France) In CHAMPAGNE, lightly sparkling. Elsewhere, e.g. Crémant de Bourgogne, de Loire and d'Alsace, METHODE CHAMPENOISE sparkling wines Cremant de Bourgogne, Vire (MWW) Cremant de Cramant, Mumm (OD) 7

Criado y Embotellado (por) (Spain) Grown and bottled (by)

Crianza (Spain) Literally 'keeping' — 'con crianza' means aged in wood

Crisp Fresh, with good acidity

Crozes-Hermitage (RHONE) A few nutty white wines — better known for pleasing SYRAH reds in a light style, which drink young but will keep. Hermitage's kid brother 78 79 82 83 85 88 89 ££-££££ 336 343

Cru artisan Antiquated classification for sub-CRU BOURGEOIS wines

Cru bourgeois (BORDEAUX) Wines beneath the CRUS CLASSES, satisfying certain requirements, which can be good value for money and, in certain cases, better in quality than supposedly classier classed growths 289 295 298 299 305

Cru classé (BORDEAUX) The best wines of the MEDOC are *crus classés*, divided into five categories from first (top) to fifth growth (or *cru*) in

1855. The GRAVES, ST EMILION and SAUTERNES have their own classifications 306 313 319 320 321

Cru grand bourgeois (exceptionnel) An estate-bottled HAUT MEDOC cru bourgeois, which is aged in oak barrels. *Exceptionnel* wines must come from the area encompassing the *crus classés* . Future vintages will not bear this designation, as it has fallen foul of the EC 302

Crusted (port) Affordable alternative to vintage port, a blend of different years bottled young and allowed to throw a deposit 485

Curico (CHILE) Up-and-coming wine region 159 236 270 282

Cuve close (CHILE) The third best way of making sparkling wine, where the wine undergoes secondary fermentation in a tank and is then bottled. Also called the CHARMAT or TANK method

Cuvée Most frequently a blend, put together in a process called ASSEMBLAGE

Cuvée de Prestige What the producer considers a finer blend, or cuvée

Dão (Portugal) DO reds and whites, fairly full. 75 80 83 85 £-££ 426

Dealul Mare (ROMANIA) Carpathian region once known for whites, now producing reds from 'noble' varieties

Dégorgée (dégorgement) The removal of the deposit of inert yeasts from CHAMPAGNE after maturation. See RD

Deidesheim (RHEINPFALZ) Distinguished wine town producing quality, flavoursome RIESLING 83 85 86 88 89 £-££ 194

Demi-sec (France) Medium dry 19 150 156

Deutscher Tafelwein (Germany) Table wine, guaranteed German as opposed to Germanic-style EC TAFELWEIN

Deutches Weinsiegel (Germany) Seals of various colours awarded for merit to German wines, usually present as neck labels

Diabetiker Wein (Germany) Indicates a very dry wine with most of the sugar fermented out (as in a Diät lager), thus suitable for diabetics

DLG (Deutsche Landwirtschaft Gesellschaft) Body awarding medals for excellence to German wines

DO Denominaci/on/ão d'Origen (Spain, Portugal) Demarcated quality area, guaranteeing origin, grape varieties and production standards

DOC(G) Denominazione di Origine Controllata (é Garantita) (Italy) Quality control designation based on grape variety and/or origin. 'Garantita' is supposed to imply a higher quality level but it is not a reliable guide. All BAROLO is DOCG, as is the dull ALBANA DI ROMAGNA

Dolcetto (d'Alba, di Ovada) (PIEDMONT) Red grape making anything from soft, full everyday wine to more robust, long-keeping DOCs 83 85 86 88 £££ 385 404

Dôle (SWITZERLAND) Light reds from the PINOT NOIR and/or GAMAY

Domaine (France) Wine estate, can encompass a number of vineyards 58 65 68 71 140 141 154 173

Dosage The addition of sweetening syrup to CHAMPAGNE, which is dry in its natural state

Douro (Portugal) The great port region and river, producing much demarcated and occasionally good table wines 80 82 83 85 ££ 435 438 480 481 482 483 485 486 488 491 493 494

Doux (France) Sweet

Dumb As in dumb nose, meaning without smell

Duras (Côtes de) (BORDEAUX) Inexpensive whites from the SAUVIGNON, often better value than basic Bordeaux Blanc 87 88 89 £-££ Côtes de Duras Sauvignon 89, Caves des Peyrieres (TH)

Durbach (BADEN) Top vineyard area of this ANBAUGEBIET

Edelfäule (Germany) BOTRYTIS CINEREA, or 'noble rot'

Edelzwicker (ALSACE) Generic name for white wine from a blend of grape varieties, increasingly rare

Eger (HUNGARY) Official wine district best known for 'Bulls' Blood'

Einzellage (Germany) Single vineyard; most precise and often the last part of a wine name, finer by definition than a GROSSLAGE

Eiswein (Germany) The finest QMP wine, made from BOTRYTIS-affected grapes naturally frozen on the vine. Concentrated, delicious, rare but often underpriced. Can only now be made from grapes of BEERENAUSLESE or TROCKENBEERENAUSLESE quality

Eitelsbach (MOSEL-SAAR-RUWER) One of the top two Ruwer wine towns, site of the famed Karthauserhofberg vineyard

Elaborado y Anejado Por (Spain) 'Made and aged for'

Elba (Italy) Island off the Tuscan coast making full, dry reds and whites

Elbling Inferior Germanic white grape

Elever/éléveur To mature or 'nurture' wine, especially in the cellars of the BURGUNDY NEGOCIANTS, who act as *éléveurs*

Eltville (RHEINGAU) Town housing the Rheingau state cellars and the German Wine Academy, producing good RIESLING with backbone

Emerald Riesling (California) Bottom of the range white hybrid grape, at best fresh, fruity but undistinguished

Emilia-Romagna (Italy) Region surrounding Bologna best known for LAMBRUSCO 230

En primeur New wine, usually BORDEAUX — specialist merchants buy and offer wine 'en primeur' before it has been released; customers rely on their merchant's judgement to make a good buy

English wine Produced from grapes grown in England, as opposed to BRITISH WINE, which is made from imported concentrate 179 183 184 186 188 189 190 193 195 210 211 214 219 224 456

Enoteca (Italy) Literally, wine library or, nowadays, wine shop

Entre-Deux-Mers (BORDEAUX) Up-and-coming source of much basic Bordeaux Blanc, principally dry SAUVIGNON 86 87 88 89 £-££ 67 72

Epernay (CHAMPAGNE) Central of Champagne production, where many famous houses are based, such as Mercier, Moët & Chandon, Perrier Jouët and Pol Roger

Erbach (RHEINGAU) Town noted for fine, full, weighty RIESLING, notably from the Marcobrunn vineyard 83 85 86 88 89 £££

Erden (MOSEL-SAAR-RUWER) Northerly village producing full, crisp, dry RIESLING. In the Bernkastel BEREICH, includes the famous Treppchen vineyard 83 85 86 88 89 £££ Erdener Treppchen Riesling Kabinett 86 Bischöflishes Priesterseminar (TAN)

Erzeugerabfüllung (Germany) Bottled by the grower/estate

Espum/oso/ante (Spain/Portugal) Sparkling

Esters Chemical components in wine responsible for a variety of odours, many fruity

Estufa The vats in which MADEIRA is heated, speeding maturity and imparting its familiar 'cooked' flavour

Eszencia (HUNGARY) Essence of TOKAY, once prized for miraculous prpoerties. Now virtually unobtainable 57 68 £££££ State Cellars (ADN)

Etna (Italy) From the Sicilian volcanic slopes, hot-climate, soft fruity DOC reds, whites and rosés. Can be flabby

Fattoria (Italy) Estate, particularly in Tuscany

Fat Has a silky texture which fills the mouth. More fleshy than meaty

Faugères (MIDI) Good, full-bodied AC reds, some whites and rosés, a cut above the surrounding COTEAUX DU LANGUEDOC 81 82 83 85 86 88 89 £-££ L'Estagnon 87 (TH)

Fendant (SWITZERLAND) The CHASSELAS grape and its white wines, so called in the VALAIS area

Fermentazione naturale (Italy) 'Naturally sparkling', but in fact indicates the CUVE CLOSE method

Fining The clarifying of young wine before bottling to remove impurities, using a number of agents including ISINGLASS and BENTONITE

Finish What you can still taste after swallowing

Fino (Spain) Dry, delicate sherry, the finest to aficionados. Drink chilled and drink up once opened ££-££££ 466 472

Fitou (MIDI) Reliable southern AC, making reds from the CARIGNAN grape. Formerly dark and stubborn, the wines have become more refined, with a woody warmth
81 82 83 85 86 88 89 £-££ Dom du Vieux Moulin 81 (MWW)

Fixin (BURGUNDY) Northerly village of the COTES DE NUIT, producing lean, tough, uncommercial reds which can mature splendidly
78 80 82 83 85 88 89 £££-££££ Dom Pierre Gelin 86 (OD)

Flabby Lacking balancing acidity

Flagey-Echezeaux (BURGUNDY) Prestigious red COTE DE NUITS COMMUNE. Echezeaux and Grands Echezeaux are the two superlative GRANDS CRUS 78 80 82 83 85 86 88 89 £££££ Grands Echezeaux, Dom de la Romanée-Conti 82 (ADN,L&W)

Fleurie (BURGUNDY) One of the ten BEAUJOLAIS CRUS, fresh and fragrant as its name suggests. Much admired but the most expensive cru
83 85 87 88 89 £££ 365

Flor Yeast which grows naturally on the surface of some maturing sherries, making them potential FINOS

Flora Grape, a cross between SEMILLON and GEWURZTRAMINER best known in Brown Brothers Orange Muscat and Flora (174)

Folle Blanche Widely planted workhorse white grape, high in acidity. Known as the GROS PLANT in MUSCADET. Some success in California

Folle Noir (MIDI) Grape used to make BELLET

Forst (RHEINPFALZ) Wine town producing great, concentrated RIESLING. Famous for the Jesuitengarten vineyard
75 76 79 83 85 86 88 89 ££-££££ 221

Franciacorta (LOMBARDY) DOC for good, light, French-influenced reds and a noted sparkler, Franciacorta Pinot 83 85 86 88 £-££ 398

Franken (Germany) ANBAUGEBIET making characterful, sometimes earthy, dry whites, traditionally presented in the squat, flagon-shaped 'bocksbeutel' on which the Mateus bottle was modelled
83 85 86 87 88 89 ££-£££ Weingut Hans (BWC)

Frascati (Italy) Cliched dry or semi-dry white from LATIUM, at best soft and clean, more usually dull. Drink within twelve months of vintage
£-££ Colle Gaio, Villa Catone (WGA)

Friuli-Venezia Giulia (Italy) Northerly region containing a number of DOCs and notably successful with MERLOT, PINOT BIANCO and GRIGIO
82 83 85 86 87 88 ££-££££ 59

Frizzante (Italy) Semi-sparkling 2

Fronsac/Canon Fronsac (BORDEAUX) Below ST EMILION, producing comparable but tougher, often robust reds. Canon Fronsac is better and often good value 78 79 81 82 83 85 86 88 £££-££££ Ch la Rivière 85 (HUN) Ch La Rose Cheuvrol 85 (UC)

Frontignan (Muscat de) (PROVENCE) Rich, sweet, grapey fortified wine from the Bandol area in Provence. More forceful (and cheaper) than BEAUMES DE VENISE. Also a synonym for Muscat a Petits Grains ££-£££ Jose Sala (A,MWW)

Frontonnais (Côtes du) (SW France) Up-and-coming, inexpensive red (and some rosé), full and fruitily characterful 85 86 88 89 ££ 235

Fruska Gora (YUGOSLAVIA) Hilly wine region best known for white wines, improving success with French grape varieties

Fume Blanc Name invented by Robert Mondavi for the SAUVIGNON grape, derived from POUILLY BLANC FUME

Adler Fells Fume Blanc 88 (OD) Taltarni Fume Blanc 88 (RD)

Fürmint Eastern European white grape, used for Tokay in Hungary

Füts de Chêne (France) Oak barrels, as in *'elévé en'* ('matured in')

Gaillac (SW France) Light, fresh, good-value reds and whites, the result of an invasion of the Gamay and Sauvignon grapes. Perle is lightly sparkling 85 86 88 89 ££ 357

Galestro (Tuscany) A light, grapey white ££ Antinori 88 (TH)

Gamay The Beaujolais grape, making wine with youthful, fresh, cherry / plummy fruit. Also successful in the Loire 357 358

Gamay Beaujolais A misnamed variety of Pinot Noir grown in California

Gamey Smell or taste reminiscent of hung game

Gard (Vin de pays du) (Midi) Huge Vin de Table producing area with one fair VDQS, Costieres du Gard
85 86 88 89 £-££ Costières du Gard, Domaine St Cyrgues (OD)

Garganega (Italy) Uninspiring white grape used chiefly for Soave

Garrafeira (Portugal) Indicates a producer's 'reserve' wine, selected and given extra ageing 78 80 82 83 85 ££ 424

Gascogne (Côtes de) (SW France) Source of Armagnac and good value fresh and floral whites. Source of our White Wine of the Year in 1989, made by Grassa 87 88 89 27 28 29 248

Gattinara (Piedmont) Red DOC from the Nebbiolo, varying in quality but at least full-flavoured and dry
78 80 82 85 88 89 ££-££££ Riserva Nervi (L&W)

Gavi (Tuscany) Full, dry white from the Cortese grape. Compared to white Burgundy (often for no good reason). Gavi and Gavi di Gavi tend to be creamily pleasant and overpriced
86 87 88 ££ Banfi (AB)

Geelong (Australia) Vine growing area of Victoria, cool climate, well suited to Chardonnay and Pinot Noir. Look for Bannockburn, Idyll and Hickinbotham 370

Geisenheim (Rheingau) Town and the home of the German Wine Institute, the most famous wine school in the world 76 79 83 85 86 ££-££££

Generoso (Spain) Fortified or dessert wine

Gevrey Chambertin (Burgundy) Best known red Cote de Nuits Commune, much exploited but still capable of superb, plummy rich wine from the best vineyards. The Grand Cru is Le Chambertin
78 80 82 83 85 88 89 ££££-£££££ Armand Rousseau 85 (ADN) Burguet 85 (D)

Gewürztraminer White grape making dry, full, fleshy, spicy wine, best in Alsace but also grown in Australasia, Italy, USA and E Europe
158 159-161 163 166-168 207

Gigondas (Rhone) Côtes du Rhône Commune producing reliable, full-bodied, spicy / peppery, blackcurrant reds, best with food
78 79 82 83 85 86 88 89 ££-£££ Jaboulet 86 (OD) Roger Combe 86 (MWW)

Giropalette Machines which, in the Methode Champenoise, automatically perform the task of Remuage

Gisborne (New Zealand) North Island vine growing area since 1920s. Cool, wettish climate, mainly used for whites
85 86 87 89 ££-££££ 49 155 226

Givry (Burgundy) Cote Chalonnaise commune, making typical and affordable, if sometimes unexciting, Pinot Noirs and creamy whites 83 85 88 89 £££ Baron Thenard 85 (LAY)

Graach (Mosel-Saar-Ruwer) Mittelmosel village producing fine wines. Best known for Himmelreich vineyard 83 85 86 88 89 ££ Graacher Himmelreich Riesling Kabinett, Zentralkellerei (TO)

Gran reserva (Spain) A quality wine aged for a designated number of years in wood and only produced in the best vintages

Grand cru (France) The finest vineyards. Official designation in BORDEAUX, BURGUNDY and ALSACE. Vague in Bordeaux and Alsace, but in Burgundy denotes single vineyard with its own AC, eg Montrachet

Grandes marques Syndicate of the major CHAMPAGNE houses

Grave del Friuli (Friuli-Venezia Giulia) DOC for young-drinking reds and whites. CABERNET and MERLOT increasingly successful
85 86 87 88 ££ Cabernet Sauvignon 86, Collavini (WGA)

Graves (BORDEAUX) Large, southern region producing vast quantities of white, from good to indifferent. Reds have a better reputation for quality (Red) 78 79 81 82 83 85 86 88 89 (White) 79 82 83 85 86 87 88 ££-£££££ Ch Fieuzal 86 (HUN)

Greco di Tufo (Italy) From Campania, best-known white from the ancient GRECO grape; dry, characterful southern wine
Mastroberardino 87 (SAS)

Grenache Red grape of the RHONE (the GARNACHA in Spain) making spicy, peppery, full-bodied wine 233 243

Grignolino (PIEDMONT) Red grape and its modest, but refreshing, wine, eg the DOC Grignolino d'Asti 85 86 87 88 ££-£££

Gros Plant (du Pays Nantais) (LOIRE) Light, sharp white VDQS wine from the same region as MUSCADET, named after the grape elsewhere known as the FOLLE BLANCHE
87 88 89 £ Gros Plant Sur Lie 87, Ch de la Noe (WGA)

Groslot/Grolleau Workhorse grape of the Loire, particularly ANJOU, used for white, rose and base wines for sparkling SAUMUR

Grosslage (Germany) Wine district, the third subdivision after ANBAUGEBIET (eg RHEINGAU) and BEREICH (eg NIERSTEIN). For example, Michelsberg is a GROSSLAGE of the Bereich PIESPORT

Gruner Veltliner White grape of AUSTRIA and Eastern Europe, producing light, fresh, aromatic wine 87 88

Gumpoldskirchen (AUSTRIA) Town near Vienna famous for full, rather heady characterful wines 83 85 86 87 ££

Gutedel German name for the CHASSELAS grape

Halbtrocken (Germany) Semi-dry. Rising style intended to accompany food 194

Hallgarten (RHEINGAU) Important town near Hattenheim producing quite robust wines (for Germany)
Hallgartener Schonhell Riesling Green Gold QbA 81, Schloss Volrads (EP)

Haro (Spain) Town at the heart of the RIOJA region, home of many BODEGAS, eg CVNE, La Rioja Alta

Hattenheim (RHEINGAU) One of the greatest Johannisberg villages, producing some of the best German RIESLINGS
76 79 83 85 88 89 ££-££££ Hattenheimer Heiligenberg Riesling Kabinett 85 (HV)

Haut-Médoc (BORDEAUX) Large APPELLATION which includes nearly all of the well-known CRUS CLASSES. Basic Haut-Médoc should be better than plain MÉDOC 78 79 81 82 83 85 86 88 89 ££-£££££ 295 298 299 302

Haut Poitou (LOIRE) Often boring VDQS red but reliable, good value SAUVIGNON and CHARDONNAY whites 85 86 87 88 89 ££ Gamay du Haut Poitou 88 (L&W)

Hautes Côtes de Beaune (BURGUNDY) Sound, soft, strawberry PINOT NOIR from a group of villages 82 83 85 88 89 ££

Hautes Côtes de Nuits (BURGUNDY) Slightly tougher than HAUTES COTES DE BEAUNE, particularly when young
80 82 83 85 88 89 ££-££££ Hautes Côtes de Nuits 1986, M.Gros (MWW)

Hawkes Bay (New Zealand) Major North Island vineyard area
85 86 87 88 89 ££-££££ 40

Hérault (Vin de pays de l') (France) Largest vine growing *département*, producing some 20 per cent of France's wine, nearly all VIN DE PAYS or VDQS, of which COTEAUX DU LANGUEDOC is best known. Also home of the extraordinary Mas de Daumas Gassac where no expense is spared to produce easily the best of France's 'country wines' 86 87 88 89 £-££ 264

Hermitage (RHONE) Top-class, long-lived northern Rhône wines; superb, complex reds and sumptuous, nutty whites. Also Australian name for the SYRAH grape and, confusingly, the South African term for CINSAULT 76 78 79 82 83 85 88 89 ££££-£££££ Chave 86 (OD,YAP,ADN)

Hessische Bergstrasse (Germany) Smallest ANBAUGEBIET, wines rarely seen in the UK

Hochfeinste (Germany) 'Very finest'

Hochgewächs QbA Recent official designation for RIESLINGS which are as ripe as a QMP but can still only call themselves QBA. This from a nation dedicated to simplifying what are acknowledged to be the most complicated labels in the world

Hochheim (RHEINGAU) Village whose fine RIESLINGS gave the English the word 'Hock'
Hochheimer Holle Riesling Kabinett 1987, Domdechant Werner (VW)

Hock English name for Rhine wines, derived from HOCHHEIM in the RHEINGAU
Hattenheimer Wisselbrunnen Kabinett 1985, Schloss Reinhartshausen (OD,HW)

Hospices de Beaune (BURGUNDY) Charity hospital, wines from whose vineyards are sold at an annual charity auction on the third Sunday in November, the prices setting the tone for the COTE D'OR year. Beware that although price lists often merely indicate 'Hospices de Beaune' as a producer, all of the wines are bought at the auction are matured and bottled by local merchants, some of whom are more scrupulous than others

Huelva (Spain) DO of the Estremadura region, producing rather heavy whites and fortified wines

Hungary Country best known for its legendary TOKAY, and Bulls Blood. The source of much 'party wine', particularly OLASZ RIZLING 454

Hunter Valley (Australia) Famous wine region of New South Wales, producing many reds (often from SHIRAZ) and full, fleshy whites from SEMILLON and CHARDONNAY (Red) 82 84 85 86 87 88 (White) 84 85 86 87 88 ££-£££££ 107 291 307

Huxelrebe Minor white grape, often grown in England 183

Hybrid Cross-bred grape, usually *Vitis vinifera* (European) x *Vitis labrusca* (N American)

Hydrogen sulphide Naturally occurring gas given off by especially young red wine, resulting in smell of bad eggs. Often caused by insufficient racking

Imbottigliato nel'origine (Italy) Estate bottled

Imperiale Large bottle containing six litres of wine

Inferno (Italy) LOMBARDY DOC, chiefly red from NEBBIOLO, which needs at least five years ageing

Institut National des Appellations d'Origine (INAO) French administrative body which designates and polices quality areas

Irancy (BURGUNDY) Light reds and rosés made near CHABLIS from a blend of grapes. Little known 82 83 85 88 89 £££ Bourgogne Irancy 1987, Leon Bienvenu (HFW)

Irouléguy (SW France) Pyrenees/Basque area producing white, rosé and slightly better red

Isinglass FINING agent derived from the sturgeon fish

Israel Once the source of appalling wine, but the new-style VARIETAL wines are improving 1985 Cabernet Sauvignon, Gamla (SEL)

Italian Riesling Not the great RHINE RIESLING, but a lesser version, going under many names, and widely grown in Northern and Eastern Europe

Jardin de la France (Vin de pays du) Marketing device to describe VINS DE PAYS from the LOIRE

Jasnières (LOIRE) Rare, sweet CHENIN BLANC wines from TOURAINE
83 85 86 87 88 89 £££ Caves aux Tuffieres 83/85 (YAP)

Jeunes Vignes Term occasionally seen in BURGUNDY, denotes wine from vines too young for their classified destiny, eg CHABLIS

Jerez (de la Frontera) (Spain) Centre of the SHERRY trade, gives its name to entire DO sherry-producing area 465-478

Jeroboam Large bottle containing three litres, usually containing CHAMPAGNE

Jesuitengarten (RHEINGAU) One of Germany's top vineyards 221

Johannisberg (RHEINGAU) Village making superb RIESLING, which has lent its name to a BEREICH covering all of the Rheingau
75 76 79 83 85 88 89 £-£££££ Johannisberger Klaus Riesling Kabinett 87, Schloss Schonborn (HAR)

Johannisberg Riesling Californian name for the RHINE RIESLING
Jekel 87 (OD)

Jug wine American term for quaffable VIN ORDINAIRE

Juliénas (BURGUNDY) One of the ten BEAUJOLAIS CRUS producing classic, vigorous wine which often benefits from a few years in bottle
83 85 87 88 89 ££-£££ Bernard Sante 1989 (OD)

Jumilla (Spain) Improving DO region, traditionally known for heavy, high alcohol wines 82 83 84 85 86 87 £-££ Taja (WSO) Sainsbury's (JS)

Jura (E France) Region containing ARBOIS and SAVOIE, best known for specialities such as VIN GRIS, VIN JAUNE and VIN DE PAILLE
Ch d'Arlay (HAR) Ch Chalon (GNW)

Jurançon (SW France) Dry, spicy white, some rosé and very good sweet wines 86 87 88 89 ££-££££ 36 154

Kabinett First step in German quality ladder, for wines which fulfil a certain sweetness rating. Semi-dry wines
185 203 204 212 213 215 216 221 225

Kaiserstuhl (BADEN) Finest BADEN BEREICH with top villages producing rich, spicy RIESLING from volcanic slopes

Kallstadt (RHEINPFALZ) Village containing the best known and finest vineyard of Annaberg, making luscious, full RIESLING

Kalterersee (Italy) Germanic name for the LAGO DI CALDARO in the SUD TIROL/ALTO ADIGE

Keller/kellerei/kellerabfüllung (German) Cellar/producer/estate-bottled 205 206 207

Keppoch/Padthaway (Australia) New vineyard area north of COONAWARRA 84 85 86 87 88 ££-££££ Lindeman's Padthaway Sauvignon Blanc 1987 (WSO,AUC,UC)

Kerner White grape, a RIESLING cross, grown in Germany and now England 219

Kiedrich (RHEINGAU) Top village high in the hills with some renowned vineyards 75 76 79 83 85 88 89 £-£££££ Kiedricher Sandgrub Riesling Spätlese 83, Dr Weil (TO)

Kir White wine with a dash of cassis syrup, good for disguising a disappointing buy. With sparkling wine (properly CHAMPAGNE), a 'Kir Royale'

Klusserath (MOSEL-SAAR-RUWER) Small village best known in UK for Sonnenuhr and Konigsberg vineyards 76 79 83 85 88 89 £-£££££ 206

Krajina Yugoslavian region noted for its PINOT NOIR
Pinot Noir Krajina 1986 (JEH)

Krems (AUSTRIA) Town and WACHAU vineyard area producing Austria's most stylish Rieslings from terraced vineyards

Kreuznach (NAHE) Northern BEREICH, with fine vineyards around the town of Bad Kreuznach 220

La Mancha (Spain) Over a million acres of vineyard on the central plain. Mostly VIN ORDINAIRE, but with some startling exceptions, for example, the Guide's Wine of the Year in 1989
82 83 85 86 87 88 89· £ 419 422

Labrusca *Vitis labrusca*, the North American species of vine, making wine which is always referred to as 'foxy'. All VINIFERA vine stocks are grafted on to PHYLLOXERA-proof labrusca roots, though the vine itself is banned in Europe

Lacryma Christi (Campania) Literally, 'tears of Christ'; melancholy name for some amiable, light, rather rustic reds and whites. Those from Vesuvio are DOC
85 86 87 88 ££ Lacryma Christi del Vesuvio Bianco 86, Mastroberardino (L&W)

Lago di Caldaro (TRENTINO-ALTO ADIGE) Also known as the KALTERERSEE, making cool, light reds with slightly unripe, though pleasant fruit
85 86 87 88 £-££

Lagrein Red grape grown in the TRENTINO-ALTO ADIGE region making dry, light, fruity DOC reds and rosés

Lake County (California) Vineyard district salvaged by improved irrigation techniques and now capable of some fine wines
84 85 86 87 88 89 ££-£££ Fetzer Cabernet Sauvignon 86 (TO)

Lalande de Pomerol (BORDEAUX) Bordering on POMEROL with similar, but less fine wines. Some good value PETITS-CHATEAUX
78 79 81 83 85 86 88 89 ££-££££ Château les Templiers 1987 (HV)

Lambrusco (EMILIA-ROMAGNA) Famous, rather sweet red fizzy wine, and now some white versions produced for the Anglo-Saxon palate. Variable quality but the best are the dry, Italian-style versions, ideal for picnics 87 88 £-££ 230 498

Landwein (Germany) A relatively recent quality designation — the equivalent of a French VIN DE PAYS from one of eleven named regions (ANBAUGEBIET). Often dry

Langhe (PIEDMONT) A range of hills

Languedoc (Coteaux du) (MIDI) Big VDQS, a popular source of everyday reds from RHONE and southern grapes 84 85 86 87 £-£££££ 264

Laski Riesling/Rizling YUGOSLAV name for poor quality white grape, unrelated to the RHINE RIESLING. Aka WELSCH, OLASZ and Italico

Late-bottled vintage (port) (LBV) Bottled either four or six years after a specific vintage; the time in wood softens them up to be ready to drink younger 483 488

Late Harvest Made from grapes which are picked after the main vintage, giving a higher sugar level ££-£££££ 169 174 217

Latium/Lazio (Italy) The vineyard area surrounding Rome. Avoid most of its Frascati although there are some exciting Bordeaux-style reds
85 86 87 88 £-££ B.Violo Frascati 87 (EP)

Laudun (RHONE) Named village of COTES DU RHONE, with some atypical fresh, light wines and attractive rosés

Layon, Coteaux du (LOIRE) Whites from the CHENIN BLANC grape, slow to develop and long lived. Lots of lean dry wine but the sweet BONNEZEAUX and QUARTS DE CHAUME are superior
75 76 83 85 88 89 ££-£££ 151

Lazio SEE LATIUM

Lean Lacking body

Lebanon Chiefly represented in the UK by the remarkable Chateau Musar, made in BORDEAUX style but from CABERNET SAUVIGNON,

CINSAULT and SYRAH 61 64 67 70 72 78 79 80 81 82 ££-£££££

Lees Or *lies*, the sediment of dead yeasts let fall as a white wine develops. See SUR LIE

Length How long taste lingers in the mouth

Léognan (BORDEAUX) GRAVES COMMUNE containing many of the finest white CHATEAUX 64 70 71 79 83 85 86 88 89 ££-£££££ Ch de Fieuzal (HUN)

Leon (Spain) North-western region producing acceptable dry, fruity reds and whites ££ Palacio de Leon (HUN)

Liebfraumilch (Germany) The most seditious exploitation of the German QbA system — a good example is perfectly pleasant but the vast majority, though cheap, is money down the drain. Responsible for the ruination of the German wine market in the UK
87 88 £ F&W Schmitgen Rheinpfalz (DRI)

Lie(s) See LEES/SUR LIE

Liqueur de Tirage (CHAMPAGNE) The yeast and sugar added to base wine to induce secondary fermentation (bubbles) in bottle

Liqueur d'Expedition (CHAMPAGNE) The sweetening syrup used for DOSAGE

Liquoreux (France) Rich and sweet

Liquoroso (Italy) Rich and sweet

Lirac (RHONE) Confident, peppery, TAVEL-like rosés, though its deep, red-fruit reds are becoming increasingly popular
78 82 83 85 88 89 ££ Lirac 'Les Queyrades' 85, Dom A.Majan (ADN,AB)

Listrac (BORDEAUX) Look out for Châteaux Fourcas-Hosten, Fourcas-Dupré, Chasse-Spleen and Maucaillou
78 79 81 82 83 85 86 88 89 ££-££££

Livermore (Valley) (California) A warm climate vineyard area with fertile soil producing full, rounded whites, including increasingly fine CHARDONNAY Wente Brothers Zinfandel 86 (AB)

Loir (Coteaux du) Clean vigorous whites from a LOIRE tributary; JASNIERES is little seen but worth looking for
83 85 86 87 88 89 £££ Jasnières 'Clos St Jacques' 86, Dom Joel Gigou (ADN)

Loire (France) An extraordinary variety of wines emanate from this area — dry whites such as MUSCADET and the classier SAVENNIERES, SANCERRE and POUILLY FUME; grassy, summery reds; buckets of rosé, some good, mostly dreadful; glorious sweet whites and very acceptable sparkling wines 58 89 117 118 119 120 122 124 125 127 128 131 137 139 132 140-2 145-51 153 156 238

Lombardy (Italy) Milan's vineyard, known mostly for sparkling wine but also for some increasingly interesting reds. See LUGANA 47 398

Loupiac (BORDEAUX) Bordering on SAUTERNES, with similar, but less fine wines 80 81 83 85 86 88 89 ££-£££ 450 451

Luberon (Côtes du) (RHONE) Reds, like light COTES DU RHONE, pink and sparkling wines; the whites CHARDONNAY-influenced. A new APPELLATION and still good value 85 86 87 88 89 £-£££ 232

Ludon (BORDEAUX) HAUT-MEDOC VILLAGE and COMMUNE
78 79 81 83 85 86 88 89 £££-£££££ Ch La Lagune 85 (HUN)

Lugana (LOMBARDY) grown on the shores of Lake Garda, smooth, pungent white wine, a match for food. Lombardy's best wine
87 88 89 ££ 47

Lugny (BURGUNDY) See MACON

Lussac-St-Emilion A satellite of ST EMILION
78 79 81 82 83 85 86 88 89 £££ Ch du Tabuteau (WSO)

Lutomer (YUGOSLAVIA) Wine producing area known mostly for its LUTOMER RIESLING, but now doing good things with CHARDONNAY Lutomer Laski Rizling (AB)

Luxembourg Source of pleasant, fresh white wines from ALSACE-like grape varieties ££-£££ Cuvee de l'Ecusson NV, Bernard Massard (EP)

Lyonnais (Coteaux du) (RHONE) Just to the south of BEAUJOLAIS, making some very acceptable good value wines from the same grapes 85 86 88 89 £-££

Macau HAUT-MEDOC COMMUNE possessing some useful CRUS BOURDEOIS 82 83 85 86 88 89 £££-££££ Villeneuve de Cantemerle 85 (M&S)

Macération carbonique Technique in which uncrushed grapes burst and ferment under pressure of a blanket of carbon dioxide gas, producing fresh, fruity wine. Used in BEAUJOLAIS, South of France and becoming increasingly popular in the New World

Mâcon/Mâconnais (BURGUNDY) Avoid unidentified 'rouge' or 'blanc' on restaurant wine lists. Mâcons with the suffix VILLAGES, SUPERIEUR or PRISSE, VIRE, LUGNY or CLESSE are better and can afford some pleasant, good value CHARDONNAY 85 86 87 88 89 ££-£££ 44 48 54 58

Madeira Atlantic island producing famed fortified wines, usually identified by style: BUAL, SERCIAL, VERDELHO or MALMSEY £££-££££ 487 489 490

Maderisation Deliberate procedure in MADEIRA, produced by the warming of wine in ESTUFAS. Otherwise undesired effect, commonly produced by high temperatures during storage, resulting in a dull, flat flavour tinged with a sherry taste and colour

Madiran (SW France) Heavy, robust country reds, tannic when young but age extremely well 82 85 86 88 89 ££ 263

Maître de chai (France) Cellar master

Malaga (Spain) Andalusian DO producing dessert wines in varying degrees of sweetness, immensely popular in the 19th century £££ Solera Scholtz 1885 (MOR)

Malbec Red grape that plays a cameo role in BORDEAUX but stars in CAHORS, where it is known as the COT or AUXERROIS

Malmsey Traditional, rich MADEIRA — the sweetest style, but with a dry finish £££-££££ 490

Malolactic fermentation Secondary effect of fermentation in which 'hard' malic acid is converted into the softer lactic acid

Malvasia MUSCATTY white grape vinified dry in Italy, but far more successfully as good, sweet traditional MADEIRA 490

Malvoisie (LOIRE) Local name for the PINOT GRIS 87 88 89 ££ J Guindon (YAP)

Manzanilla Dry, tangy SHERRY — a FINO-style wine widely (though possibly mistakenly) thought to take a salty tang from the coastal BODEGAS of SANLUCAR DE BARRAMEDA ££-£££ 473

Marc Residue of pips, stalks and skins after grapes are pressed — often distilled into a woody and unsubtle brandy of the same name, eg Marc de Bourgogne

Marches (Italy) Central region on the Adriatic coast best known for ROSSO CONERO and good, dry, fruity VERDICCHIO whites (Red) 85 86 87 88 (White) 86 87 88 89 ££-££££ 406

Marcillac (SW France) Full-flavoured country reds principally from the Fer grape — may also contain CABERNET and GAMAY Cave de Valady 86 (BD)

Margaret River (Australia) Recently developed cool vineyard area on Western Australia coast, gaining notice for CABERNET SAUVIGNON and CHARDONNAY. Also, Australia's only ZINFANDEL from Cape Mentelle (best known wineries are Moss Wood, Cape Mentelle, Leeuwin, Vasse Felix and Chateau Xanadu) 85 86 87 88 £££-££££ 105 106

Margaux (BORDEAUX) COMMUNE that boasts a concentration of CRUS CLASSES, the most famous being the first growth Château Margaux 78 82 83 84 85 86 88 89 ££-££££ Ch Marquis de Terme 1984 (TO)

Marlborough (New Zealand) Newest but increasingly important wine area, with cool climate making excellent white wines
86 87 88 89 ££-££££ 40 81 95 129 134 135 138 448

Marmandais (Côtes du) (SW France) Uses the BORDEAUX grapes plus GAMAY, SYRAH and others to make a variety of pleasant, inexpensive wines

Marsala Dark, rich, fortified wine from SICILY crucial to a number of recipes, such as zabaglione ££-£££££ Vecchio Samperi, de Bartoli (WCE)

Marsannay (BURGUNDY) Sought-after, delicate pale red and rosé from the PINOT NOIR 83 85 86 87 88 89 £££-££££ Philippe Charlopin 86 (ADN)

Marsanne Along with Roussanne, grape responsible for most whites of the northern RHONE. Also planted successfully in the Goulburn Valley in VICTORIA by Chateau Tahbilk and Mitchelton 85 86 88 78 79

Master of Wine (MW) One of a small number (under 200) who have passed a gruelling set of trade exams

Mavrodaphne Greek red grape and its wine, full-bodied, dark and strong, needs ageing ££ 479

Mavrud (BULGARIA) Traditional red grape and characterful wine

Médoc (BORDEAUX) As a generic term, implies sound, everyday claret to be drunk young. As an area, that region of Bordeaux south of the Gironde and north of the town of Bordeaux 85 86 88 89 £-££ 274 289

Melon de Bourgogne White grape producing a dry, not very exciting wine but can be good in the LOIRE. Also known as MUSCADET (Loire), WEISSBURGUNDER (Germany) and PINOT BLANC (California)
86 118 124 127 128

Mendocino (California) Northern, coastal wine county successfully exploiting cool microclimates to make 'European-style' wines
83 84 85 86 87 88 89 ££-£££ Fetzer Cabernet Sauvignon 86 and Barrel Select Chardonnay 87 (MWW)

Ménétou-Salon (LOIRE) Bordering on SANCERRE making similar, less pricy SAUVIGNON and some PINOT NOIR red
87 88 89 ££-£££ Clos de Marsay 87, Guy Saget (GI)

Mercaptans See HYDROGEN SULPHIDE

Mercurey (BURGUNDY) Good value wine from the Côte CHALONNAISE — tough, full reds worth waiting for, and nutty, buttery whites
83 84 85 86 87 88 89 £££ Michel Juillot 85 (HAR)

Merlot Red grape making soft, honeyed, even toffeed wine with plummy fruit. Used to balance the TANNIC CABERNET SAUVIGNON throughout the MEDOC but the main grape of POMEROL and ST EMILION. Also successful in VENETO, HUNGARY and Australia
243 245 276 284 268 308

Merlot di Pramaggiore (VENETO) Excellent, plummy red wine from the BORDEAUX grape

Méthode Champenoise As a term, now restricted by law to wines from CHAMPAGNE but in effect used by all quality sparkling wines; labour-intensive method where bubbles are produced by secondary fermentation in bottle

Methuselah Same as an IMPERIALE, usually applied to CHAMPAGNE

Meursault (BURGUNDY) Superb white Burgundy; the CHARDONNAY showing off its nutty, buttery richness in mellow, full-bodied dry wine 83 84 85 86 87 88 89 £££-£££££ 112 115

Midi (France) Vast and vastly improved region of southern France, including CORBIERES, ROUSSILLON, LANGUEDOC, MINERVOIS and the VIN DE PAYS departments of GARD, AUDE and HERAULT 17 26 71 170 173 241 245 246 249 250 251 253 255 256 258 259 260 262 267 268 328 442 492 500

Millesime (France) Year or vintage

Minervois (SW France) Suppertime reds, satisfyingly firm and fruity

85 86 87 88 89 £-££ 255

Mis en Bouteille au Château/Domaine (France) Bottled at the estate

Mittelhaardt (RHEINPFALZ) Central and best BEREICH
86 87 88 89 ££ Deidesheimer Hergottsacker (PD)

Mittelmosel (MOSEL-SAAR-RUWER) Middle and best section of the Mosel,
including the BERNKASTEL BEREICH 85 86 87 88 89 £-£££ 200 225 228

Mittelrhein (Germany) Small, northern section of the RHINE. Good
RIESLINGS little seen in the UK 83 85 86 88 89 ££-£££

Moelleux (France) Sweet 154

Monbazillac (SW France) BERGERAC AOC, using the grapes of sweet
BORDEAUX to make improving inexpensive alternatives to SAUTERNES
83 85 86 88 89 ££-£££ Ch Monbazillac 86 (HUN)

Monica (di Cagliari/Sardegna) (Italy) Red grape and wine of SARDINIA
producing dry and fortified spicy wine
£ Monica di Sardegna 86, Cantina Sociale di Dolianova (WCE)

Monopole (France) Literally, exclusive — in BURGUNDY denotes single
ownership of an entire vineyard

Montagne St Emilion (BORDEAUX) A satellite of ST EMILION
83 85 86 88 89 ££-£££ Ch Bertin 85 (MWW)

Montagny (BURGUNDY) Tiny Côte CHALONNAISE COMMUNE producing
good, lean CHARDONNAY, a match for many POUILLY FUISSES
86 87 88 89 £££ Ch de Davenay, Montagny 1er Cru (JS,WWI,VW)

Montalcino (TUSCANY) Village near Siena known for BRUNELLO DI
MONTALCINO

Montepulciano (Italy) Red grape making red wines in central Italy; also
see VINO NOBILE DI MONTEPULCIANO and ABRUZZI 387

Monthélie (Burgundy) Often overlooked COTE DE BEAUNE village
producing potentially stylish reds and whites
84 85 86 87 88 89 £££ Dom Garaudet 84 (LAY)

Montilla (-Moriles) (Spain) DO region producing SHERRY-type wines in
SOLERA systems, often so high in alcohol that fortification is
unnecessary £-££ Dos Reinos Dry Montilla (OD)

Montlouis (LOIRE) Neighbour of VOUVRAY making similar wines
84 85 86 87 88 89 ££-£££ Montlouis Moelleux 85, Berger Frères (L&W)

Montravel (Cotes de) (SW France) Dry and sweet whites from, and
comparable to, BERGERAC ££

Mor (HUNGARY) Hungarian town making clean, aromatic white wine —
Mori Ejerzo

Morey St Denis (BURGUNDY) COTES DE NUIT village which produces
deeply fruity, richly smooth reds, especially the GRAND CRU Clos de
la Roche 82 83 85 86 88 89 £££-£££££ Clos Sorbets 85, J Truchot Martin (HUN)

Morgon (BURGUNDY) One of the ten BEAUJOLAIS CRUS, worth maturing,
when it can take on a delightful chocolate/cherry character 85 86 87
88 89 ££-£££ 364

Morio Muskat White grape grown in Germany making full, fragrant
wine 87 88 89 £-££ 199

Mornington Peninsula (VICTORIA) Some of Australia's newest and most
southerly vineyards which are producing minty CABERNET, tasty,
slightly thin PINOT and fruity CHARDONNAY 84 85 86 87 88 £££ 84

Moscatel de Setúbal (Portugal) Delicious, honeyed fortified dessert
wine from a peninsula south of Lisbon. Ages indefinitely
£££-£££££ 20 year old Moscatel de Setubal, JM Fonseca (HAS)

Moscato The MUSCAT grape in Italy, at its best in fruity, low strength
Spumante wines (eg Moscato d'Asti) or in sumptuous dessert wines
££-££££ 1 171

Moselblumchen Generic light, floral TAFELWEIN from the MOSEL-SAAR-
RUWER, equivalent to the Rhine's LIEBFRAUMILCH

Mosel/Moselle River and loose term for MOSEL-SAAR-RUWER wines, equivalent to the 'HOCK' of the Rhine 85 86 87 88 89 £-£££££ 198

Mosel-Saar-Ruwer (MSR) (Germany) Major ANBAUGEBIET capable of superb RIESLINGS, differing noticeably in each of the three regions 198 200 206 216 222 228 225

Moulin-à-Vent (BURGUNDY) One of the ten BEAUJOLAIS CRUS, big and rich at its best and, like MORGON, benefits from a few years ageing 85 86 87 88 89 ££-£££ Moulin-a-Vent 1989, Jean-Georges (AF)

Moulis (BORDEAUX) Red wine village of the HAUT-MEDOC; like LISTRAC, some good value lesser growths 82 83 85 86 88 89 ££-£££ Ch Maucaillou 83 (JS)

Mourvèdre RHONE grape usually found in blends. Increasingly popular

Mousseux (France) Sparkling. *Vin mousseux* tends to be cheap and unremarkable

Mousse The bubbles in CHAMPAGNE and sparkling wines

Mudgee (Australia) High altitude, isolated region undergoing a revival; previously known for robust, often clumsy wines. (Botobolar and Montrose are probably the best known producers) 76 344

Müller-Thurgau Workhouse white grape, a RIESLING/SYLVANER cross, making much unremarkable wine in Germany. Very successful in England 201 210

Murfatlar (ROMANIA) Major vineyard and research area having increasing success with the CHARDONNAY
Murfatlar Gewürztraminer 1983 (Touchstone Wines, tel:0562 74678)

Murray River Valley (Australia) Vineyard area between VICTORIA and NEW SOUTH WALES producing much wine which ends up in boxes 73

Murrumbidgee (Australia) Area formerly known for bulk dessert wines, now improving irrigation and vinification techniques to make good table wines and some stunning BOTRYTIS-affected sweet wines (look out for de Bortoli)

Muscadet (LOIRE) Large area at the mouth of the Loire making dry, appley white wine from the Melon de Bourgogne. Clean and refreshing when good but varies in quality. SUR LIE is best 86 87 88 89 £-£££ 86 118 124 127 128

Muscat à Petits Grains A.k.a. FRONTIGNAN, the grape responsible for MUSCAT DE BEAUMES DE VENISE, ASTI SPUMANTE, Muscat of Samos, Rutherglen Muscats and Alsace Muscats 169 170 444

Muscat of Alexandria Grape responsible for MOSCATEL DE SETUBAL, Moscatel de Valencia and some sweet South Australian offerings. Also known as Lexia and not of as high quality as MUSCAT A PETITS GRAINS 173

Muscat Ottonel Muscat variety grown in Middle and Eastern Europe
Murfatlar Muscat Ottonel 1979 (HUN)

Must Unfermented grape juice

MW See MASTER OF WINE

Nackenheim (RHEINHESSEN) Village in the NIERSTEIN BEREICH, producing good wines but better known for its debased GROSSLAGE, Gutes Domtal

Nahe (Germany) ANBAUGEBIET producing underrated wines, gaining in popularity, combining delicacy of flavour with full body 87 88 89 £-£££ 197 201 220 223 229

Naoussa (Greece) Rich, dry red wines from the Xynomavro grape ££-£££ Ch Pegasus, Marlovitis (GWC)

Napa Valley (California) Established, top-quality vineyard area. 'Napa' is the American-Indian word for 'plenty'
(Red) 84 85 86 87 88 (White) 85 86 87 88 89 ££-££££ 108 312 317

Navarra (Spain) Northern DO, traditionally for rosés and heavy reds

but now producing some good value, exciting wines to rival RIOJA
81 82 85 86 87 £-£££ Gran Feudo 87, Bodegas J Chivite (SAF)

Nebbiolo Great red grape of Italy, producing wines which are slow to
mature, then richly complex and fruity, epitomised by BAROLO
396 405 411 416 417

Négociant (-Eléveur) A BURGUNDY merchant who buys, matures and
bottles wine

Négociant-manipulant (NM) Buyer and blender of wines for CHAM-
PAGNE, identifiable by NM number mandatory on label

Neusiedlersee (AUSTRIA) Burgenland region on the Hungarian border,
best known for its fine, sweet, BOTRYTISED wines

New South Wales (Australia) Major wine-producing state including the
HUNTER VALLEY, MUDGEE and MURRUMBIDGEE regions

New Zealand New, super-star nation, especially successful with
Sauvignon Blanc

Nierstein (RHEINHESSEN) Village and, with PIESPORT, BEREICH best known
in the UK. Some very fine wines, obscured by the notoriety of Gutes
Domtal 86 87 88 89 £-£££ 204 213

Noble rot Popular term for BOTRYTIS CINEREA

Nose Smell

Nouveau New wine, most popularly used of BEAUJOLAIS

Nuits St Georges (BURGUNDY) COMMUNE producing the most claret-like
of red Burgundies, properly tough and lean when young but glorious
in age 82 83 84 85 88 89 £££-£££££ 374

NV Non-vintage, meaning a blend of wines from different years

Oaky Flavour imparted by oak casks. 'Woody' is usually less complimentary

Ockfen (MOSEL-SAAR-RUWER) Village producing the best wines of the
Saar-Ruwer BEREICH, especially from the Bockstern vineyard
££-£££££ Max Grunhauser Herrenberg Riesling (LV)

Oechsle (Germany) Sweetness scale used to indicate the amount of
sugar in grapes or wine

Oenology The study of the science of wine

Oidium Insidious fungal infection of grapes, causing them to turn grey
and shrivel

Olasz Rizling (HUNGARY) Term for the inferior WALSCHRIESLING

Oloroso (JEREZ) Style of full-bodied SHERRY, dry or semi-sweet
££-£££ 467 468 476

Oltrepó Pavese (Italy) Red and white LOMBARDY DOC for a range of
wines from varying grape varieties
££ Barbera 86, Fugazza; Bonarda 86, Fugazza (WCE)

Opol (YUGOSLAVIA) Source of dry, light, slightly spicy rosé

Oppenheim (RHEINHESSEN) Village in NIERSTEIN BEREICH best known,
though often unfairly, for Krotenbrunnen vineyard. Elsewhere
produces soft wines with concentrated flavour 76 83 85 86 88 89 ££-
££££ Oppenheimer Kreuz Riesling Kabinett 87, Carl Koch (MWW)

Orange Muscat Yet another member of the MUSCAT family, best known for dessert
wines in California and VICTORIA 174 175

Oregon (USA) Fashionable wine-producing state best known in the UK
for its skill with the PINOT NOIR
83 85 86 87 88 ££-£££££ Bethel Heights Pinot Noir 86 (HFW)

Oriahovitza (BULGARIA) Major source of reliable CABERNET SAUVIGNON and
MERLOT 81 84 85 £-££ Reserve Cabernet Sauvignon 83 (MWW,TH)

Orvieto (Italy) White Umbrian DOC responsible for a quantity of dull
wine. Orvieto CLASSICO is better
86 88 89 ££-£££££ Antinori 'Campo Grande' Orvieto Classico 88 (MWW)

Oxidation The effect (usually detrimental) of oxygen on wine

Pacherenc-du-Vic-Bilh (SW France) Dry or fairly sweet white wine, a speciality of MADIRAN growers. Very rarely seen, worth trying ££-£££

Padthaway See KEPPOCH/PADTHAWAY

Pais CHILEAN red grape and its wine

Palate The taste of a wine

Palatinate (Germany) Region (ANBAUGEBIET) now known as the RHEINPFALZ

Pale Cream (Spain) A slightly sweetened FINO sherry ££ Duke of Wellington Pale Cream (SEL)

Palette (PROVENCE) AC rosé, a cut above the average. Also some fresh white 82 83 85 86 88 89 ££-£££££ Ch Simone 84 Rouge, 85 Rosé (LV,YAP)

Palo Cortado (Spain) A rare SHERRY-style wine pitched between an AMONTILLADO and an OLOROSO ££-££££ The Wine Society Palo Cortado (WSO)

Palomino White grape responsible for all fine SHERRIES

Pasado/Pasada (Spain) Term applied to old or fine FINO and AMONTILLADO sherries £££-££££ Manzanilla Pasada, Hidalgo (TAN) Tanners Very Fine Old Sanlucar Amontillado (TAN)

Passe-Tout-Grains (BURGUNDY) Wine made of two-thirds GAMAY, one third PINOT NOIR 83 85 86 87 88 89 ££-£££ Henri Jayer (THP) Rion 87 (M&V)

Passito (Italy) Sweet, raisiny wine, usually made from sun-dried grapes ££££-£££££ Moscato Passito di Pantelleria, Bukkuram, de Bartoli (WCE)

Pauillac (BORDEAUX) The home of Châteaux Lafite, Latour and Mouton — the epitome of full-flavoured, blackcurranty Bordeaux, very classy (and expensive) wine 78 79 81 82 83 85 86 88 89 £££-£££££ 306 309 313 319 320

Pécharmant (SW France) In the BERGERAC area, producing light, Bordeaux-like reds. Worth trying 83 85 86 88 89 Ch de Tiregand 86 (JS)

Pedro Ximenez (PX) White grape dried in the sun for sweet, curranty wine, added to produce the mellower SHERRY styles. Also produces one very unusual wine at de Bortoli's in Australia £££-£££££ Garvey's Pedro Ximenez (MWW) de Bortoli Botrytis Pedro 82 (BWS)

Pelure d'Oignon 'Onion skin'; distinctive, orangey tint of some rosé

Peñafiel (Portugal) District producing some good VINHOS VERDES 86 88 89 Paco de Teixero 88 (WCE)

Penedés Largest DOC of Catalonia, with improving table wines following the example of the Torres BODEGA. More importantly, the centre of the CAVA industry 82 83 85 86 87 ££-£££££ 314 429

Perlé/Perlant (France) Lightly sparkling

Perlwein (Germany) Sparkling wine

Pernand-Vergelesses (BURGUNDY) COMMUNE producing rather clumsy, jammy reds but fine whites, some of the best buys on the COTE D'OR 82 83 85 88 89 £££-££££ Dom Chanson 1er Cru 'Les Vergelesses' (TAN)

Pessac-Léognan (BORDEAUX) GRAVES COMMUNE recently given its own APPELLATION and containing all the better Graves CHATEAUX.

Pétillant (FRANCE) Lightly sparkling

Petit Chablis (BURGUNDY) Less fine than plain CHABLIS 85 86 87 88 89 ££-£££ Dom Gallois (FWC)

Petit château (BORDEAUX) Minor property, beneath CRU BOURGEOIS

Petite Sirah Red grape, a.k.a. Durif in the MIDI and grown in California. Has nothing to do with the SYRAH Inglenook Petite Syrah 81 (PD)

Petrolly A not unpleasant overtone often found in mature RIESLING

Pfalz (Germany) See RHEINPFALZ

Phylloxera Dastardly louse that wiped out Europe's vines in the 19th century. Foiled by the practice of grafting VINIFERA vines onto American roots. Isolated pockets of pre-PHYLLOXERA vines still exist, eg in Chile and Portugal

Piave (VENETO) Area covering a number of DOCs, including reds made from a Bordeaux-like mix of grapes 82 83 85 86 87 88 89

Piedmont (Italy) North-western region producing many fine and popular wines, including BAROLO, BARBARESCO, OLTREPO PAVESE, ASTI SPUMANTE and DOLCETTO D'ALBA
1 4 171 231 385 388 392 296 404 405 410 411 416 417

Piemonte See PIEDMONT

Piesport (MOSEL-SAAR-RUWER) With its GROSSLAGE Michelsberg, infamous for dull wine. Try one of its single vineyards — Guntersley or Goldtröppchen — for something eminently more drinkable
83 85 86 87 88 89 £-£££

Pineau d'Aunis Red grape grown in the LOIRE valley for red and rosé

Pineau de la Loire The CHENIN BLANC grape

Pineau des Charentes (SW France) White grape juice fortified with cognac — best chilled as an aperitif or with cheese ££-£££

Pinot Blanc Not as classy or complex as its PINOT NOIR or CHARDONNAY relations, but fresh and adaptable. Widely grown, at its best in ALSACE (Pinot d'Alsace) and the ALTO ADIGE in Italy (as Pinot Bianco). In California, a synonym for MELON DE BOURGOGNE 41 43 59

Pinot Chardonnay Misleading name for the PINOT BLANC

Pinot Gris White grape of uncertain origins, making full, rather heady, spicy wine. Best in ALSACE (also known as TOKAY D'ALSACE) and Italy (as Pinot Grigio) Pinot Gris Reserve Spéciale 85, Schlumberger (L&W)

Pinot Meunier Dark pink-skinned grape that plays an unsung but major role in CHAMPAGNE, where it is the most widely planted variety. In England, it is grown as the Wrotham Pinot or Dusty Miller; Bests in VICTORIA produce a VARIETAL wine from it

Pinot Noir Noble red grape with the unique distinction of being responsible for some of the world's greatest red (BURGUNDY) and sparkling white (CHAMPAGNE) wine. Also grown, with varying degrees of success, in the New World
9 366 367 368 370 371 373 377 378 382

Pinotage Red grape, a PINOT NOIR-CINSAULT cross used in South Africa and New Zealand Montana Cabernet Sauvignon/Pinotage (OD)

Pomerol (BORDEAUX) With ST EMILION, the Bordeaux for lovers of the MERLOT grape, which predominates in its rich, soft, plummy wines. Château Pétrus is the big name 78 81 82 83 85 86 88 89 £££-£££££ 318

Pommard (BURGUNDY) COMMUNE blessed with a higher proportion of old vines, making slow to mature, then solid and complex reds
83 85 88 89 £££-£££££ 375

Port (Portugal) Fortified, usually red wine made in the upper Douro valley. Comes in several styles; see TAWNY, RUBY, LBV, VINTAGE, CRUSTED and WHITE

Pouilly Fuissé (BURGUNDY)Fine white beloved by the Americans, with consequent vastly inflated prices. Other Mâconnais wines are affordable and often its equal, unless you can stretch to the finest examples
85 86 87 88 89 ££-£££££ 93 142

Pouilly Fumé (LOIRE) Distinguished, elegant SAUVIGNON BLANC with classic gooseberry fruit and 'flinty' overtones
86 87 88 89 ££-£££££ 137 145 146

Pourriture noble (France) BOTRYTIS CINEREA or NOBLE ROT

Prädikat (Germany) Short for QUALITATSWEIN MIT PRADIKAT (QMP), the best German wines

Precipitation The 'throwing' or, more properly, dropping, of a harmless deposit, usually of tartrate crystals, in white wine

Premier Cru Principally a BURGUNDY ranking, indicates wines second only to a GRAND CRU 60 61

Primeur (France) New wine, eg BEAUJOLAIS Primeur

Propriétaire (-Récoltant) (France) Vineyard owner-manager

Prosecco (VENETO) Dry and sweet sparkling wines, less boisterous than ASTI SPUMANTE and often less fizzy
££-£££ Sainsbury's Prosecco (JS) De Col Prosecco (BI)

Provence (France) Southern region producing a quantity of honest, country wine with a number of minor ACs. Rosé de Provence should be dry and fruity with a hint of peppery spice 241 259 332

Puisseguin St Emilion (BORDEAUX) Satellite of ST EMILION 82 83 85 86 88 89
££-££££ Ch la Croix de Mouchet (BI) Ch Durand Laplagne 85 (ADN,TAN)

Puligny-Montrachet Aristocratic white COTE D'OR COMMUNE that shares the Montrachet vineyard with CHASSAGNE
78 79 81 83 85 86 88 89 ££££-£££££ 110

Putto (Italy) As in CHIANTI PUTTO, wine from a consortium of growers who use the cherub ('*putto*') as their symbol

Puttonyos (HUNGARY) The measure of sweetness (from 1 to 6) of TOKAY

PX See PEDRO XIMENEZ

QbA (Germany) *Qualitätswein bestimmter Anbaugebiet*: basic quality German wine meeting certain standards from one of the eleven ANBAUGEBIET, eg RHEINHESSEN

QmP (Germany) *Qualitätswein mit Prädikat*: QBA wine with 'special qualities' subject to rigorous testing. The QMP blanket designation is broken into five sweetness rungs, from KABINETT to TROCKENBEERE- NAUSLESEN plus EISWEIN

Qualitätswein (Germany) Loose 'quality' definition to cover QBA and QmP wines, whose labels will carry more informative identification of their exact status

Quarts de Chaume (LOIRE) Luscious but light sweet wines, uncloying, ageing beautifully, from the COTEAUX DU LAYON
76 83 85 88 89 £££-££££ Ch de l'Echarderie 85 (YAP)

Quincy (LOIRE) Dry white SAUVIGNON, lesser-known and often good value alternative to SANCERRE or POUILLY FUME 85 86 87 88 89 ££-£££ 131

Quinta (Portugal) Vineyard or estate, particularly in port where 'single quinta' wines are much prized 491 493

Racking The drawing off of wine from its LEES into a clean cask or vat

Rainwater (MADEIRA) Light, dry style of Madeira popular in the US

Rancio Term for the peculiar yet prized oxidised flavour of certain fortified wines, particularly in France and Spain

Rasteau (RHONE) Southern village producing sound, spicy reds with rich berry fruit, and some dessert wine 83 85 86 89 ££-£££ 331

RD (CHAMPAGNE) Récemment DEGORGEE — a term invented by Bollinger to describe their delicious vintage Champagne, which has been allowed a longer than usual period on its LEES. Other producers make their own versions but may not call them 'RD' £££££ Bollinger RD (HAR)

Recioto (Italy) Sweet or dry alcoholic wine made from semi-dried, ripe grapes 397 409 461

Récoltant-manipulant (RM) (CHAMPAGNE) Individual winegrower and blender, identified by mandatory RM number on label

Récolte (France) Vintage, literally 'harvest'

Refosco (FRIULI-VENEZIA GIULIA) Red grape and its DOC wine, dry and full-bodied, benefits from ageing

Régisseur In BORDEAUX, the manager of a CHATEAU and its wine production

Regnié (BURGUNDY) Recently created the tenth BEAUJOLAIS CRU
85 86 87 88 89 ££-£££ 363

Reichensteiner Hybrid white grape popular in England

Reims (CHAMPAGNE) Capital town of the area, base of many GRANDES MARQUES, eg Krug, Roederer **79 82 83 85** £££-£££££

Remuage (CHAMPAGNE) Part of the METHODE CHAMPENOISE, the gradual turning and tilting of bottles so that the yeast deposit collects in the neck ready for DEGORGEMENT

Reserva (Spain) Indicates the wine has been aged for a number of years specific to the DO 74 431

Réserve (France) Legally meaningless, as in 'Réserve Personelle', but implying a wine selected and given more age 16 83 188 193 284 317

Residual sugar Tasting term for wines which have retained sugar not converted to alcohol by yeasts during fermentation

Retsina (Greece) Distinctive dry white wine characterised by a piney, resinated flavour 157

Reuilly (LOIRE) White AC for dry SAUVIGNONS, good value alternatives to Sancerre. Some spicy PINOT rosé **85 86 87** 88 89 ££-£££ 132

Rheingau (Germany) Produces the finest German RIESLINGS of the eleven ANBAUGEBIETE, some extremely expensive **83 85** 88 89 £-£££££

Rheinhessen (Germany) Largest of the eleven ANBAUGEBIET, producing fine wines but better known for LIEBFRAUMILCH and NIERSTEINER **83 85 88** 89 £-£££££ 176 180 203-205 212 213 218 495 497

Rheinpfalz (Gemany) Formerly known as the Palatinate, southerly ANBAUGEBIET noted for riper, spicier RIESLING **83 85 88** 89 £-£££££ 178 185 194 202 207-209 215 221 227 257 459

Rhine Riesling/Rheinriesling Widely used name for the noble RIESLING grape 181

Rhône (France) Rich, round, warm, spicy reds from the GRENACHE and SYRAH, mostly underappreciated and hence undervalued. Some highly prized (and rightly so) rich, peachy, nutty wines **83 85 86 88** 89 £-£££££ 6 232 323-326 329-331 334 336 340-343 347 348 350-354 378

Ribatejo (Portugal) DO area north of Lisbon making much white wine and good, full-bodied reds, especially GARRAFEIRAS 82 83 85 £-£££ 141

Ribera del Duero (Spain) Northern DO region bordering Portugal, source of VINHO VERDE-type whites and newer stylish reds 82 83 85 86 ££-£££££ 427 437 Pesquera (C&B)

Riesling The noble grape producing Germany's finest offerings, ranging from light, floral everyday wines to the delights of the BOTRYTIS-affected sweet wines, which still retain their freshness after several years. Also performs well in ALSACE, California and the BAROSSA/ EDEN VALLEY (Australia) 182 185 187 191 192 196 212 215 217 218 221- 223 255-259 448 455

Riesling Italico See ITALIAN RIESLING

Rioja Alavesa (Spain) Minor subregion of the RIOJA area, with some fine reds 81 82 85 86 87 ££-£££££ 63 74 434 Contino Reserva 85 (ADN)

Rioja Alta (Spain) The best subregion of the RIOJA area 81 82 84 85 86 87 ££-£££££ 430 432 433 436

Rioja Baja (Spain) Largest subregion of the RIOJA area, producing less fine wines, most of which are blended with wine from the Alta and Alavesa regions 81 82 85 86 87

Ripasso (Italy) VALPOLICELLA which, having finished its fermentation, is pumped into fermenting vessels recently vacated by RECIOTO and AMARONE, causing a slight refermentation. This increases the alcohol and body of the wine 399

Riquewihr (ALSACE) Town and COMMUNE noted for RIESLING Riesling d'Alsace 86, Marcel Deiss (WC,BD)

Riserva (Italy) DOC wines aged for a specified number of years

Rivaner The MULLER-THURGAU grape with reference to its RIESLING/SYLVANER parents

Rivesaltes (Muscat de) (MIDI) Grapey, fortified dessert wine, lighter and more lemony than that of BEAUMES DE VENISE
££-£££ Muscat de Rivesaltes, Dom Bresson (ADN)

Rolle (MIDI) Variety used to make BELLET

Romania Traditionally making sweet reds and whites, but trying to develop drier styles from classic European varieties
£-£££ Sainsbury's Romanian Pinot Noir (JS)

Rosato (Italy) Rosé

Rose d'Anjou (LOIRE) Widely exported, usually dull pink from the CABERNET FRANC. Semi-sweet but getting drier
Marks & Spencer Rosé d'Anjou (M&S)

Rosé des Riceys (CHAMPAGNE) Rare and delicious AC still rosé from the PINOT NOIR £££ Bonnet 85 (CDV)

Rosso Conero (Italy) Big DOC red from the MARCHES, from the MONTEPULCIANO and SANGIOVESE grapes with a hint of bitter, herby flavour. Needs five years 406

Roussillon (Côtes du) (MIDI) Sturdy red wines, soft amber-coloured whites and some rosé. Pleasant country wines, but not always worthy of their AC. Côtes du Roussillon Villages is better
86 87 88 89 £-££ 249

Rubesco di Torgiano (UMBRIA) Popular red DOC
82 83 85 88 ££-£££££ Torgiano Riserva Monticchio 79, Lungarotti (ADN,WSO)

Ruby Cabernet (California) A cross between CABERNET SAUVIGNON and CARIGNAN producing big, fruity wines which tend to lack subtlety

Ruby (port) Cheapest, basic port; young, blended, sweetly fruity wine
480 481 482

Rudesheim (RHEINGAU) Tourist town producing, at their best, rich and powerful RIESLINGS 85 88 89 197

Rueda (Spain) DO for clean dry whites and a traditional, FLOR growing sherry-type wine 82 84 85 86 £-£££ Marques de Griñon 89 (HAS)

Rufina (TUSCANY) Subregion of the CHIANTI DOC
81 83 85 86 88 ££-£££££ Chianti Rufina 86, Villa de Vectrice (ADN,WCE)

Ruländer German name for the PINOT GRIS grape

Rully (BURGUNDY) COTE CHALONNAISE COMMUNE, the 'poor man's Volnay'. Much white is destined for Crémant de Bourgogne
£££-££££ Faiveley 86 (J&B)

Ruppertsberg (RHEINPFALZ) Top-ranking village with a number of excellent vineyards making vigorous, fruity RIESLING
83 85 88 89 Ruppertsberger Geisbohl Riesling Kabinett 85, Burklin-Wolf (L&W)

Russia See USSR

Russian River Valley (California) Cool vineyard area north of SONOMA and west of NAPA

Rust (AUSTRIA) Wine centre of BURGENLAND, famous for Ruster AUSBRUCH, sweet white wine

Rutherglen (Australia) VICTORIA wine area on the MURRAY RIVER noted for rich, MUSCATTY dessert and port-style wines, and for incredibly tough reds £££-£££££ 441 443

Saar (Germany) Tributary of the MOSEL river 83 85 86 87 88 89 ££-££££

Sablet (RHONE) A named COTES DU RHONE village
Sablet Cotes du Rhone Villages 1982, Chamfort (WH,LHV)

Sacramento Valley (California) Another name for the CARNEROS region

St Amour (BURGUNDY) One of the ten BEAUJOLAIS CRUS, tends to be light and delicately fruity 83 85 86 87 88 89 ££-£££ Portenin (ADN)

St Aubin (BURGUNDY) Underrated COTE D'OR VILLAGE for reds and rich, flinty, nutty whites, affordable alternatives to MEURSAULT

81 83 85 86 87 88 89 £££ 151

St Bris (Sauvignon de) (BURGUNDY) Burgundy's only VDQS, an affordable alternative to SANCERRE from the CHABLIS region **86 87** 88 89 ££ 130

St Chinian (SW France) AC in the COTEAUX DU LANGUEDOC producing mid-weight, good-value wines ££ Dom de Soulie 86 (HFW)

St Emilion (BORDEAUX) COMMUNE for soft, MERLOT-dominated claret. Its lesser satellite neighbours — LUSSAC, PUISSEGUIN, etc — often prefix the name with theirs **78 79** 81 82 83 85 86 88 89 ££-£££££ 293 301 322

St Estèphe (BORDEAUX) Northern MEDOC COMMUNE, often a shade more rustic than its neighbours, tough when young but very long-lived **78 79** 81 82 83 85 86 88 89 ££-£££££ Ch Cos d'Estournel 85 (J&B)

St Georges St Emilion (BORDEAUX) Satellite of ST EMILION **78 79** 81 82 83 85 86 88 89 ££-£££ Ch Macquin-St-George 85 (MWW)

St Joseph (RHONE) Vigorous, fruity reds from the northern Rhône, with the spice of the SYRAH. Generally good value **78 79** 82 83 85 88 89 £££-£££££ 342 Le Grand Pompée 88, Jaboulet (JS)

St Julien (BORDEAUX) Aristocratic MEDOC COMMUNE producing classic rich wines, full of cedar and deep, ripe fruit **78 79** 81 **82 83** 85 86 88 89 £££-£££££ 296 321

St Nicolas de Bourgueil (LOIRE) Summery, lightly fruity CABERNET FRANC, needs a warm year to ripen its raspberry fruit **83 85 86** 87 88 89 ££ Les Gravières 87, J-P Mabileau (MWW)

St Péray (RHONE) AC for full-bodied, still white and METHODE CHAMPENOISE sparkling wine £££

St Pourçain (Central France) The local wine of Vichy, AC for red, white and rose

St Romain (BURGUNDY) High in the hills of the HAUTES COTES DE BEAUNE, a village producing undervalued fine whites and rustic reds **83 85 86** 87 88 89 £££ Barolet 87 (TO)

St-Véran (BURGUNDY) Affordable alternative to POUILLY FUISSE, delicious young. Head and shoulders above its MACONNAIS neighbours **83 85 86** 88 89 £££-££££ Marcel Vincent (EP)

Sainte Croix-du-Mont (BORDEAUX) Neighbour of SAUTERNES, with comparable though less fine wines **83 85** 86 88 89 ££-£££ 445 449

Sakar (Mountain) (BULGARIA) Source of much of the best CABERNET SAUVIGNON **81** 84 85 ££ Sakar Mountain Cabernet, Vinimpex (MWW)

Samos (Greece) Aegean island producing sweet, fragrant, golden MUSCAT once called 'the wine of the Gods' ££-£££ 440

Sancerre (LOIRE) Much exploited AC, but at its best the epitome of elegant, steely dry SAUVIGNON. Quaffable pale reds and rosés from the PINOT NOIR **86 87** 88 89 ££-£££ 139 140 141

Sangiovese The red grape of CHIANTI, used elsewhere but not to such great effect

Sanlúcar de Barrameda (Spain) Town neighbouring JEREZ, centre of production for MANZANILLA sherry

Santenay (BURGUNDY) Pretty white CHARDONNAYS and good, though occasionally rather clumsy, reds from the southern tip of the COTE D'OR **82 83** 85 86 £££-£££££ 369

Sardinia (Italy) Good, hearty, powerful reds, robust whites and a number of interesting DOC fortified wines 384 403

Saumur (LOIRE) White and rosé METHODE CHAMPENOISE sparklers which are reliably clean and appley, fresh fruity whites plus reds and pinks made from CABERNET FRANC ££-£££££ 5 119 120

Saumur Champigny (LOIRE) Crisp, refreshing CABERNET FRANC red; like BEAUJOLAIS, serve slightly chilled **85 86** 88 89 ££-£££ Clos Rougeard 86 (HFW)

Sauternes (BORDEAUX) Nobly rich, honeyed dessert wines, SAUVIGNON and SEMILLON blends, properly BOTRYTIS-affected. Worth splashing out on 83 86 88 89 £££-£££££ 458 460 464

Sauvignon (Sauvignon Blanc) White grape making gooseberry-fruity wine with a steely backbone, classically elegant in fine LOIRE but equally successful in the New World, particularly New Zealand 77 116 122 123 129 130 133 134 135 136 138 143 144

Savagnin Jura variety used for VIN JAUNE and blended with CHARDONNAY for ARBOIS. Also, confusingly, the Swiss name for the GEWURZTRAMINER

Savennières (LOIRE) Fine, rarely seen, vigorous and characterful whites, very long-lived. Coulée de Serrant and La Roche aux Moines are the top names 82 83 84 85 86 88 89 £££-££££ La Roche Aux Moines 86 (LV)

Savigny-lès-Beaune (BURGUNDY) Rarely seen whites and delicious plummy/ raspberry reds, at their best can compare with neighbouring BEAUNE 82 83 85 86 87 88 89 £££-£££££ 372

Savoie (E France) Mountainous region best known for crisp, floral whites such as APREMONT, Seyssel and Crépy

Scharzhofberg (MOSEL-SAAR-RUWER) Top-class Saar vineyard, producing quintessential RIESLING Scharzhofberger Kupfergrube Riesling Kabinett 86, Reichsgraf von Kasselstadt (EP)

Schaumwein (Germany) Low-priced sparkling wine

Scheurebe White grape, RIESLING SYLVANER cross, grown in Germany and in England, where it imparts a grapefruity tang

Schloss (Germany) Literally 'castle', often (as in CHATEAU) designating a vineyard or estate

Schlossbockelheim (NAHE) Village giving its name to a large Nahe BEREICH, producing elegant, balanced Riesling. Best vineyard: Kupfergrube ££-£££ Schlossbockelheimer Kupfergrube Riesling QbA 83/85 (Staatliche Weinbaudomanen) (RAE)

Schluck (AUSTRIA) Generic term for a light, blended white wine from the WACHAU

Sciacarella (CORSICA) Corsican red grape variety, making smooth, aromatic, RHONE-style wine 85 86 Domaine Peraldi, Clos du Cardinale (BD,WC)

Second label (BORDEAUX) Wines produced principally by Bordeaux CHATEAUX which, because of the youth of the vines or a lessening of quality in a particular year, are sold under a 'second' name 301 309

Sec/secco/seco (France/Italy/Spain) Dry

Sekt (Germany) Not dry, but sparkling wine. Only the prefix 'DEUTSCHER' guarantees German origin

Sélection de Grains Nobles (ALSACE) Equivalent to German BEERENAUSLESEN: rich, sweet BOTRYTISED wine from selected grapes 168

Sémillon White grape blended with the SAUVIGNON in BORDEAUX to give fullness — vinified separately in the New World, particularly in the HUNTER VALLEY, produces fat, savoury, peachy-buttery wine 31 39 40 49 64 77 82

Sercial Grape used for MADEIRA, making the driest and some say the finest wines 489

Servir frais (France) Serve chilled

Setúbal See MOSCATEL DE SETUBAL 172 423 425 428

Sèvre-et-Maine (Muscadet de) (LOIRE) Demarcated area producing a cut above plain Muscadet. (Actually, it is worth noting that this 'higher quality' region produces the vast majority of each Muscadet harvest) ££ 86 127 128

Seyval blanc Hybrid grape, a cross between French and American vines, successful in eastern US and England Thames Valley Vineyard 88 (HFW)

Shiraz The Syrah grape in Australia 297 333 337 338 339 345 346 355

Sicily (Italy) Best known for Marsala, but produces a variety of unusual fortified wines, also much sturdy 'southern' table wine 386 393

Sin crianza (Spain) Not aged in wood

Skin contact The longer the skins are left in with the juice after the grapes have been crushed, the greater the Tannins and the deeper the colour

Soave (Veneto) Irredeemably dull white wine; the best one can hope for is that it is fresh and clean. Soave Classico is better, single vineyard versions are best. Sweet Recioto di Soave is delicious 86 87 88 89 £-£££££ 46 50 397 461

Solera Sherry-ageing system, a series of butts containing wine of ascending age, the older wine being continually 'refreshed' by the younger

Somlo (Hungary) Ancient wine district, now source of top-class whites. See Furmint

Sonoma Valley (California) Region containing some of the state's top wineries, subdivided into the Sonoma, Alexander and Russian River Valleys and Dry Creek 92 136 166

Spanna (Italy) In Piedmont, the Nebbiolo grape, main ingredient of Barolo Spanna del Piemonte 87, A Vallana (MWW,GHW)

Spätburgunder The Pinot Noir in Germany Spätburgunder 86, Lingenfelder (WCE)

Spätlese (Germany) Second step in the QmP scale, late-harvested grapes making wine a notch drier than Auslese 205 208 218 220 222 227 228

Spritz Slight sparkle or fizz. Also Petillance

Spritzig (Germany) Lightly sparkling

Spumante (Italy) Sparkling

Stalky or stemmy Flavour of the stem rather than of the juice

Steely Refers to young wine with evident acidity. A compliment when paid to Chablis and dry Sauvignons

Steen Grape grown widely in South Africa, thought to be the Chenin Blanc of the Loire

Structure All the component flavours fit well together. A young wine with structure should age well

Suhindol (Bulgaria) Source of good reds, particularly Cabernet Sauvignon 84 85 £-££ 243

Sulfites (America) American term now featuring as a labelling requirement alerting those suffering from an (extremely rare) allergy to the presence of sulphur compounds

Supérieur (Bordeaux) Technically meaningless in terms of discernible quality, but denotes wine with 1-2 per cent more alcohol 281 300

Superiore (Italy) As in France, indicates a degree or two more alcohol but not necessarily finer wine

Sur lie 'On its Lees', most commonly seen of Muscadet, one of the few wines that benefits from ageing with its own dead Yeasts 86 127

Süssreserve (Germany) Unfermented grape juice used to bolster sweetness and fruitiness in German and English wines, in a process known as back-blending

Swan River (W Australia) Well-established but not generally too exciting vineyard area. (Best known wines come from Houghton and Evans and Tate) 52

Switzerland Produces, in general, enjoyable but expensive light, floral wines for drinking when young Chicla Trevelin 1987 (TAN)

Sylvaner/Silvaner White grape, originally from Austria but adopted by other European areas, particularly Alsace, as a prolific yielder of young, crisp, quaffable wine 42 202

Syrah The red RHÔNE grape, an exotic mix of ripe fruit and spicy, smokey, gamey, leathery flavours. Skilfully adopted by Australia where it is called SHIRAZ or HERMITAGE 345 346 350-355

Tafelwein (Germany) Table wine. Only the prefix 'DEUSTCHER' guarantees German origin

Tannat Rustic French grape variety used in CAHORS

Tannin Astringent component of red wine which comes from the skins, pips and stalks and helps the wine to age

Tarry Red wines from hot countries often have an aroma and flavour reminiscent of tar. The SYRAH grape in particular exhibits this characteristic

Tartrates Harmless white crystals that are often deposited by white wines in the bottle

Tasmania (Australia) Up-and-coming area with great potential which is producing more than adequate CHARDONNAY, PINOT NOIR and CABERNET SAUVIGNON. (Look out for Heemskerk, Moorilla, Piper's Brook) Piper's Brook Chardonnay 87 (BWS)

Tastevin The silver BURGUNDY tasting cup. Much adopted as an insignia by vinous brotherhoods *(confréries)* and much used as ashtrays by wine buffs. The Chevaliers de Tastevin organise an annual tasting of Burgundies; successful wines may bear an ugly *Tastevinage* label

Taurasi (CAMPANIA) Big red from the AGLIANICO grape, needs years to soften. Develops a characteristic cherryish taste 83 85 88 ££-£££ Aglianico del Vulture (WGA)

Tavel (RHÔNE) Spicy, peppery, characterful dry rosé, usually (wrongly) said to age well 85 86 87 88 89 ££ Maby (BLS)

Tawny (port) Either ruby port that has been barrel-matured to mellow and fade or a cheap blend of RUBY and WHITE PORT. Examples with an indication of their age (eg 10-year-old) are the real thing 493

Tempranillo (Spain) The red grape of RIOJA, whose sturdy fruit is a match for the vanilla/oak flavours of barrel-ageing 429

Tenuta (Italy) Estate or vineyard 51

Terlano/Terlaner (TRENTINO-ALTO-ADIGE) Northern Italian village/its wines, usually fresh and crisp and carrying the name of their grape variety 87 88 89 £-££££ Cabernet Riserva 85, Lageder (WCE)

Teroldego (TRENTINO-ALTO-ADIGE) Dry reds, quite full-bodied with lean, slightly bitter berry-like flavours 83 85 86 87 88 £-££ 391

Tête de Cuvée (France) A producer's finest wine, or the one he is proudest of

Thouarsais (Vin de) (LOIRE) VDQS for a soft, light red from the CABERNET FRANC and whites from the CHENIN BLANC ££ Vin de Thouarsais Rouge 1989, M Gigon (YAP)

Tinta Negra Mole Versatile and widely used MADEIRA grape, said to be a distant cousin of the PINOT NOIR

Tocai White grape and its wines of northern Italy, of Venetian origin 87 88 89 £-££££ Friulano 87, Schioppetto (WCE)

Tokay (HUNGARY) Legendary dessert wine made only from NOBLE ROT-affected grapes 76 79 81 £££-£££££ 454

Tokay d'Alsace See PINOT GRIS 38 164 165

Toro (Spain) Region on the Portuguese border lying on the DOURO producing up-and-coming wines £-££ Sainsbury's Toro 85 (JS)

Toscana See TUSCANY

Touraine (LOIRE) Area encompassing the ACs CHINON, VOUVRAY and BOURGUEIL, also an increasing source of quaffable VARIETAL wines — SAUVIGNON, GAMAY DE TOURAINE etc 122

Touriga (Nacional) Red port grape, also seen in the New World

Traminer Alternative name for the GEWURZTRAMINER grape, particularly in Italy and Australia

Trebbiano Much appreciated and widely planted white grape in Italy, though less vaunted in France where it is called the UGNI BLANC TREBBIANO D'ABRUZZO 1989 (WCE)

Trentino-Alto Adige (Italy) Northern wine region variously known as the Italian Tyrol or Süd Tirol. Cool, fresh VARIETAL wines, non-Italian in style and often with Germanic labels 86 87 88 89 £-££££ 34 55 56 390 391 394 400

Tricastin (Coteaux du) (RHONE) Southern Rhône APPELLATION, emerging as a source of good value, soft, peppery/blackcurranty reds 323 324 329

Trittenheim (MOSEL-SAAR-RUWER) Village whose vineyards are said to have been the first in Germany planted with RIESLING, making soft, honeyed wine 76 79 83 85 86 88 89 ££-££££ 446

Trocken (Germany) Dry

Trockenbeerenauslese (Germany) Fifth rung of the QMP ladder, wine from selected dried grapes, with concentrated sugar and usually BOTRYTIS-affected. Only made in the best years, rare and expensive

Trollinger The German name for the Black Hamburg grape, used in Wurttemburg to make light red wines

Tunisia Best known for dessert MUSCAT wines

Turkey Producer of big, red, often oxidised table wine which is rarely seen in the UK

Tursan (Vin de) (SW France) MADIRAN VDQS whose big, country reds are most likely to be seen in the UK

Tuscany (Italy) Major wine region, the famous home of CHIANTI and some of the more intractable reds, BRUNELLO DI MONTALCINO and VINO NOBILE DI MONTEPULCIANO 111 304 407 408 412 413 414 418

Ugni Blanc Undistinguished white grape of southern France — comes into its own as the TREBBIANO in Italy, particularly in TUSCANY 65

Ull de Llebre (Spain) Literally 'hare's eye' — a pink wine from the TEMPRANILLO in Catalonia

Ullage Space between surface of wine and top of cask or, in bottle, cork. The wider the gap, the greater the danger of OXIDATION

Umbria (Italy) Central wine region, best known for white ORVIETO 86 87 88 89 ££-££££ Orvieto Classico Muffa Nobile 86,Az Ag Barberani (WGA) Orvieto Classico Campo Grande 88, Antinori (MWW)

USSR A vast wine producer, exporting very little to the UK except heavy Crimean reds and sweet red and white 'Champanski'; horrible or amusing depending on your point of view

Utiel-Requeña (Spain) DO of VALENCIA, producing heavy reds widely used for blending and some of Spain's best rosé

Vacanzay (LOIRE) Near CHEVERNY, making comparable whites, light, clean and rather sharp

Vacqueyras (RHONE) COTES DU RHONE VILLAGE and COMMUNE producing fine, full-bodied, peppery reds 83 85 86 87 88 89 ££-£££ 341

Valais (SWITZERLAND) Vineyard area on the upper RHONE, making good FENDANT (CHASSELAS) and some reds Fendant Pierrafeu 87

Valdepeñas (Spain) LA MANCHA DO striving to refine its rather hefty, alcoholic reds and whites 78 81 82 83 84 86 87 £-££ 421

Valencia (Spain) Produces quite alcoholic red wines and also MOSCATEL DE VALENCIA. Can your fridge afford not to have a bottle? 439

Valle d'Aosta (Italy) Small wine-producing area between PIEDMONT and the French/Swiss border

Valpolicella (VENETO) Light red very similar in composition to BAR-

DOLINO; should be nuttily pleasant but more often, in UK, is rather dull. It really is worth paying more for a bottle of AMARONE or RECIOTO **78 79 81 83 85 86 88 £-£££££ 383 395 409**

Valréas (RHONE) Peppery and inexpensive red AOC **83 85 86 88 89 ££**

Valtellina (LOMBARDY) Red DOC from the NEBBIOLO grape, of variable quality but improves with age Grumello 84 (WGA)

Varietal A wine made from and named after a single grape variety, eg California CHARDONNAY, GAMAY DE TOURAINE

Vaucluse (RHONE) COTES DU RHONE region producing much rosé and good reds from certain villages, eg VACQUEYRAS

VDQS (France) *Vin Délimité de Qualité Supérieur*; official designation for wines better than VIN DE PAYS but not fine enough for an AC. Source of much good value everyday drinking

Vecchio (Italy) Old

Vegetal Often used of SAUVIGNON BLANC and CABERNET FRANC, like 'grassy'. Frequently complimentary

Velho/velhas (Portugal) Old, as of red wine

Veltliner See GRUNER VELTLINER

Vendange (France) Harvest or vintage

Vendange Tardive (France) Particularly in ALSACE, wine from late harvested grapes, usually fairly sweet
Gewürztraminer Vendange Tardive 83, Caves de Bennwihr (THP)

Vendemmia (Italy) Harvest or vintage

Vendimia (Spain) Harvest or vintage

Venegazzú (VENETO) Remarkably good VINO DA TAVOLA from the CABERNET SAUVIGNON, almost claret-like. Needs five years
Venegazzú della Casa 1984, Conte Loredan (VW,TAN,UBC)

Veneto (Italy) North-eastern wine region, the home of SOAVE, VALPOLICELLA and BARDOLINO **46 50 94 383 389 395 397 399 409 461 462**

Ventoux (Côtes du) (RHONE) Improving source of everyday, country reds **86 87 88 89 £-££ 326**

Verdelho White grape used for MADEIRA and WHITE PORT **52**

Verdicchio (Italy) White grape seen as a number of DOCs in its own right; in UMBRIA, a major component of ORVIETO **86 87 88 89 £-££ 70**

Verduzzo (FRIULI-VENEZIA GIULIA) White grape making a dry and a fine AMABILE style wine in the COLLI ORIENTALI

Vermentino (LIGURIA) The dry white wine of the Adriatic. Best drunk *in situ* with seafood

Vernaccia White grape making the Tuscan DOC Vernaccia di San Gimignano and Sardinian Vernaccia di Oristano, at best with a distinctive, characterful flavour **86 87 ££-££££** Vernaccia di San Gimignano 'Terre di Tufo' 88, Teruzzi e Puthod (WCE)

Victoria (Australia) Huge variety of wines from the liqueur MUSCATS of Rutherglen to the peppery SHIRAZES of Bendigo and the elegant CHARDONNAYS of the YARRA VALLEY. See these, plus MURRAY RIVER, MORNINGTON PENINSULA, GOULBURN VALLEY, GEELONG and PYRENEES **174**

VIDE (Italy) A marketing syndicate formed by enterprising producers for their estate wines

Vieilles Vignes (France) Wine from a producer's oldest, best vines **137**

Vigneto (Italy) Vineyard

Vignoble (France) Vineyard; vineyard area

Villages (France) The suffix *'villages'* after e.g. Côtes du Rhône or Mâcon generally indicates a slightly superior wine (in the way that CLASSICO does in Italy)

Vin de Corse Corsican wine

Vin de garde (France) Wine to keep

Vin de paille (JURA) Speciality of the region; rich and sweet golden wine from grapes laid out and dried on straw mats

Vin de pays (France) Lowest/broadest geographical designation, simple country wines with certain regional characteristics
26-30 116 170 173 234 258 264 267 268 328 356

Vin de table (France) Table wine from no particular area

Vin doux naturel (France) Fortified dessert wines, best known as the sweet, liquorous MUSCATS of the south, eg BEAUMES DE VENISE

Vin gris (France) Chiefly from ALSACE and the JURA, pale rosé from red grapes pressed before, not after, fermentation

Vin jaune (JURA) A speciality of ARBOIS, golden yellow, slightly oxidised wine, like a dry SHERRY

Vin santo (Italy) Powerful white dessert wine from grapes dried on the vine and after picking, especially in TUSCANY. Takes its name from a similar style from the Greek island of Santorini
75 80 84 £££££ Capezzana 84, Avignonesi 80 (WCE)

Vinho Verde (Portugal) Young, literally 'green' wine, confusingly, red or pale white often tinged with green. At best delicious, refreshing, slightly fizzy 87 88 89 £-££ Sainsbury's Vinho Verde (JS)

Vinifera Properly *Vitis vinifera*, the species name for all European vines

Vino de pasto (Italy) Table wine

Vino da tavola (Italy) Table wine, but the DOC quality designation net is so riddled with holes that many superb wines slip through with merely this modest APPELLATION

Vino Nobile di Montepulciano (TUSCANY) CHIANTI in long trousers; truly noble, made from the same grapes, ages superbly to produce a traditional full red 80 82 83 85 86 88 £££-££££ 402

Vino novello (Italy) New wine from this year's harvest, equivalent to French NOUVEAU

Vintage (port) Only produced in 'declared' years, the best quality, aged in wood then in bottle for many years. Must be decanted
Vintage Port 78 (JS)

Vintage Champagne Made from the wine of a single, good 'declared' year

Vintage character (port) Inexpensive alternative to vintage, a blend of more than one year's wines. Pleasant enough £££-££££ 486

Viognier The white grape of the finest RHONE wines (eg Condrieu) making richly nutty, peaches-and-cream wine
Ch Grillet 86 (YAP) Condrieu 86, George Vernay (LNR)

Viticulteur (-Propriétaire) (France) Vine grower/vineyard owner

Viura (Spain) White grape of the RIOJA region

Vivarais (Côtes du) (PROVENCE) Light southern reds, a great deal of fruity rosé and occasional fragrant, light whites

Volnay (BURGUNDY) Great village, producing reds of such delicacy and complexity that tasters wax lyrical 78 80 82 83 85 88 89 ££££-£££££ 1er Cru Les Caillerets 1986, Pousse d'Or (D,GH,GHS)

Vosne Romanée (BURGUNDY) Buy only the finest when you can afford it from the village which numbers Romanée-Conti among its many grand names 78 80 82 83 85 88 89 ££££ 379 380

Vougeot (BURGUNDY) COTE DE NUITS COMMUNE comprising the famous GRAND CRU Clos de Vougeot and a great number of growers of varying skill 78 80 82 83 85 88 87 ££££-£££££ 381

Vouvray (LOIRE) White wines from the CHENIN BLANC, from clean, dry whites and refreshing sparklers to astonishingly long-lived, sweet wines with massive acidity
69 71 75 76 83 85 88 89 ££-£££££ 8 150 153 156

Wachau (AUSTRIA) Major wine region, producing some superlative

RIESLING from steep, terraced vineyards

Wachenheim (RHEINPFALZ) Full, rich, unctuous RIESLING in all but the best years from this superior MITTELHAARDT village **75 76 79 83 85** 86 88 89 ££-£££££ Wachenheimer Gerumpel Riesling Kabinett 85, Burklin Wolf (HAR)

Walschriesling/Welschriesling The ITALIAN RIESLING or OLASZ RIZLING, unrelated to the great RHINE RIESLING, but widely cultivated in Central Europe

Washington State US region to watch, particularly for its RIESLING and MERLOT

Wehlen (MOSEL-SAAR-RUWER) MITTELMOSEL village making fresh, sweet, honeyed wines, particularly from the Sonnenuhr vineyard **75 76 79 83 85** 86 88 89 ££-£££££ 225

Weingut (Germany) Wine estate

Weinkellerei (Germany) Cellar or winery

Weissburgunder The PINOT BLANC in Germany and Austria 220

White port (Portugal) Made from white grapes, an increasingly popular dry or semi-dry aperitif

Wiltingen (MOSEL-SAAR-RUWER) Distinguished Saar village, making elegant, slaty wines. Well-known for the Scharzhofberg vineyard **76 79 83 85** 86 88 89 ££-£££ Wiltinger Kupp Riesling Kabinett 88, Zentralkellerei (TAN,ADN)

Winkel (RHEINGAU) Village with an established reputation for complex, delicious wine, housing the famous Schloss Vollrads estate **75 76 79 83 85** 86 88 89 ££-£££££ Winkeler Jesuitgarten Riesling Kabinett 85, J Spreitzer (EP)

Wintrich (MOSEL-SAAR-RUWER) MITTELMOSEL village neighbouring PIESPORT, most often seen in UK coupled with Kurfurstlay GROSSLAGE

Winzerverein/Winzergenossenschaft (Germany) Cooperative

Wurttemburg (Germany) ANBAUGEBIET surrounding the Neckar region, producing more red than any other. Little seen in the UK

Yarra Valley (Australia) Revived historic wine district of VICTORIA, re-populated by small, adventurous, 'boutique' wineries using mostly noble varieties **82 84 86** 88 ££££-£££££ 97 104 113 371 382

Yeasts Naturally present in the 'bloom' on grapes, their function is to convert sugar to alcohol, or, in the case of sparkling wines, to create carbon dioxide. Some wines, eg CHAMPAGNE and MUSCADET — benefit from being aged in contact with their yeasts — or 'SUR LIE'

Yonne (BURGUNDY) Wine department, home of CHABLIS 60 61

Yugoslavia Established suppliers of mostly very average wines, white and fast-improving red, almost all made in giant cooperatives 247

Zell (MOSEL-SAAR-RUWER) BEREICH of lower Mosel and village, making pleasant, flowery RIESLING. Famous for the Schwarze Katz (black cat) GROSSLAGE **76 79 83 85** 86 88 89 Zeller Petersborn Kabertchen Spatlese 83, Kloster Machem (EP)

Zentralkellerei (Germany) Massive, central cellars for groups of cooperatives in six of the ANBAUGEBIET — the MOSEL-SAAR-RUWER is Europe's largest 206

Zinfandel (California) Versatile red grape producing everything from dark, jammy, leathery reds to pale pink, spicy 'blush' wines. Also grown by Cape Mentelle in MARGARET RIVER, Australia **82 84 85 86** 88 ££-£££££ 237 335 349

INDEX TO WINES

Wines that appear in bold type are particularly recommended. Those that appear printed in red are the *Guide*'s Wines of the Year.